The Austrian Socialist Experiment

Westview Special Studies

The concept of Westview Special Studies is a response to the continuing crisis in academic and informational publishing. Library budgets for books have been severely curtailed. Ever larger portions of general library budgets are being diverted from the purchase of books and used for data banks, computers, micromedia, and other methods of information retrieval. Interlibrary loan structures further reduce the edition sizes required to satisfy the needs of the scholarly community. Economic pressures on university presses and the few private scholarly publishing companies have greatly limited the capacity of the industry to properly serve the academic and research communities. As a result, many manuscripts dealing with important subjects, often representing the highest level of scholarship, are no longer economically viable publishing projects--or, if accepted for publication, are typically subject to lead times ranging from one to three years.

Westview Special Studies are our practical solution to the problem. As always, the selection criteria include the importance of the subject, the work's contribution to scholarship, and its insight, originality of thought, and excellence of exposition. We accept manuscripts in camera-ready form, typed, set, or word processed according to specifications laid out in our comprehensive manual, which contains straightforward instructions and sample pages. The responsibility for editing and proofreading lies with the author or sponsoring institution, but our editorial staff is always available to answer questions and provide guidance.

The result is a book printed on acid-free paper and bound in sturdy, library-quality soft covers. We manufacture these books ourselves using equipment that does not require a lengthy make-ready process and that allows us to publish first editions of 300 to 1000 copies and to reprint even smaller quantities as needed. Thus, we can produce Special Studies quickly and can keep even very specialized books in print as long as there is a demand for them.

About the Book and Editor

The first comprehensive reevaluation of the Austrian Republic and the role of Austrian social democracy between the two world wars, this volume presents new research on the events and personalities that led from the renowned social and cultural accomplishments of "Red Vienna" to the bloody civil war of 1934. In particular, the contributors analyze "Austromarxism" within the context of the historical limitations of an Austrian Republic divided into ideologically rigid and militarized camps and beset with political violence. At the center of the debate is whether Austromarxism truly represented a new concept of politics. The volume concludes with a comparative assessment of the strengths and weaknesses of other interwar Socialist parties in combatting the threat of fascism.

Anson Rabinbach is a member of the Institute for Advanced Study, Princeton, New Jersey, and an assistant professor of history, Cooper Union for the Advancement of Science and Art, New York.

Published with the support of the
Federal Ministry for Science and Research in Vienna and
in cooperation with the Center for European Studies,
Harvard University

The Austrian Socialist Experiment

Social Democracy and Austromarxism, 1918–1934

edited by
Anson Rabinbach

Westview Press / Boulder and London

Westview Special Studies in West European Politics and Society

Copyright © 1985 by Westview Press, Inc.

Published in 1985 in the United States of America by Westview Press, Inc.;
Frederick A. Praeger, Publisher; 5500 Central Avenue, Boulder, Colorado 80301

Library of Congress Cataloging in Publication Data
The Austrian socialist experiment: social democracy
and austromarxism, 1918-1934
   (Westview special studies in West European politics and society)
   Bibliography: p.
   1. Austria--Politics and government--1918-1934.
2. Socialism--Austria. I. Rabinbach, Anson.
DB97.A935 1985   320.5'31'09436   85-3307
ISBN 0-8133-0186-6

Printed and bound in the United States of America

10 9 8 7 6 5 4 3 2 1

Contents

The Austrian Socialist Experiment

Introduction

Anson Rabinbach

The greatest achievement of postwar European socialism, the modern welfare state--which was achieved
without revolution, with the overwhelming support of the
working classes, and within the framework of capitalism
and democracy--may be showing signs of age. Some observers have even suggested that the eclipse of the Social Democratic governing parties in Scandinavia and
West Germany, after more than a decade of electoral triumph, signals the permanent passing of the socialist
idea which is tied to progress and the ideals of the Enlightenment. Socialism, it has been said, is a "victim
of success."[1]
The socialist experiments of the 1960s and 1970s,
like those of the 1920s and early 1930s, have been vulnerable to the nemesis of economic instability. When
faced with the end of growth or the problem of balancing
long-term economic policy with social benefits, Social
Democratic governments often find themselves in crisis.
Nevertheless, social democracy, with its emphasis on the
electoral arena, the steadily increasing demographic and
economic power of the working class, and the gradual
conversion of the middle classes to the security-
oriented welfare state was a success story in the postwar era until very recently in such diverse countries of
northern and central Europe as Britain, Sweden, Denmark,
Norway, Austria, and West Germany. Moderate nineteenth-
century socialists like the Webbs, Karl Kautsky and
Eduard Bernstein appear to have been vindicated far beyond their own rather limited expectations: capitalism,
it turns out, was not destined to be consumed in a final
crisis; the expansion of the suffrage changed the social
basis of political power; the modern capitalist state
proved malleable enough to embrace economic planning and
redistributive social engineering; and, most important,
socialist governments have ruled within the framework of
capitalist democracy.
These achievements all had their roots in the less
successful but more adventurous socialist experiments of

1

2

the interwar years. By the mid-1920s Social Democratic
parties throughout Europe began to experiment with new
conceptions of economic planning and investment, social
welfare, public housing, and collective social institutions. Of these early experiments two stand out: the
Swedish economic experiment and the Austrian experiment
in cultural and social policy. The postwar model of the
Scandinavian "middle way"--as Marquis Childs called it--
was presaged by the prewar Swedish Social Democrats who,
after assuming power in 1932, pioneered in state regu-
lated economic planning, and ultimately created the
first successful Keynesian economy. After 1922 the Austrian Social Democrats made their capital, Vienna, the
most innovative example of a progressive urban culture
and society to be attempted by any major socialist or
communist organization outside of Russia. The Austrian
experiment of the 1920s and 1930s called Red Vienna was
the cutting edge of the Social Democratic experiment in
central Europe between the wars. It carried earlier and
more modest reform ideas farther. Social Democrats in
Vienna hoped that it would incorporate the best that
Marxist theory had to offer, thereby providing an example for socialists around the world. But its ultimate
fate, which was bound up with the events of February
1934, also demonstrates the concrete political limits
posed by any socialist experiment.
    In light of the new crisis of European socialism,
it may be useful to reflect on the problems encountered
by one of the first great European socialist experiments, that of the Austrian Socialist Party in the First
Republic. This volume represents the efforts of specialists in modern Austrian history to reassess the
tragic and consequential events of the Austrian Civil
War of February 1934 on the occasion of its fiftieth anniversary. From the 12-15 February the city of Vienna
and smaller industrial cities in the provinces were consumed by a short but bloody struggle between the Schutzbund (the armed forces of Social Democracy) and the
troops of the government of Engelbert Dollfuss, who had
established an authoritarian rule eleven months earlier.
Within a few days both the troops of the Austrian army
and the paramilitary organizations of the Austrian fascist Heimwehr shelled into submission the magnificent
Viennese housing blocks which were the pride of the Socialists between the wars, thereby defeating the
workers' resistance. In the words of the British journalist G. E. R. Gedye, the housing projects became
"fallen bastions" reminiscent of the destruction of
World War I. But they were also a portentous sign of
both the victimization and the resistance of civilian
populations in the even bloodier destruction to come.
    This sparse summary provides only the barest sketch
of the events of February 1934. But those days of re-

sistance in Vienna were remarkable--and not simply because they marked the beginning of the end of the Austrian First Republic, adding yet another to the growing
list of former democracies in central Europe in the mid-
1930s. The Austrian Civil War of 1934 marked the first
active European working-class struggle against fascism.
It drove the strongest and most popular Social Democratic labor movement into illegality and exile. The events
of 1934 also fundamentally altered the political culture
of postwar Austria; however, the nature of the party
that was defeated may ultimately be more significant
than the regime that proved victorious. The purpose of
this book is to consider the nature of Austrian Social
Democracy in the context of the First Republic.

Austrian Social Democracy was unique among the
parties of the European left, especially after 1918. It
was characterized by unrivaled intellectual dynamism,
remarkably innovative cultural and social policies, and,
in the early years of the republic, by a series of
striking political achievements. The party's leaders--
dubbed the "Austromarxists" before World War I by the
American Socialist Louis Boudin--included Victor and
Friedrich Adler, Otto Bauer, Rudolf Hilferding, Karl
Renner, Max Adler, and somewhat later, Käthe and Otto
Leichter. Together they represented what was certainly
the most fertile strain in Marxism to emerge from the
established Social Democratic orbit. Austromarxism was
notable for its undogmatic view of Marxism as an empirical social science that had programmatic implications for the development of socialist institutions and
for the creation of a new type of individual.

The intellectual fecundity of Austromarxism was
applied to the very real afflictions of both pre- and
post-World War I Austria: the national question; the
problem of law; the formation and basis of the state;
the social infrastructure; and cultural politics. In
each of these domains, Austria constituted what Helmuth
Plessner called "a belated nation." Less industrialized
than Germany or western Europe, lacking in any experience of republicanism or democracy, and plagued by a
political climate that preferred dramaturgical artifice
to reasoned discourse, prewar Austria provided a legacy
that the First Republic could not easily renounce. For
the Austrian Marxists, the problems of nationalism, the
failure of the imperial state, the conservatism of the
Austrian peasantry, and the new irrationalist mass politics of the fin de siècle underscored the theoretical
importance of culture, ideology and the structure of the
state.

After 1917 Austromarxism found itself pressed between the extremes of conservative German Social Democratic reformism and a radical Leninist Bolshevism in
Russia. In its attempt to find a middle road, to demon-

strate that democratic socialism was a viable alternative, Austromarxism represents the most far-reaching
and sustained attempt to find a "third way" for western
socialism in the era of revolution and counterrevolution. Otto Bauer, the party's most brilliant thinker
and its leader throughout the interwar years, was in
fact the first to characterize the authoritarian regimes
of both the right and the left as products of the general European crisis between the wars. His diagnosis of
that crisis as a stalemate of class forces was one of
the most profound analyses of the interwar situation to
emerge from the European left.

Yet, despite the considerable intellectual achievements, this was no mere socialism of the professors.
The Austromarxists took their cue from the motto of the
young Engels: "whatever science condemns should not
exist in reality." They contributed to Marxist theory
while attempting to realize a new type of socialism,
centered--for a variety of reasons that will be noted
shortly--in the capital of Vienna. As Tom Bottomore
pointed out, Austrian Social Democracy "provides the
material for an especially interesting case study of the
relations and reciprocal influence between theoretical
conceptions and practical policies."[2] The practical
side of Austrian Socialism was its attempt to create a
new working-class culture and institutional infrastructure in Vienna. As a result of Article 114 of the
Federal Constitution adopted in 1920, the capital, Vienna, achieved for the first time the status of a Province or State (Land), which allowed it to operate with
some independence of the federal government in matters
of finance and administration. Though the Socialists
could not achieve an electoral majority on the national
level, after the 1919 municipal elections their political hegemony in Vienna was absolute. This state of affairs permitted them to establish a municipal showcase,
an experimental form of "socialism in one city." But
Red Vienna was limited to remaining a socialist bastion
in a country where the forces of clerical conservatism,
Heimwehr fascism and Nazism enjoyed wide appeal and support in the provinces.

On 29 December 1921 the provisions of the constitution granting Vienna state status went into effect.
Having also secured control over the municipality of
Vienna, the Socialists immediately embarked on an ambitious program of social welfare, including dental and
health care; infant, child and youth clinics; public
swimming pools; and sports facilities. But the centerpiece of the party's achievement in Red Vienna was its
radical housing policy: a property and luxury tax
placed on the affluent financed a huge municipal building project. Responding to a postwar housing crisis,
the party utilized land owned by the city to construct

an extraordinary array of new housing projects widely
known as the Vienna "Superblocks" and "People's Palaces." These housing complexes were almost self-sufficient, with stores, communal laundries, communal
kitchens, kindergartens and schools, libraries, meeting
rooms, clinics and many other innovative collective facilities. Architecturally the great Wiener Höfe--
especially the impressive Karl Marx Hof, the Karl Seitz
Hof and the Reumann Hof--were symbols of the Socialists'
power in Vienna, for they resembled proletarian fortresses rather than the streamlined modern urban housing
so typical of Weimar Germany.

But these social improvements represented only one
side of the new municipal socialism. Equally important
was the broad educational function of the party in the
capital: its attempt to create "neue Menschen" through
its youth organizations, adult education, lending libraries, bookstores, publications, theaters, festivals,
and cultural organizations. On a given day a worker
might hear a worker's chorus, read a socialist news-
paper, or attend a lecture on the socialist implications
of the theory of relativity. The creation of a culture
to counter the bourgeois, Catholic, conservative influences represented by the Christian Social Party was one
of the most original features of Austrian Socialism in
the First Republic.

Compared with its intellectual and cultural
achievements, however, Austrian Socialism's political
record is far more ambiguous. Certainly, before 1920--
while the Socialists maintained their position in the
coalition government--they were able to win a number of
substantial concessions in parliament, especially concerning labor legislation and worker's control. By
curbing the workers' council movement, and by supporting
a radical program of socialization of industry, the Socialists successfully avoided the emergence of a strong
Communist party, thereby averting the split characteristic of all other European Social Democratic parties in
the aftermath of World War I. Finally, by reducing the
size of the federal army, and through their control over
the popular militias (Volkswehr), the Austrian Social
Democrats were also able to prevent a repetition of the
German situation in which a Socialist government struck
an alliance with the forces of militarism.

Significant as these accomplishments were, the Socialists could do little to forestall the rise of the
Austrian right and the emergence of authoritarian and
fascist movements throughout the late 1920s and early
1930s. Powerless to effect events at the national
level, the Social Democrats increasingly saw Red Vienna
as an "island of freedom" in an otherwise hostile sea.
The Socialists retreated to their "fortress" in Vienna
and watched as the parties of the right gradually took

control of the political structure of the country. By
the mid-1920s officially tolerated political violence
had become endemic to the politics of the First Republic; from its dynamic came the final outburst on 12
February.

The papers collected here represent, for the most
part, the results of a colloquium entitled Austrian
Social Democracy 1918-1934: A Socialist Experiment and
its Collapse, which was held 10-12 February 1984 at the
Harvard University Center for European Studies.[3] This
conference to commemorate the fiftieth anniversary of
the Austrian Civil War was sponsored by the Austrian Institute in New York, under the direction of Dr. Fritz
Cocron and Dr. Peter Marboe. Some fifty experts on modern Austrian history from the United States, Great
Britain and Europe--including six specialists from Austrian universities--gathered to discuss the reasons for
the crisis of the First Republic and the origins of the
civil war. Thanks to the unique format of the Harvard
Colloquium series, which emphasizes short and provocative presentations and a maximum of audience participation, the conference became three days of both invigo-
rating and exhausting discourse on the subject at hand.
The relative brevity of these papers as well as the moments of intellectual passion reflect the nature of that
experience.

This Harvard Colloquium, which was not only lively
and well-informed, but often intellectually heated,
attests to a decade of important new research and scholarship on the history of the First Republic.[4] Not all
of the participants were simply scholars, however.
Some, like Hans Zeisel, Adolf Sturmthal, and Fritz
Kaufmann, were also closely associated with Austromarxism in the 1930s. Their contributions add a human
dimension which is often lacking in scholarly exchange.

From the outset of the colloquium there was wide
agreement that the events of February 1934 had to be
placed within a broad framework which emphasizes the
limits on the First Republic. This standpoint is assumed by the contributors to this book as well. In
assessing the events of 12 February 1934 one cannot
gloss over the circumstances that the First Republic
faced: the social and psychological effects of both the
breakdown of the monarchy and the war years; Austria's
weak geopolitical position in central Europe, especially
after 1933; the widely shared belief that the First Republic was "incapable of survival"; the political structure of the Republic, which was characterized by tensions among three competing "camps," each with its own
private army and ideology; and, finally, a general lack
of loyalty to the Austrian "nation."

Far wider is the spectrum of opinion on the degree
of Socialist commitment to both the Republic and democ-

racy, and about the role of internal versus external
forces--especially Hitler and Mussolini--in sealing the
fate of the Republic. Some of the conference participants wanted to see responsibility for the collapse of
the Republic distributed more generally; they point to
the shared resort to political violence, to the authori-
tarianism inherited from the Habsburg Empire, and to the
ambivalent attitude of the Socialists themselves towards
the new democracy. Others stressed that a commitment to
democracy and to the Republic was the special virtue of
the left; as Karl Stadler put it, the Social Democrats
were not "Jacobins masquerading as Girondists." The
limits of the Socialists' room to maneuver was yet
another unresolved issue at the colloquium. Scholars
agree only that these questions are still the most controversial and passionately contested in the historiog-
raphy of the First Republic.

Another question discussed extensively at the conference and in this volume is the contribution of Austromarxism to the development of the First Republic.
The acknowledged theoretical and practical achievements
of Austrian Socialists must be weighed against their
political consequences. The party's real and symbolic
failure to respond to the Vienna riots of July 1927
brought about a decisive turning point in its fortunes
and so raises this question most dramatically. In the
interwar period Austromarxism and Red Vienna both represented attempts to find a way out of the dilemmas posed
by the realities of global and Austrian politics. Although, as Josef Weidenholzer argues, Red Vienna was not
"the first choice" of the leaders as a way out of the
crisis, it served in part as a substitute for the Social
Democrats' lack of political power in the national
arena.

The essays in this book propose some answers as to
why the Austrian Socialists were so successful as theorists, so acute in their diagnosis of the circumstances
they faced, so able as leaders of what was (in per
capita terms) the most powerful European Social Democratic party, and yet so unable to translate their ideas
into a politically successful strategy. On this there
is no consensus either. Whereas various contributors
place a strong emphasis on the psychological inadequacies of the party's leaders (especially Otto Bauer),
others consider Red Vienna itself to be the source of
the party's difficulties. Some are even more sceptical
of the party's cultural policies, questioning whether,
by single-minded attention to the institutional development of Red Vienna, means had not been turned into ends.
Radical rhetoric and Bildung were counterproductive when
they led to the avoidance of reality and to an excessive
concern for the future over the difficulties of the
present. As Karl Kraus put it in his unflattering por-

trait of the Socialist leaders: "over the defeat they
are constantly building an arch of triumph, invisible to
profane followers, who can only be told of its existence."[5] The displacement of politics into culture
created a paradoxical situation, but the paradox could
not be avoided, as William McGrath has noted: "if it
was a flight from reality, it was because the time as a
whole had taken flight." If the cultural and political
achievements of Red Vienna secured a great deal of loyalty for the party among the rank and file, the price of
that loyalty was very high. The success of the Socialists in this domain may also have been overestimated, as
Peter Marcuse and Helmut Gruber argue with respect to
housing and to the party's efforts to create a working
class culture.

Neither in our colloquium nor in this volume did we
neglect the implications of the events of the First Republic for the Second Austrian Republic. Although this
question is naturally of greater concern for Austrian
historians, it remains a constant motif throughout. In
two respects Austromarxism and Austrian Socialism have
become relevant to the present. First, the ideas of the
Austromarxists have experienced a renaissance of sorts
in the last decade, especially in renewed efforts to
find a "third way." Both the Eurosocialist and Euro-
communist movements of the 1970s saw in the democratic
emphases and ideological pluralism of the Vienna Socialists a model for a new nonSoviet left. But the most
lasting impact of the Austrian experience of February
1934, most historians agree, has been the remarkable
stability and harmony of the Second Republic, especially
in recent years under the stewardship of the SPO. The
unique parity system of the Austrian government and
economy is, to no small extent, a result of the trauma
of the civil war experience; there has been a concerted
attempt to convert the hostile camps of the First Republic into the "social partnership" of the Second. In
short, the political tragedy of the First Republic seems
to have had a salutary effect on the future of Austria.

Since any book of this nature is a collaborative
enterprise, recognition is due, first and foremost, to
all those who attended the colloquium and made it a success. They are too numerous to list; nonetheless, Professors William Wright and Andrei S. Markovits deserve
special thanks for their important contribution to the
success of the endeavor. I would also like to thank the
Austrian Institute for sponsoring the colloquium, for
providing the financial support, and above all for the
enthusiasm and attention that its directors, Dr. Fritz
Cocron and Dr. Peter Marboe, respectively, brought to
the project. Mr. Karl Koehldorfer also contributed
enormously through his expert handling of technical
arrangements for the colloquium. Dr. Thomas Nowotny,

former Consul General of Austria in New York, was the
originator of the idea of a colloquium and its devoted
supporter it even after he returned to Vienna and assumed new responsibilities. The Austrian Ministry of
Science and Research under Dr. Heinz Fischer kindly
provided the financial assistance for the publication of
this volume.
    At the Harvard University Center for European
Studies I would like to thank Professors Charles Maier
and Guido Goldman, the Center's Director, for cosponsoring the colloquium and for extending the hospitality
of the Center. Abigail Collins, the Center's Assistant
Director, was indefatigable in her close supervision of
all of the requirements of both the colloquium and this
publication. For the typing of the manuscript, I thank
Amy Gluckman, Michael Heller, and Dove Scher. Last but
not least I would like to express my gratitude and
appreciation to Dr. Karen Rosenberg whose excellent
editorial work on the manuscript was surpassed only by
her ability to steer a firm course through all of the
storms that such an endeavor necessarily calls forth.

Notes

1. See Alan Wolfe, "The Death of Social Democracy,"
The New Republic (25 February 1985), pp. 21-23.

2. Tom Bottomore, Austro-Marxism, trans. Tom
Bottomore and Patrick Goode (Oxford, 1978), p. 37.

3. Jack Jacobs, who participated in the colloquium,
wrote his paper expressly for this volume.

4. See Professor Rath's contribution in this volume
and Helmut Gruber, "History of the Austrian Working
Class: Unity of Scholarship and Practice," International Labor and Working Class History No. 24 (Fall
1983), pp. 49-66.

5. Karl Kraus, Die Dritte Walpurgisnacht (Munich,
1967), p. 222.

1.The Habsburg Heritage: Some Pointers for a Study of the First Austrian Republic

Klemens von Klemperer

In the field of contemporary history there is a natural tendency to argue in terms of guilt--in the Austrian case the guilt of a Seipel, a Dollfuss, even an Otto Bauer--and at the 1974 Viennese conference on the year 1934 the emphasis fell precisely on that.[1] I suggest that the time has come for us to move away from recriminations for they do not lead anywhere. I have no intention of transferring to Austria the futile argument between "intentionalists" and "functionalists" concerning Nazi Germany. I have no intention of whitewashing any one culprit (assuming there was one) or of trying compulsively to "equalize guilt." Neither do I intend to fall back upon Schicksal, which is the resort of the scoundrel. Rather, I propose to examine the objective, structural conditions affecting all the actors on the scene, including the scoundrels, fools, and knaves. They obviously acted in a context, and that above all is what we should explore here; therefore, I propose that we use this first session of our deliberations to find ways of accounting for the February days of 1934.

Among historians there is also a tendency to look at the little Austria of the period after World War I in isolation--as an Alpine republic with parochial problems, with a "yodling" or Lederhosen perspective, and with a proverbial "shortage of non-illiterate politicians," to quote Hermann Bahr. But even the problems of this seemingly insignificant state should be seen in the context of events happening elsewhere, and especially in Germany, Central Europe as a whole, and Italy. Austria will then appear once again as the "kleine Welt in der die grosse ihre Probe hält."

Might I also suggest that in tracing the road to 1934 it is not enough to concentrate on the role of Social Democracy in the political landscape of the First Republic. Vienna may have been a "red fortress," but the country at large was not. We must keep in our purview the "other half"--which in fact constitutes more than half--of the country: the urban middle and upper clas-

ses, the peasant population, and last but not least, the
Church. Only a broad focus which includes their interests, their sensitivities, and their interaction with
each other, as well as with Social Democracy, will help
us in our proceedings. There are crucial questions that
must be asked in this connection: why after October
1920 did all efforts toward a Black-Red coalition fail?
Why did the Pan-Germans never link up with the Social
Democrats? What developments account for the estrange-
ment of the Church from the Republic and especially, of
course, of the Church from the Socialists? Ignoring the
"other half"--let alone implicitly assuming its cul-
pability--will not help us trace the unfolding of the
Austrian tragedy. Let us then take note at the outset
of the wise words which none other than Karl Renner
spoke in parliament in the fall of 1928: "We all have
failed, all without exception. By the force of things,
by the dialectics of the civil war psychosis were we
driven, all of us, to commit follies."[2]

In putting our problem in the broadest context, I
would like to propose some themes which we might keep in
mind:

1. Going back into the Austrian past, there is the
problem of empire. Republican Austria was a post-imperial structure. With this statement I mean to point to
the shift not from monarchy to republic, but from empire
to small Alpine republic. Austria was what was left
over after "dismembration," and the new republic had to
come to terms with this reality. Indicative of the
postwar Austrian frame of mind is the fact that the
Social Democratic Party and even the Workers' and Soldiers' Councils and the Schutzbund kept convening what
they still called Reichskonferenzen. The loss of empire
was not psychologically assimilated and acknowledged;
hence the phantom presence of the Reich in politics and
culture.

Of course the political dimension is what interests
us most here. Dean Acheson said in the 1950s that Great
Britain had lost its empire but had not yet found a
role. After World War I such was the predicament of
Russia, Turkey, Hungary and, of course, Austria. Russia
found a new "idea" and, ultimately, legitimacy in revolution; Turkey (under Atatürk) in nationalism, secular-
ization, and the idea of state. Hungary, after the Bela
Kun fiasco, found its guiding principle in restoration
(Reichsverwesertum). Austria either was not able to go
any of these routes or did not choose to; hence the
identity problem--which was also a legitimacy problem--
of the new Austria. Even after the second war Renner
referred to Austria as the "Land ohne Namen."[3] After
November 1918 there was a general debate over the name
of the new state: was it to be called "Deutsches Alpen-
land" or "Südostdeutschland" or "Deutschösterreich"?

Many other names, most of them on the awkward side, were
proposed in response to a poll conducted by the Inns-
brucker Nachrichten in March 1919.[4]   All were symptoms
of what Hugo von Hofmannsthal had called the "agony" of
the thousand-year-old Roman Empire of the German Nation.[5]   In fact, Austria was still searching for
alternatives to a Kleinstaatdasein.
     However different the new Austria was from the old
supranational structure, someone like Ignaz Seipel
clearly saw the connection between the two. He perceived the continued, if paradoxical, relevance of his
wartime work Nation und Staat which had argued the case
of a Christian commonwealth in which nation and state
were not identical. As successor to the supranational
empire, an "infranational" state, as Barbara Ward put
it,[6] was created, cut off from the main body of the
Germans as well as from the Germans of the South Tyrol
and the Sudetenland. Thus nation and state were as
little identical as they had been in the old monarchy.
Seipel was fully aware of the strange connection between
the "old great supranational state"[7] and the small
republic. For him, a fulfillment policy meant, in the
last analysis, to be "condemned to live, for a while,
the hard life of a small state"[8] while keeping all
other options open. Hence his ruminations about a
"reconstructed Austro-Hungarian Monarchy" and a "Central
European empire".[9]   Towards the end of 1919 and the
beginning of 1920 Renner was still exploring the possibilities of an Anschluss of Austria with the Successor
States and a Danubian Confederation of sorts.[10]   Even
the Anschluss movement was not solely a chapter in German nationalism but a manifestation of Grossraumdenken.
Otto Bauer cruelly dismissed the "miserable peasant
state"[11] in which making politics would not be worth
one's while. In front of parliament, Johann Hauser did
not shy away from calling the new state a "cripple."[12]
Austrians of virtually all strata and political persuasions had their eyes trained outside the borders of
the new Alpine Republic. They all lived in a never-
never land, not in the here and now. Hence the incidence of the "politics of unreality" and the ascendency
of myth over reality, of metapolitics over politics. It
took Seipel some self-control to abide by the phrase
which he often repeated: "hic Rhodos, hic salta!" Not
until the summer of 1927, moreover, did the Socialists'
journal Der Kampf tone down its Anschluss stance, and
not until 1933 did the Socialists eliminate the Anschluss paragraph from their party program.
     2. There is also the militarization of the spirit
to which Adam Wandruszka has already pointed[13] and the
emphasis on power and violence on the part of the right
as well as the left. This has to be seen, of course, in
the context of such developments as the Carinthian

defense struggle, the fight against the partisans in the
Burgenland, and the many other militant confrontations
in Central Europe after World War I. In this connection, it also should be remembered that a large arsenal
of weapons had found its way into circulation after the
demobilization of the old army and that many of these
weapons were used in the February and July crises of
1934. The political vocabulary in Austria became increasingly militaristic; there was the Heimatblock, the
Einheitsfront, and then in May 1933 the Grossdeutsche
and the Nazis formed their Kampfgemeinschaft. In 1932,
speaking before parliament, even as measured and peace-
loving a person as Karl Seitz urged the workers to
militancy (Wehrhaftigkeit) and to bless (heilig halten)
their weapons.

    3. Austria between the two world wars has to be
seen in the context of what Karl Dietrich Bracher has
called the "era of ideologies."[14] Politics were
increasingly removed from the realm of the practical and
subordinated to a ready-made ideological schema. The
function of politics changed from the realization of a
given objective to the legitimation of a closed and
infallible prescription. One example of Otto Bauer's
acrobatics was his insistence on a balance of class
forces in postwar Austria--which was a Volkstaat or
peoples' state; this was a forced and unsubstantiated
ideological argumentation. His chief antagonist Ignaz
Seipel no doubt started out as a pragmatist and a pioneer of an Austrian policy of accommodation with secu-
larism. However, the rigid division which he made in
October 1927 between those in the "army camp of Christ"
and those in the "army camp of the enemies of
Christ"[15] smacked of ideology as well as of martial
values. (Seipel later came into the orbit of Othmar
Spann, a fanatic ideologist and apologist of a corporative order.) Ernst Karl Winter was correct when he
juxtaposed Bauer's doctrinaire form of Austromarxism to
Seipel's "Austroscholasticism"[16] in which the pragmatic approach to politics was replaced by a priori
rigidity.

    4. We might also take notice of the concept of im-
provised democracy which Theodor Eschenburg, falling
back on Hugo Preuss, has applied to the European middle
zone between the world wars, and especially to Germany
and Austria.[17] Democratization occurred in these two
German states as a result not of long-standing tradition
and political development but of the collapse of the old
authority and of defeat. Democracy, then, had no legitimacy in this area after World War I. Germany and Austria did not develop a democratic consensus and were
unable to live with political, social and economic conflict. Moreover, both rejected the Bolshevik model of
democracy and veered towards semi- and neo-right-wing

experiments. This holds true for Central Europe in
general, with the exception of Czechoslovakia.

5. Now for one caveat against a too catastrophic or
deterministic view of the history of the First Austrian
Republic. Such a view is bound to be misleading.
Austria has habitually been looked upon as a junior
partner of the Weimar Republic which, rightly or wrongly, has been envisaged as headed for disaster. While
this view of Weimar is not up for discussion here, what
about the First Austrian Republic? In a recent article
on the op-ed page of the New York Times, Flora Lewis addressed herself to the phenomenon of "Sweden's Quiet
Way"[18] which led after World War II towards democratic
socialism. Can we not speak about a corresponding
"quiet way" of the First Austrian Republic? The relevant question is not why the republic was destroyed by
extremists but rather why and how, despite all its
handicaps, it held out so long.

To begin with, the Austrian revolution, unlike the
German, was not a revolution manquée. Certainly we must
acknowledge its real social accomplishments. Otto Bauer
went so far as to compare the Austrian revolution with
the American model[19] as a revolution without terror,
but a revolution nevertheless, and as a revolution by
general consensus--though to be sure, the consensus of a
crisis situation. He took pride in the fact that the
new state was "fundamentally the product of a contrat
social, arrived at between the various classes of the
German-Austrian people, as represented by the political
parties."[20] Renner spoke of "the community of the
great parties"[21] and he described the Black-Red coalition metaphorically as a "snow pit" in which two wander-
ers caught in a storm find temporary shelter.[22]

In assessing the viability of the new republic
some considerations must be kept in mind:
a. The Black-Red coalition which ushered the republic
   into existence and lasted until October 1920.
b. The absence in Austria of an Ebert-Gröner pact. The
   very fact that the Austrian army was in dissolution
   contributed to Austria's military weakness and political strength. The new republic, in other words,
   did not depend on the old army. It created its own
   army, the Volkswehr, which was loyal to the repub-
   lic--Otto Bauer saw it as the first act of the proletarian revolution which would catapault itself into a
   national revolution--and also able to keep down the
   Rote Garde (Volkswehrbataillon 41). In the long run,
   the drawback of this setup was that the Austrian army
   became an "army in the shadow of the parties" and
   eventually a tool of reaction.
c. The fact that in republican Austria the regime
   (Staatsform) was never seriously questioned as it was
   in Weimar Germany. In this regard, the position of

the Catholic camp was decisive. Cardinal Piffl in
his instructions to the Viennese clergy of 12 Nov.em-
ber 1918 and then in the pastoral letter to the
Austrian Catholics of 23 January 1919 set the tone
for Catholic acceptance of the republic. This course
contrasted markedly to the one pursued by the German
Protestant churches which adhered strictly to the
formula of "throne and altar." Seipel himself played
a major part in the transition from monarchy to
republic in his "programmatic" articles of November
1918 for the Reichspost.[23] He dismissed publicly
the narrow dynastic view of legitimacy as "useless"[24] and prided himself on the absence of an
obstructionist right in Austria. He wrote:

We have been reproached for having evaded the issue
of the form of government....In our fatherland...
the new form of government, which came about almost
by itself, cannot be changed without...civil war
....What would have happened had our party not recognized the Republic and not tried to cooperate
with it? What would have happened had the only
conservative party of Austria...counted itself out?
It would be forced today to try to assert itself
outside the floor of Parliament. But then we would
have civil war.[25]

d. The fact, on which Seipel once again prided himself,
   that Austria did not experience a Kapp Putsch.[26]
e. The absence in Austria of any Flaggenstreit, since
   the old Babenberg colors were generally accepted by
   the population.
f. The fact that the Austrian left emerged after the
   war undivided. This was certainly a factor in helping the Austrians to stave off the Bolshevik experiment in Hungary. In Austria, the Communist Party
   never amounted to anything. In turn, of course, it
   was precisely because the Socialists embraced both a
   moderate and radical faction that they were torn
   between pragmatic statesmanship and the "radical
   phrase," a dilemma that incapacitated the party in
   1927 and in 1934. But then came the breakup of the
   coalition in October 1920, a crucial event. The
   crisis consensus simply did not hold up against the
   structural strains of the new republic. The coalition did not break up over a minor issue, as Norbert
   Leser has argued.[27] On the contrary, it broke up
   over a central issue, namely the control of the army.

   6. Economic conditions naturally played a role in
the collapse of the consensus; they were, according to
David Landes, the worst in all Europe.[28] Though the
question of the myth or reality of Austria's viability
is not my assignment, I should like to mention for con-

sideration Victor Adler's suggestive distinction between
viability (<u>Lebensfähigkeit</u>) and potential (<u>Entwicklungs-
fähigkeit</u>).[29]

7. Inevitably, the dimension of the quality of
statesmanship will have to enter in to our general equa-
tion and again we should steer away from recrimination
as much as possible. There is no doubt that the titanic
rivalry between Ignaz Seipel and Otto Bauer overwhelmed
and squashed the republic; they were "too big for Austria." There is good and obvious reason to assign blame
to Seipel and the Heimwehr, but let me remind you that
the Christian Socials were not alone in their criticism
of Bauer. Renner, who, of course, had pleaded unsuccessfully for a pragmatic coalition policy, exposed his
party comrade's "messianic outlook"[30] and revolutionary romanticism--qualities which he considered "fatal."
How are we to assess Bauer's statement: "Infinitely
better to err with the masses than to be proved right in
opposition to them?"[31] Even Karl Seitz said on 20
October 1932: "Democracy is to us no absolute value but
only the road to socialism. We must sanctify the
weapons."[32]

8. A final vital consideration which we shall have
to keep in mind is the impact on Austria of outside
pressures, especially those coming from fascist Italy
and Nazi Germany during the Dollfuss era. The Dollfuss
policy of outdoing the fascists in order to outflank
them certainly did not pay--much to the contrary. The
February events of 1934 destroyed the last chance of an
anti-Hitler coalition between the Catholic and Socialist
camps and led directly to Schuschnigg's capitulation to
Hitler in Berchtesgaden on 12 February 1938.

As late as November and December 1933 Otto Bauer
launched the proposition that, after all, the workers
could live with a non-fascist corporative order that
would complement but not replace democracy.[33] But
this was written in the thirteenth hour of the Austrian
state. Was this statesmanship on the part of Otto
Bauer, a counsel of despair or yet more of Bauer's
mental acrobatics? At any rate, the switches had long
been set for the fatal clash of February 1934.

NOTES

1. Ludwig Jedlicka and Rudolf Neck, eds., <u>Das Jahr
1934: 12. Februar. Protokoll des Symposiums in Wien am
5. Februar 1974</u> (Munich, 1974).

2. <u>Sten. Prot. über die Sitzungen des Nationalrates
der Republik Österreich (1920-1932)</u>, III, G.P., 3 Octo-

ber 1928, p. 1624.

3. Karl Renner, "Austria, Key for War and Peace",
Foreign Affairs, Vol. 26 (Jul. 1948), p. 595.

4. See Friedrich F.G. Kleinwächter, *Von Schönbrunn
bis St. Germain. Die Entstehung der Republik Österreich*
(Graz, Vienna, and Cologne, 1964), p. 146; also Walter
Goldinger, "Der geschichtliche Ablauf der Ereignisse in
Österreich 1918-1945," in Heinrich Benedikt, ed., *Ge-
schichte der Republik* (Vienna, 1954), p. 30.

5. Hugo von Hofmannsthal to Eberhard von Bodenhausen, Rodaun, 10 July 1917, in Freifrau von Bodenhausen,
ed., *Briefe der Freundschaft* (Berlin, 1953), p. 235.

6. Barbara Ward, "Ignaz Seipel and the Anschluss",
Dublin Review, Vol. 203 (July-Sept. 1938), p. 42.

7. *Sten. Prot.*, 73. *Sitzung d. konstituirenden
Nationalversammlung*, 20 Apr. 1920, p. 2122.

8. Seipel to Dr. W. Bauer, 30 Jul. 1928, Haus-,
Hof- und Staatsarchiv, Neues Politisches Archiv, 1918-
1938 (St.A.), Liasse Deutschland I/1, Geheim, K. 456 (ad
Z. 23808/13).

9. Strictly Secret Dispatch Z. 25941, "Verlegung
des Völkerbundes", Österreichische Vertretung beim
Völkerbund in Genf (Pflügl), 17 Dec. 1927; St.A., Liasse
Völkerbund, Innere Organisation, K. 162.

10. R. Schüller, *Das Erbe Österreichs* (Typescript,
St.A.), p. 54.

11. Otto Bauer to Karl Kautsky, 6 May 1919, Inter-
nationales Institut für Sozialgeschichte, Amsterdam,
quoted in Herbert Steiner, "Otto Bauer und die 'An-
schlussfrage' 1918/19," in Richard G. Plaschka and Karlheinz Mack, eds., *Die Auflösung des Habsburgerreiches*
(Vienna, 1970), p. 477.

12. Schulthess' *Europäischer Geschichtskalender*,
1919, Vol. I, p. 542.

13. Adam Wandruszka, "Die Erbschaft von Krieg und
Nachkrieg," in Ludwig Jedlicka and Rudolf Neck, eds.,
*Österreich 1927-1938. Protokoll des Symposiums in Wien
23. bis 28. Oktober 1972* (Vienna, 1973), pp. 23ff.

14. See Karl Dietrich Bracher, *Zeit der Ideologien*
(Stuttgart, 1982).

15. Neue Freie Presse, 18 Oct. 1927, morning edition.

16. Ernst Karl Winter, "Am Beispiel Österreichs" in Christentum und Zivilisation (Vienna, 1957), p. 405; in fact, Winter attributed a relatively greater ideological rigidity to Austromarxism.

17. Theodor Eschenburg, Die improvisierte Demokratie. Gesammelte Aufsätze zur Weimarer Republik (Munich, 1963).

18. New York Times, 24 Jan. 1984.

19. Otto Bauer, The Austrian Revolution (London, 1925), p. 168.

20. Ibid., p. 54.

21. Goldinger, "Der geschichtliche Ablauf,"p. 48.

22. See Friedrich Funder, Vom Gestern ins Heute. Aus dem Kaiserreich in die Republik (Vienna and Munich, 1952), pp. 638ff.

23. Ignaz Seipel, Der Kampf um die österreichische Verfassung (Vienna and Leipzig, 1930), pp. 49ff.

24. Reichspost, 3 Apr. 1922.

25. Ignaz Seipel, "Österreichs wirtschaftliche und politische Lage," Reichspost, 24 Oct. 1921.

26. Seipel, Kampf, p. 80ff.

27. Norbert Leser, "Austro-Marxism: A Reappraisal," Journal of Contemporary History, No. 2 (1966), pp. 117-133.

28. David Landes, The Unbound Prometheus. Technological Change and Industrial Development in Western Europe from 1750 to the Present (Cambridge, 1969), pp. 375-80; I owe this reference to Anson Rabinbach, The Crisis of Austrian Socialism: From Red Vienna to Civil War 1927-1934 (Chicago, 1983), p. 65.

29. Quoted in Karl Renner, Der Anschluss Österreichs an Deutschland als europäisches Problem (Berlin, 1926), p. 31.

30. Leser, "Austromarxism," p. 130.

31. Ibid., p. 128.

20

32. Das Jahr 1934, p. 108.

33. Arbeiter-Zeitung, 24 Nov., 9 and 27 Dec. 1933.

2. The Social and Economic Background of Austria's *Lebensunfähigkeit*

Bruce F. Pauley

The question of Lebensunf<u>ähigkeit</u> was central to both the economic and political history of the First Austrian Republic. If the country was not economically viable then clearly it had to seek some kind of association with one or more other states: Germany; the Little Entente states of Czechoslovakia, Yugoslavia, and Rumania; or with Italy and Hungary. All three possibilities were pursued at various times depending on which political party was in power and the international balance of power.

Nearly all Austrians at one time or another--though never all at the same time--believed that their country was, indeed, not capable of existing as an independent state due to the smallness of its domestic markets and its lack of natural resources.[1] In view of the impressive economic performance of the Second Republic-- once the most economically depressed of the Danubian states, it is the most prosperous one today--it is tempting to conclude that these convictions were grossly in error. But were they?

The First Republic had almost exactly the same territory as the Second and therefore presumably the same economic potential. Geography, however, is only one aspect of viability, and perhaps not even the most important. No economist would argue that psychological factors are not a significant aspect of a country's economic health. If a people does not have faith in its economic future, this fact alone is likely to become a self-fulfilling prophecy. In 1919, and to only a somewhat lesser extent in succeeding years, the Austrians' pessimism was, at the very least, understandable.

AUSTRIA AT THE PARIS PEACE CONFERENCE

Aside from desperate food shortages, to be discussed later, the most important early source of the national malaise was the country's treatment at the

Paris Peace Conference. By the time the Austrian delegation was permitted to state its case before the conference in June 1919, the meeting was four and one-half
months old. The South Tyrol had been assigned to Italy,
and the Historic Provinces of Bohemia, Moravia, and
Austrian Silesia had been given to Czechoslovakia in
their entirety.[2] Lacking military force and bargaining power, the Austrians wisely chose to rely on the
ethnographic principle and the Wilsoninan concept of a
just peace in asking for only those territories of the
old monarchy inhabited by German-speaking majorities.[3]
Although the Austrian proposals were modest, concessions
were made by the Allies in only two areas--southern
Carinthia (which was awarded to Austria after a plebi-
scite in 1920) and German West Hungary, or the Burgenland. The final peace terms left the country with only
26.3 percent of the population and 23 percent of the
territory of the Austrian half of the Dual Monarchy. No
less than a third of the German-speaking people of old
Austria was left under foreign rule, including roughly
650,000 in compact areas just beyond the new frontiers.[4]

The Austrian people had been prepared for a hard
peace, but St. Germain came as a brutal shock. They had
hoped that the elimination of the dynasty and the old
army would produce reasonable terms. When these expectations were disappointed, the Socialists, who had led
the fight against monarchism and militarism, were held
responsible by their rivals, as were the Social Democrats in Germany.[5]

VICTORS AND VANQUISHED

Impartiality was not practiced in Paris because the
Allies regarded the secessionist states (Czechoslovakia,
Yugoslavia, Rumania, and Poland) as the "victors," while
Austria and Hungary were seen as the "vanquished." Actually, the secessionist states had little to do with
the Allied victory, and only the Czechs could legiti-
mately claim political traditions in harmony with the
western democracies. With the exception of the Czechs
and possibly the Poles, the secessionist states were no
more the natural allies of the West than were the Austrians or Hungarians who had never considered Britain,
France, or the United States to be their enemies in any
meaningful sense. At the end of the war, Wilsonianism
was as popular in Vienna and Budapest as elsewhere in
east central Europe.[6]

Only France had anything like a general program for
east central Europe and it was simple: to reward their
new friends, the secessionist states, with what were to
be strong and strategic frontiers, and to punish the

Central Powers. Thus, for example, 3,250,000 German
Austrians were left in Czechoslovakia compared to
100,000 Czechs in Austria (mostly in Vienna). With only
25 percent of the population of the fallen Austro-
Hungarian Monarchy, Czechoslovakia was left with 96
percent of the Monarchy's coal, 75 percent of its textile and chemical factories, 92 percent of its sugar
refineries, and 75 percent of its breweries, to cite
only a few examples.[7]

France usually considered the economic needs only
of its would-be allies. Thus, Czechoslovakia and
Rumania were given wide strips of the Hungarian Plain to
facilitate their east-west and north-south communica-
tions, respectively, but Austria was given no similar
territory for the Burgenland. The best rail connection
from Vienna to Innsbruck was cut by the awarding of
almost purely German-speaking territory to Yugoslavia
and Italy. The weaving looms for Austria's textile
industry, located near Vienna and in Vorarlberg, were
now cut off from the spindles which were manufactured in
Czechoslovakia. The steel mills of northern Styria were
likewise separated from their coal supplies in Czechoslovakia.[8]

By dividing the Successor States into victors and
vanquished, have and have-not states, the Great Powers,
and above all France, made cooperation between these
states a virtual impossibility. Austria and Hungary had
next to nothing with which to bargain and the Little
Entente states had no need to make concessions. Consequently, a Danubian federation, which France itself
wanted as a counterweight to Germany, especially after
the rise of Hitler, had little chance of success. By
default, an Austro-German Anschluss therefore appeared
to many Austrians to be the only possible alternative.

The Little Entente states and Poland were able to
begin the postwar era with a sense of euphoria. Austrians, by contrast, considered their country little more
than a rump state, a punishment for losing the war.
"Apathy pervaded every class, and this loss of hope was
proving the greatest psychological and political obsta-
cle to reconstruction. The Austrians had no pride in
being Austrians and took little interest in their small
country."[9]

ECONOMIC NATIONALISM

In theory a country of almost any size and population, with many or no natural resources and industries,
can survive as an independent state if it can purchase
the goods it is unable to produce itself with money acquired from the sale of its own surpluses. This fact
has been amply demonstrated by the history of the Second

Austrian Republic which has flourished although burdened
by the same liabilities in natural resources as its pre-
decessor between the wars.

What prevented this trade--vital for all the Successor States, but especially for Austria with its inadequate food supplies--was nationalism. Nationalism
was nothing new to the Danubian Basin in the interwar
years. It had been growing before the war, particularly
among the Czechs and the Hungarians. Food shortages
brought on during the war by the British naval blockade
and the conscription of millions of Austro-Hungarian
peasants caused every nationality within the monarchy to
hoard whatever foodstocks it possessed, even at the expense of other imperial nationalities, especially the
German-Austrians, and most especially the two million
Viennese.

The Paris Peace Conference aggravated already hy-
per- nationalistic feelings in east central Europe by
creating new states and new boundary disputes and by fa-
voring some states at the expense of others. When these
feelings were transferred to the economic sphere, they
resulted in a desire for self-sufficiency or autarky.
Unfortunately, Austria was in the poorest position of
any Danubian state to pursue such a policy.

FOOD AND COAL SHORTAGES

At the very heart of Austria's economic plight--and
therefore at the core of the viablility question--was
its shortage of food and coal, and the unwillingness of
its neighbors to sell these products in exchange for
Austrian industrial commodities. Austria, in fact, was
subjected for years to a virtual economic blockade by
its neighbors.[10]   Consequently, in 1923 Austrian industries were able to produce at only 48 to 60 percent
of capacity. If exports could have been increased to
make possible the full use of Austria's industrial capacity the country would have been able to pay for all its
necessary imports.[11]   Instead, Austria was underpro-
ducing and overconsuming.[12]

Only 4.5 percent of the new republic's land consisted of plains and just 28 percent was arable (compared with 47 and 18 percent respectively for Czechoslovakia, and 68 and 19 percent for Hungary). Just 42 percent of Austria's land was under cultivation.[13]   To
make matters worse, the demands of the world war had
reduced the number of horses and cattle in 1919 to only
about two-thirds of the prewar level, and the number of
pigs, sheep, and goats to only about half of the 1914
standard.[14]   Moreover, Austrian agriculture in the
early years of the Republic was extremely inefficient.
If it had had the efficiency of neighboring Switzerland

in 1925 it could have been self-sufficient in food.[15]
    Agricultural production was raised considerably
during the First Republic. The production of potatoes,
sugar, and dairy products was so substantial that Austria became either self-sufficient in these areas or
showed a surplus, as in the case of dairy products. The
production of wheat and barley also improved by 50 percent, although Austria still needed to import 37 percent
of its requirements of these foodstuffs in 1936.[16]
The trouble was that these gains were made in part because of protective tariffs, even though free trade was
in Austria's best interest. The result of the tariff
policy was higher food prices for consumers and less
capital to invest in more profitable sectors of the
economy.[17] Moreover, the large number of peasants,
who made up about a third of the country's population,
kept the potential labor supply for industries low. By
contrast, less than 10 percent of the population of the
Second Republic is engaged in agriculture.[18]
    Even more than for food, Austria was dependent on
imports for its coal; domestic resources filled less
than one-tenth of its needs in 1937.[19] The new
republic, which acquired 12 percent of the total population of Austria-Hungary and 30 percent of its industrial workers, was left with only 0.5 percent of the
monarchy's coal reserves.[20] In the early postwar
years coal supplies were often not even sufficient for
the transporting of available foodstuffs.[21] Ironically, imported coal became more plentiful only in 1920
when a brief world boom came to an end and a prolonged
economic crisis ensued.[22] During the inflation of
1922-1923, however, the Austrian crown fell so drastically that it became difficult for entrepeneurs to gain
the necessary foreign exchange with which to purchase
raw materials.[23] To make matters worse, Poland and
Czechoslovakia, Austria's two most important suppliers
of coal, exploited the situation by charging Austria
higher prices than their other customers.[24]

TRADE AND TARIFFS

    Economic nationalism inevitably led to tariff wars.
The newly independent states, along with Hungary, were
eager to protect their infant industries with ever-
increasing tariffs and import restrictions which deliberately discriminated against the old established industries of Austria.[25] Whereas Austria's tariffs rose
from 22.8 percent in 1913 to 36 percent in 1931, those
of Czechoslovakia and Hungary rose from the same 22.8
percent to 50 and 45 percent respectively, while
Rumania's skyrocketed from 30.3 percent to 63 percent.[26] Austria's industries had enjoyed a tariff-

free domestic market of over fifty-two million people
before the war, a market which was also protected
against outside competition. Now its domestic market
had shrunk to one-eighth of its former size and Austrian
industries had to face world-wide competition.[27] The
net result of these tariffs was that Austria's trade
declined dramatically, especially after the start of the
Great Depression. By 1933 Austrian exports were only 35
percent of their 1929 level.[28] In 1935, trade between
Austria and Czechoslovakia was only one-sixth of the
prewar volume.[29] Although Austria's trade subsequently recovered to a certain extent, by 1937 imports were
still only 45 percent of their 1929 value, while exports
amounted to just 55 percent of the pre-Depression standard. Moreover, import surpluses continued and were not
fully offset by such "intangibles" as tourism, transit
fees, and banking services.[30]

THE SHORTAGE OF CAPITAL

     One of the most serious obstacles to prosperity in
the First Republic was the persistent shortage of capital. The discovery of oil in northeastern Austria compensated in part for Austria's coal stortages in the
Second Republic, but these fields were not discovered
until 1932, and were still producing at only modest
levels in 1937.[31] Austria also had vast quantities of
potential water power which was to make the Second
Republic an exporter of hydroelectricity; however, the
First Republic lacked the necessary capital to develop
this potential. This shortage of capital for the development of the country's natural resources, industry and
agriculture was, in fact, a major cause of the profound
pessimism which permeated the whole country during the
First Republic, especially in its early years.
     There were numerous reasons for this shortfall of
capital. First and foremost, war loans had absorbed
most of the country's domestic capital and were now absolutely worthless.[32] Second, the social reform program of the Socialist chancellor, Dr. Karl Renner, was
very costly. Frightened by the Bolshevik governments in
neighboring Hungary and Bavaria, the Socialist-dominated
parliament approved an eight-hour day, higher wages,
holidays with pay, subsidized rail fares, collective
contracts, and workers' councils in factories.[33]
Moreover, the maintenance of 233,000 civil servants and
120,000 state pensioners--legacies of the monarchy--fur-
ther contributed to huge deficits and runaway inflation,
which resulted in revenues covering less than half of
federal expenditures until 1922.[34]
     This ambitious social program--the most radical in
the world outside the Soviet Union--not only worsened

Austria's financial predicament, but also created a vicious circle. The Socialists tried to fight apathy and to give workers faith in their country's future through social welfare, but they paid for it in high taxes and inflation which alienated and further discouraged the middle class--the class already hardest hit by the breakup of the monarchy. And potential foreign and domestic investors, horrified by the Socialists' unorthodox social, economic, and financial policies, and worried about domestic political divisions, were unwilling to give Austria anything more than short-term credit for food as long as the Socialists remained in power.[35] What little domestic capital Austrian bankers had to lend could be obtained only at high rates of interest, around 16.15 to 18.65 percent in 1925, for example.[36]

The cycle was at least partially broken when the priest-politician and leader of the conservative and Catholic Christian Social Party, Ignaz Seipel, became chancellor in 1922. The Allies were willing to loan Seipel what they had denied the Socialists because he was financially orthodox and--unlike the Socialists who favored an Anschluss with Germany--believed at least outwardly in the viability of Austria and promised to maintain its independence.[37] Therefore, the League of Nations loaned Austria 126 million dollars in 1922, but not without strings. Austria had to repeat the renunciation of the Anschluss which it had made in the Treaty of St. Germain and turn over its budgetary sovereignty to a League commissioner. To help balance the budget, the commissioner insisted on the dismissal of almost 85,000 civil servants and public employees, many of whom then entered radical politics, including the Nazi Party.[38]

Seipel, in the words of his foremost biographer, Klemens von Klemperer, "had cured Austria's finances, but not after all, its economy. The stabilization of the currency brought about an increase in prices which was a blow to the workers and impoverished middle classes. Unemployment...jumped from 38,000 in September 1922 to 161,000 in January 1923."[39] The hard currency policy imposed on Austria hampered the capture and even the retention of foreign markets. In succeeding years the value of imports exceeded exports by a ratio of about five to three.[40] Finally, the stipulation connected with the loan amounted to foreign interference in Austria's domestic affairs, which only confirmed the doubts many people already had as to whether Austria could really be an independent state.[41]

However, the loan from the League as well as other foreign credits which Austria received during the First Republic proved to be of only limited economic value. The League's loan was only sufficient to rescue the currency and repair the country's railroads and highways.

[42] Nearly two-thirds of Austria's foreign purchases still had to go for fuel and other basic raw materials. [43] Foreign and domestic credit continued to be either too little, too expensive, or too short-term for the modernization of already existing industries or the exploitation of the abundant potential water power or forests. (Forests covered 38 percent of the country, the third highest percentage in Europe.)[44] The development of heavy industry, which is vital to the foundation of a healthy modern economy, was hampered particularly by the shortage of long-term, low-interest capital. Some progress was made in the exploitation of water power and, as we have seen, in agriculture, and to a certain extent even in heavy industry, thanks to the developing iron and steel plants of northern Styria. But none of this was as yet sufficient to change the demographic structure of the country, let alone to create any semblance of prosperity.[45] The percentage of people engaged in the low-income areas of agriculture and forestry declined only slightly from 39.5 percent in 1910 to 37.1 percent in 1934 while those engaged in industry and crafts barely increased from 35.2 percent in 1910 to just 36.2 percent in 1934.[46]

OVERCOMING LEBENSUNFÄHIGKEIT IN THE POST-ANSCHLUSS YEARS

A glimpse at Austria's industrial development after 1938 helps us understand more clearly the problems of the First Republic. During the Anschluss years Nazi Germany invested huge amounts of capital in order to establish heavy industry in the vicinity of Linz, in central Austria. The number of industrial enterprises employing between one hundred and one thousand workers increased by 52 percent between 1937 and 1946.[47] Capital goods industries, of which Austria was in particularly short supply, were expanded at the expense of consumer industries.[48] These new industries, as well as the war economy, helped create a reservoir of skilled and disciplined workers. And, finally, the Germans introduced advanced new industrial and administrative techniques which were to prove especially useful after liberation.[49]

After the war, between 1948 and 1951, Austria was the recipient of 1.6 billion dollars of Marshall Plan aid, of which 1.4 billion dollars came from the United States. Not only was this amount sufficient to repair the considerable war damage, but much of it could also be invested in hydroelectrical development, the modernization of industry, and the mechanization of agriculture. Already by mid-1949 total production exceeded the prewar level by 26 percent, and this was only the begin-

ning of Austria's "economic miracle."[50]   Unemployment
has never risen above 8 percent in the Second Republic
(as compared to 29 percent in 1933) and inflation has
never gotten out of control.[51]

THE SPECIAL STATUS OF VIENNA

        The economic and demographic changes brought on by
industrialization in central and western Austria during
and after the World War II went far in solving Austria's
single most important economic, social, and political
problem: the problem of Vienna. The status of Vienna
was especially difficult for the First Republic. Its
population in 1910 of 2.1 million was modest for the
capital of an empire of over fifty-two million people.
Geographically it was also located near the center of
the Dual Monarchy. With the monarchy gone, however, it
had a hinterland of only 4.4 million people and found
itself at the eastern extremity of the country. Austria's entire urban population was not especially large
compared with those of Switzerland or the United Kingdom. But Vienna was the home of most of Austria's
superfluous civil servants and of light industries rendered superfluous by the loss of most of their markets.
The larger part of Austria's unemployed, in fact, lived
in Vienna. To a considerable extent the question of
Austria's viablility was really the question of Vienna's
viability.[52]
        The problem of Vienna was solved in large measure
by war and time. By 1937 the Austrian birthrate had
fallen below the death rate,[53] and nowhere more so
than in Vienna. Two hundred thousand Viennese Czechs
returned to Czechoslovakia and another two hundred thousand Viennese Jews either emigrated after the Anschluss
or were slaughtered in the Holocaust. By 1950 most of
the retired imperial civil servants who had lived in
Vienna were dead. The Russian occupation also contributed to the fact that the city lost 16.4 percent of
its population between 1934 and 1951. During this period, however, the western provinces grew between 22.8
and 24.6 percent.[54] Today Vienna has a population of
only 1.6 million out of a total Austrian population of
7.5 million.

ASSETS OF THE FIRST REPUBLIC

        In 1918 Austria's economic plight was so desperate
that it was all too easy for its citizens to forget the
country's genuine assets. Nevertheless, as distinguished from Austria in 1945, it had suffered no material war damage to its buildings, rails, or highways and

its soldiers returned quickly from the front.[55] Although drastically reduced in size, it was still more
than twice the area of Switzerland and Denmark, about
three times the size of both Belgium and the Netherlands, and far larger than the Baltic States of Estonia,
Latvia, and Lithuania. It had a larger population than
most of these states and all the Scandinavian countries.
With its population now 96 percent German-speaking, it
was by far the most linguistically homogeneous of the
Successor States. Only about 10 percent of its land was
totally unproductive, 38 percent was covered with valuable forests, 28 percent consisted of pastures and
meadows, and 22 percent was arable.[56] The country's
towering mountains and charming baroque cities continued
to have great tourist appeal. Vienna, with its two
million people, although for too large for its hinterland, was still a great financial, scientific, artistic,
and cultural center. The city's unique geographic
location, on one of the major crossroads of Europe,
attracted transit trade beneficial to the city's commercial life.[57]

     By 1937 Austria, despite several years of economic
warfare waged by Nazi Germany, had made considerable
progress. The country's finances were on a thoroughly
sound basis and its economic dependence on Germany was
less than that of the Balkan states. Industrial production was 103 percent of the 1929 level, compared to
only 96 percent for Czechoslovakia and 92 percent for
the USA (but 117 percent for Germany and 124 percent for
Great Britain).[58] Pessimists, however, including
Nazis who were determined to prove Austria's Lebensunfähigkeit, could point out that employment was still
only 67.4 percent of the already low 1929 level compared
to 104.3 percent in Germany.[59] Of course, Nazis ignored Germany's role in Austria's plight, which included
the virtual cessation of German tourism and trade between 1933 and 1936.[60] But few Austrians could forget
that their per capita income on the eve of the Anschluss
was still substantially behind the level of 1913[61] and
that the country's gross national product, after having
surpassed the 1913 standard by 5 percent in 1929, still
stood in 1937 at only 91 percent of the prewar
level.[62]

THE QUESTION OF NATIONAL IDENTITY

     To a very large extent, however, the question of
Austria's viability or lack of it was not simply a question of size, population, natural resources, trade, employment, or cost of living. Perhaps even more important was the lack of national identity both before and
after 1918. Before 1918 many Hungarians, Czechs, and

Poles living in the Austro-Hungarian Monarchy (although
by no means all of them, or even a majority) had wanted
to have an independent state of their own; however, this
desire did not exist among the German-speaking Austrians. Many saw themselves as strictly Tyroleans, Stryri-
ans, Carinthians, etc.; a few wanted to join the German
Empire. But none of them wanted or envisioned a separate German-speaking Austrian state.[63]

As late as 1938 most Austrians did not regard themselves as a separate nationality with a separate culture, but simply as part of the larger German "race."
In 1918 it was taken for granted that only distinct
nationalities could or should have a state of their
own.[64]   This is why Chancellor Kurt von Schuschnigg
could readily refer to Austria as a "second German
state" in his July Agreement with Germany in 1936.[65]
Loyalty toward one's political party and social class
(the three Lager) proved to be much stronger than loyalty toward the state during the First Republic. "Bargaining between leaders of the two main Lager [the Socialists and Catholic Christian Socials] was suspected
as appeasement of the 'class enemy' and thus fraught
with the possibility that followers might defect."[66]
It was fortunate for the Second Republic that by 1945
most of the left-wing Socialist leaders and the interwar
leaders of the Catholic party were either dead or in
exile.[67]   Those leaders of the Second Republic who did
remain in or return to Austria had established contact
with one another in Nazi concentration camps, and there
they had become aware of their Austrian identity and of
their differences with Germans from the Reich. These
personal contacts continued with the establishment of
the Second Republic.[68]

Since the World War II the idea that a political
nation need not be identical with a cultural nation has
gained popularity in the western world and with most of
Austria's leaders.[69]   Unprecedented prosperity helped
create a sense of self-reliance and well-being among the
Austrians.[70]   Their brief experience as part of the
Third Reich cured all but a few of them of their
Anschluss sentiments. A poll in 1971 revealed that only
7 percent still favored union with Germany; among those
under thirty the figure was only 3 percent.[71]   And
with the dying out of the pre-World War I generation,
the Austrians' longing for their imperial past has also
passed away--except for a sentimental dream--and been
replaced by "an honest and successful search for an
active role in international affairs as a small
power."[72]

CONCLUSION

No simple answer can be provided for the question: "Was the First Austrian Republic Lebensunfähig?" An almost unlimited potential for water power, considerable oil reserves, and a rapidly improving agricultural scene gave optimists some grounds for believing that the country might indeed be viable, at least at some distant point in the future. But by 1938 that future had still not arrived and immediate reality always appeared cloudy; the hostile attitude of Austria's neighbors and their unwillingness to trade with Austria, the chronic shortage of investment capital, the surplus of civil servants, the inflation, and the Depression all prevented the establishment of anything like a stable economy.

Perhaps even more important than economic factors in preventing the emergence of a truly viable state were political and psychological considerations. Until the Austrian people could think of themselves as a distinct people, and place the interests of the state and people as a whole above the interests of the political parties to which they belonged there was little likelihood of Austria's becoming a workable state. No one could have foreseen at any time during the First Republic that it would take eight years of German restructuring of the Austrian economy, a second world war, a ten-year military occupation, and massive foreign assistance to give the Austrian people a sense of national identity, a prosperous economy, and hope for the future.

NOTES

1. For example, Otto Bauer, the leader of the left wing of the Social Democratic Party and Austria's foreign minister during the first part of the Paris Peace Conference, reflected the views of most Socialists in that he was a consistent proponent of an Anschluss with Germany (before Hitler came to power) on the grounds that Austria could not grow its own food, had insufficient coal and had no export industries. Consequently, it would have to be the servant of foreign capitalists. See Walter Goldinger, Geschichte der Republik Österreich (Vienna, 1962), p. 118. Even Ignaz Seipel, the leader of the conservative and Catholic Christian Social party and twice chancellor of Austria, questioned the viability of the new republic when he said in November 1918 that "'the German Austrians have been members of a great state for so long that they cannot suddenly confine their spirit to the narrow inter-

ests of a small state.'" Quoted in William T. Bluhm, Building an Austrian Nation: The Political Integration of Western Nation (New Haven, 1973), p. 26. Seipel and most other Christian Socials were later to take a more positive stand on Austrian independence, but always they retained a certain ambivalence.

2. Claude Roberts, "The Austrian Reaction to the Treaty of St. Germain." The Southwestern Social Science Quarterly, Supplement to Vol. XL (1959), p. 88.

3. Friedrich Kleinwächter, Von Schönbrunn bis St. Germain: Die Entstehung der Republik Österreich (Graz, 1964), pp. 199-200; David F. Strong, Austria (October 1918-March 1919) (New York, 1939), p. 155; Malbone W. Graham, New Governments of Central Europe (New York, 1925), p. 138.

4. Leo Pasvolsky, Economic Nationalism of the Danubian States (New York, 1928), p. 95; Strong, Austria, p. 131.

5. Karl R. Stadler, The Birth of the Austrian Republic (Leyden, 1966), p. 24; C. A. Macartney, The Social Revolution in Austria (Cambridge, England, 1926), p. 108; Hans Rogger and Eugen Weber, The European Right: A Historical Profile (Berkeley and Los Angeles, 1966), p. 329.

6. Malcolm Bullock, Austria, 1918-1938; A Story in Failure (London, 1939), p. 54; Professor A. C. Coolidge to the Commission to Negotiate Peace, Budapest, 19 January 1919, Foreign Relations of the United States, Paris Peace Conference, XII: 375.

7. Harriet Wanklyn, Czechoslovakia (New York, 1954), pp. 272-73; Pasvolsky, Economic Nationalism, p. 36.

8. Pasvolsky, Economic Nationalism, p. 96; Julius Braunthal, The Tragedy of Austria (London, 1938), pp. 37-38.

9. Bullock, Austria 1918-1938, p. 184.

10. Friedrich Hertz, Zahlungsbilanz und Lebensfähigkeit Österreichs (Munich and Leipzig, 1925), p. 22.

11. Ibid., p. 33.

12. Ibid., p. 25.

13. K. W. Rothschild, Austria's Economic Develop-

34

ment Between Two Wars (London, 1947), p. 5.

14. Friedrich Hertz, The Economic Problem of the Danubian States: A Study of Economic Nationalism (London, 1947), p. 136.

15. Hertz, Zahlungsbilanz und Lebensfähigkeit, pp. 10-11.

16. Rothschild, Austria's Economic Development, pp. 66-67.

17. Hertz, Economic Problem, pp. 118, 220.

18. Eduard März and Maria Szecsi, "Austria's Economic Development, 1945-1978," in Kurt Steiner, ed., Modern Austria (Palo Alto, 1981), p. 131.

19. Rothschild, Austria's Economic Development, p. 6.

20. Charles A. Gulick, Austria from Habsburg to Hitler, Vol. I, Labor's Workshop of Democracy (Berkeley and Los Angeles, 1948), p. 144.

21. Ibid., p. 93.

22. Ibid., p. 150.

23. Ibid., p. 156.

24. Hertz, Economic Problem, p. 77.

25. Fritz Machlup, "The Development of the Austrian Economy since the Second World War," in William E. Wright, ed., Austria Since 1945 (Minneapolis, 1982), p. 48.

26. Hertz, Economic Problem, p. 72.

27. Ibid., p. 137; Pasvolsky, Economic Nationalism, p. 189.

28. Rothschild, Austria's Economic Development, p. 54.

29. Hertz, Economic Problem, p. 84.

30. Pasvolsky, Economic Nationalism, p. 142. See also Hertz, Zahlungsbilanz und Lebensfähigkeit, p. 54.

31. Rothschild, Austria's Economic Development, p. 7.

32. Hertz, Economic Problem, p. 86.

33. For a comprehensive account of this social legislation see Judit Garamvölgyi, Betriebsräte und sozialer Wandel in Österreich 1919/1920: Studien zur Konstituierungsphase der österreichischen Betriebsräte (Vienna, 1983).

34. Elizabeth Barker, Austria, 1918-1972 (Coral Gables, Fla., 1973), p. 49; Pasvolsky, Economic Nationalism, pp. 101-102; Lajos Kerekes, "Wirtschaftliche und soziale Lage Osterreichs nach dem Zerfall der Doppelmonarchie," in Rudolf Neck and Adam Wandruszka, eds., Beiträge zur Zeitgeschichte (St. Pölten, 1976), p. 87.

35. Antonin Basch, The Danube Basin and the German Economic Sphere (New York, 1943), pp. 130-31; Barker, Austria, 1918-1972.

36. Hertz, Economic Problem, p. 165.

37. Klemens von Klemperer, Ignaz Seipel: Christian Statesman in a Time of Crisis (Princeton, 1972), p. 177; Goldinger, Geschichte der Republik Osterreich, p. 118; Barker, Austria, 1918-1972, p. 53.

38. Karl R. Stadler, Austria (New York and Washington, 1971), p. 123; Gerhard Jagschitz, Der Putsch: Die Nationalsozialisten 1934 in Osterreich (Graz, 1976), p. 15.

39. von Klemperer, Ignaz Seipel, p. 217.

40. The World Almanac and Book Of Facts, 1929 (facsimile edition), pp. 588-89; Ferdinand Lacina, "Developments and Problems of Austrian Industry," in Steiner, ed., Modern Austria, p. 156.

41. Kurt Steiner, Politics in Austria (Boston, 1972), p. 77.

42. Kurt Wessely, "Zisleithaniens Wirtschaft und die Nachfolgestaaten," in Richard G. Paschka and Karlheinz Mach, eds., Die Auflösung des Habsburgerreiches: Zusammenbruch und Neuorientierung im Donauraum (Vienna, 1970), pp. 447-48.

43. Pasvolsky, Economic Nationalism, p. 173.

44. Ibid., p. 172; Alfred Werner, "Is Austria 'Lebensfähig'?, Journal of Central European Affairs,

36

Vol. V, No. 2 (July 1945), p. 114.

45. Bluhm, Building an Austrian Nation, p. 44.

46. Ibid., pp. 24, 83.

47. Herman Freudenberger and Radomir Luza, "National Socialist Germany and the Austrian Industry, 1938-1945," in Wright, ed., Austria Since 1945, p. 94.

48. Ibid.

49. Ibid., p. 96.

50. Stadler, Austria, pp. 267, 281.

51. Steiner, Politics in Austria, p. 81; Rothschild, Austria's Economic Development, p. 52.

52. Pasvolsky, Economic Nationalism, pp. 178-79.

53. Hertz, Economic Problem, p. 101.

54. Bluhm, Building an Austrian Nation, pp. 83-84.

55. Goldinger, Geschichte der Republik Österreich, p. 288.

56. Pasvolsky, Economic Nationalism., p. 149.

57. Rothschild, Austria's Economic Development, pp. 42-43.

58. Ibid., pp. 65-66, 69.

59. Hertz, Economic Problem, p. 147.

60. Other Nazi attempts to undermine Austria's economy included the refusal to import Austrian films or books which did not conform to Nazi racial laws. Moreover, some of Austria's meager heavy industry, including the Alpine Montan steel works of Styria, were owned by Germans who concentrated their investments in Germany. See Rothschild, Austria's Economic Development, pp. 84, 96.

61. Hertz, Economic Problem, p. 221.

62. Wessely, "Zisleithaniens Wirtschaft," p. 443.

63. Stadler, Austria, p. 106.

64. Steiner, Politics in Austria, p. 7.

65. Bluhm, Building an Austrian Nation, p. 42.

66. Steiner, Politics in Austria, pp. 410-11.

67. Bluhm, Building an Austrian Nation, p. 42.

68. Steiner, Politics in Austria, pp. 172-73.

69. Bluhm, Building an Austrian Nation, p. 10.

70. Ibid., p. 85.

71. Steiner, Politics in Austria, p. 158.

72. von Klemperer, Ignaz Seipel, p. 44.

3. The Heimwehr and February 1934: Reflections and Questions

C. Earl Edmondson

It seems appropriate to me, in view of the role that the paramilitary Heimwehr played in the events of February 1934, to consider the Heimwehr phenomenon in a conference devoted primarily to the place of Austria's Social Democratic Party in the history of the First Republic. In these brief remarks I will first comment on the contributions of the Heimwehr to the demise of the Republic. Then for the sake of argument I will raise several "what if" questions about the course of interwar Austria and about the role of the Heimwehr role in particular.

I see no grounds for revising the generally held view that the only force holding Austria's various Heimwehr groups together was their antipathy to Marxism as an ideology and to the Social Democratic Party (SDAP) as a significant political force. Since Austria's Socialists were the country's major proponents of republican institutions, the Heimwehr was perforce also anti-republican. Those few Heimwehr leaders who, like Richard Steidle, had flirted with republicanism before the war, turned decidedly against it in the wake of the Russian Revolution and events in Austria at the end of the war. In any case, the Heimwehr could not destroy the SDAP without destroying the Republic, so it early became bent on destroying both, even if the Heimwehr leaders could never fully agree on how a post-republican regime should be shaped.

Most Heimwehr leaders also succumbed to the generally prevailing belief that Austria was lebensunfähig. Their attitudes were determined in large measure by their nostalgia for the old empire and its social order, or by their commitment to pan-Germanism. Even had they been emotionally prepared to accept the independence of the little Austria that emerged from World War I, however, most Heimwehr leaders would have preferred to see the country merge with or become thoroughly dependent upon some larger entity than to permit the Socialists an enduring role in governing the country. One can only

regret that they placed greater value on the destruction
of the SDAP, hence of the Republic, than on the maintenance of Austrian independence. (Their counter-argu-
ment, of course, was that the Socialists would make
Austria dependent on the inimical Western democracies
or, worst of all, on Soviet Russia.)

Regardless of the extent to which the Heimwehr
proper represented only a radical fringe, or however
much it served merely as the tool of vested interests,
it repeatedly succeeded in fomenting discord, in keeping
nerves raw, in narrowing the options. Even before July
1927 some of its leaders wanted to emulate Mussolini
with a "march on Red Vienna." From the perspective of
the Social Democrats, Heimwehr machinations before the
elections of April 1927 could be said to justify that
part of the Linz Program that usually gets so much attention. This is not to say, of course, that in the
spring of 1927 the Heimwehr would have been in a position to act forcefully, even had the Socialists won a
majority in the Nationalrat. As it was, the Linz Program's rhetoric about "dictatorship," however qualified
or justified, provided powerful ammunition to Heim-
wehr--and other--propagandists who appealed to an all-
too-credulous non-Socialist population.

Note the salient Heimwehr contributions to the
turmoil of the republic: the vigorous opposition to the
general strike in July 1927; the energetic Aufmarsch
activities, with their attendant tension and violence,
in 1928 and 1929, especially in industrial regions; the
bombastic, even if largely abortive, campaign in 1929
for a revision of the Austrian constitution along authoritarian lines; the open avowal of fascism at Korneu-
burg in 1930; Starhemberg's entry into Vaugoin's minority cabinet in September 1930 with his brash announce-
ment that he would not surrender power; the participation of the Heimatblock in the national elections in
November 1930 under the banner of anti-parliamentary
goals; Pfrimer's lamentable putsch in September 1931;
re-entry into the government in May 1932 on the strength
of the Heimatblock's eight crucial seats in the Nationalrat; the incessant use, first of ministerial portfo-
lios to harass, weaken, and provoke the Socialists and
their paramilitary Schutzbund, and second of the Heimwehr's key position after the demise of Parliament to
browbeat Dollfuss into eliminating the Social Democrats
from public life. Even after the Nazi Party emerged as
a major competitor, the Heimwehr intensified its anti-
Socialist campaign, which the Nazis were perfectly happy
to see it do. Finally, there is, it seems to me, little
reason to doubt that the Heimwehr, pushed hard by Mussolini, was the driving force in bringing the country to
the point of civil war in February 1934. This is not to
say that all Heimwehr leaders wanted a shooting war with

the Socialists, although Emil Fey, then the state secretary for security affairs, may well have. Nevertheless, in its own eyes, the Heimwehr's greatest achievement came in those mid-February days fifty years ago. What a sad commentary!

One of the major features of the two weeks before the shooting started was the Heimwehr's so-called "rolling putsch" at the provincial level which began in the Tyrol late in January. There is, unfortunately, still a great deal of uncertainty about the genesis of this effort "to roll up Austria from the west." What, for example, was Dollfuss's relationship to the putsch during its opening stages? Did it begin as an isolated event that sparked a spreading brushfire or was there an overall plan and timetable? Was it directed chiefly against the Socialists or against the Nazis, those increasingly potent rivals then about to celebrate the first anniversary of Hitler's accession to power in Germany? I tend to think that the Heimwehr's real concern in the Tyrol was with the Nazis. In the face of that competition, the Heimwehr leaders felt that they had to "out-Nazi" the Nazis in two ways. They had (1) to prove themselves vis-à-vis the Nazis by intensifying their anti-Socialist campaign, and (2) to secure power at various levels of government for themselves before the Nazis achieved a breakthrough. Thus, it seems plausible that the major aim of the "rolling putsch" was to secure a leading role for the Heimwehr in newly authoritarian provincial governments before the Nazis could become too strong. Clearly they could not create authoritarian governments in provinces like Lower Austria and Styria, not to mention Vienna, without crushing the SDAP--the destruction of which in any event remained a primary goal. Indeed, as the spreading operation got closer to Vienna, where Fey had his locus of power, the whole affair necessarily took on a more anti-Socialist character.

In a number of ways, the Heimwehr's provincial coups were rather daring. For one thing, Christian Social officeholders--not just Socialists and Nazis-- took umbrage at the Heimwehr's demands. Many of them, too, would have to be displaced in the creation of dictatorial provincial regimes. That a civil war against the Socialists would help divert attention from the differences between the Heimwehr and the Christian Social Party no doubt occurred to some Heimwehr leaders, even though such a conflict may not have been the original purpose of the provincial operations. Nevertheless, despite the fact that the Socialists and their underground military units had been gravely weakened in the preceding two years, a shooting war with them entailed great risks. No one knew how widespread resistance might prove to be, or how the Nazis might seek to

exploit the situation, or how the governments in London
and Paris would react (at least not before the advent of
a right-leaning government in France following the riots
in Paris on 6 February).[1]   Thus, in trying to restruc-
ture the provincial governments and to get the Socialists removed from the Vienna Rathaus, the Heimwehr was
playing a dangerous game for high stakes. As it turned
out, when war came the government's regular forces contributed more to the armed effort against the Socialist
resisters than did the Heimwehr, although the latter
proved most zealous in trying to exploit the "victory"
over the "Reds." After the fact, Heimwehr leaders were
probably pleased that the conflict had come about; after
all, it was the culmination of their anti-Socialist
"mission." In view of the risks involved and the role
of the executive forces in the fighting, however, many
Heimwehr leaders probably would have been almost as
happy had they achieved the desired results without a
war--with the exception, perhaps, of Major Fey.
     There still remain several questions concerning the
exact relationship between the "rolling putsch" and the
civil war. To what extent did the Heimwehr action help
bring nerves to a fever pitch? Without it, would Fey's
harassing raids against Socialist centers have succeeded
in provoking armed resistance in Linz? Without it, what
would have been the Socialists' response to a "quiet"
appointment of a federal commissioner to administer
Vienna--even though Socialist leaders had said that
tampering with their control of the capital would be a
casus belli?
     When one gets into the "what if" game--which, I
take it, we are at least in part invited to play at a
conference of this sort--one naturally comes up against
the question of inevitability. I suspect most of us try
to resist the assumption that historical developments
are absolutely determined, either in the long or short
run, on either the social or the individual level. I,
for one, do not much like the notion of inevitability.
But I have to confess that in interwar Austria the room
for the kind of maneuvering that would have produced a
different course appears to have been very narrow indeed. Austria was so much at the mercy of other powers,
so overwhelmed by the forces swirling around her, that
her interwar history seems to bear the stamp of inevitability more than does the history of interwar Europe
as a whole. On the wider map, different decisions in
London, in Paris, in Berlin, in Rome, even in Washington, would probably have made a much greater difference
in the way things turned out in Austria than any decisions made in Vienna could have made. But surely none
of us wants to leave it at that. I hope that this conference will address, among other things, the issue of
alternative decisions and developments that might have

been initiated within Austria itself, especially by the
Socialist party and leadership, since their role is the
major object of our consideration.

For my part, I would like to pose a couple of additional "what if" questions in connection with the Heimwehr's role in interwar Austria, only two among the many
questions that together we could conjure. I want to
point to unique events and specific decisions, the absence of which would have made a major difference. In
doing this, I am fully aware that conditional history is
an "iffy" proposition. Historians are called upon primarily to examine what actually occurred, even if not to
determine categorically wie es eigentlich gewesen ist.
For limited purposes, however, the effort to imagine
different scenarios can be instructive. It seems to me
that this is especially the case when one is trying to
assess the role of a radical group like the Heimwehr.
In what follows I am assuming that basic social forces
and attitudes are "givens" but that within these "givens" events could have taken different turns and that
Austria could have had a different history, at least up
to a point.

Not surprisingly, the first problem centers around
the "inevitable" question that all of us have no doubt
contemplated at one time or another: what if the verdict in the Schattendorf murder trial had been different? Thus, what if there had been no occasion for a
"turning point" on 15 July 1927? (At least for the purpose of speculation I am assuming that a different verdict was possible, though you may counter that it was
the unavoidable result of those "givens" of which I
spoke a moment ago. Should I ask, instead, a "what if"
question about a different response to the verdict on
the part of workers?) In any case I find the question
particularly relevant to the Heimwehr, for I seriously
doubt that the Heimwehr could have become anything like
the Volksbewegung that it liked to call itself in 1928
and 1929 without the July events. In my view the Linz
Program alone would have been insufficient to stimulate
rapid growth of the Heimwehr during the late 1920s, even
had Mussolini provided the same subsidies (which he
might not have done without the July Days).

A related queston is this: what if the Heimwehr
had not already been well established when the Great
Depression struck? It is true that the Heimwehr found
itself in considerable disarray following its failure to
achieve a more radical revision of the constitution in
1929. Even so, however, it retained the preeminent position on the far right as economic conditions worsened
rapidly in 1930. Had it not already been so well established, might not the Nazis have been even more directly
the chief beneficiaries of the Depression than they
were? Keep in mind the fact that, as it was, the Heim-

wehr almost fell apart during the Depression. Thus
without the developments of the late 1920s that hinged
on July 1927, the Heimwehr as such might well not have
played a major role in the death of the Republic--which
is not to say, however, that the Republic would have
survived.
    The second problem to which I would like to point
is closely linked to the first. What if Starhemberg had
not decided to sanction the formation of the Heimatblock
in 1930? That is, what if after the expansion of the
late 1920s and the confusion of 1929-1930 there had
still been no separate Heimwehr participation in the
parliamentary elections of November 1930? Of course, a
number of factors, including the impact of the Depression and the failure to work out an electoral pact with
the Nazis, lay behind Starhemberg's decision to campaign
separately, but it can hardly be considered an inevitable or necessary event.
    Consider how things might have been different had
the Heimatblock not campaigned. Who would have garnered
those eight mandates which the Heimatblock won and which
became so critical in 1932? Surely not the Social Democrats. The Christian Socials? Perhaps in the Tyrol and
Lower Austria. The Pan Germans? Not likely, except
perhaps in Carinthia. The Nazis? Might not the Nazis
have won a Grundmandat in Styria and then several other
seats there and elsewhere? If that had happened, then
when the newly elected Nationalrat convened in December
1930 there would have been several Hakenkreuzler instead
of Hahnenschwänzler on the far right. Imagine, Frau-
enfeld instead of Starhemberg, the Frauenheld!
    Now, project the impact of different election re-
sults into the years after 1930. While the field for
speculation on the possible fate of Austria's parliamentary and constitutional institutions under different
circumstances is a rich one, I shall limit my questions
to the Heimwehr's role after 1930. I contend that,
without those eight Heimatblock mandates in the Nationalrat and the leverage they provided, the Heimwehr, or
what was left of it, would not have been able to play
such a significant role in the events of the 1930s. Had
the Heimwehr, through the Heimatblock, not been Regier-
ungsfähig, it would have been much more difficult for
Mussolini to use it as his anti-Socialist bludgeon in
Austria's internal affairs or for Fey to be in a position to goad the Socialist paramilitary into a fury.
Indeed, one might even argue that there would have been
no civil war in February 1934 had the Heimatblock not
campaigned in 1930! Furthermore, without the results of
that campaign, would the Heimwehr have been in a position to demand equal billing in whatever authoritarian
regime might have emerged in the mid-1930s--a role that
conceivably made the Dollfuss-Schuschnigg regime more

"fascist" and that kept it more internally divided than
such a regime might otherwise have been? Or would the
absence of an ostensibly powerful Heimwehr presence
merely have strengthened the Nazi opposition during the
early and mid-1930s, with incalculable consequences for
political relationships within Austria?

In raising such questions, I am trying to provoke
debate about the possible effects of conceivable alternative developments and decisions given Austria's general situation within an economically destabilized and
ideologically divided Europe. I have raised these questions primarily with the Heimwehr in mind. How much
more momentous might have been fundamentally different
decisions and deeds on the part of larger and more significant groups and of more eminent personalities in
Austria's public life! In the last analysis, my "what
if" game becomes a lament that different paths were not
taken, that even within their constricted space Austrians allowed events to produce the civil war of February
1934. Whatever the constraints imposed by the general
European conditions, Austrians of all persuasions had it
within their power to pursue a path less confrontation-
al, less violent. Would that they had done so!

NOTES

1. This emendation to my original remarks
reflects an observation made during discussion by Prof.
Adolf Sturmthal.

4. Writings on Contemporary Austrian History, 1918-1934

R. John Rath

When I heard the news of the February 1934 civil war in Austria, I was a graduate student at the University of California. My shock and anger at that turn of events were similar to the feelings of most of my friends at Berkeley. We regarded Chancellor Engelbert Dollfuss' suppression of the Republican Schutzbund as an outright attack by a fascist government on the great mass of Austrian workers. Since the full impact of the National Socialist revolution had still not been felt in Germany by early 1934, I, at least, regarded Dollfuss as a more calamitous monster than Adolf Hitler.

The comments of British and American journalists, some of whom--such as G.E.R. Gedye[1]--were excellent observers, reinforced these conclusions. So did the first impressive, well-documented study of the First Republic published shortly after the end of the Second World War: the large two-volume Austria from Habsburg to Hitler written by Charles A. Gulick and published by the University of California Press in 1948. Mary MacDonald's factual, brief analysis, The Republic of Austria, 1918-1934: A Study in the Failure of Democratic Government, brought out two years earlier by Oxford University Press, tended to do the same. Walter Goldinger and Adam Wandruszka added important details to the historical narrative and clarified prevailing concepts about political ideologies during the First Republic in their contributions to Heinrich Benedikt's Geschichte der Republik Österreich published by Oldenbourg Verlag in 1954, but what they wrote, solid as it was, provided no compelling impetus to revise prevailing views about this era in Austrian history.

Insofar as I can tell, the only important studies published during the twenty-five years immediately following the end of World War II that gave momentum to reevaluations of various aspects of Austrian history between 1918 and 1938 were those by an American political scientist, an American historian, and a Hungarian historian and diplomat. Alfred Diamant induced scholars

to pay more attention to the influence of Catholic social ideas and movements on Austrian political life
through his Austrian Catholics and the First Republic:
Democracy, Capitalism, and the Social Order, 1918-1934
published by Princeton University Press in 1960. Paul
R. Sweet furnished irrefutable documentary evidence of
Mussolini's complicity in the February 1934 civil war in
an appendix to Julius Braunthal's The Tragedy of Austria
which was published in London in 1948. And in the 1960s
Lajos Kerekes produced a number of articles and books
based on documents in the Hungarian archives which provided proof that Mussolini had contributed financial
support to the Austrian Heimwehr since 1928.[2]

Apart from the volume edited by Benedikt, relatively little was written in Austria about the First Republic before the 1970s. The many historians who had been
tainted with National Socialism and the few who had been
avowed champions of the Dollfuss-Schuschnigg government
found it politically wise to hide whatever interest they
may have retained in the immediate prewar era. Only the
pre-1938 proponents of democracy and socialism seemed to
be regarded with favor after 1945. Moreover, the bitter
political antagonisms of the 1920s and 1930s had still
not subsided enough to make possible a dispassionate
evaluation of Austria's recent history. Then, too, the
era of the First Republic was still regarded by orthodox
historians as a period worthy of only superficial attention by journalists and popularizers. Until the latter
half of the 1960s Ludwig Jedlicka was fighting an uphill
battle to make contemporary history respectable. With
the establishment of the Institute for Contemporary
History at the University of Vienna in 1966, largely as
a result of his tireless efforts, the Rubicon was finally crossed in the campaign to make contemporary history
worthy of esteem.[3] Two years later the Ludwig Boltzmann Institute for the History of the Working-Class
Movement was founded at what is now the University for
Social and Economic Studies at Linz. Under the direction of Karl R. Stadler, the Institute has sponsored a
large number of studies dealing with various aspects of
Austrian social democracy and the working-class movement.[4]

Perhaps the most significant step in stimulating
research on the history of the First Republic was the
creation in 1972 of the Scientific Commission for Research on the History of Austria between 1927 and 1938.
At the first plenary session of the Commission in October 1972, a number of papers based largely on archival
sources were presented. The hypotheses which were proffered led to animated discussions by the historians and
the political leaders of the 1930s who particpated in
the session.[5] The proceedings of this colloquium and
of six others held between 1974 and 1978 have been pub-

lished. Five of these volumes deal directly with the
subject under discussion at our own colloquium.[6] Many
of the new hypotheses and conclusions of Austrian historians during the past decade either were presented at
these colloquia or else were inspired by discussions at
these meetings. Other interesting reinterpretations can
be found in the large volume entitled Vom Justizpalast
zum Heldenplatz: Studien und Dokumentationen 1927 bis
1938 which was brought out by the Commission to commemorate the thirtieth anniversary of the establishment of
the Second Republic.

Some of the most stimulating findings reported at
the above conferences were gleaned from the protocols of
the ministerial council between 1918 and 1938, which the
Commission will eventually publish. Thus far, five
volumes covering the period of the Dollfuss chancellor-
ship from May 1932 to 16-17 February 1934 have appeared
in print.[7] In addition, the Commission has published
the highly revealing Protokolle des Klubvorstandes der
Christlichsozialen Partei 1932-1934 edited by Walter
Goldinger (Vienna, Verlag für Geschichte und Politik,
1980). These volumes, as well as the memoirs of various
participants in key events of the 1920s and 1930s, and
the enormous mass of documents dating up to 1938 in the
Austrian State Archives that were recently made available to scholars have served as the key sources for most
of the contributions made thus far at the colloquia
organized under the auspices of the Commission.

Limitations of time prevent me from making more
than hasty mention of a handful of what I believe are
some of the most interesting new findings and reinterpretations presented at the above-mentioned conferences
by such Austrian scholars as Adam Wandruszka, Ludwig
Jedlicka, Rudolf Neck, Norbert Leser, Gerhard Botz,
Gerhard Jagschitz, Karl Haas, Anton Staudinger, Karl
Ausch, and Verena Lang. Among them is Wandruszka's
reference to the potent influence exerted on postwar
Austria by the military mentality of officers from the
First World War.[8] Karl Ausch advances the thesis that
the deflationary policy which the Austrian government
followed as a result of the Geneva loan agreement of
1922 led directly to 12 February 1934.[9] A rather
unusual variation of this supposition can be found in
Klerikal-Fascismus, a volume published in 1979 by the
pro-Communist German political scientist Klaus Jörg-
Siegfried, who argues that the Geneva loan was a device
of Western European finance capital to subjugate the
Austrian economy to the control of Western European
banks.[10]

Gerhard Botz has pointed out that the numerous
efforts to influence the course of Austrian politics
through the use of force had a deleterious effect on the
stability of the Republic.[11] Studies by Anton

Standinger, Ludwig Jedlicka and Karl Haas have revealed
the systematic and successful endeavors by War Minister
Carl Vaugoin to transform the Austrian military forces
from a democratic, neutral army into a professional
organization controlled by the Christian Socials.[12]
Highly illuminating is Peter Huemer's revelation of the
invaluable assistance provided to Vaugoin in this matter
by Robert Hecht, the head of the legal bureau of the
army ministry, who also influenced Chancellor Dollfuss'
decision to resort to the old 1917 war emergency decree
after the abolition of Parliament in March 1933.[13]
    Anton Staudinger, Karl Stuhlpfarrer, Karl Haas and
others have pointed out the importance of the National
Socialist successes in the 24 April 1932 diet elections
in Vienna and other provinces in persuading more and
more Christian Social politicians of the need to resort
to authoritarian methods. These gains also encouraged
the Social Democrats to increase their demands for new
elections, though it should have been evident to them
that only the National Socialists would really profit
from any new elections.[14] In Staudinger's opinion, as
early as 1930 the Vaugoin ministry used tactics that at
least bordered on authoritarian [15], and by 1931 Kurt
von Schuschnigg was convinced that a parliamentary government could no longer safeguard the political interests of Catholicism.[16] Moreover, both Staudinger and
Verena Lang have pointed out that shortly before Parliament was formally abolished in March 1933, key Christian
Social Party leaders had concluded that the ministry
should govern in an authoritarian fashion at least until
the constitution could be changed to limit the authority
of Parliament.[17] Dollfuss was of the same opinion although, as Gerhard Jagschitz has stated, when Dollfuss
had become chancellor ten months earlier there had been
no indication that he would turn to an authoritarian
course. He was then regarded as a technocrat and an
agricultural reformer, a leader of the Lower Austrian
agrarian movement which had strong democratic traditions.[18]
    Austrian historians have described not only the
cleavages in the Dollfuss government but also the increasing divergences between the left and right wings of
the Social Democratic Party, and the serious differences
between Theodor Körner and Alexander Eifler over the
organization of the Schutzbund.[19] Everhard Holtmann,
Karl Haas and most recently, Fritz Weber have noted the
readiness of the more conservative Social Democratic
party leaders to make far-reaching concessions in order
to come to terms with Dollfuss.[20]
    During the past decade, scholars outside of Austria
also have made important contributions to the literature
on the First Republic. We all know about the recent
works by the four other participants on this panel about

Chancellor Seipel,[21] the Austrian Heimwehr,[22] the
Austrian National Socialists,[23] and Austrian political
parties and elections.[24]   Let me also call your attention to the disclosures by Eric C. Kollman and Martin
Kitchen about the growing rifts in the Schutzbund,[25]
the studies by Stanley Suval and Alfred D. Low on the
Anschluss movement,[26] and particularly to The Crisis
of Socialism by Anson Rabinbach published last year by
the University of Chicago Press,[27] which I believe is
the best balanced, most objective study on the demise of
the First Republic that I have seen anywhere.
        Yet, much more still needs to be done. To mention
just a few of the areas, we still need more insightful
investigations of the psychological,[28] economic, and
sociological factors that led to the breakdown of social
democracy and the development of right-wing authoritarian and fascist movements not only in Austria but in all
of Central and East-Central Europe in the 1920s and
1930s. A study comparing developments in Austria with
those in Germany would be particularly enlightening. As
for Austria itself, the focus of historians, I believe,
has been concentrated too exclusively on factors bearing
on the breakdown of democracy and the rise of fascism.
We need more and better analyses of the basic economic
and social policies of the governments dominated by the
Christian Socials: their agricultural policies, their
efforts to conclude tariff agreements which would stabilize or increase food prices for the benefit of agricultural interests, their attempts to cut down on unemployment benefits, and their pursuance of deflationary fis-
cal policies. Then, too, although Rainer Nick and Anton
Pelinka have published a useful comparative study of the
First and Second Republics,[29] we need more in-depth
explanations of how the very failures of democracy in
the 1920s and 1930s may have contributed to the development of healthy democratic life in the Second Republic.
And more important, what factors in the First Republic
contributed to what I personally think is the real Austrian miracle of the past half century: the development
of a strong feeling of Austrian nationalism.

NOTES

        1. See especially his Betrayal in Central Europe:
Austria and Czechoslovakia: The Fallen Bastions (New
York, 1939). First published in England under the title
Fallen Bastions.

52

2. See especially "Akten des Ungarischen Ministeriums des Ausseren zur Vorgeschichte des Annexion Osterreichs," Acta Historica, Vol. 7, no. 3-4 (1960), pp. 355-390; "Italien, Ungarn und die Osterreichische Heimwehrbewegung 1928-1931," Osterreich in Geschichte und Literatur, Vol. 9, no. 1 (1965), pp. 1-13; "Akten zu den geheimen Verbindungen zwischen der Bethlen-Regierung und der österreichischen Heimwehrbewegung," Acta Historica, Vol. 11, no. 1-4 (1965), pp. 299-339; Abenddämmerung einer Demokratie: Mussolini, Gömbös und die Heimwehr (Vienna, 1966); and Allianz Hitler-Horthy--Mussolini: Dokumente zur ungarischen Aussenpolitik (1933-1944) (Budapest, 1966).

3. On the founding of the Institute and other earlier efforts to stimulate research in Austrian contemporary history, see especially Ludwig Jedlicka, "Die Entwicklung der zeitgeschichtlichen Forschung von der Reichenauer Tagung 1960 bis heute," in Osterreich 1927 bis 1938. Protokoll des Symposiums in Wien 23. bis 28. Oktober 1972, in Wissenschaftliche Kommission des Theodor-Körner-Stiftungsfonds und des Leopold-Kunschak-Preises zur Erforschung der österreichischen Geschichte der Jahre 1927 bis 1938, Veröffentlichungen, ed. Ludwig Jedlicka and Rudolf Neck, Vol. I (Vienna, 1973), pp. 9-17. Reprinted in Vom Justizpalast zum Heldenplatz. Studien und Dokumentationen 1927 bis 1938 (Vienna, 1975), pp. 17-20.

4. For the work and publications of the Institute for the first ten years of its existence, see Gerhard Botz, Hans Hautmann, and Helmut Konrad, Karl R. Stadler, Rückblick und Ausschau. 10 Jahre Ludwig Boltzmann Institut für Geschichte der Arbeiterbewegung, in Materialien zur Arbeiterbewegung, No. 12 (Vienna, 1978).

5. For a more detailed review of the discussions at this colloquium, see my brief report entitled "First Plenary Meeting of the Commission for Research on the History of Austria between 1927 and 1938," Austrian History Yearbook, Vol. 8 (1972), pp. 389-396.

6. Osterreich 1927 bis 1938; Das Jahr 1934: 12. Februar. Protokoll des Symposiums in Wien am 5. Februar 1974, in Wissenschaftliche Kommission des Theodor-Körner-Stiftungsfonds und des Leopold-Kunschak-Preises zur Erforschung der österreichischen Geschichte der Jahre 1927 bis 1938, Veröffentlichungen, ed. Ludwig Jedlicka and Rudolf Neck, Vol. II (Vienna, 1975); Das Jahr 1934: 25. Juli. Protokoll des Symposiums in Wien am 8. Oktober 1974, in Ibid., Vol. III (Vienna, 1975; Die Ereignisse des 15. Juli 1927. Protokoll des Symposiums in Wien am 15. Juni 1977, in Wissenschaftliche Kommission des

Theodor-Körner-Stiftungsfonds und des Leopold-Kunschak-Preises zur Erforschung der österreichischen Geschichte der Jahre 1918 bis 1938, Veröffentlichungen, ed. Rudolf Neck and Adam Wandruszka, Vol. V (Vienna, 1979); and Die österreichische Verfassung von 1918 bis 1938. Protokoll des Symposiums in Wien am 19. Oktober 1977, in Ibid., Vol. VI (Vienna, 1980).

7. Gertrude Enderle-Burcel, ed., Protokolle des Ministerrats der Ersten Republik, Pt. 8: 20. Mai 1932 bis 25. Juli 1934 (Vienna, 1980-1984).

8. Adam Wandruszka, "Die Erbschaft von Krieg und Nachkrieg," in Osterreich 1927 bis 1938, pp. 23-28.

9. Karl Ausch, "Genfer Sanierung und der 12. Februar 1934," Ibid., pp. 97-103.

10. Klaus-Jörg Siegfried, Klerikal Faschismus. Zur Entstehung und sozialen Funktion des Dollfussregimes in Osterreich. Ein Beitrag zur Faschismusdiskussion, in Sozialwissenschaftliche Studien, Vol. II (Frankfurt am Main, 1979), especially pp. 11-19 and 30-44.

11. Gerhard Botz, Gewalt in der Politik: Attentate, Zusammenstösse, Putschversuche, Unruhen in Österreich 1918 bis 1934 (Munich, 1976).

12. Anton Staudinger, "Bemühungen Carl Vaugoins um Suprematie der Christlichsozialen Partei in Osterreich (1930-33)," Mitteilungen des Osterreichischen Staatsarchivs, Vol. XXIII (1970), pp. 297-376; Ludwig Jedlicka, Ein Heer im Schatten der Parteien: Die militärpolitische Lage Osterreichs 1918-1938 (Graz, 1955), especially Chapter III; Karl Haas, "Zur Wehrpolitik der österreichischen Sozialdemokratie in der Ersten Republik," Osterreich 1927 bis 1938, pp. 75-84.

13. Peter Huemer, Sektionschef Robert Hecht und die Zerstörung der Demokratie in Österreich. Eine historisch-politische Studie (Munich, 1975).

14. Ludwig Jedlicka, Vom alten zum neuen Oster-reich. Fallstudien zur österreichischen Zeitgeschichte 1900-1975 (St. Pölten, 1975), pp. 238-239.

15. Anton Staudinger, "Christlichsoziale Partei und Errichtung des 'Autoritären Ständestaates' in Osterreich," Vom Justizpalast zum Heldenplatz, p. 65.

16. Anton Staudinger, "Die Mitwirkung der christlichsozialen Partei an der Errichtung des autoritären Ständestaates," Osterreich 1927 bis 1938, p. 72.

17. Ibid., pp. 68-70; Staudinger, "Christlichsoziale Partei und Errichtung des 'Autoritären Ständestaates' in Österreich," pp. 68-69; Verena Lang, "Die Haltung des Bundespräsidenten Miklas gegenüber der Sozialdemokratischen Partei 1933/34," Das Jahr 1934: 12. Februar, pp. 9-11.

18. Gerhard Jagschitz, "Bundeskanzler Dollfuss und der Juli 1934," Vom Justizpalast zum Heldenplatz, pp. 233-234. As late as 21 September 1933, the German chargé d'affaires in Italy wrote the German Foreign Ministry that already "at Riccione the Duce...urged [Dollfuss], who until very recently seems to have been convinced of the need for retaining a parliamentary system in Austria, even though it be a limited one, is supposed to have been deeply impressed with Mussolini's forceful representations." Documents on German Foreign Policy 1918-1945, ser. C (1933-1937), Vol. I (Washington, D.C., 1959), p. 829. The italics are mine. On 28 April 1933, the French ambassador in Austria wrote Foreign Minister Paul-Boncour that Dollfuss, who was aware that France would not approve a loan to a fascist regime, had told him "that he was considering the reintroduction of the parliamentary regime in July." As cited in Karl Haas, "Der '12. Februar 1934' als historiographisches Problem," Vom Justizpalast zum Heldenplatz, p. 162. These evaluations of Dollfuss's views by foreign diplomats, of course, do not prove that the Austrian chancellor was a convinced democrat in the spring and summer of 1933, but they seem to indicate that at that time Dollfuss may perhaps not have been a rigid adherent of fascist or authoritarian principles.

19. Rudolf Neck, "Thesen zum Februar. Ursprünge, Verlauf und Folgen," Das Jahr 1934: 12. Februar, especially pp. 15-16 and 20-21; Norbert Leser, Zwischen Reformismus und Bolschewismus: Der Austromarxismus als Theorie und Praxis (Vienna, 1968), pp. 464-509; Norbert Leser, "12 Thesen zum 12. Februar 1934," Das Jahr 1934: 12. Februar, pp. 58-64; Ilona Duczynska, "Theodor Körner und der 12. Februar," Österreich 1927 bis 1938, pp. 109-121.

20. Everhard Holtmann, "Sozialdemokratische Defensivpolitik vor dem 12. Februar 1934," Vom Justizpalast zum Heldenplatz, pp. 116-120; Karl Haas, "Der '12. Februar 1934' als historiographisches Problem," Ibid., pp. 159-168; Fritz Weber, "Karl Renner über die sozialdemokratischen Bemühungen um einen Kompromiss mit Dollfuss, das Aufgeben der 'Anschluss'-Orientierung und die soziale Basis des Austrofaschismus," Zeitgeschichte, Vol. 11, (March 1984), pp. 256-258.

21. Klemens von Klemperer, Ignaz Seipel, Christian Statesman in a Time of Crisis (Princeton, 1972).

22. C. Earl Edmondson, The Heimwehr and Austrian Politics, 1918-1936 (Athens, Ga., 1978); Bruce F. Pauley, Hahnenschwanz und Hakenkreuz: Steirisches Heimatschutz und österreichischen Nationalsozialismus 1918-1934 (Vienna, 1972).

23. Bruce F. Pauley, Hitler and the Forgotten Nazis: A History of Austrian National Socialism (Chapel Hill, 1981).

24. Melanie A. Sully, Political Parties and Elections in Austria: The Search for Stability (New York, 1981).

25. Eric C. Kollman, Theodor Körner, Militär und Politik (Vienna, 1973), especially pp. 202-228; Martin Kitchen, The Coming of Austrian Fascism (London and Montreal, 1980), especially pp. 124-140. The reader's attention should also be called to Ilona Duczynska's interesting and informative Workers in Arms: The Austrian Schutzbund and the Civil War of 1934 (New York, 1978).

26. Stanley Suval, The Anschluss Question in the Weimar Era: A Study of Nationalism in Germany and Austria, 1918-32 (Baltimore, 1974); Alfred D. Low, The Anschluss Movement 1918-1919 and the Paris Peace Conference (Philadelphia, 1974).

27. Anson Rabinbach, The Crisis of Austrian Socialism: From Red Vienna to Civil War 1927-1934 (Chicago, 1983).

28. It should be noted that Peter Loewenberg is making some interesting and pioneering studies of psychological aspects of limited facets of the history of the First Republic. See, for instance, his articles on "Victor and Friedrich Adler: Revolutionary Politics and Generational Conflict in Austro-Marxism," in Peter Loewenberg, Decoding the Past. The Psychohistorical Approach (New York, 1983), pp. 136-160; and "Austro-Marxism and Revolution: Otto Bauer, Freud's 'Dora' Case, and the Crises of the First Austrian Republic," Ibid., pp. 161-204.

29. Rainer Nick and Anton Pelinka, Bürgerkrieg-Sozialpartnerschaft: Das politische System Österreichs 1. und 2. Republik. Ein Vergleich (Vienna, 1983).

5. Social Democracy and the Political Culture of the First Republic

Melanie A. Sully

Among the most striking aspects of the political culture of Austria are the importance and stability of the three main camps: the Social Democratic, the Catholic Christian Social, and the Pan-German nationalist Lager. After both world wars, they were instrumental in shaping new political values and institutions and their influence has persisted throughout the Second Republic. As a comparison of the voting behavior in the First and Second Republics indicates, the potentially disruptive forces of civil war, dictatorship, occupation and war were unable significantly to dislodge the Lager loyalties of the population. The militaristic, aggressive nature of the Lager in the interwar period had been replaced by a mood of consensus and reconciliation rooted in a realization of the disasters which can result from senseless conflict. Although the multifarious associations of the Lager remain, their totalistic claims on the individual and their pedantic mission to convert are weaker. The great coalition (1945-1966) and the system of social and economic partnership have been the vehicles for the transmission of this atmosphere of peace and domestic harmony. A new, positive working relationship between employers and trade unions has been crucial in enabling the political system to adapt smoothly to the change from the great coalition to one-party governments (1966-1983) and, more recently, to a small "red-blue" coalition.

The willingness of the Socialists to cooperate with former political and economic rivals and their integration in the political system also contributed to the stability of the Second Republic. The responses of the Socialists were influenced by the tragedies of the interwar period, including the civil war of 1934, and the eclipse of the party and its affiliated organizations from 1934-1945. A reappraisal was necessary to explain the failures of the prewar party and to avoid a repetition of those mistakes. Many were critical of the

ineptitude of the prewar leadership, and the Socialist
Party (SPÖ) of the Second Republic seemed determined to
avoid confrontations or an ideology which could reopen
old wounds. The new, fragile Republic established after
1945 was considered to be particularly vulnerable to
collapse or division, the longer the Allied occupation
continued. External threats, the experiences of the
Nazi occupation, and later the presence of foreign,
Allied troops encouraged Austrians to develop a positive
awareness of their own identity as a nation. The Lager
pulled together under these circumstances in a way which
had never been experienced in the First Republic.

The Socialists played their part in developing this
new spirit, demonstrating whenever possible their commitment to western democracy and the existing state.
Although some in the party look back with nostalgia to
the courageous Kampfgemeinschaft of the old SDAP and,
like the veteran Austromarxist Josef Hindels, regret the
loss of a specifically "socialist" purpose in the aims
and actions of the present SPÖ, few would question the
positive advantages brought by the new mood compared
with the collapse of the First Republic and its replace-
ment by tyranny and dictatorship. These considerations
have deterred the Lager from sinking back into the feuds
of the past. In short, the bloodshed and horror of the
events of February 1934 survive in memories and shape
contemporary political attitudes.

Throughout their history, the Austrian Social Democrats have demonstrated their respect for the state and
appreciated the need for law and order. The fact that
these elements have often seemed incongruous in a party
the declared aim of which has been to change and re-
structure society represents only one aspect of Austromarxism's dualism. Even before World War I, the party
had led no major attack on the existing system but had
concentrated on modifying the positive aspects of the
economic structure of the Habsburg empire. Both Otto
Bauer and Karl Renner hoped in their different ways to
salvage the best from the existing state and thus resolve political conflict. An SPÖ publication summed up
the efforts of the early Social Democrats in this way:
"They did not want to destroy the house in which they
lived but wished to make it inhabitable for all its
residents."[1] By 1914, the SDAP was dedicated to the
goal of improving the condition of the working class,
but drastic measures to achieve this were relegated to
long-term aims.

The outbreak of war confirmed the SDAP as a staats-
treu party, and opposition to the imperialist conflict,
voiced by a minority under Friedrich Adler, grew only
slowly. Apparently dejected by the persistent law-and-
order mentality of the party executive, Adler complained
at his trial for the assassination of the Minister Pre-

sident Stürgkh that a revolution would only be possible against the wishes of the leadership, and he even went so far as to say that the party executive acted as a brake on revolutionary initiative.[2]

There was some discontent at this lack of militancy in the party's central direction, as the controversies concerning the attitude to the war show. Yet a tragic split in the labor movement, as in Germany, was avoided by the restraint and flexibility of both the left and the right. The fear, which was prevalent throughout the party, that disunity could wreck all its achievements originated in the nineteenth century and has persisted to the present day. During 1918 the empire steadily disintegrated, more through its own inadequacies and the efforts of nationalist movements than as a result of socialist pressure. On 12 November the First Republic was created in the hope that an increase in revolutionary activity along Leninist lines would be forestalled. Communist agitation and propaganda increased in 1919 as food supplies and conditions for the workers deteriorated. The SDAP concluded that a soviet-type putsch would only lead to an invasion by the Entente powers, a blockade and the isolation of Vienna from the provinces and, eventually, a counterrevolution. Common sense, self-discipline, a return to order, and unity were urged by the party in an effort to avoid further bloodshed and a disruption of the system. Eager to rebuild after the ravages of war, the party had little time for revolutionary adventurists, while the workers remained loyal to the SDAP and unimpressed by the factional squabbles of the new Communist Party.

In the first election of the Republic in February 1919 the Social Democrats gained 40.8 percent of the vote, emerging as the strongest party, but lacking an absolute majority. A coalition was formed with the Christian Socials which enabled the Social Democrats to pass some welfare legislation. In its position towards the bourgeois state, the party remained ambivalent and sought to combine reformist practice with radical rhetoric, for it was aware of its vulnerability to external pressure and of the country's dependency on the international economic system.

After the war, the Social Democrats became convinced that their revolutionary ardor had led to the collapse of the monarchy; thus they confirmed the red scare propagated by the right. But, in practice, the party had sought to avert the establishment of a soviet republic and had shown an aptitude for negotiation rather than revolutionary activity; it had preferred democracy and the ballot box to chaos and bloodshed. But despite the fact that the party had such intentions throughout the First Republic, it could not dispel its image as the incarnation of the red terror. Social

Democracy found itself in this position through its
inability to define clear perspectives on the nature of
the state, democracy, the winning of power, and governmental participation. Serious ambiguities resulted from
this lack of clarity which confused the party's own supporters and caused them mistakenly to believe that a
greater revolutionary will existed during times of crisis.

The party's allegiance to the Republic led it to
support the status quo against conservatism and the
right wing; however, in 1920 under Bauer's guidance the
party opted for an oppositional policy which seemed the
"natural" position for the proletariat. Failure to stay
in the coalition has been described by the historian
Robert Kann as a major blunder which led to "twelve
years of increasingly violent internecine domestic conflict, five years of an authoritarian regime and ultimately the catastrophe of the German occupation."[3]
Preoccupation with unity and the fear of defections to
the Communists prompted the party to break with the
coalition which Bauer, in any case, had always regarded
as a temporary measure justifiable when the classes were
in a state of equilibrium. But the self-imposed isolation which accompanied opposition was considered a sui-
cidal policy, especially after 1945, and the SPO more
readily accepted coalition government. The coalition
experiment of 1919-1920 had secured important reforms
for the workers but had not fundamentally changed the
economic order, and though some concessions had been
won, the SDAP was acutely aware of the limitations
placed upon it by the hostile capitalist environment.
Throughout the 1920s the SDAP found itself in the opposition, praising the virtues of a Republic despised by
the government, a Republic which was also predominantly
capitalist. The party did not fulfill the role of a
"loyal opposition" and continued to mount, at least
verbally, an attack on the "system." Confusion resulted
from this paradoxical position, but the party seemed
unaware of the dangers which were mounting to threaten
its very existence.

During the first years of the Republic the party
seemed optimistic about its chances and believed that
its power base, centered in Red Vienna, would inevitably
expand. A concerted battle for votes was initiated with
the intention of attracting the Kleinbürgertum, although
it was made clear to potential supporters and reiterated
by Bauer at the 1926 party conference that the leadership of the SDAP would remain with the proletariat. The
party had an impressive record in mobilizing its traditional clientele which was the industrial working class,
but realized this segment of the population could not
provide it with an absolute majority in Parliament. It
concentrated on wooing agricultural workers, the peas-

antry, small farmers, tradesmen, white-collar workers
and even civil servants and intellectuals who could be
considered allies in the struggle to break the power of
the capitalists and landowners; however, this strategy
was attempted at a time when Lager loyalties were extremely rigid, social cleavages were acute, and the
classes were becoming increasingly more polarized.
Competition for votes in the middle ground was to be
more successful under the sober political conditions of
the Second Republic, but in the 1920s it was an unreal-
istic ploy. Furthermore, the SDAP's emphasis on the
primacy of the urban proletariat made the party's over-
tures to the lower middle class less convincing. In
addition, the comprehensive network of associations and
the distinct political culture which acted as a barrier
(Abgrenzung), shielding conscious socialists from bourgeois influences, might have seemed frightening to members of the petit-bourgeoisie who showed more sympathy
for the class enemies of the SDAP, especially as economic conditions worsened. The elements which the SDAP
had hoped to integrate ultimately sought refuge in the
bourgeois camp.
  The efforts of the party were thus based on false
assumptions restricting maneuverability in so far as the
leadership hesitated to implement radical policies which
would alienate the petit-bourgeoisie. But this alienation occurred anyway, partly as a result of the contradictions inherent in Austromarxism. At the same time as
it appealed to nonproletarian sections of society, the
party was assiduously constructing an elaborate counter-
culture in which a socialist being would be able to
develop, free from all bourgeois contamination. This
cultural policy hardened the already existing opposition
of the Catholic associations and cut the party off from
all but the most committed. After 1945, and particularly in the Kreisky era, the bridge-building efforts of
the SPO gradually found a response, although ambiguities
persisted. A recent article in the party's theoretical
journal Die Zukunft noted that the SPO still wished to
be a staatstragend party in a capitalist system yet also
showed nostalgia for the idea of a class party with a
Gegenkultur.[4] In the First Republic the inability to
resolve this kind of tension was an outstanding characteristic of the Social Democratic Party.
  The SDAP consistently maintained that it sought
power in the Republic in order to preserve democracy and
to quell the forces of tyranny. A paramilitary organization, the Schutzbund, was conceived for the purpose of
defending the Republic with disciplined cohorts, but was
envisaged by the party executive as a deterrent which
should not have to be mobilized. Nevertheless, opponents of socialism and of Bolshevism could construe its
existence as the beginnings of the red revolution, and

misunderstandings grew after the SDAP party conference
at Linz in 1926 and the tragic July days of 1927.

At Linz, the party inserted the unfortunate reference to a dictatorship into its program. It came out of
the assumption that the party would come to power with
the backing of the country but right-wing forces would
proceed to mount a counterrevolution and the workers
would then be forced to retaliate with a dictatorship,
which would be necessary not to subvert democracy but to
protect it from reactionary enemies. Thus dictatorship
was not envisaged as the means for a dramatic seizure of
power but as a last resort to defend a position which
had been democratically won. Nevertheless, the reference had unpleasant connotations of Bolshevism which the
right fully exploited in order to gain financial support
from industry for their efforts to stamp out the "reds."
Bauer and the party abhorred the thought of violence and
human suffering and deplored the worst aspects of the
Russian revolution. It would have been more pertinent
for the party to have developed a strategy which would
have secured power before discussing the hypothetical
aftermath, but the strong element of determinism in
Austrian Social Democracy worked against this. The
party felt it was on the brink of success and was preparing for the tasks which would confront it once in
government. The reference to a "dictatorship" was misleading and gave the impression to the party's own members, as well as to its opponents, that it was more
inclined to radicalism than it in fact was.

In 1927, after the acquittal of right-wing Frontkämpfer members who had opened fire on and killed socialist workers, there were frantic demonstrations in
Vienna and pleas that the SDAP fight back. The party
was reluctant to use force, fearing that the escalation
of an explosive situation could lead to bloodshed and
defeat. Yet the rank and file, apparently frustrated by
the procrastination of the leadership, continued the
demonstrations, only to be mercilessly shot down by
police forces better equipped for conflict. Shock and
disillusionment reverberated throughout the party which
no longer seemed as invincible as it had taught itself
to believe. The Schutzbund, halfheartedly and belatedly
mobilized, was called in, more to maintain order than to
take the offensive. The party wished at all costs to
avoid a civil war, although an article in its paper Die
Arbeiter-Zeitung of 15 July 1927 implied that this was
the situation which already prevailed in the republic:
"The bourgeois world is constantly warning against
starting a civil war; but is not this provocative release, scot-free, of men who have killed workers (indeed
because they killed workers) in itself tantamount to a
civil war?" Yet, despite this assessment, no call for a
strike action came from the party, and supplies of arms

were not released.

The masses felt badly let down by the leadership's lack of positive direction during the events in 1927 and some concluded that uncoordinated action without the official blessing of the party would always end in failure. After 1927, the masses waited in vain for a signal from party headquarters which would be the battle cry to reverse the rightist onslaught. Apparently dazed after 1927, the party was unable to grasp the essence of the new power relationships. A short spell in government after World War I, an indomitable position in Vienna and electoral progress (in 1927 the party had gained 42.3 percent), had given the Social Democrats an illusion of strength. By 1929 10 percent of the population were members of the SDAP; the right wing, by contrast, seemed weak, divided, and frightened. But the events of 1927 taught the party to think less ambitiously and the possession of power no longer seemed imminent. As has been noted by Anson Rabinbach, the mood became more defeatist and no offensive strategy was devised to reflect the real power situation.[5] Bauer rejected a coalition with the bourgeoisie but also refused to contemplate a civil war or revolutionary action. Both courses, it seemed, were equally repugnant, and immobilism spread throughout the party apparatus; in 1934 everyone was still "waiting for Godot."

In the last years of the Republic the party persisted with its negative dualism, refusing to consider either governmental participation or a revolutionary overthrow of the system. It steadfastly adhered to formal democratic procedures at a time when they were being undermined by extraparliamentary activity and by bitter class hatred. The theoretical sentiments of the SDAP continued to be more radical than its reformist practice, but unity and organizational strength were maintained. The bourgeois bloc was prone to internal factional disputes and personal rivalries which led the Socialists to hope that the right contained the seeds of its own destruction and would ultimately collapse.

After the events of 1927 and scenes of angry workers demonstrating in street battles, the right became even more convinced of the need to stamp out the threat of the red menace, and industrialist financing of the Heimwehr increased. Throughout 1933 the government stepped up its war of nerves in a desperate effort to reduce the influence of the Social Democrats. Workers were deprived of basic, hard-won rights and felt vulnerable, frightened of losing their jobs. Trade union bargaining power was steadily reduced. The Renner men in the SDAP urged the party to explore some kind of arrangement with Dollfuss which would help the position of the workers and forestall the possibility of a brown-black alliance. Bauer opposed the idea of a coalition

with a right-wing dictatorship, believing that the party
would only incur blame for the economic crisis and would
not be strong enough to utilize effectively its position. The gulf between the camps seemed too great for a
realistic consideration of a viable coalition. Even
members of the Christian workers' movement were too committed to their Lager to make meaningful cooperation
with the SDAP possible and, as a political force, this
wing carried too little weight with the government to
influence social or constitutional policies and improve
the workers' position.

In his pamphlet Der Aufstand der österreichischen
Arbeiter, Otto Bauer assumed personal responsibility for
the defeat of the party in the civil war. He referred
to the intransigent opposition of the party to the calling of new elections in 1932 which drove the Christian
Socials into a coalition with Fey and the Heimwehr in
order to stave off the Nazi threat. The SDAP had been
afraid of repeating the mistakes of the Tolerierungs-
politik of the German Social Democrats, Bauer explained.
One of the most fateful errors, he reflected, had been
the failure to call a general strike on 15 March 1933
when Dollfuss prevented parliament from reassembling.
Apparently, Bauer had been hoping for a peaceful settlement with Dollfuss and the party had not wanted to abandon this chance and lurch prematurely into the carnage
of a civil war. Bauer had also worried that a general
strike would have fomented a brown-black alliance which
would have been detrimental to the interest of the working class. The government continued to whittle away the
power of the Social Democrats, depriving them of the
Schutzbund, a free press and the right to strike. Meanwhile, in September 1933, the SDAP executive confined
the party to using armed force only if the government
proclaimed a fascist constitution, violated the autonomy
of Vienna, or attempted to dissolve either the trade
unions or the party. Thus the government could avoid
provoking conflict with the Socialists yet could reduce
their power in areas where it seemed the party was not
prepared to fight. It increased the powers of the police and intensified control of the press. Leaders of
the workers' movement, often those who knew where arms
were being stored, were imprisoned and weapons were confiscated. The party became trapped in a mood of hopeless defeatism, its confidence shattered and its leadership lacking conviction that a general strike would be
effective given the high numbers of unemployed. As
Martin Kitchen points out in his book, The Coming of
Austrian Fascism, the Social Democrats had devised a
brilliant recipe for inaction: they demanded obedience
from the masses and, at the same time, waited for them
to take the initiative.[6]

The civil war that the party dreaded came in any

case and under less favorable conditions than in 1933.
The final call to arms in February 1934 came not from
the headquarters of the party but from desperate and
frustrated members in Linz who could no longer tolerate
the "wait and see" policy of the leadership. Rather
than surrender their arms to the police, they decided to
use them, thereby throwing the Viennese party into utter
disarray and inspiring others to follow their example.
Inferior in arms, the workers were quickly thrown on the
defensive in the capital and cornered in the magnificent
municipal flats of "Red Vienna." The last stand was
made in many of these apartment blocks which had been
portrayed by the right as the launching sites for the
"red revolution." Built like fortresses (with convenient open courtyards, thick walls, narrow windows) and
strategically located near railway stations, these flats
could plausibly be construed as part of a grand design
to seize power. But, once again, appearance contrasted
markedly with the actions, or inaction, of the party
leadership. A humanitarian strain, predominant in the
party since the days of Victor Adler, as well as voli-
tional weakness made it reluctant and even horrified to
countenance the thought of violence, however much its
radical rhetorical bluffs incensed the opposition and
misled its own supporters. External factors as well as
internal contradictions contributed to the disasters of
1934, and the Austrians had good reason to feel that,
with Hitler in power in Germany, a fascist Italy to the
south, and no offers of outside assistance, the situation was hopeless.

To summarize, it can be said that the failure of
the SDAP leadership to act decisively was one of the
major factors responsible for its defeat in the civil
war. The government was by no means united or strongly
entrenched in power and the reliability of the troops
was considered problematic, but the party did not contemplate using the full force of the Schutzbund and
hoped these units would be a sufficient deterrent to
avoid conflict. Actually, the overall perception of the
role of the Schutzbund varied amongst leading Social
Democrats: whereas Deutsch stressed military putschist
tactics, Körner advocated a politicized guerilla-type
formation. The masses imagined that the Schutzbund
existed in order to fight and were disillusioned by the
inadequacies which were exposed during the February battles. Many in the party were confused by the fact that
the initiaitive to fight had been taken against the
wishes of the SDAP executive and were reluctant to support rebels breaking with party discipline.

Also, by 1934, the workers were already demoralized
by the effects of the economic depression and the lack
of any solutions or cause for hope. The call for a
general strike during the civil war was not effective

and the government continued to circulate its propaganda
and newspapers. The fact that the railways continued to
run enabled the executive to move in supplies from Hungary. The SDAP could not coordinate the sporadic action
of its members in the provinces and was particularly
hindered by the lack of response in Lower Austria, which
contained industrial areas that could have formed a link
with comrades fighting in neighboring Styria and Upper
Austria. Given these circumstances, the extent and
resilience of the fighting workers is impressive; however, the tragic end to the bitter battles which was
followed by the establishment of a corporate state,
showed that courage alone is not enough to defend democracy. In his introduction to Karl Stadler's book Opfer
verlorener Zeiten, Bruno Kreisky remarked that one of
the lessons to be learned from these events was that it
was better to live for an idea than to die for one.[7]
The spirit of the Austrian workers could not be crushed,
and the battles and sacrifices provided hope for those
who survived. For over a decade afterwards, the rank
and file clung to memories of the heroism shown in the
fight against oppression and tyranny. Most remained
loyal to the ideals of Social Democracy and believed
that the party would one day be rebuilt to fulfill these
dreams.

The illegal Revolutionary Socialist group which
succeeded the SDAP retained communication with Bauer and
the old party, even if at times the relationship was
strained. Some continuity was maintained and a mass
drift of members to the Communist Party was avoided.
The fighting workers of 1934 were accepted by the new
SPO after 1945 and glamorized as a valiant chapter in
its history; the fact that the February heroes had
fought and died in spite of party instructions found
little mention. The eleventh-hour stand of the Schutzbund and the subsequent fighting provided the SPO with a
glorious tradition of which it could be proud.

The immediate result of the civil war was the dissolution of the party and its organizations and the establishment of an authoritarian regime which ultimately
paved the way for Nazism. This inaugurated a reappraisal of social democratic aims and methods and led to a
period of introspective speculation which included criticisms of the past. Such reassessment also took place
in the conservative Catholic camp, particularly during
the Nazi occupation. By 1945 a specific "Austrian"
national consciousness was in the making which had been
absent before the civil war. A spirit of patriotism,
rooted in a need to free Austria from external controls
and to avoid the feuds of the past, developed in both of
the main Lager, whereas in the First Republic a readiness to look outside of Austria, particularly to Germany, had undermined confidence in a fragile, new poli-

tical system increasingly attacked by economic crises.
The Moscow Declaration of 1943, which indicated that the
Great Powers were willing to help an independent Austria, contributed to the growing awareness of the positive aspects of nationhood.

The leaders of Austrian socialism after 1945 were
more pragmatic and more concerned with administration
than their predecessors. There was a disinclination to
engage in idle theoretical debates and a preference for
solid, constructive work. Many of the old militants had
died or lost their revolutionary zeal, and a mood of sober realism replaced ideological politics. Part of the
reevaluation process involved a different attitude to
democracy. In the First Republic, the SDAP was accused
by its opponents of pursuing undemocratic aims, although
the party adhered faithfully to democratic norms and
procedures even when they were moribund. The SDAP had
tended to qualify its enthusiasm for democracy, often
referring to it as a means to the ultimate goal of socialism. The party's clearer commitment to democracy
after 1945 helped to stabilize the political system but
also made it vulnerable to criticisms from the left that
the socialist goal has been abandoned.

The presence of a greater Demokratieverständnis,
detectable in both of the major Lager since 1945, does
not automatically enhance the democratic nature of the
state. The political scientist Anton Pelinka has pointed out that a new vigilance may be necessary to guard
against the dangers of oligarchy, since the democratic
consciousness which has developed in the Second Republic
among the political elites has not been paralleled by a
similar process among the masses.[8] A pattern of stable voting behavior and strong loyalty to one of two
parties and their associations indicate this ongoing
conservatism. The political system is managed by a
bureaucratic cartel of elites manifest in the operation-
al mode of social partnership. There is more stability
than in the First Republic, but the influence of the
ordinary citizen on the decision-making process has not
increased correspondingly.[8]

The experience of civil war contributed to the belief that open conflict in the political system could
only be a negative and ultimately crippling influence.
After World War II, the SPO became devout supporters of
the Great Coalition, showing none of the reservations on
the matter which had characterized Bauer's thinking. At
the party conference in 1948 Eduard Weikhart, later
state secretary in the Ministry of Trade, reminded party
members of the disasters which ensued after the SPO left
the coalition in 1920, surrendering the management of
the state to its opponents.[9] And in 1961 Oskar
Helmer, former Minister of the Interior, referred to the
specter of civil war when he advocated a continuation of

the coalition with the OVP.[10] Throughout the 1950s the SPO continued to rid itself of ambiguities in its attitude toward the bourgeois state, communism and democracy. The revision of the Linz program which was finally adopted in Vienna in 1958 totally rejected all forms of dictatorship and acknowledged the integration of the party in the Republic; the determinism of the party was replaced by a belief that the working people had to take positive action to overthrow capitalism.

Under Kreisky's leadership, the SPO continued to affirm its faith in western democracy and unequivocally rejected communism. Bauer's old dream of winning over 51 percent in an election was eventually fulfilled and the great progress which Austria made in social welfare legislation brought it closer to the goal of achieving humanitarian social democracy on an eminently peaceful basis. Some left-wing socialist intellectuals and the Socialist Youth think that the SPO did not use its absolute majority in the 1970s to its fullest potential and that the international economic environment once again restricted the scope of the Austrians. But the party believes in the gradual build-up of democratic power centers within the system and is not discouraged by the fact that this process will be painstaking and slow. A new program adopted in 1978 showed a greater understanding for and sympathy with Christian values--the party is eager to foster contacts with the Church and avoid the narrow, doctrinaire approach of the SDAP. And despite some reversals in fortune, the SPO can be proud of its achievements.

Some ghosts of the past continue to haunt Austrian politics, however, occasionally causing the party some embarrassment. Since the old party was brutally repressed by presumed "fascists," the latter have often been considered a greater danger than their common enemy, National Socialism. Although the SPO remains acutely sensitive on the Austrofascist chapter in the country's history, it has been accused of comparative tolerance on the Nazi question. In 1949 the League of Socialist Freedom Fighters was established within the party to remind it of the dangers of fascism and Nazism and the sufferings of old comrades. In 1982 it had over 4,000 members who ensure that the party's glorious traditions and past sacrifices will never be forgotten. On appropriate occasions, they lay wreaths on the graves of those who perished at the hands of the fascists. This organization urges constant vigilance to avoid the growth of right-wing radical organizations in the future.

After the war, the Socialist Helmer was eager to revive the third force in Austrian politics--that with pronounced Pan-German sympathies--in order to offset the monopoly of the Catholic and conservative OVP on the

right. Under Kreisky, the SPÖ came to an arrangement
with the successor to the third Lager, the Austrian
Freedom Party (FPÖ), and introduced a reform of the
electoral system which was benficial to this small party. Although Friedrich Peter, the leader of the FPÖ at
the time, was attacked for his activities as an officer
in the Waffen SS, one of his main protectors proved to
be Bruno Kreisky. In the 1979 election campaign, the
SPÖ resurrected the ghost of the anti-socialist Bürgerblock of the First Republic by implying that the ÖVP
would ally with the FPÖ if the SPÖ did not win an absolute majority, and this strategy, which played on old
fears, was successful and the party gained 51 percent of
the vote, its best results during the Second Republic.
In 1983 the SPÖ lost seats and votes and entered a coalition with the FPÖ which proved to be an uneasy alliance: one of the new government's decisions, which was
sanctioned by the FPÖ Minister of Defence, was to swear
in soldiers of the Bundesheer at Mauthausen, once a
concentration camp. A similar ceremony took place at
Karl Marx Hof, scene of some of the battles of February
1934. It was hoped that this action would help overcome
the divisions of the past, yet tensions remain and the
ÖVP is suspicious of the SPÖ's commemoration of the
civil war. It resents what it considers to be Socialist
insinuations that the Christian Social camp was solely
responsible for the war and the corporate state. The
SPÖ, on the other hand, rejects the theory that responsibility for the conflict must be shared and is particularly determined to explode the myth that Dollfuss was a
patriot who saved the fatherland from Nazi marauders.
These emotive views and the periodic resurgence of old
controversies demonstrate that the civil war and its
consequences left an indelible mark on the country's
history.

NOTES

1. Das grosse Erbe, p. 30

2. Friedrich Adler vor dem Ausnahmegericht (Berlin,
1919), p. 51.

3. Robert Kann, "Karl Renner," Journal of Modern
History, Vol. 23, Part 3 (1951), pp. 243-49, esp. p.
247.

4. H. Berger and H. Tieber, "Die Partei politisie-
ren--die Diskussion demokratisieren!" Die Zukunft (Nov.
1983), p. 17.

70

5. Anson Rabinbach, The Crisis of Austrian Social-ism (Chicago, 1983).

6. Martin Kitchen, The Coming of Austrian Fascism (London, 1980), p. 128.

7. Karl R. Stadler, Opfer verlorener Zeiten (Vienna, 1974), p. 10.

8. Anton Pelinka, Zeitgeschichte, Bericht über die gesamtösterreichischen Seminare, Zeitgeschichte I,II, III: Beiträge zur Lehrerfortbildung, Vol. 22 (Vienna, 1982), p. 92.

9. Protokoll, SPO, (Vienna, 1948), p. 142.

10. Jacques Hannak, Ausgewählte Reden und Schriften (Vienna, 1963), p. 98.

6. Otto Bauer as an Ambivalent Party Leader

Peter Loewenberg

> Zwischen der Verdrängung und der normal zu nennen-
> den Abwehr des Peinlich-Unverträglichen durch
> Anerkennung, Überlegung, Urteil und zweckmässiges
> Handeln liegt eine grosse Reihe von Verhaltungs-
> weisen des Ichs von mehr oder weniger deutlich
> pathologischem Charakter.
>
> Between repression and what we call the normal me-
> thod of defending against what is painfully unbear-
> able--through recognition, planning, judgment, and
> appropriate action--there lie a great many modes of
> ego behavior that are more or less clearly of a
> pathological character.
>
> --Sigmund Freud, "Eine Erinnerungsstörung
> auf der Akropolis" (1936)

I wish to offer the following four propositions for
discussion in addressing the issues of "Politics, the
State and Violence" in "Austrian Social Democracy, 1918-
1934: The Socialist Experiment and Its Collapse."
These are: (1) "Socialism" was limited to Vienna; (2)
the Social Democratic Party was captive to a rigid ideology of class war; (3) the Socialists were genuine hu-
manitarians, not an instrument of violent combat; and
(4) the party leadership, particularly Otto Bauer, was
ambivalent and inept.

The first proposition is that the "socialist experiment" was structurally limited to one city and one
state (Land) in the Republic. Vienna had taxing and
borrowing power which enabled the Land Wien to finance
bold social and housing programs. However, the built-in
structural conflict of one urban Social Democratic state
and small pockets of industry elsewhere counterpoised
against a conservative agrarian society was a formula
for Socialist frustration and defeat. The Social Democrats were unable to break out of their urban industrial
constituencies and power bases to appeal to other

71

classes and social groups.

Otto Bauer was the articulate and charismatic leader whose programmatic formulations became the policy of the Socialist Party in the First Austrian Republic. His theory of the "balance of classes" was presented to the Social Democratic Parteitag in 1921. Applying the phrase from Friedrich Engels to the political situation of the First Republic, he argued that the result of the Austrian revolution was that "the conflicting classes held each other in equilibrium." There was a "balance" of power between the industrial areas of Vienna, Lower Austria, and Upper Styria which could not be governed against the will of the workers and the agrarian areas, which could not be governed against the will of the peasants. This inherent ideological, economic and political conflict between the socialist state (Land) of Vienna and the conservative central government of Austria created one of the tragic structural dilemmas of the First Republic.

Bauer also developed other "balances." He perceived a contradiction between the power of the proletariat within the Austrian nation and the total powerlessness of the nation as a whole beyond its boundaries. After 1920 he saw a balance between the government and the bourgeois parliamentary majority, on the one hand, and the extraparliamentary power position of Social Democracy, on the other; this he termed a balance of "parliamentary democracy" of the bourgeoisie and "functional democracy" which made the government dependent in its most important decisions upon the cooperation of proletarian organizations.[1] Even in the new Austrian Army, the command of the bourgeois officers was limited by the socialist consciousness and organization of the troops and of the Soldiers' Councils. According to Bauer, the middle-class paramilitary formations and the proletarian order-keeping force were "holding each other in check," and the republic was a "compromise between the classes, a result of the balance of class forces" ("Gleichgewichts der Klassenkräfte").[2] "It was a republic in which no class was strong enough to rule the other classes, and therefore all classes had to share the power of state with each other."[3]

As early as the spring of 1914, Bauer looked forward to the class-conscious proletariat becoming both a majority of the population and a parliamentary majority.[4] Then the ruling classes would have to choose between permitting peaceful reforms in the ownership of the means of production or staging a counterrevolution, which in turn would instigate a proletarian revolution that would be indominable as soon as the class-conscious workers constituted a majority of the population.

The second proposition states that the Social Democratic Party was hamstrung by an ideology of Marxist

revolutionary theory which was interpreted, particularly
by Otto Bauer, as a guide to action. Its premise was
fatalistic: the automatic accession of socialists to
power upon the collapse of bourgeois capitalism. The
language of the party's Linz Program of 1926 which suggested class warfare and "dictatorship of the proletariat" served to alienate the peasantry and the middle
classes from Social Democracy. Unlike the National
Socialists, the party leadership and intellectuals had
contempt for the affective situation of the farmer,
small-town shopkeeper, and petty bureaucrat. The party
ideologists also mistakenly identified the real threat
of the early 1930s as bourgeois capitalist democracy
rather than fascism. This misjudgment, combined with
Bauer's analysis that the social alternatives were capitalism or socialism, led in the early 1930s to a refusal of coalitions with the middle class.

Otto Bauer's special contributions to the ideology
of ambivalence in the 1920s were four: (a) in 1921, the
theory of "balance of class forces"; (b) in 1926, a particular variant of the "dictatorship of the proletariat"
dependent on the 1914 theory of a 51 percent majority;
(c) in 1928, the theory of the "pause"; and (d) in 1930,
the theory of "obstruction." In all of these formulations we see a connection between the man and his intellectual product: Bauer is the cautious, balancing, ob-
sessional theoretician who uses his superior intellect
to avoid making decisions. His conclusion in each case
is that the optimal and "correct" current position for
Austrian Marxists is to wait and do nothing until the
constellation of forces naturally moves in their direction so that conflict will be resolved without danger or
confrontation.

Bauer's special theory of the "dictatorship of the
proletariat" was incorporated in the Linz Program
adopted at the Parteitag in November 1926 with the immediate purpose of diverting the attempts of the extreme
left, led by Max Adler, to promote an endorsement of the
tactics of violence. The formulation was Bauer's and
his phrasing is a tour de force in the adroit expression
of ambivalence, for it ingeniously manages to contain in
one statement the acquisition of power both through majority rule as well as through civil war and the dictatorship of the proletariat:

The Social Democratic Workers' Party must...main-
tain for the working class the possibility of destroying the class rule of the bourgeoisie by democratic methods. If, however, despite all these
efforts of the Social Democratic Workers' Party, a
counterrevolution of the bourgeoisie should succeed
in shattering democracy, then the working class
could only conquer the power of the state by civil

war....If, however the bourgeoisie should resist
the social revolutionary change, which will be the
task of the state power of the working class, by
planned constriction of economic life, by violent
uprising, or by conspiracy with foreign counterrevolutionary powers, then the working class would
be compelled to break the resistance of the bourgeoisie by means of dictatorship.[5]

Bauer's special theory of the "dictatorship of the
proletariat" was so hemmed in by qualifications--it
would only take place after the democratic election of a
Socialist government and only if the bourgeois forces
engaged in a "violent uprising, by conspiracy with foreign counterrevolutionary powers"--that it would never
take place. In fact, it claims nothing more than the
right of a government to self-defense against sabotage,
violence and insurrection. Yet at the same time the
language was so provocative and inflamatory, and was
perceived as so threatening by the middle class and the
peasantry, that these segments of the population were
even further alienated from Social Democracy.
    In the crisis of 1927, when Karl Renner advocated a
policy of coalition, saying, "This theory of pauses is a
desolate, enervating conception of Socialism....A general socialization is a general nonsense,"[6] Bauer
steadfastly opposed a coalition, holding that it would
only disappoint the workers and strengthen the Communists.[7] But by 1928 events had made his earlier
theory untenable and Bauer was ready to reevaluate his
theory of balance and to redefine the revolution of
1918. He did this with the theory of "the pause" ("die
Pause") which was defined as the period between the
former revolution and the next revolution. Whereas in
the early 1920s he had viewed the Austrian Republic as a
compromise balance of class forces, now, in the light of
the shattering defeat of July 1927, Bauer reassessed the
1918 revolution as a triumph of the entire bourgeoisie
over the privileged feudal forces of monarchy, dynasty,
and industrial aristocracy. Since the present was a
phase of the stabilization of capitalism, no Social
Democrat should serve as minister in a coalition government, for whatever he achieves will be won at the expense of the broad mass of the proletariat.[8]
    Bauer identified the party's "weapon" as that of
"obstruction" ("das Kampfmittel der Obstruktion"), by
which he meant that the Socialist minority would ob-
struct the bourgeois majority in parliament. He thought
that the middle class parties would not dare to break
the obstruction and enforce their will upon the Socialists for fear of provoking an uprising by the working
masses outside of the parliament.[9] After 1927 Bauer
conceded that the bourgeoisie no longer feared prole-

tarian recourse to the streets, for they had superiority
of force there as well as in government, so in 1930 he
turned to the parliament as the hope for the Socialist
future. As before, Bauer's emotional stance is one of
passive waiting: he said if the Socialists can
strengthen their parliamentary position, their opponents
will "be forced to come to us and to share the power of
state."[10] Furthermore, since the issue is no longer
whether Austria is to be a bourgeois republic--since
that issue has been settled and the republic stabi-
lized--now the bourgeois political alliances among middle class and peasants would fall apart, to the benefit
of the working class.

Will the triumphant bourgeoisie which has now
achieved power turn against democracy? Bauer asked. His
answer was decidedly negative. No land presents less
attractive prospects for a violent resolution of class
war than Austria, for it would result in famine, the
destruction of foreign credit, and industrial standstill. He was convinced the bourgeoisie would decide to
share power, not with fascism against democracy, but
with the Socialists to defend the democratic republic.[11]

According to my third proposition, the Socialists
abhorred violence and were a truly humanitarian party.
They predicated their strategy on a policy of bluff by
threatening military action by the Schutzbund. After
the disastrous events of the failed general strike of
July 1927 it should have been as obvious to the Social
Democratic leadership as it was to the opposition that a
tactic of confrontations with the state and its Heimwehr
auxiliaries was an ineffectual bluff. Some Socialist
leaders such as Theodor Körner saw this and predicted
the failure of a military policy, but Körner's voice was
not heard and he resigned.

As events moved toward the demise of Austrian democracy, Bauer repeatedly used the rhetorical symbol of
"responsibility to mothers" to rationalize inaction. At
the 1929 Socialist Parteitag he said: "We will continue
our policy of prudence and consciousness of responsibility, however the fascists jeer at it, that we simply owe
to the mothers of this land, and that we also owe to the
requirements of the working class itself, which must be
protected from falling into traps set for it by fascism."[12] The anticipated crisis came to a head in
March 1933 with an Austrian reflection of the Nazi
seizure of power in Germany. On 10 March, responding to
the first attempt by the Dollfuss government to end
Austrian democracy, Bauer gave a speech to 1,500 members
of the Socialist Party which, behind its very superficial tone of militance, already signalled despair and
defeat:

> One thing I want to say, without wishing to sound
> pathetic--in this difficult time there is only one
> thing which still makes this sad life bearable:
> the sole fact that in our country we can at least
> still get together to promote our thoughts, ideas
> and ideals. At least we can still fight for an-
> other, better, greater future. The bourgeoisie
> shall know this and from it understand our deter-
> mination: if they also take this from us, then
> life would be worthless for us.[13]

The ultimate issues are posed in the idioms of German
Romanticism and idealism, and Bauer is only one step
away from insisting on the right of the mind to hold
thoughts, ideas and ideals. This speech, so reminiscent
of the "inner emigration" of some Germans of the 1930s,
was a concession of emotional defeat before the battle.
Bauer depicted the international scene to the party
assemblage in terms of a hopeless encirclement by fascism: in the south, fascist Italy; a military dictatorship in Yugoslavia; a fascist "Hungary of the Hangmen"
to the east; and now Hitler's Germany on the western
border. "In this situation, in which we are surrounded,
it will be the great, difficult, but therefore all the
more glorious task of the Austrian working class to
maintain Austria as an island of democracy, an island of
freedom, in the midst of this fascist sea." [14]. Bauer
then prophesied that if fascism did triumph in Austria,
it would be inescapably bound to the fascist alliance,
and this would sooner or later mean that we "would be
sent to the slaughter bench for the glory of Misters
Hitler, Mussolini and Horthy...."[15] Again he spoke of
the "responsibility to the mothers of the land" ("Ve-
rantwortung vor den Müttern des Landes").[16]
    On 15 March Chancellor Engelbert Dollfuss forcibly
prevented the convening of the Parliament in which his
government had a majority of one vote. Thus Austrian
democracy ended in a coup d'état which all observers,
including Bauer and the Socialists, had anticipated.
This was the moment in the history of the First Republic
at which the Social Democrats stood before the decision
to fight. The working class was in a stronger position
to do battle in March 1933 than it was to be in February
1934. Bauer subsequently said the Socialists should
have responded with a general strike and their own offensive. Analyzing these events eleven months later,
from exile, he implied that he had been blind and now
could see clearly. "We were then still stupid enough to
trust Dollfuss' promise. We backed out of the fight
because we wished to spare the country the catastrophe
of a bloody civil war. The civil war broke out eleven
months later anyway, but under what were for us essentially more unfavorable conditions. It was an error,

the most fatal of our errors," he stated.[17]   "The
working masses awaited the signal to fight. At that
time the railway workers were not yet as battered as
they were twelve months later. The military organization of the government was then much weaker than it was
in February 1934. We, then, might have been able to
win. But we shrank back before the fight at that time.
We still believed we could come to a peaceful solution
through negotiations."[18]

The Socialists convened an extraordinary Parteitag
in October 1933 to make policy for what was viewed as a
critical situation. Bauer formulated "Four Points"
which were absolute limits, for if they were breached,
the Socialists would fight: (1) the suspension of the
rights of the city of Vienna and the imposition of a
government commissioner; (2) attacks on the trade
unions; (3) dissolution of the party; and (4) the imposition of a fascist constitution.[19]   By the promul-
gation of these four points or "triggers" to resistance,
the Socialists did two disastrous things. They in
effect told the government that their other positions of
strength, for example the Schutzbund, were vulnerable to
attack and would not be defended; and most important,
they left further initiatives to the government.

The fourth proposition above is that the party
leaders were ambivalent as to how social change was to
be accomplished. Coming from a bifurcated tradition of
revolutionary theory wedded to meliorism in practice,
they constantly talked violent revolution while passive-
ly waiting for the decomposition of the class enemy.
Bauer's obsessing was the important historical symptom
of an ambivalence toward revolutionary action in the
European socialist tradition. Obsessing is of course
not inherent in Marxism, for Marxist ideology has not
prevented other leaders from taking decisive steps at
critical junctures to ensure that they or their movements survive or even succeed. This was a direct
expression of Bauer's character and that of his party.
He exhibited constant ambivalence and doubt in the emotional sphere, using intellectual twisting and turning
to avoid conflict. He placed events in an explainable,
albeit retrospective, Marxist theoretical pattern as
though when he had done so he could control the world.
He had a strong belief in the power of his own thought
to structure the world and influence events. Bauer
followed a political and a psychological strategy of
passivity in dealing with the class enemy in Austrian
politics, a strategy of waiting until the apple falls
into his lap. He assumed a stance of expectant and intellectual receptivity with the confidence that sooner
or later events were determined to move in the direction
of socialism.

The passive, expectant stance of "do nothing, they

will have to come to us" is characteristic of both his
personality and his political style. Successful states-
men--whether revolutionaries, such as Lenin, or conservatives, such as Bismarck--used opportunities that
others did not see and then molded events through decisive interventions. Successful party leadership and
diplomacy are generative activities. When openings for
action are created, the moment must be seen and used,
the development of history shaped by sensing and in-
voking latent potentials. If these creative initiatives
are not taken, the dynamic possibilities will be left to
other protagonists who will use them for their own ends,
as happened in Austria fifty years ago.

NOTES

1. Otto Bauer, Speech to the Social Democratic
Party Congress, 1921, in Otto Bauer, Die Osterreichische
Revolution (Vienna, 1923), p. 243.

2. Ibid., p. 244.

3. Ibid., p. 245.

4. Otto Bauer, "Gewerkschaften und Sozialismus,"
Der Kampf, Vol. 7, No. 6 (March 1914), p. 241.

5. Protokoll des sozialdemokratischen Parteitages
1926 (Vienna, 1926), p. 248.

6. Charles A. Gulick, Austria from Habsburg to
Hitler, Vol. 2, Fascism's Subversion of Democracy (Berkeley and Los Angeles, 1948), p. 1394.

7. Ibid., p. 1396.

8. Otto Bauer, "Hoppla, wir leben," Der Kampf, Vol.
21, No. 1 (January, 1928), pp. 1-4.

9. Otto Bauer, "Die Bourgeois-Republik in Osterreich," Der Kampf, Vol. 23, No. 5 (May, 1930), pp. 195-
202.

10. Ibid., p. 200.

11. Ibid., p. 201.

12. Protokoll des sozialdemokratischen Parteitages
1929 (Vienna, 1929).

13. Arbeiter-Zeitung, 10 March 1933, as quoted in Julius Braunthal, "Otto Bauer: Ein Lebensbild," in Otto Bauer: Eine Auswahl aus seinem Lebenswerk (Vienna, 1961), p. 85; Otto Leichter, Otto Bauer: Tragödie oder Triumph (Vienna, 1970), p. 16. The Braunthal version is more complete.

14. Braunthal, p. 84

15. Ibid., p. 85.

16. Leichter, p. 29.

17. Otto Bauer, Der Aufstand der österreichischen Arbeiter (Prague, 1934) as quoted in Herbert Steiner, Käthe Leichter: Leben und Werk (Vienna, 1973), p. 148.

18. Bauer, Der Aufstand der österreichischen Arbeiter, p. 12ff., as cited in Steiner p. 116.

19. Norbert Leser, Zwischen Reformismus und Bolshewismus: Der Austromarxismus als Theorie und Praxis (Vienna, 1968), p. 478; and Anson Rabinbach, The Crisis of Austrian Socialism: From Red Vienna to Civil War, 1927-1934 (Chicago, 1983), pp. 144-145; 244, n. 88.

7. Austrian Social Democracy: The Image and the Facts

Karl R. Stadler

It is highly significant that the historic event
which is being remembered in Austria in this year of
1984 is not the outbreak of World War I, which surely
marked the end of an era, but the fiftieth anniversary
of the ill-fated rising of parts of the socialist working class against the forces of Chancellor Dollfuss.
The explanation is, of course, that there is little
argument about the causes and consequences of the Great
War, and few of those who participated in it are still
alive. The question of responsibility for the events of
12 February 1934, however, is far from settled; the
political parties that were the chief antagonists then
have their successors today and enough contemporaries
have survived to keep the discussion going.
        Actually, the desire to discuss the February events
is rather one-sided. The People's Party, heirs to the
Christian Socials of Dr. Dollfuss, are none too happy
about the suspension of parliamentary government and the
crushing of the labor movement, while the Socialist
Party, heirs to the Social Democrats, consider it a
moral obligation and a political duty to study the
causes of these events and draw the right conclusions.
The Church, of course, through Cardinal König, has expressed regret over its share of historic responsibility. The conservative camp, while regretting the
actual events, uses the martyrdom of Dollfuss, whom Nazi
putschists killed in July 1934, as a means of vindi-
cating his policies; they consider Dollfuss a dedicated
patriot who was left no other choice by the doctrinaire
and extremist Socialists under Otto Bauer. This, however, is an untenable position: the Social Democrats
were not Jacobins masquerading as Girondists. To their
historic misfortune, they operated in a country that in
1918 had become too small for their visions and were
confronted by opponents who had never reconciled themselves to the democratic revolution of 1918 and who misunderstood the nature of reformist socialism.
        Their main criticism of the ideological position

and the policies of Austrian Social Democracy in the
First Republic can be summarized as follows: .
    1. The alleged ambivalence of the party towards
"bourgeois democracy" and its secret sympathy towards
the Bolshevik system--sympathy which for tactical
reasons was never openly admitted.
    2. Radical policies, proclaimed in extremely in-
temperate language and backed by threats of violent
action, which deepened the divisions between the political groups and prevented the formation of a common
stand on issues of national interest.
    3. The refusal to shoulder responsibility at crit-
ical moments when the very existence of the nation was
at stake. In situations like these the party is said to
have favored its own interests to the exclusion of national interests.
    4. Finally, in the last phase of Austrian indepen-
dence, the failure to recognize the sources of the main
threat. This led to the pursuit of sectional interests
rather than a policy of a united stand against National
Socialism.
    Since the time when these criticisms were formu-
lated and believed by a considerable number of Austrians, historical research--aided by the opening of archives and the publication of memoirs by the principal
actors in the Austrian tragedy--has invalidated every
one of these accusations. Unfortunately, all too many
authors of historical works, both inside Austria and
abroad, have taken little notice of this fact.
    For the purposes of this conference of experts in
Austrian history, it will suffice briefly to mention the
historical background against which the events of February 1934 have to be studied. We are in agreement that
these events originated in the social and psychological
consequences of World War I. There was a widely shared
disbelief in the viability of the First Republic. In
addition, there were political tensions between a radi-
calized working class and the formerly privileged classes, each with strong ideological orientations, private
armies, and a "camp mentality." The nonsocialist parties were attached to fascist regimes in neighboring
countries--Hungary, Italy, and Germany--while some socialists pinned their pathetic hopes on the western
democracies.
    For reasons of geography and of ideology, the Sovi-
et Union played no part in the calculations of either
side; the "Bolshevik menace" was a useful propaganda
slogan for the right, but the left, which was denounced
as "social fascists" in the terminology then current in
the Comintern, followed developments in the Soviet state
with critical interest. It is generally accepted today
that the Social Democratic policy of 1918-1919 spared
Austria the experience of a brief soviet regime--such as

those in Hungary and Bavaria--which would almost certainly have led to civil war and the establishment of a Horthy-type regime. While the Social Democratic leadership expressed sympathy with the overthrow of Russian czarism and the revolutionary struggles of the Hungarian and other peoples, party leaders showed great skill in directing the ardor of the workers' and soldiers' councils into constitutional channels. The introduction of parliamentary democracy and Ferdinand Hanusch's imposing labor legislation (soon followed by the renowned social reforms of "Red Vienna") were intended to be the Social Democratic alternative to Bolshevism.

It was inevitable that after the breakup of the coalition in 1920 and the consolidation of conservative and reactionary rule, disappointment should set in within the ranks of the labor movement. Short-lived oppositional groups and especially members of the youth organizations continued to demand a more radical, socialist policy from a leadership which was fully committed to winning power by democratic means and which insisted that the magic figure of 51 percent of the electorate would one day mark the beginning of socialist government in Austria.

There can be no lack of democratic reliability in a party which hopes to alter the existing social order by democratic means. For Socialists to work for a socialist order is no more reprehensible than for conservatives to seek to preserve the existing order. It is hard to see any ambivalence towards democracy in the slogan of Socialist activists: "Demokratie, das ist nicht viel;/ Sozialismus ist das Ziel." Admittedly, after the fascist experience we would not put it quite that way.

Likewise, with wisdom after the fact, no Social Democratic party today would adopt the tactics and employ the language of the prewar labor movement. (Politicians--and historians--do sometimes learn from history.) Although these tactics were forced upon the prewar labor movement by its opponents, they did help prevent the growth of a significant communist party. Misconceptions about the alleged practice of threatening violence and civil war must be refuted. A case in point is the famous Linz Program of the Austrian Party which was adopted in 1926--one of the historic documents of Austromarxism, and also one of the most often cited, particularly for its passage on the "dictatorship of the proletariat":

> The [Party] will exercise power in a democratic way and with all the guarantees of democracy...But if the bourgeoisie were to resist the social changes which the working class in power will have to bring about, by systematic sabotage of the economy, by

violent resistance, by conspiring with counterrevolutionary forces abroad, then the working class
would be compelled to overcome bourgeois resistance
by means of a dictatorship.

It may have been unwise to run the risk of being
misunderstood or wilfully misinterpreted, but in view of
the style of political controversy then prevalent, opponents of the Social Democrats would probably have cited
any other formulation by the party as proof of its advo-
cacy of civil war and dictatorship. Even Otto Bauer's
interpretation of this passage--"Democratic as long as
we can, dictatorial only when we are forced and insofar
as we are forced"--did not make it sufficiently clear
that this was not a threat but a warning based on the
underlying hope that such a situation would never arise.
To underline the essentially peaceful, i.e., constitutional, tactic of the Social Democratic Party, one
may cite its reaction to the events of 15 July 1927. A
mass protest against the acquittal of right-wingers on
trial for the killing of two persons led to violent
clashes with the Vienna police and the death of eighty-
nine people. Far from calling out its own defense
corps, the Republikanischer Schutzbund, the party pro-
tested by means of a brief general strike and a great
deal of parliamentary oratory. It was certainly not a
"dress rehearsal for a Marxist revolution," as its opponents claimed, but a disastrous tactical error, for it
allowed the spontaneity of the masses free play. We now
know what soul-searching went on in the party leadership
after the event. 15 July 1927 was a turning point in
the history of the First Republic; it marked the beginning of Austrofascism and of the decline of Social Democracy.
Once again, external factors accelerated the process. The beginning of the world economic crisis had
tragic consequences for the working classes: an increase in the number of unemployed and a consequent
weakening of the labor unions. There was a serious situation which only a change in governmental economic and
social policy could have calmed. The fact that, in June
1931, the Social Democrats turned down Chancellor
Seipel's offer of a coalition in which Otto Bauer would
be deputy premier gave rise to the accusation that Socialists shunned responsibility at a time of national
crisis. Yet it can be argued that this was no genuine
"offer" but a clever tactical move on the part of
Seipel: the Socialists were to be led into the trap of
cosponsoring extremely unpopular measures only to be
dismissed--weakened and demoralized--when they had done
their "patriotic duty."
It was not just the "intransigence" of Otto Bauer
that led to the unanimous rejection of the "offer";

even the very moderate Karl Renner, for reasons of his
own, supported the refusal. Bauer found a plausible
explanation for the party's decision on this occasion,
as he so often did: "It is not the duty of Social Democracy to run a capitalist system about to collapse."
But only a year later, at the party congress of 1932, he
warned delegates that the issue of the moment was not
capitalism or socialism, but how to maintain Austria as
an island of democratic freedom threatened by increasingly fascist and authoritarian forces. There is no
contradiction in this case between the recognition of a
growing danger and the refusal to shoulder responsibility for unpopular policies, as some historians appear
to think; the extremes of accommodation and compromise
to which the German Social Democratic Party went could
not prevent the rise of Hitler. Defending the interests
of the working classes in the Austria of those days did
more to prevent the growth of Nazism than unprincipled
concessions would have done.

And so we come to the last and perhaps the most
serious criticisms of socialist policy. It has been
said that the party did not recognize the deadly threat
which Nazi Germany posed to Austrian independence but
continued the traditional game of opposition tactics.
And it has been charged that the Social Democrats did
not distinguish between the traditional bourgeois parties and the new fascist mass party but saw them both as
"one reactionary mass." Both as an historian and a contemporary I cannot accept this critique.

The rise of the NSDAP in Germany from 1930 onward
gave its sympathizers in Austria a tremendous boost;
they began to become serious rivals of the other fascist
movement--the Heimwehr, which was oriented toward
Italy--and of the bourgeois parties at whose expense
they made spectacular gains in the provincial elections
of 1932. A year later, with Hitler already in power,
the NSDAP became the strongest party in Innsbruck with
40 percent of the votes. It was clear that the government no longer had a majority in the country, and the
Socialists therefore demanded a general election in the
summer of 1932, which would undoubtedly have resulted in
a number of Nazis entering parliament. The party's hope
was that this would give the Socialists a relative
majority, result in a coalition under their leadership,
and show up the comparative weakness of Hitler's followers.

The conservative camp under Chancellor Dollfuss
still saw the main enemy in the Socialist Party and
hoped to come to some arrangement with the NSDAP, even
contemplating the inclusion of some "moderate" Nazis in
the government. It was only in June 1933, when the
radical wing of the Nazi movement started a campaign of
violence, that the Nazi party was banned, but even this

could not induce Dollfuss (who had suspended parliament
and was governing by emergency decrees) to seek the ·
cooperation of his main opponents. The Socialists repeatedly offered to help in the struggle against the
Nazis and criticized the government for its halfhearted
measures. In September a conference of local Socialist
parties of the provinces which bordered on Germany
issued an appeal for national unity against the growing
menace, and in October the Social Democratic Party removed the demand for an Anschluss from its program, but
it was all to no avail.

In the deadlock situation between the suspension of
parliament in March 1933 and the Schutzbund uprising of
February 1934 significant developments took place inside
the main political blocs. Dollfuss came under mounting
pressure both from Mussolini and his Austrofascist Heimwehr allies to crush the socialists and to do away with
the last remnants of constitutional life in Austria, and
he readily yielded; the democratic elements in his
Christian Social Party, which were mostly to be found in
its labor and farmers' organizations, lost all influence. In the Socialist Party--which had weathered all
storms from World War I through the revolution to the
breakup of the coalition without any risk of a split or
of even serious divisions--it was not the governing Austromarxist faction under Otto Bauer which took the initiative but the right wing led by Karl Renner.

The dividing line between the factions ran roughly
between Vienna and the provinces; between the younger
generation and the old; between intellectuals, journalists and activists on the one hand, and the party's
institutional and parliamentary "establishment" on the
other. The left wing, with the implied threat of force,
demanded a firm stand against further encroachments on
democratic liberties. The right wing blamed the deadlock on the leftist course of the party led by Bauer and
sought an understanding with the democratic elements
among their opponents with whom they had long cooperated
in several provincial governments. In this endeavor the
right sometimes went so far as to virtually abandon traditional socialist positions--all in the name of Real-
politik.

The initiative was first taken by the leaders of
the party in Lower Austria, notably Oskar Helmer, who
obtained the consent of the central executive to contact
conservative leaders. A "position paper" prepared by
Helmer in the summer of 1933 spoke of the need for new
persons in the leadership who were prepared to place the
"ethical orientation of the movement above its rational
economic basis"; the masses should be told with complete
frankness that "democratic socialists could under no
circumstances be revolutionaries." Statements like
these antagonized the left wing without appeasing the

enemy, and opponents of the Social Democrats read them,
quite rightly, as signs of the deep divisions within the
party.

How little influence the Social Democrats wielded
among the Christian Socials was shown by the fate of the
last two offers that Renner was authorized to make. In
November 1933 he submitted to President Miklas and a few
others the draft of a Staatsnotstandsgesetz which a-
mounted to an act of surrender to Dollfuss' authoritarian style. This law would have provided for parliament
to be convened once more so that it could pass a "solemn
declaration for Austrian independence against the Hitler
movement," grant Dollfuss full power to continue government by decree, and then adjourn indefinitely. Only its
constitutional committee was to act as a sort of parliamentary watchdog, but without the right to veto legislation. Since Dollfuss ignored this offer, Renner and
Helmer obtained the agreement of the party executive to
a program for a reform of the constitution which would
have legalized the authoritarian regime of Dollfuss and
provided only a few democratic safeguards. It was now
clear that the party was prepared to pay almost any
price for its continued existence, but even this could
not avert the tragedy of 12 February 1934, for no one in
the government camp paid the draft the compliment of
even an acknowledgment. Ironically, the first Social
Democratic leaders to be arrested once fighting broke
out in Linz were Renner and his Lower Austrians.

Otto Bauer's article "Klassenkampf und
Ständeverfassung" in the penultimate issue of the
theoretical journal Der Kampf, published in January
1934, shows how far even he was prepared to use his
authority with the rank and file to avoid civil war and
to tide the party over these critical times. With his
usual brilliance, he analyzed the historical roots and
the development of the corporatist idea; he expressed
his doubts that the corporate state which the bourgeoisie now desired would create a new social order
without class antagonism. However, he concluded, there
was no reason why the working class should oppose at all
costs the corporatist institutions which were now being
established. In the following issue, the last to appear
in Austria, Otto Leichter formulated the position of the
left: "Keine Stände-Illusionen!" Within a few days the
controversy became a purely academic question, and on
May Day 1934 Austria was proclaimed a "Christian-German
corporate state" by the victor in the civil war.

8. Learning from the Civil War: The Political System of the First and Second Republics

Anton Pelinka

12 February is the most decisive turning point in
the history of Austria since 1918. The civil war shows
the great distance between the two main streams of Austrian political culture which had crystallized in two
parties. After the civil war, however, the tide turned
in favor of an alignment between these two currents, for
the failure of an authoritarian, corporate state as well
as the German occupation had brought to the fore certain
tendencies towards elite cooperation and towards a grand
coalition. Indeed, it is remarkable that smaller European democracies such as Austria, which had been strongly influenced by the experience of deep fragmentation
and political violence caused by such fragmentation,
later became "consociational."[1]

FROM POLARIZATION TO CONSOCIATIONALISM

Austria would have no consociational democracy--
including the tendency of political parties to compromise and neocorporatist decision-making by economic
pressure groups[2]--without the experience of civil war.
12 February 1934 is the thesis without which the Second
Republic could not have been founded and modelled as an
antithesis. To shoot, to imprison, to execute is to
reach the extremes of competition; to bargain, to compromise, to divide powers is to arrive at the height of
consensus. If 12 February represents the thesis, then
the Austria of today is the antithesis.

The two parties SPO/OVP have dissented in their official opinions concerning the civil war, not only as a
result of the fact that, historically speaking, they
were located on different sides, but also because of the
political culture established in both parties after
1945.[3] To justify a high degree of consensus, it is
necessary to emphasize some differences; and to justify
consensus in the daily life of politics, it is best to
underline differences far away from day-to-day politics.

12 February provides a framework for this, and so is
used in a kind of ritual fashion in Austria today.
     The Socialists tend to place all responsibility for
the civil war on the other side--a fact which is not
only understandable, but as far as "responsibility" and
not "reason" is concerned seems also to be correct. The
People's Party tends to argue not in terms of "responsibility" but in terms of "reason" and to find "reasons"
on both sides. That too is understandable. But in both
"camps," only a small minority at best is really concerned with the history and the meaning of the Austrian
civil war. In the SPO it is the purview of the traditional left wing, and in the OVP there is not even a
minority seriously interested in this question. Besides
its ritual function--as a way of saying "you never had
it so good"--12 February has no real meaning for real
policy matters today.
     In discussing the turn towards fascism, a compara-
tive dimension should also be considered: Austria is
one of the European countries with a dearth of parliamentary tradition. Though it fell into the fascist trap
together with many other European countries, there were
clear distinctions among those nations: the better established, the longer accepted, and the more self-evi-
dent was parliamentary rule, the better immunized a
country was against fascism. Economy was, and still is,
only one independent variable used to explain fascism;
political culture is the second.[4] Austria can and
must be grouped with politically underdeveloped countries which couldn't resist fascism--countries like
Bulgaria and Rumania, Hungary and Portugal, and also
Italy and Germany. It differed distinctively from
Switzerland and Belgium, the Netherlands and all the
Scandinavian countries. The parliamentary rule established in Austria in 1918--one of the last in Europe[5]
--couldn't bear the burden of centuries of feudal and
military rule.
     It is obvious that small European countries with a
background of Protestantism did not tend towards fascism
with the same intensity as Catholic or Orthodox countries. Of course, Protestantism and parliamentary tradition were strongly linked; however, it is interesting
that in Germany, the NSDAP, which was originally based
in the Catholic south, had its great electoral breakthrough in the Protestant north while, on the other
hand, fascism in power was mainly a Catholic phenomenon.
A comparative approach clearly indicates a difference
between fascism in various coalitions with the Catholic
church (Spain, Portugal, Austria, Hungary, Slovakia,
Croatia) and National Socialism, the specifically German
kind of fascism.
     Another factor which produced Austrian fascism was
electoral stratification, as demonstrated by a lack of

centrist voting. For example, the language of the Linz
Program, especially the reference to a defensive
"dictatorship of the proletariat," must be seen as the
result of the fragmentation of the electorate. The term
"dictatorship of the proletariat" was supposed to integrate different views and wings within the party; its
function, therefore, was an internal one. The Socialists' other option--the orientation towards centrist
public opinion and centrist voting behavior which occurs
in Austria today--did not succeed during the First
Republic, and for very good reasons. As opposed to
Socialists in the Scandinavian countries, in Britain and
also in France, the SDAP was not able to find a centrist
position for social democracy. The deeply fragmented
society did not permit the "catch-all party" strategy
which was achieved at that very time in other countries,
and which is possible and necessary in Austria today.[6]
    Using a concept which Berelson, Lazarsfeld and
McPhee and also Lipset developed in the 1950s and
1960s,[7] we can say that the average Austrian voter was
an "ideological" man because he was characterized by a
high degree of political interest and activity, and also
by "black and white" thinking. Thus the parties were
"ideological parties" as well as "class parties." The
parties did change, however, and after 1945 became
"catch-all-parties" directed at a changing electorate.
They reflected the transformation of "ideological" to
"political" man, or, as some critical data gathered by
Barnes and Kaase indicate;[8] to "sociable" man. "Political" or "sociable" man has almost no interest in
politics and ignores the differences between the parties; he tends instead to perceive the parties as
"them." In 1934 "catch-all-parties" already existed,
mainly in the Anglo-American systems: the ability of
the Democratic Party to build the broad "F.D.R. coalition" of underdogs from around the nation is perhaps the
best example. The political parties in Austria in 1934
were thus in a condition resembling underdevelopment
which reflected the underdevelopment of the political
and social system.
    After 1934 and especially after 1945 Austria had to
pay for its state of development: it traded stability
and integration for instability and disintegration.
Concommittantly, the country lost much of the motivation
for its high level of political participation and political activity--activity which had come to a tragic but
nevertheless impressive climax on 12 February. The differences between the parties, especially between the
SDAP and the present-day SPO, tell us about what we have
won--but also about what we have lost.

THE CONSTITUTION AND PARTY SYSTEM

Austria is an example of the ability to adapt and to learn, for it has established consociational instead of centrifugal democracy and changed from extreme instability to extreme stability. In 1984 it is characterized by depolarized mass nonparticipation, not the polarized mass participation of 1934; thus a country which, en route to civil war, demonstrated an overwhelming interest in politics now has citizens who sometimes show a significant lack of interest in politics.[9] All of these adaptations occurred without any change in the constitution. Created in 1920 by an interparty compromise, the constitution changed in 1929 as a result of antiparliamentary pressure from the right and cannot explain the drift toward civil war. There is a paradox in Austrian history: the constitutional change of 1929 was intended to strengthen the position of the federal president and make him independent of parliamentary majorities, according to the "Weimar pattern."[10] However, it was not the strong president created by the changed constitution but the federal chancellor--who had been weakened by it, and was still dependent on parliament and on the president--who became the spearhead of antidemocratic tendencies and overthrew restrictions which the constitutions had tried to provide. If any position provided the springboard for a dictator, it would seem to be that of the federal president, but, ironically, it was the chancellor who succeeded in playing a dictatorial role.

All this happened without any dramatic changes within the party system, defined as a quantitative relationship among different parties. In 1907 and 1911 the two major parties managed to establish themselves as the leading political factors. And in 1920, 1930, 1945, and 1955 the same parties and "camps" dominated the political system. Even fifty years after the civil war, the Socialist Party and the Christian-conservative camp, the latter now represented by the People's Party, are stll the dominant political factors in Austria. The parties, deeply rooted in the nineteenth century,[11] did not change and party elites, too, have been characterized by continuity; not even the years between 1938 and 1945 interrupted the flow of "red" and "black" elites who represented the separate, fragmented subsystems. But while the party system didn't change, the impact of party politics changed significantly.

The only relative political significance of the Austrian constitution is its function as a screen masking the central importance of consensus. The lack of consensus, in spite of the existence of a constitution, helps to explain the developments from 1 October 1920 to 12 February 1934. What we can learn and have already

learned is that it isn't the constitution which creates
a political system, but the political system which
creates a constitution and constitutional reality. We
are aware of the many examples of this which the Second
Republic has produced. For example, the decisive role
of the social partnership has been developed without
integrating the system of institutionalized compromise
into the constitution.[12] And Adolf Schärf's words,
"Don't touch the constitution," reflect a high degree of
ability to separate the constitution from political
decision-making.[13]

The First Republic collapsed with a party system
which was dominated by two big parties and a relatively
small number of third parties, while the Second Republic
flourished in spite of a party system which was almost
unchanged. The experience of 1945 demonstrates that it
isn't the party system which makes the difference, it's
the party elites' behavior. Julius Raab, the leader of
the Lower Austrian Heimatschutz, a member of the 1930
Parliament and of Kurt Schuschnigg's last cabinet is
only one example of the continuation and identity of the
Christian-conservative elite. The phrase chosen by the
SPO in 1945 as a symbol of integration--"Social Democrats and Revolutionary Socialists"--is a token of the
same situation within the socialist camp.

SOURCES OF POLITICAL INSTABILITY

After almost four decades of the Second Republic,
of stabilization and of integration, we can look back
and ask: what was the reason for the inability of the
First Republic to survive? First, there was the lack of
a democratic tradition, expressed by a lack of democratic theory. The party platforms which the Social Democrats and the Christian Democrats produced in the 1920s
didn't present a deep analysis of the nature of democracy. The Linz Program defined democracy as majority
rule and respect for minority rights, while the Christian Social manifesto expressed even less interest in
democracy.[14] The development of Hermann Broch seems
to be typical: in 1919 he published a very stimulating
article about the possible combination of parliamentary
rule and council system (Rätesystem), but he came out
with no further publications in this field all the way
up to 1938. Only in exile in the United States did
Broch, influenced by American discussions, become one of
the first Austrian thinkers--perhaps, the second after
Hans Kelsen--to develop some sort of "democratic
theory."[15]

In addition, there was a lack of self-confidence.
Between reactionary nostalgia for the old empire and the
tendency towards the Anschluss there was no room left

for an Austrian or republican patriotism. And between
the "Italian way" (which meant, in reality, a semi-
colonial dependence on fascist Italian imperialism) and
the "German way" (perfect integration into totalitarian
National Socialist German imperialism), there was no
room for an "Austrian way." It was only outsiders like
Ernst Karl Winter and Alfred Klahr who tried to form a
concept of an Austrian nation,[16] but up to 1945,
reality was not mature enough for this concept.

And there was a lack of economic vitality not so
much in the economy itself, but in the economy mirrored
in the attitudes of public opinion. The economic situation in Austria during the First Republic was not substantially worse than that of other comparable countries, but the belief in the potentially imperialistic
Lebensunfähigkeit--Austria's inability to survive economically within the borders of a small state[17]--
weakened policy performance and limited political
options. Theories of self-sufficiency and of Grossraum
(extraterritorial sphere of influence) did not fit the
reality of a small republic, and these ideological perceptions, which were the result of an outdated imperial
mentality and not a reflection of the real economy,
destabilized the republic. In 1945 smallness began to
be considered preferable to conceptions of the old
empire and the Reich, and after 1945 countries like
Switzerland or Sweden became models and examples for
Austria.

There was also a lack of efforts towards reconciliation on the part of the force usually thought to
have been established as a conciliator: the church.
The Catholic Church did not try to soften an already
polarized situation. On the contrary, the church--
defined as the bishops who spoke for it--was a radi-
calizing force.[18] The church put pressure on the
Christian-conservative camp to destroy any possibility
of compromise. For example, public pastoral letters,
such as that released in 1930 during the general election campaign, interpreted democratic competition as a
choice between the realm of God and the domain of
evil.[19] "Quadragesimo anno," which was soft on
fascism, neutral toward democracy, but extremely hostile
to and outspoken against socialism--including social
democracy--was intensively discussed on the eve of the
civil war; thus the pope himself seemed to justify the
war against the republic. Bishops and the Catholic
Action helped to legitimize the authoritarian state,
permitting the conceptualization of the Austrian dictatorship as Christian rule. Catholics, including such
bishops as Gföllner from Linz and Hudel from the Anima
in Rome, deepened pre-existent Christian anti-Semitism.
Some of them tried to "outnazi the Nazis" by crude anti-
Semitic propaganda, while others such as Hudal argued

that it wasn't anti-Semitism which separated National
Socialism from Christianity.[20]
  Finally, there was a lack of balance between Vienna
and the other provinces. Vienna and the other parts of
the republic were politically disintegrated, socially
different and culturally hostile, so that Vienna seemed
an isolated island within a sea of conservative provinces. Federalism failed to provide balance; the Social Democratic party had over 50 percent of its members
in Vienna, while in Vorarlberg, on the other extreme,
they won fewer votes than the two small parties of the
German national camp. Vienna was proletarian, while the
other provinces were still agricultural, and the small
industrial potential outside Vienna--in Styria, for
example--was manipulated by special interests; German
capital worked as an instrument of Hitler's foreign
policy. Vienna and the Viennese were full of prejudice
against the "provinces" (as if Vienna itself wasn't a
province) while the other provinces were biased against
the Wasserkopf (hydrocephalus), against "Red Vienna."
  Though the civil war, the events of 12 February and
the days which came after it were the dramatic watershed
which brought about the failure of the republic, the
fate of the republic had been decided long before. If
12 February has generally been a symbol, it is now more
of a contradiction. It was a symbol of the strength of
antidemocratic intentions and the weakness of democratic
forces, but it also stands in contradiction to 1945 and
to postwar Austrian development.

NOTES

  1. For the concept of "consociational democracy"
see Arend Lijphart, Democracy in Plural Societies. A
Comparative Exploration (New Haven, 1977).

  2. For the concept of "corporatism" or "neocor-
poratism" see Philippe C. Schmitter and Gerhard Lehm-
bruch, eds., Trends Toward Corporatist Intermediation
(Beverly Hills, 1979) and also Gerhard Lehmbruch and
Philippe C. Schmitter, eds., Patterns of Corporatist
Policy-Making (Beverly Hills, 1982).

  3. Kurt Steiner, Politics in Austria (Boston, 1-
972), especially pp. 155-188; William T. Bluhm, Building an Austrian Nation. The Political Integration of a
Western State (New Haven, 1973), especially pp. 46-81.

  4. Wolfgang Wippermann, Faschismustheorien: Zum
Stand der gegenwärtigen Diskussion (Darmstadt, 1975);

Pierre Aycoberry, The Nazi Question. An Essay on the Interpretation of National Socialism (1922-1975) (New York, 1981).

5. For the development of European parliamentary rule, see Klaus von Beyme, Die parlamentarischen Regierungssysteme in Europa (Munich, 1970). For the Austrian situation, emphasizing comparative aspects, see Rainer Nick and Anton Pelinka, Parlamentarismus in Österreich (Vienna, 1984).

6. For the concept of "catch-all parties" see Otto Kirchheimer, The Transformation of the Western European Party Systems, in Joseph La Palombara and Myron Weiner, eds., Political Parties and Political Development (Princeton, 1966), pp. 177-200; Richard Rose, Do Parties Make a Difference? (Chatham, N.J., 1980).

7. Bernard R. Berelson, Paul F. Lazarsfeld and William N. McPhee, Voting: A Study of Opinion Formation in a Presidential Campaign (Chicago, 1954), especially pp. 305-323; Seymour Martin Lipset, Political Man: The Social Bases of Politics (New York, 1960).

8. Samuel H. Barnes, Max Kaase et al., eds., Political Action. Mass Participation in Five Western Democracies (Beverly Hills, 1979), Leopold Rosenmayr, ed., Politische Beteiligung und Wertwandel in Österreich: Einstellungen zu Politik und Demokratieverständnis im internationalen Vergleich (Munich and Vienna, 1980).

9. For several survey data, see Peter Gerlich and Karl Ucakar, Staatsbürger und Volksvertretung: Das Alltagsverständnis von Parlament und Demokratie in Österreich (Salzburg, 1981); Roland Deiser and Norbert Winkler, Das politische Handeln der Österreicher (Vienna, 1982); Fritz Plasser and Peter A. Ulram, Unbehagen im Parteinestaat: Jugend und Politik in Österreich (Vienna, 1982).

10. Steiner, Politics, pp. 111-113.

11. Steiner, Politics, pp. 119-154; Anton Pelinka, Political Parties, in Kurt Steiner, ed., Modern Austria (Palo Alto, 1981), pp. 223-239.

12. Anton Pelinka, Modellfall Österreich? Möglichkeiten und Grenzen der Sozialpartnerschaft (Vienna, 1981); Bernd Marin, Die Paritätische Kommission: Aufgeklärter Techno-korporatismus in Österreich (Vienna, 1982).

13. Information given by Jacques Hannak, Adolf Schärf's personal friend, to the author in 1971. About Schärf in general, see Karl R. Stadler, Adolf Schärf: Mensch, Politiker, Staatsmann (Vienna, 1982).

14. For the development of political manifestos in Austria, see Klaus Berchtold, ed., Osterreichische Parteiprogramme 1868-1966 (Vienna, 1967), Albert Kadan and Anton Pelinka, Die Grundsatzprogramme der österreichischen Parteien: Dokumentation und Analyse (St. Pölten, 1979).

15. Hermann Broch, Politische Schriften (Frankfurt am Main, 1978), especially pp. 11-23, 72-80.

16. Felix Kreissler, La Prise de Conscience de la nation Autrichienne: 1938-1945-1978, 2 vols. (Paris, 1980).

17. Norbert Schausberger, Der Griff nach Osterreich: Der Anschluss (Vienna, 1978), especially pp. 81-87.

18. Alfred Diamant, Austrian Catholics and the First Republic: Democracy, Capitalism and Social Order 1918-1934 (Princeton, 1960).

19. August M. Knoll, ed., Kardinal Fr. G. Piffl und der österreichische Episkopat zu sozialen und kulturellen Fragen 1913-1932 (Vienna, 1932), pp. 167-177.

20. Anton Pelinka, Stand oder Klasse? Die Christliche Arbeiterbewegung Osterreichs 1933-1938 (Vienna, 1972), pp. 213-233.

9. Strategies of Political Violence: Chance Events and Structural Effects as Causal Factors in the February Rising of the Austrian Social Democrats

Gerhard Botz

In this paper I wish to discuss three different aspects of the February 1934 rising of the Austrian Socialists: first, its origins in the complementary strategies of violence practiced by the fascist Heimwehr movement and the paramilitary defense organization of the Socialists, the Republican Schutzbund; second, the causal role of chance in unleashing the civil events on 12 February 1934; third, and most important, some long- and mid-term socioeconomic causes as expressed in a quantitative model of conflict. These three aspects imply a point of view which stresses the similarities between a single event, the February 1934 rising, and many other, less tragic violent incidents during the whole interwar period in Austria.

During the First Republic, violence was a frequent phenomenon which occurred in many different forms.[1] The number of victims of political violence varied greatly from year to year. In quantitative terms, the evolution of political violence formed a typical three-peaked curve. The initial period of the First Republic (1918-1920), the so-called Austrian Revolution, displayed a high level of violence, while the following years (1921-1926) were a period of relative political peace and stability. The burning of the Vienna Palace of Justice in 1927 signalled the abrupt beginning of the so-called latent civil war (1927-1933) which led to the climax of political violence and to open civil war on 12 February 1934. The final years of an independent Austria, the authoritarian semi-fascist dictatorship of Dollfuss and Schuschnigg, are not considered in this context.[2]

Frequent or excessive incidents of political violence were, obviously, generally the result of strategies of political violence. During the interwar period each major participant on the battlefield of intensified political struggle adopted specific forms and strategies of violence. Space does not permit a discussion of the early Communist putsch strategies of 1918-1919 or the

use of violence among the Nazis.[3]   I will restrict
myself to the Christian Social Party and the Heimwehr,
on the side of the government, and the Social Democratic
paramilitary self-defense organization, the Republican
Schutzbund, on the side of the Social Democratic opposition.

For some years after 1918 the middle-class Catholic
and conservative camp did not develop its own strategies
of violence.[4]   Ever since the foundation of the republic, at first timidly and later with growing self-assur-
ance, it had formed close relations with virtually all
levels of the state apparatus, with the exception of the
Viennese municipal and regional administrations. The
state executive--or at least sections of it--had always
been at its disposal. This may create the impression
that the camp had a strictly legalistic orientation
throughout this period. No doubt, quite a few middle-
class politicians recoiled from openly breaking with
legality, even at a time when--as in the early 1930s--
notions about "true democracy," "the authoritarian
state," and undemocratic, dictatorial forms of government had already gained strong currency among Christian
Socials as well as German Nationalists. This is not to
say, however, that in 1920 the same group of politicians, in cooperation with Hungarian counterrevolu-
tionaries had not already entertained serious plans for
the overthrow of a coalition government that gave them
only a half share of power.[5]   In later years, plans
for a coup d'état also played an important role among
large sections of the middle-class parties at various
times. When Dollfuss set aside parliamentary democracy
in March 1933 this constituted a sort of "cold" coup
d'état, conducted in stages.[6]
In the day-to-day political skirmishes of the
interwar period, this camp did employ auxiliary troops
which operated outside the law and used violent means:
the early Heimwehr formations, the monarchist Ostara,
the War Veterans' Association, etc. were without exception proto- or semi-fascist organizations. The fact
that the heterogeneous organizations that had come together in the Heimwehr had been able to operate inde-
pendently since 1927 and to build up their own party
organizations shows that the essential criteria for a
fascist movement had already been met.
In the early 1920s radical right-wing organizations
had already practiced an offensive version of the Social
Democrats' defensive strategy of violence, especially in
those regions of Austria where they could command a
broad social base.[7]   Thus there was a constant interplay between the left's and the right's strategies of
violence which determined their further development. As
time went on, the Heimwehr--influenced by Italian fascists and Hungarian reactionaries--developed a strategy

of mass marches which were designed to encircle "Red
Vienna" and other citadels of Social Democracy and to
make them ripe for a takeover, as in the Italian model.
Such provocative displays of Heimwehr formations in the
middle of industrial centers and working-class districts
(with the blessing of the Catholic clergy and the protection of the state authorities) were meant to break
the "Reds' monopoly of the street," at least symbolical-
ly, and thus to weaken the Austromarxists psychologically. The Social Democrats did indeed perceive it in this
way, yet when they took up the challenge and deployed
their Schutzbund, often only a minor incident provoked
shooting and violent street-fighting. Virtually every
Sunday during the late 1920s there were collisions between marchers and countermarchers, especially in the
industrial regions of Upper Styria and Lower Austria.

A plan for a putsch by the Heimwehr may well have
taken into account this automatic triggering of violence. However, sections of the Christian Social and
German Nationalist parties, despite their sympathy with
the Heimwehr, were still hostile to the idea of a dictatorship established by the paramilitary organization.
For this reason, many Heimwehr leaders as well as some
of their backers among the Christian Socials (such as
the head of the Styrian government, Anton Rintelen)
hoped that by provoking clashes with the Schutzbund they
might tempt it into larger-scale hostilities or even an
attempted coup d'état.[8] This in turn was to be
answered by a counter-blow from the Heimwehr, acting in
conjunction with police and army. The expected defeat
of the "Reds" was to lead to an Austria reconstructed on
fascist lines and unfettered by any constitutional constraints. Without the active participation of the state
executive, most Heimwehr leaders did not feel strong
enough to attempt a putsch.[9] This was the political
background of the street fights such as the one at the
Styrian village of St. Lorenzen on 18 August 1929.

It was also the background of the attempted Heimwehr putsch on 13 September 1931. The leader of the
radical, pro-Nazi Styrian Heimatschutz, Walter Pfrimer,
fearing a possible defeat of the Heimwehr by the Nazis
who were growing in number and influence, had decided to
"march on Vienna." The Schutzbund, however, took coun-
termeasures and the army, after its initial neutrality,
intervened--albeit hesitantly--against the Heimwehr, so
that Pfrimer's attempt at a putsch failed miserably.[10]

There is strong evidence that the political actions
of the Dollfuss government and particularly of the Heimwehr during the last weeks before the 12 February 1934
were aimed at provoking the outbreak of a decisive
battle with the Social Democrats. The dictatorial anti-
Socialist government took various measures, including
the arrest of the leaders of the Schutzbund, provocative

searches for weapons, the confiscation of organs of the press, a prohibition on demonstrations, and the appointment of state commissioners for the Chambers of Labor. These acts were accompanied by a threatening political offensive by the Heimwehr. Starting in the Tyrol, the Heimwehr leaders organized marches through several capitals of Austrian federal states and tried to press the Dollfuss government into moving further against democracy and the Socialists. There were rumors, not unfounded, that the Heimwehr was preparing a "march on Vienna" if the Dollfuss government would not meet demands for a corporate state and for the outlawing of the Social Democratic Party. The ominous words spoken by Vice Chancellor Emil Fey on 11 February 1934 also belong to this context--although we cannot be certain that he really was referring to the next day when he announced: "We will go to work tomorrow and finish the job for the sake of our fatherland."[11]

The thesis that the Schutzbund's attempted insurrection of February 1934 had been deliberately provoked by the Heimwehr still remains a matter of controversy among scholars of Austrian history, but is certainly a probability.[12] In any case, the Schutzbund, weakened by mass unemployment, by the political retreat of the party leadership, and by a ban of eleven months would have been defeated if attacked jointly by the executive and the Heimwehr, even if circumstances had been a little more favorable.

A nearly perfect complement to the Heimwehr's use of violence is the role of violence in Austromarxist political strategy. Although proletarian militancy and the use of violence played only a defensive role in Austromarxist theory in general and in the Linz party program in particular, when it came to the actual situation of armed marches and street fighting, the battle rules of the Schutzbund did not differ very much from those of its opponents. The Social Democrats' strategy of violence flowed from their party's reformism which, while attentist in character, was nevertheless based on socialist goals. While the majority of the party did not reject violence in principle as a political instrument, it nevertheless wished to restrict it to a merely defensive function. Even the ominous formulations in the Linz Program of 1926, which spoke of breaking the "bourgeoisie's resistance with the instruments of a dictatorship," ought to be understood as a mainly defensive statement. It was intended to force the bourgeois side to keep to the democratic rules, if it should prove unwilling to give up political power peacefully once the Social Democrats had won their expected overwhelming election victory.[13]

This strategy was also imposed on the Republican Schutzbund, which was founded in 1923 to serve as the

armed executive organ of the Socialist camp. After all,
ever since the end of the so-called Austrian Revolution,
the Social Democrats had had sound reasons for not believing that the state apparatus was absolutely reliable
when it came to repulsing counterrevolutionary strata-
gems, monarchist plans for a putsch, and the influence
of Bavarian and Hungarian right-wing extremists. In
these circumstances, the party leadership felt constrained to turn the "proletariat's fighting fitness"
into the reality of a counter-army--and this is precisely what the Schutzbund became after 1927. Strict
military discipline, uniforms, training in the use of
weapons, military staff exercises, the establishment of
arms depots, etc. turned this organization, which originally had been opposed to militarism, into a militaristic one. This also meant that its strategy of violence
began to resemble more closely that of its opponents.
In effect, the Schutzbund increasingly had its fighting
methods imposed on it by others, especially by the Heimwehr which developed a strategy of marches towards the
end of the 1920s. Almost every Sunday from 1928 on,
several thousand Schutzbund members tested and demonstrated the proletariat's readiness to defend itself in
large-scale manoeuvres and marches. Naturally this led
to collisions with the Heimwehr's opposing strategies,
collisions which frequently ended in bloodshed. The
Schutzbund, however, cannot be accused of directly provoking clashes on large scale, a charge which might be
levelled against its opponents with some justification.

It was, however, not an accident that the military
spirit within the Schutzbund prompted a modification of
the conditions governing the use of violence by the Social Democrats. The Schutzbund leadership around Alexander Eifler and Julius Deutsch took the view that the
Schutzbund would have to counter right-wing efforts to
establish a dictatorship even before the Social Democrats had gained a parliamentary majority. As early as
1928 they reckoned with the ever-present possibility of
civil war.

Such deviations from the theoretical principles
contained in the party program of 1926 were bound to be
very much more marked and less differentiated among the
rank and file than among the leaders of the party's
paramilitary organization. What tended to happen in the
day-to-day practice of political conflict--what Karl
Renner called the "class struggle with pitchforks"[14]--
was precisely what Otto Bauer had warned against when
referring to the Linz Program: "Violence does not mean
a street brawl!"[15] Violence used as a defensive strategy degenerated into the partly offensive tactics of
brawling.

Theodor Körner, a former general and the Social
Democrats' defense expert, denounced this development in

the sharpest terms and, at an early stage, predicted its
consequences: it would suppress the Socialist camp's
will to fight, make their various opponents seem to a be
a single and undifferentiated enemy, and produce an
almost exclusive reliance on violent means which the
Social Democrats, despite their numerical superiority,
would always use in a manner inferior to their opponents. Körner suggested that socialist military strategy take into account the possibility of politically
mobilizing the entire working population and of employing spontaneous passive resistance; however, this sug-
gestion went unheeded, as did his exhortation to try
every means available within a parliamentary, democratic
constitutional state before resorting to defensive
violence.[16]

But, in contrast to Körner, I do not believe that
the socialist paramilitary defense strategy was the
result only of the shortsightedness of the party's
executive committee or the Schutzbund leadership.
Rather it was the consequence of the party's process of
marginalization. In other words, the ideology and behavior of the Austrian socialist labor movement was de-
formed by the attempts of the Christian conservatives to
roll back the Social Democrats' quasi-revolutionary
gains in social influence and power which followed the
breakup of the coalition government. In conjunction
with the structural deficiencies and the downswing in
economic and social developments during the First Repub-
lic--to which I will refer later--this marginalization
process had two effects for socialist policy.

First, it enabled them to build up a counter-
society in "Red Vienna." On the one hand, "Red Vienna"
was different from the reactionary state, but on the
other, it was an attempt to continue on the level of the
land or town the same kind of politics from which the
Socialists had been excluded at the state level. A
similar role was played by the Schutzbund organization:
it gave many former army officers a renewed social role
and an identity in a paramilitary hierarchy.[17] Thousands of the young unemployed, seeking new social and
political backing after having been uprooted by the
consequences of the world economic crisis, also poured
into the Schutzbund organizations after 1930. Given the
background of the leadership and of the rank and file,
it is not at all surprising that the Schutzbund as a
whole could only continue the strategy of a regular
army.

Furthermore, the isolation of Austromarxism in
sociological and electoral strongholds led almost inevitably to its voluntary withdrawal from those positions of political power and public influence which were
not yet firmly in the hands of fanatical anti-Marxists.
Such marginalization or incapsulation made the Austro-

marxists incapable of finding potential allies for a
democratic solution to the aggravated economic and
political crises of the 1930s. Moreover, as Austromarxist theories of fascism show, marginalization resulted in an inability even to recognize differences in
the anti-Marxist camp. In my opinion, the whole discussion among Austrian Socialist leaders about entering a
coalition government during the early 1930s was condemned to be ineffective as long as the questions were
posed only in terms of a decision about participation in
government.[18] At the same time, the problem arises
whether the fascinating success of cultural and social
policy in Vienna did not carry with it the failure of
Austromarxism in the state. The Austrian political
scientist Norbert Leser has already posed this question
in similar terms.[19]

I will now only briefly mention the second main
point of my presentation: the role of chance in setting
off the civil war of February 1934. By identifying the
elements of strategy and the rules for the use of violence, I do not mean to advocate the misleading volun-
taristic interpretation of historical events. Towards
the end of January 1934, when sociopolitical tensions
had reached their climax, the eruption of civil war no
longer required consciously planned political action.

Linz on the night of 11-12 February 1934 confirms
this assertion. In accordance with the anti-Socialist
actions of the Heimwehr, during the week preceding 12
February 1934, Fey and others who had been members of
the Dollfuss government since the beginning of 1934 as
well as Hans Hammerstein-Equord, the director of the
security forces of Upper Austria, had already managed to
disarm the regional Socialist paramilitary and political
organizations and to provoke the outbreak of fighting.
The measures included searches for hidden Schutzbund
weapons, the setting up of a register of all Socialist
activists, and preparatory measures for their arrest and
imprisonment in internment camps similar to concentration camps.[20]

Against the wishes of the majority of the Upper
Austrian Social Democratic leadership, the regional
Schutzbund and its leader, Richard Bernaschek, decided
to alert the units, make weapons available, and prepare
for violent resistance. This was, as Anson Rabinbach
has pointed out, "the result of a gradual process of
emancipation from the hegemony of the party executive
that had been developing in Upper Austria for at least
six months before the insurrection."[21] If there were
any more searches for weapons or arrests in Linz, the
capital of the province of Upper Austria, the Schutzbund
would no longer stand still; instead of giving way to
disgraceful capitulation, it would struggle to the
bitter end. The hesitant Viennese party leadership and

Social Democrats throughout Austria were to be carried
along by the Upper Austrian offensive into a general
strike and a political upheaval.

Bernaschek informed three party leaders in Vienna
whom he thought capable of supporting his plans, i.e.,
Otto Bauer, Theodor Körner and the chairman of the
unions, Johann Schorsch. But Otto Bauer and the
Viennese party leadership advised Bernaschek to hold
back. A coded telephone call as late as 2 AM on 12
February giving this order to Bernaschek was monitored
by a post officer and immediately reported to the
police.[22] The police were preparing to search for
weapons in the building of the Linz swimming pools and
baths, but the police commander, after he had been
informed of the content of Otto Bauer's message, decided
to divert the search to Social Democratic headquarters
at the Hotel Schiff, where the Schutzbund and Bernaschek
also had their headquarters. When police units entered
the Hotel Schiff in the early morning of the same day,
fighting started and spread to Vienna and most industrial regions of Austria.

The conventional interpretation of these events is
that both sides--the Schutzbund as well as the police--
clearly wanted to commence fighting during the final
hours before the first shots were fired on 12 February
1934. The crucial points of this argument are that
Bernaschek, on the one hand, persisted in his plans and
disobeyed Otto Bauer's orders, and that the police department, on the other, anticipated Bernaschek's behavior. I believe, however, that both assumptions are
wrong.

First, there was little probability that in a centralized paramilitary formation like the Schutzbund, an
important but nevertheless only regional leader like
Bernaschek would have disregarded Vienna's expressed
order, even if Bernaschek's preparedness during the
previous weeks initiated the uprising, contrary to the
strategy of the Social Democratic executive committee.
In addition, one has to take into account that an isolated upheaval would have had no chance at all. My
hypothesis is therefore that Bernaschek gave up his
plans or hesitated to put them into action during the
last decisive hours before the beginning of the fighting. Indeed, there is strong evidence supporting this
view in published documents[23] and in oral sources
which have been collected recently by the Linz labor
historian Peter Kammerstätter.[24] Bernaschek's memoirs, published in 1934, describe his chaotic and inconsistent behavior when the police knocked at the door
of his office: on the one hand, the Schutzbund leader
gave the order, "To arms!" and on the other hand, he
tried to negotiate by phone with Landeshauptmann Josef
Schlegel.[25] This Christian Social politician, in

contrast to many of his party friends, was strongly
committed to the principles of democracy and was prepared to intervene for a withdrawal of the police from
Bernaschek's headquarters, but his action came too
late.[26] Only after some decisive minutes, just before
the police broke down Bernaschek's door, did this
Schutzbund leader telephone the order that fighting
begin outside the Hotel Schiff. Surprisingly, Bernaschek himself surrendered, without having fired one
shot, at the beginning of the uprising of his followers.[27]

Second, the assumption that the outbreak of the
February uprising had been meticulously planned is weak
because it implies that the Upper Austrian police director knowingly sent his units into a battle for which
they were not properly prepared. The Linz police had
detached only a few units and had informed its superior
command and the military forces only shortly before it
began the operation against the Hotel Schiff. Furthermore, this is no evidence that the police commander,
after having been informed of Otto Bauer's phone message, diverted the search for weapons into the Hotel
Schiff merely in order to start the final battle with
the Social Democrats. On the contrary, as a careful
observer of his antagonists, he might well have assumed
that Bernaschek would obey Otto Bauer's orders.

One can therefore conclude that the commencement of
fighting on 12 February 1934 was the result of a reciprocal error by each partner in a conflict on the local
level. It can reasonably be assumed that the fighting
could easily have broken out in places other than Linz,
for instance in Upper Styria,[28] and at other moments
during that period. While one cannot reduce the outbreak of fighting in February 1934 to chance events, one
should note that strategic planning, regional sociopolitical factors or socioeconomic structures alone
cannot explain the actual course of the historical
events.[29]

This leads me to my third point: had it not been
for long-term structural tendencies, the given political
strategies could never have been developed and a simple
accident in conflict management could not have produced
far-reaching historical events. These tendencies must
be considered the real causes of the civil war of 1934.
In macrohistorical perspective, the February 1934 events
are nothing but the peak of the oscillating curve of
political violence which went on throughout a twenty-
year period. Hence, from this point of view, it is
meaningful to develop a quantitative model of the causal
factors of political violence in Austria since 1918.

I have done this by calculating multiple regression
equations from a total of about two dozen variables
which indicate annual changes in the economic, social,

sociopsychological, political and state conflict potentials on the state level, for each year from 1919 through 1937.[30] Theoretical considerations and empirical testing recommended the use of the following variables as potential explanatory factors:[31]

1. The average rate of <u>unemployment</u> (as compared with the whole labor force) during the preceding year. The assumption for this was that the sociopolitical consequences of unemployment are often somewhat delayed; in the First Republic of Austria (not in the Second Republic) this variable is highly negatively correlated with economic growth rates.

2. The numbers of <u>suicides</u> for each year: this variable was considered an indicator of the anomic situation, isolation and desperation.

3. A ratio of the <u>stability of government</u>, standardized (0.0 - 1.0) and calculated for each year. The duration from one change of the whole government (or more than one minister) to the next one could indicate the level of political stability or conflict inside the ruling classes.

4. The ratio of <u>expenses for police</u> and the Ministry of Interior as compared with the whole annual state budget. This measures, to some extent, the ability and the preparedness of the state and the politically dominant classes to use violence against groups which present a (violent) challenge to their rule.

5. The average ratio of <u>union members</u> as compared with all the employed by year. This is meant to measure the strength of the traditional organizations of the labor movement.

6. The total numbers of working-days lost through <u>strikes</u> by all strikers, each year. This variable is theoretically and empirically highly positively correlated with the immediately preceding one and is considered to be an expression of the level of conflict and tension in labor relations and economic distribution.

The variable to be explained is the annual change in the level of political violence as measured by the logarithm of the numbers of deaths involved by year. Although one can distinguish different types of political violence causing deaths among the conflicting partners, the overall sum of those killed is taken to be a multidimensional--but nevertheless the best available--quantitative indicator of the amount of political violence occurring in a given period. The same can be said of the number of severely injured which is highly positively correlated ($r = 0.98$) with the number of deaths. Because of the assumption of linearity in the regression model, the annual figures for deaths are used as logarithms in this analysis. This numerical transformation can also be justified by theoretical considerations, namely that a factor of self-intensification is immanent

in political violence up to a specific point. (See the
bivariate correlation matrix shown in Table 9.1; these
elements are built into that model.)

TABLE 9.1
Bivariate Correlation Matrix

	1	2	3	4	5	6	7
1. Unemployment in previous year	1						
2. Suicides	0.89	1					
3. Government stability	-0.13	0.16	1				
4. Internal force	0.79	0.79	0.27	1			
5. Labor union strength	-0.74	-0.60	-0.02	-0.72	1		
6. Strikes	-0.59	-0.65	-0.06	-0.50	0.73	1	
7. Political deaths (logarithm)	0.49	0.16	-0.20	0.26	-0.54	-0.22	1

Source: Aggregate data, collected by the author for the
data collection "Interwar Period," Ludwig Boltzmann
Institute of Social Scientific History, Salzburg. For
assistance in computer computations I am indebted to
Bernd Lohmöller (West Berlin), Günther Klawora, Franz
Maier and Albert Müller (Salzburg).

There is no doubt that cyclical economic downswings
and the severe worsening of economic and social conditions over a period of some years produced an increased
degree of social discontent as well as a greater inclination and organizational ability to use violence. During the democratic phase of the First Republic, periods
of economic growth and relatively low unemployment went
hand in hand with low annual figures for the casualties
of violence. Conversely, any decline in the GNP and any
increase in unemployment was accompanied by an increase
in political violence. Unemployment must be regarded as

the key factor in transposing the area of conflict from
the industrial-economic sphere to the extraparliamentary
political level.

Long-term and hopeless unemployment was the experience which, directly or indirectly, shaped the attitudes
of hundreds and thousands of Austrians. Those who had
not yet suffered this fate were politically mobilized
and more inclined towards the use of violence, while the
unemployed tended to be depoliticized and alienated from
the traditional Social Democratic workers' organizations
which had been opposed to violence.[32] The number of
union members in general and the Socialist union members
in particular decreased drastically as unemployment
grew. The weakened position of workers on the labor
market and the organizational weakening of the unions
also led to a decline in strike activities. Those
political parties (such as the Christian Socials) which
were strongly rooted in politicocultural networks outside the firms were affected to a lesser degree by this
mechanism, at least before the world economic crisis
approached its bottom in Austria. This in turn explains
the large percentage of unemployed in the paramilitary
organizations of all political orientations.

The link with unemployment appears significant in
another respect as well. Its negative effect both on
the attitude to strikes and on trade unions may have
blocked the settlement of primarily economic conflicts
within the orderly confined of labor relations. It may
thus have banked up a conflict potential on the economic
level which spilled over into the political one. And it
is this which, arguably, was the cause of the particular
ideological loading and the ferocity with which violent
political conflicts were fought out in the First
Republic.

In the First Republic, unemployment was particularly acute because the slump caused by the world economic
crisis further exacerbated an already high degree of
long-term, structural unemployment. This fact is significant in accounting for the casualty figures on violence. If one examines the degree to which violence was
determined by the time lag between economic growth and a
reduction in unemployment, one finds that a one-year
time lag alone accounted for 20 percent of the total
violence.[33]

Another result of the analysis is that anomic situations linked with high rates of suicide, although
positively correlated with unemployment, cannot be considered as a direct social-psychological cause for political violence. On the contrary, it seems to indicate
the importance of another intermediate causal factor:
the organizational strength of political militants or
paramilitary activism. It is obvious that there are
strong causal connections between the numerical strength

of paramilitary organizations and political violence in
the postrevolutionary period (after 1920). This also
brings into this model the strategies of violence
mentioned above.

It is therefore to be expected that political
violence cannot be accounted for in purely economic,
social or psychological terms. A quantitative explanatory model that would also include the organizational
strength of the parties in the conflict might lead us
into the area of political explanations. The numerical
strength of political organizations engaged in hostilities and violence played an important role, though one
that cannot yet be ascertained in quantitative terms.

As a result of the growing ideological and political polarization and the instability of the political
system--at least as perceived by the ruling classes--
police expenses were raised. This also indicates an
increase in the organizational strength of one of the
main conflict partners in the First Republic: the conservative and bourgeois-dominated state. It is obvious
that a high level of political violence is usually
linked with police and/or military intervention. This
is shown by a (relatively low) positive regression coefficient of political deaths with police expenses;
instability inside the government, however, did not
affect violence at all.

The aspect of organizational strength also enters
into any explanation of why, in the First Republic, the
statistical incidence of violence was subject to considerable annual fluctuations. It can be concluded that a
high incidence of political violence weakened the material and organizational potential of one of the parties
to the conflict--the loser--to such a degree that the
avoidance of political violence in the period immediately following became likely. Therefore there is a
negative correlation between political violence and the
amount of violence in the previous year.

Probably the most significant cause of political
violence was that its very presence in political conflicts dragged the state's apparatus of coercion into
struggles, even ones in which the executive had originally not been involved. Thus as long as conflict
potential existed within society and as long as the
necessary organizational preconditions were present,
there was a tendency for the interplay of violence and
counterviolence to escalate to dimensions approaching
civil war.[34] (For this reason, the statistical analyses summarized here do not use the crude data of the
annual death figures, but their decadic logarithm,
increased by a factor of 1).

A quantitative explanatory model, certainly still
incomplete, indicates the following relevant causal
factors for the incidence of political violence in a

particular year (Vt). Unemployment rates in the previous year (Ut-1), government stability (Gt), internal state force (Ft), anomic tendencies as measured by suicides (At), labor union strength (Lt) and strikes (St) account for 44 percent of the overall fluctuations of the annual numbers of political deaths. The model, specified in standardized beta coefficients, is:

$$Vt = 0.66 \ Ut\text{-}1 - 0.78 \ At - 0.04 \ Gt \\ + 0.18 \ Ft - 0.11 \ Lt + 0.56 \ St$$

This formula means that an increase in the annual level of violence is mainly "caused" by (unspecified effects of) a decrease of anomic tendencies and of strikes which indicate a weakening of the traditional labor movement. Each factor accounts roughly speaking for one third of the explained variance. In addition to this, there are weaker causative effects on political violence exerted by the unemployment of the previous year and the internal force potential of the state. These factors account for 20 and 10 percent respectively. Government stability and the numerical strength of the labor unions as such have no effect on political violence.

It is assumed here that these factors played an important role also in causing the violent events of 1934. But the relatively low percentage of explained variance in this formula indicates the existence of causal factors other than those listed here. On the one hand, the effect of simple chance events and of voluntary political strategies has to be considered; on the other hand, there is another type of structural cause of violence, which seem to have been invariant during the whole period of the First Republic.

In the process of transition from a predominantly agrarian to a predominantly industrial society, the First Republic occupied an interim position. Transitional stages of this kind tend to be characterized by an uneven growth (or decline) of individual sectors of the economy, by concentration in the structure of ownership, and by changes in the distribution of incomes, etc.; they are also frequently marked by great social tensions, political instability and a high level of violence. Highly developed as well as completely traditional countries, however, tend towards political stability and a low level of violence.[35] Social change, particularly if it takes place abruptly or is interrupted--which is the case in most societies at an intermediate level of development--may cause great sociopsychological and political tensions; in this connection, the determining role in the shaping of political attitudes has been ascribed to "relative deprivation."[36] The high level of violence in the Austria of the interwar period, compared with the last decades of the Habsburg monarchy and the Second Republic, may thus be linked to the accelerated modernization of Austria, a process that had already begun at the turn of the century.

If the revolutionary national and social changes which the years 1918-1919 brought in the former empire were part of a critical transitional phase in the process of modernization, the so-called Austrian Revolution, heightened the conflict. The (not unnatural) absence of consensus about the structure of state and society resulted in the calling into question of the recently established political and social system: the left thought that the revolutionary and evolutionary changes since the Great War had not been radical enough, while the various groups of the right believed that these changes had gone much too far. This explains the attempt which the large sociopolitical groupings made early on to create their own armed formations and to arrogate themselves the right to use violence. The fact that they achieved this--to a disastrous degree--reflects the weakness of a young state further restricted by the peace treaties. For this reason, the representatives of the state--both middle-class and Social Democratic politicians--were neither able nor willing to prevent the accumulation and distribution of weapons left over by the world war. Another result of World War I was that the veterans of this war as well as the rising generation had grown accustomed to the use of violence.[37] The greater inclination to employ violent means--the "front spirit"--played an important role throughout the First Republic in the expression of political and social discontent and tensions.

From a macrohistorical point of view, these long-term or constant causes of violence (and their list might be even further extended) together with medium-term causes of violence (the worsening of economic, social and political conditions over a period of a few years) go far towards explaining the February 1934 events.

Indeed, there seems to hae been a kind of a historical overdetermination for civil war and the defeat of democracy in Austria. There was little room for strategic political decision-making. If one compares Austria with Germany, one sees the same outcome of the historical process--the defeat of democracy and of the labor movement by fascism--regardless of whether in 1918 the socialist labor movement controlled the army and the state and whether or not it was split. How radical the Social Democrats were in ideology and how moderate they were in their political practice is of less importance. It has to be assumed that the character of the middle classes was much more important for the defeat of the labor movement in Austria, as in most of the countries

of central Europe. In those places where the "old" and
"new" middle classes were not separated so strictly from
the working class, where they were less "corporatistic"
and where they displayed strong liberal and democratic
tendencies, democracy did survive, even at the climax of
the world economic crisis. In countries outside of
western and northern Europe, the overthrow of democracy
by fascist and authoritarian dictatorship was almost
predetermined. Therefore, it seems to me that the main
question for the Austrian Social Democrats in 1934 was
not how to win the battle against dictatorship. It was
rather the question of how to be defeated by fascism in
a manner which opened the possibility of a revival and a
"new way" after the fascist interlude. The experience
of civil war gave the chance for a victory of democracy
and for long-term Socialist domination in the Second
Republic.

NOTES

1. See for instance H. Benedict, ed., Geschichte
der Republik Osterreich (Vienna, 1954; 2nd ed., 1977);
Karl R. Stadler, Austria (London, 1971); E. Weinzierl
and K. Skalnik, eds., Osterrich 1918-1938. Geschichte
der Ersten Republik, 2 vols. (Graz, 1983).

2. U. Kluge, Der österreichische Ständestaat
1934-1938 (Vienna, 1984); E. Talos and W. Neugebauer,
eds. "Austrofaschismus" (Vienna, 1984).

3. See G. Botz, Gewalt in der Politik. Attentate,
Zusammenstösse, Putschversuche, Unruhen in Osterreich
1918-1938, 2nd ed. (Munich, 1983), pp. 312-321.

4. Here I follow my article, "Political Violence,
its Forms and Strategies in the First Austrian Republic," in W. J. Mommsen and G. Hirschfeld, eds., Social
Protest, Violence and Terror in Nineteenth- and Twentieth-Century Europe (London, 1982), pp. 300-329. See
this article for the source of subsequent quotations.

5. L. Kerekes, "Die 'Weisse Allianz'," Osterreichische Osthefte, 7 (1965), p. 360ff.; see also H. G. W.
Nusser, Konservative Wehrverbände in Bayern, Preussen
und Osterreich 1918-1933 (Munich, 1973); L. Rape, Die
österreichischen Heimwehren und die bayerische Rechte
1920-1923 (Vienna, 1977); C. E. Edmundson, The Heimwehr
and Austrian Politics 1918-1936 (Athens, Georgia, 1978);
B. F. Pauley, Hitler and the Forgotten Nazis (Chapel
Hill, 1981).

6. P. Hümer, Sektionschef Robert Hecht und die Zerstörung der Demokratie in Österreich (Vienna, 1975); G. Botz, "Der 4. März als Konsequenz ständischer Strukturen ökonomischer Krisen und autoritärer Tendenzen" in E. Fröschl and H. Zoitl, eds., Der 4. März 1933 (Vienna, 1984), pp. 13-36.

7. F. L. Carsten, Fascist Movements in Austria: From Schönerer to Hitler (London, 1977); B. F. Pauley, Hahnenschwanz und Hakenkreuz: Steierischer Heimatschutz und Österreichischer Nationalismus, 1918-1934 (Vienna, 1972).

8. L. Kerekes, Abenddämmerung einer Demokratie (Vienna, 1966).

9. F. Winkler, Die Diktatur in Österreich (Zurich, 1953), p. 27f.; E. Ludwig, Österreichs Sendung im Donauraum (Vienna, 1954), p. 68.

10. J. Hofmann, Der Pfrimerputsch (Vienna, 1965), p. 69ff.; L. Jedlicka, Ein Heer im Schatten der Parteien (Graz, 1955), p. 90.

11. Wiener Zeitung, Vol. 231, No. 43 (2 Dec. 1934), p. 1.

12. R. Neck, "Thesen zum Februar" in L. Jedlicka and R. Neck., eds., Vom Justizpalast zum Heldenplatz (Vienna, 1975), pp. 154f.; also in L. Jedlicka and R. Neck, eds., Das Jahr 1934: 12. Februar (Vienna, 1975), pp. 15-24; Martin Kitchen, The Coming of Austrian Fascism (London, 1980), pp. 202.

13. In Protokoll des sozialdemokratischen Parteitages 1926, abgehalten in Linz vom 30. Oktober bis 3. November 1926 (Vienna, 1926); see also K. Berchtold, ed., Österreichische Parteiprogramme 1966-1968 (Vienna, 1967), p. 251ff.; H. Feichter, "Das Linzer Programm (1926) der österreichischen Sozialdemokratie," Historisches Jahrbuch der Stadt Linz 1973/74 (1975), pp. 233-239; A. Schunck and H.-J. Steinberg, "Mit Wahlen und Waffen" in W. Huber and J. Schwardtfeger, eds., Frieden Gewalt, Sozialismus (Stuttgart, 1976), p. 464ff.

14. In Parteitag 1927: Protokoll des sozialdemokratischen Parteitages abgehalten vom 29. Oktober bis 1. November 1927 im Ottakringer Arbeiterheim in Wien (Vienna, 1927), pp. 132f., 139.

15. Protokoll... 1926, p. 265.

16. E. C. Kollman, Theodor Körner (Munich, 1973), pp. 208ff.; I. Duczynska, Der demokratische Bolschewik (Munich, 1975), p. 117ff.

17. This is particularly true for Körner himself. See G. Botz, "Theodor Körner" in F. Weissensteiner, Die österreichischen Bundespräsidenten (Vienna, 1982), p. 175ff.; in general see J. Wiedenholzer, Aug dem Weg zum 'Neuen Menschen'. Bildungs- und Kulturarbeit der österreichischen Sozialdemokratie in der Ersten Republic (Vienna, 1981), p. 163ff.; B. McLoughlin, "Die Organisation des Wiener Neustädter Schutzbundes," Zeitgeschichte 11, 5 (February, 1984), pp. 135-161.

18. N. Leser, Zwischen Reformismus und Bolschewismus (Vienna, 1968), p. 449ff.; P. Kulemann, Am Beispiel des Austromarxismus (Hamburg, 1979), p. 362ff.; G. Botz, "Austro-Marxist Interpretation of Fascism," Journal of Contemporary History 11, 4 (1976), pp. 129-156.

19. Leser, Reformismus, p. 373ff.

20. J. Kykal and K. R. Stadler, Richard Bernaschek. Odyssee eines Rebellen (Vienna, 1976), p. 78ff.; J. Wiedenholzer, "Bedeutung und Hintergrund des 12. Februar 1934" in "Es wird nicht mehr verhandelt..." Der 12. Februar 1934 in Oberösterreich (Linz, 1984), pp. 22ff.

21. A. Rabinbach, The Crisis of Austrian Socialism. From Red Vienna to Civil War 1927-1934 (Chicago, 1983), p. 193.

22. Der Februar-Aufruhr 1934. Das Eingreifen des österreichischen Bundesheeres zu seiner Niederschlagung (Vienna, 1934), p. 198; Hans von Hammerstein, Im Anfang war der Mord (Vienna, 1981), p. 105ff.

23. W. Goldinger, ed., Protokolle des Klubvorstandes der Christlichesozialen Partei 1932-1934 (Vienna, 1980); R. Neck and A. Wandruszka, ed., Protokolle des Ministerrates der Ersten Republik, section VIII, 5 vols. (Vienna, 1980-1984).

24. P. Kammerstätter, Der Aufstand des Republikanischen Schutzbundes am 12. Februar 1934 in Oberösterreich, 5 vols. (Unpublished manuscript, Linz, 1984; copy in Ludwig Boltzmann Institute of Social Scientific History, Salzburg).

25. R. Bernaschek, "Die Tragödie der österreichischen Sozialdemokratie," in Osterreich, Brandherd Europas (Zurich, 1934), p. 280ff.

26. A. Schlegel, Von Katstrophe zu Katastrophe.
November 1918 bis Februar 1934, Miscellanea, New Series
32, Wiener Katholische Akademie (Vienna, 1981), part 2,
p. 255ff.

27. Kammerstätter, Aufstand, vol. 1, passim; H.
Fiereder, Der Republikanische Schutzbund in Linz und die
Kampfhandlungen im Februar 1934 (Linz, 1983), p. 11ff.

28. R. Hinteregger, K. Schmidlechner and E.
Staudinger, Für Freiheit, Arbeit und Recht. Die
steierische Arbeiterbewegung zwischen Revolution und
Faschismus (1918-1938) (Graz, 1984), p. 88; von
Hammerstein, Anfang, p. 101.

29. For recent publications, see I. Etzersdorfer
and H. Schafranek, eds., Der Februar 1934 in Wien.
Erzählte Geschichte (Vienna, 1984); H. Exenberger and H.
Zoitl, Februar 1934 in Wien (Vienna, 1984); W. R.
Garscha and H. Hautmann, Februar 1934 in Osterreich
(Berlin, 1984); for a comprehensive bibliography see
Informationen. Projektteam Geschichte der Arbeiter-
bewegung 9, 29 (1984), p. 14ff.

30. This is an extension of the models developed in
my articles "Formen und Intensität politisch-sozialer
Konflikte in der Ersten und Zweiten Republik" in
Austriaca. Cahiers universitaires d'information sur
l'Autriche, special No. 3 (1970), pp. 427-468; "Politische Gewalt und industrielle Arbeitskämpfe in Wirt-
schaftskrisen" in Bernd Marin, ed., Wachtumkrisen in
Osterreich? Vol. 2, Krisenszenarios (Vienna, 1979), pp.
260-306.

31. Sources for this can be fund in Botz, "Formen,"
p. 432ff. and Botz, "Political Violence," p. 324 and the
data collection "Interwar Period" of the Ludwig Boltzmann Institute of Social Scientific History, Salzburg.

32. M. Jahoda, P. F. Lazarsfeld and H. Zeisel, Die
Arbeitslosen von Marienthal, 2nd ed. (Allensbach, 1960),
pp. 42ff. and 83f.; D. Stiefel, Arbeitslosigkeit:
Soziale, politische und wirtschaftliche Auswirkungen am
Beispiel Osterreichs 1918-1938 (Berlin, 1979); this is
questioned in H. Safrian, "Wir ham die Zeit der
Orbeitlosigkeit schon richtig genossen auch" in G. Botz
and J. Weidenholzer, eds., Mündliche Geschichte und
Arbeiterbewegung. Eine Einführung in Arbeitsweisen und
Themenbereiche der Geschichte "geschichtsloser" Sozial-
gruppen (Vienna, 1984), pp. 293-332.

33. This value results from a comparison between
the squared multiple correlation coefficient R^2 for

regression equations of economic growth and unemployment, once inclusive and once exclusive of the time lag
in casuality figures.

34. See also C. Tilly, "Revolution and Collective
Violence" in F. I. Greenstein and N. W. Polsby, eds.,
Handbook of Political Science, Vol. 3 (Reading, Mass.,
1975), p. 515.

35. I. K. Feierabend and R. L. Feierabend, "Aggressive Behaviour within Politics, 1948-1962" in J.
Chowming Davies, ed., When Men Revolt and Why (New York,
1971), p. 236ff. Also see B. A. Nesvold, "Social Change
and Poltical Violence" in Hugh Davis Graham and Ted R.
Gurr, eds., The History of Violence in America:
Historical and Comparative Perspectives (New York,
1969), p. 653ff.; T. R. Gurr, "A Comparative Study of
Civil Strife," Ibid., p. 572ff.

36. See T. R. Gurr, Rebellion: Eine Motivations-
analyse von Aufruhr, Konspiration und innerem Krieg
(Dusseldorf, 1972), p. 33ff.

37. P. H. Merkl, Political Violence under the
Swastika (Princeton, 1975), p. 154ff.; K. Renner,
Osterreich von der Ersten zur Zweiten Republik (Vienna,
1953), p. 117ff.

10. The Austromarxists in "Red" Vienna: Reflections and Recollections

Hans Ziesel

There was something very special about that democratic socialist labor movement, something rarely captured in the political tracts and articles of the
era.[1]   Today, on the fiftieth anniversary of the
events which drove that socialist movement underground,
I will try to recapture some of the living substance of
its goals, its fights, its defeats, and of the remarkable men and women who led it.

Some of my earliest, yet most vivid memories have
to do with the way socialists resisted World War I.   For
instance, I remember well the summer of 1914 which I
spent in a small village on the Adriatic coast, in the
Italian-speaking part of the Austrian monarchy.   In July
of that year the news reached us of the murder of
Jaurès, the magnificent French socialist who had led the
fight against the impending war.   My parents were dejected; the last hope for peace seemed gone.   In August
Austria declared war on Serbia.   The day the news
reached us, my father tried to interrupt the patriotic
din in the local coffeehouse by shouting "a basso la
guerra" which resulted in our prompt if honorific ejec-
tion from the place.

Another such memory is that of Victor Adler, the
man who had led the Socialist Party during the last
three decades of the monarchy.   The occasion was a mass
meeting some time early in 1916 to which my parents had
taken me.   He spoke about the war.   He stammered a bit;
his head was bowed.   "You probably know," he reminded
his audience at one point, "the inscription over our
Ministry of War, si vis pacem para bellum."   He translated the passage, then, raising his arms high above his
ailing body, he cried out: "It is a lie, comrades; if
you want peace you must prepare for peace."   Having
prepared for peace, Victor Adler died on the eve of the
proclamation of the Republic.   Like Moses, he was not
allowed to see the new land.   "I do not mind dying," he
said, "I am just so curious."

Then there are memories of the trial of Friedrich

Adler, Victor Adler's son. In October 1916, to the
shock and surprise of everyone, this mild mannered man
had assassinated the Austrian Prime Minister Count
Stürgkh. In those times of absolute censorship, he
thought this to be the only way of bringing the issue of
war and peace before the people. A generous monarchy
obliged him: Adler's passionate defense at his trial
for murder became the fanfare of the antiwar wing of the
Socialist Party.

There is another man whose memory I should like to
invoke here because he too represented the style of
these old socialists. Herr Klatschko had left his
native Russia long before the turn of the century,
heading first for the United States where he took part
in the founding of one of the short-lived socialist
communes. After it failed, he returned to Europe and
settled in Vienna as a patent attorney. His major role,
however, was to provide a haven for the Russian socialists who escaped czarist persecution, some of them
literally through burrows they had dug from their
Siberian camps. He was a man of high personal principles, and kept a most modest standard of living. When
he died, one of his Russian friends gave the funeral
oration. My mother, who was there, told me later that
tears had rendered him unable to finish his eulogy. He
was Leon Trotsky, the future Commander of the Red Army.

The aftermath of the war brought striking opportunities and temptations. One of the fateful tasks that
confronted the Socialist Party during the very first
months of the Republic was dealing with the temptation
offered by the Russian Bolshevik revolution which had
spread to Hungary and briefly to Bavaria, both neighbors
of Austria. The Austrian Socialists fought the temptation with determination. At issue was not only the surrender of the Socialist Party's democratic principles,
but also the prevention of the fragmentation that later
would debilitate the labor movements of so many other
European countries. The Austrian Socialist Party, with
Friedrich Adler in the forefront, fought for the hearts
of its members and won. Because the Austrian Socialists
had retained their unity, Austria has remained to this
day the only central European country that, with the
exception of a few years after World War II, never had a
communist party of any significance.

The city of Vienna, in which the Socialists held a
majority, provided an opportunity for the great
socialist adventure of the two decades between the wars;
the essentially rural provinces were dominated by the
Catholic Party. By acquiring state status in the Federal Republic, Vienna was able to go its own, socialist
way. One of its key figures was Hugo Breitner, who gave
up his job as bank director to become the city's treas-
urer. Through a system of progressive taxes, he laid

the foundation for Vienna's ambitious reform work--
primarily in the fields of welfare and school reform--
and for a public housing program that became a model for
later efforts all over the world. All this took place
against the opposition of the federal government which
was dominated by the Catholic Party and within an economy in which unemployment during the depression reached
a level of 26 percent, and there was virtually no unemployment insurance.

The Socialists' economic and social endeavors were
accompanied by a vigorous effort to develop a new style
of living aimed at a higher form of life--including no
drinking, decent sexual relations, and communion with
nature. The party youth in particular carried that
spirit; meetings which occurred almost daily, weekend
excursions, vacation-time camps and retreats filled our
lives.

All these efforts were carried out by a determined-
ly democratic party whose concern for making Vienna a
model city was embedded in the vision of a not-too-
distant socialist society. The movement bore the imprint of its leaders, persons of high spirit, of humane
views, tireless men and women with modest worldly demands. They were interested, beloved and, on the whole,
exemplary persons.

There was, for instance, Wilhelm Ellenbogen, another physician who gave up doctoring for service in the
socialist movement. In 1927 at the Congress of the Socialist International which I attended as a stenogra-
pher, I was sitting near him when an unusually elegant
member of the British Labor Party walked onto the ros-
trum and was introduced, to much applause. Ellenbogen
only shook his head and murmured: "Nobody can persuade
me that this is a socialist." The man was Oswald
Mosley, who was to become the leader of the English
Black Shirts. Ellenbogen was a sensitive guardian of
his party's political morality.

There was Friedrich Austerlitz, the editor-in-chief
of the Arbeiter-Zeitung, a self-taught jurist, member of
Austria's constitutional court--which in its wisdom
allowed the participation of lay judges--and a portly,
modest bachelor. He was a powerful polemicist and an
untiring teacher of new generations of journalists.
When I told him that I intended to visit America, he
suggested I see his nephew. "He was named Fredric after
me," he said, "but he americanized his name from Austerlitz, I believe, to--Astaire."

There was Käthe Leichter, the vibrant leader of the
socialist women's movement. When the Nazis came, she
brought her family to safety, overstayed her time, was
caught, and eventually shot in Ravensbrück.

There was Theodor Körner, a distinguished general
in the old monarchy who had become a passionate social-

122

ist. He was a radiant, eternally young man who even in
deep winter never wore a coat. After World War II he
became Vienna's first mayor and later president of the
Republic. When, at the war's end, I sent food parcels
to the friends who had survived, Körner added a line to
his thank-you note: "I trust you won't mind that I
passed my parcel on to the city's poor."

And then, of course, there was Otto Bauer, the
party's ascetic leader, who through his editorials in
the Arbeiter-Zeitung, was our foremost educator, a man
of formidable intellect and moral stature who shaped our
Marxist convictions more than anyone else. His three
major historical works, The Nationality Problem, The
Austrian Revolution, and The Fight for Forest and Pasture would offer appropriate selections for an anthology
of Marxist scholarship. There was a great elegance
about these socialists of the First Republic. In the
American vernacular, they were beautiful people.

What of Marxism was a living part of that socialist
movement? We had little doubt that the theory of the
class struggle was correct and that the social betterment of the poor had to be fought for and won by the
socialist movement that represented them. The Austrian
political reality left us in no doubt about the truth of
that part of Marxism. Nor did we doubt that capitalism
was a transient phase in human development. The steadily recurring and ever deepening depressions in the business cycle threatened the very foundations of society.
Moreover, to allow profit-seeking to become the basic
economic drive seemed immoral. The labor theory of
value appeared to buttress these convictions. Socialism
was destined to supersede capitalism because those elements of an economy which were owned and operated by the
society as a whole were developing during the mature
stages of capitalism. It was thought that the people
who worked for the capitalists for wages or salaries
would gradually join the socialist movement and thereby
assure its ultimate victory. The eventual transfer of
the title for the means of production from private
owners to the society at large would cure the ills of
capitalism and preserve its achievements. To fight for
that goal was the political burden of capitalism's
exploited victims, the workers, whose self-interest
would make them the prime driving force towards socialism. This development, which we believed to be
inexorable, was but one manifestation of historical
materialism, a theory which suggested that man's political goals are significantly influenced by his place in
the economic hierarchy.

The transition to socialism would be prepared by
two developments within the capitalist society. The
continuing concentration and growth of managerial units
would facilitate the transition to community ownership.

And the institutionalization of trade unions would
prepare workers for their future participation in gov-
ernance. The socialist society, we believed, would be
different in kind from all previous ones because ex-
ploiters and exploited would no longer confront each
other. This would give humanity its first full opportunity to pursue its higher goals. In Engels' words,
the socialist society would make the "jump from the
realm of necessity into that of freedom." The piecemeal
reform efforts of the day were but the first building
blocks of that future. The ultimate justification of
socialism derived from our expectation that it would
usher in a new man, a new morality. Such were the
visions into which the constructive political tasks of
the day were embedded.

Austria was then and still is a small country, and
Vienna a comparatively small city of not quite two
million inhabitants. Nevertheless we thought of ourselves as the avant-garde of a world which we watched
with enormous interest; parochial geography did not
impede our view. When Judge Gary died, the Arbeiter-
Zeitung told us all about the steel trust he had founded. When Sacco and Vanzetti died, our flags flew at
half-mast. Of course, the international socialist
movement was of particular concern to us. We were hosts
to émigrés from fascism, including Sigmund Kunfi and
Zoltan Ronay from Hungary and Filipo Turati and Carlos
Treves from Italy.

Austromarxism at that time was challenged, infused,
and buffeted by three powerful intellectual currents.
There was the group around the economist Ludwig von
Mises, the advocate-general of the free market, who is
acknowledged as the intellectual ancestor of Milton
Friedman and the economists who follow Friedman's flag.
Mises challenged socialist theory on two grounds. He
claimed that a socialist economy with artificial prices
would not allow sound accounting, and on that score he
was shown to be in error.[2] The second current originated with Vienna's astute philosophers--the Vienna
Circle. They were linked to the socialist movement
through one of their distinguished members, Otto Neu-
rath, one of the last polyhistors: physicist, historian, statistician, and philosopher. I first encountered
his thought when I read his 1919 Dresden lectures on the
promise of socialism. He was a man of unexpected
thoughts. At one of the coffeehouse extensions of his
seminar for us socialist students, he raised his fist
and asked with a prophetic smile, "What will we do, when
all the world's energy will come from one small center?"

The Vienna of these years was also the birth place
of Freud's psychoanalysis and Alfred Adler's individual
psychology. The latter exerted a powerful influence on
the educational ideas of the socialist movement, pri-

marily through one of Adler's associates, Carl Furt-
müller, who became the leading architect of the school
reform.

Our vision of the future had two components. The
optimistic view, buttressed by the success of the many
constructive achievements of the City of Vienna and by
the response of the electorate, was the promise of
advancement through the democratic electoral process.
The dark vision flowed from the fear that the democratic
road to progress might be cut off; the fascist take-
overs in the countries bordering on Austria became a
growing threat. Hungary, our neighbor to the east, was
the first to establish a fascist regime; in the twenties, Italy followed; in the thirties, Hitler closed the
circle. Austrian fascism drew strength from these
friends: through the example they set, through their
active irredentist support backed by weapons and money
and, as we now know, through direct political conspiracy
with some members of the Austrian government. The
spirit that bound us socialists together was strengthened by the rapid deterioration of the political scene
around us.

The July days of 1927 put the optimistic and the
pessimistic vision to an unexpected test, and the
violent encounter revealed the future. When, quite
unexpectedly, some irresponsible demonstrators set the
Justizpalast on fire, the Vienna police--which was not
under the city's administration--killed some ninety
people. It was the beginning of the civil war that
ended seven years later in the February days of 1934.

In the fifty years that have since passed,
politicians and historians have devoted much effort to
the analysis of those February days and the years which
preceded them. Many of these analysts, balancing on-
the-one-hand points against on-the-other-hand points,
have come up with a verdict of shared responsiblity. My
reading of these events is different. The balanced view
derives from a failure to weigh the points. A grim joke
of World War I vintage comes to mind about the sausage
that was half chicken and half horse--one chicken, one
horse. The truth rests on the simple fact that it was
the Socialists who wanted to preserve democracy and the
Republic, and that it was the Bürgerblock which wanted
to--and did--destroy both.

The tragic end of Dollfuss, who was murdered by the
Nazis in the summer of 1934, has tended to obscure his
pivotal role in the destruction of the Republic. He
began by putting parliament out of commission; then he
dissolved the constitutional court when it threatened to
intervene; and he completed the onslaught in February
1934 by destroying the Socialist opposition. That he
did all this in the mistaken hope of taming the Nazi
movement does not alter the fact that he destroyed the

Republic, intentionally and effectively. Whatever
"Austrian vision" lay behind it, this destruction was as
criminal as it was shortsighted. When the critical hour
came four years later, the Republic lacked its most determined defenders. That Dollfuss himself became the
first victim of the National Socialist attack is a
tragic irony of history.

Some of his defenders say he did all this to
counter the threat of a socialist dictatorship. But
what evidence was there of such a threat? During an
earlier scholarly conference on the 1934 events, an
enthusiastic defender of Dollfuss reminded his listeners
that Karl Seitz, the venerated mayor of Vienna, had
threatened in a speech that democracy was not enough:
"our fight is for social democracy." To call this a
threat is malicious nonsense. Social democracy was the
universal formulation of the socialists' ultimate goal:
supplementing the equality won in the franchise by
social equality.

Recently, I came across another formulation of that
dangerous socialist threat in a pamphlet written during
the twenties by one of those terrible Austromarxists,
Robert Danneberg, whose calvary began in Buchenwald and
ended in Auschwitz: "In the new golden age the earth
will be no longer the vale of sorrows; socialism will
free the road for the ascent of humanity to luminous
heights." Not even the now-famous formulation of the
Socialist Party's program is evidence of any threat.
After firmly reiterating its unambiguous support of the
democratic process, the program voiced concern lest the
legitimate aspirations of the socialist movement be
thwarted by dictatorial intervention and stated that in
that case the socialists would have no choice but to
answer force with force and to establish a dictatorship
of their own.

Since these programmatic formulations were primarily
Otto Bauer's and since he was also the party's leader in
the political battles of the day, much of the on-the-
other-hand blame has been fastened on him. Yet no
socialist distanced himself more sharply from the Communist program than he. I cannot improve on the
pertinent statement by Professor Eduard März:

> Bauer, as is well known, resisted the revolutionary
> seizure of power in 1918 and 1919 because he be-
> lieved that socialism must rest on a broad majority
> of the working class. With regard to the "dicta-
> torship of the proletariat" as it was practiced in
> the Soviet Union, he correctly predicted that it
> would transform itself into a dictatorship over the
> proletariat. It is in this sense that one must
> also understand the Linz Program he helped write in
> which violence was assigned a strictly defensive

126

role. The "revolutionary means" the Linz program
speaks of, as the distinguished nonsocialist
scholar Franz Klein wrote (Ost. Volkswirt, 14
August 1926), are the "natural weapons of the
democratic state in defense against those who break
the law, by calling for the help of the sheriff, of
the police, of the army, and eventually, if need
be, by calling to arms its citizenry."[3]

I should like to add a personal recollection to
this analysis. Bauer was horrified by violence. His
entire policy was directed toward preventing it at any
price short of the destruction of the Socialist Party.
What is more, I believe that since 15 July he knew that
he could not lead the party if his policy failed and it
came to civil war. On that day, which was the most
violent one in the history of the Republic to that
point, while the first victims of the police shooting
were being brought on stretchers into the parliament,
Bauer, deep in thought, paced back and forth in the
socialist conference hall, chain smoking, not saying or
doing anything. The totally unexpected violence found
him helpless, or so it struck me.
When, four years later, the political situation was
reaching a crisis stage, General Körner advised the
party leadership that, in his view, with a properly
prepared strategy, the Socialists could win a civil war.
That the party rejected Körner's advice out of hand
showed how far removed it was from considering the pos-
sibiity of all-out civil war. The sole forlorn hope was
to avoid it. If one needs more proof of this intent,
one can find it in the criticism the Socialists encountered from the far left for their handling of the 1934
events.
I have never seen the advocates of shared responsibility spell out just what horrible things were
threatened by a Socialist victory. Efforts to retore
and maintain full employment? Nationalization of the
banking system (which had begun in 1931) and of heavy
industry? All this has become a reality in the Second
Republic. Yet in those years the Bürgerblock thought
the threat of a Socialist majority sufficient justification for conspiring with Austria's fascist neighbors
to destroy the socialist movement and the Republic for
which the Socialists stood. But those responsible for
the destruction cannot credibly put even part of the
blame on the Socialists who desperately tried to preserve the Republic.
As to the men and women who died on the barricades
and on the gallows in those days, they will live in
history. They have the distinction of having been part
of the one movement in the whole of Europe that offered

armed resistance to the fascist onslaught. They defended a movement and an achievement which Karl Polanyi
rightly called "one of the most spectacular triumphs of
western history."[4] I toast their memory.

The title given to our conference today betrays a
certain bias. We are asked to discuss "The Collapse of
the Socialist Experiment." Collapse suggests destruction from within; this is not what happened. The Socialists were pushed and pushed hard. Collapse also
suggests a final end; this is not what happened either.
The socialist movement under the leadership of Bruno
Kreisky has survived well into the Second Republic.

How has Marxist theory survived the last fifty
years? Both Marxist theories and political prescrip-
tions have lost some of their pristine power in the
light of that experience. To begin with, the mere
transference to public ownership was meant to insure
that decisions that affect the human substance would not
be guided solely by price and cost considerations. And
it was intended to remove--or at least to tame--the per-
nicious bottom phase of the business cycle. The class
struggle theory too has undergone reformulation. Marx's
claim to its universality over time and geography is
diminished by the reawakened power of nationalism and
religion, as well as by the population pressure of un-
imagined proportions which have overwhelmed the relevance of class structure during the last few decades.
Not even in the Western democracies has the class struggle been the predominant political issue.

The realization that the enhancement of the living
standard of the laboring claasses depends more on the
increase of a nation's productivity than on the redis-
tribution of its income is changing the traditional
forms of struggle. Austria's Second Republic has developed one new form of socialism that keeps prices, productivity and wages in balance. A tripartite communica-
tions network--the "social partnership"--that links
employers, trade unions, and the government aims at the
peaceful resolution of competing claims on the national
product. Among its side effects are the control of
inflation and a zero frequency of strikes. The Japanese
have pursued similar goals with similar means.

The reformulation of the class struggle theory is
tied to the reappraisal of the Marxist expectation that
the industrial working class, because of its exploited
position, would be the driving force towards socialist
revolution or reform. Both the American and the Russian
experience has shown that the drive for radical reform
does not always emanate from the working class. Even a
fighting working class has too often been fighting for
short term gains rather than for progressive reform.

Marx's proposition that man's value positions--
occasionally even the direction of his intellectual

pursuits--are determined by the socioeconomic order in which he lives, or even by the position he holds in that hierarchy, has stood the test of time. In a more modest form, that proposition has become an integral part of historical learning and research. But Marx's labor theory of value turned out to be an incomplete explanation of why property ownership yields unearned income; it is now essentially of historical interest. The Soviet Union paid a heavy price for taking the labor theory of value seriously. Following Marx, in its early years it did not consider transportation costs as part of the value of goods, with the result that coal, for instance, was sold at the same price in Leningrad and in the Don Basin where it was mined. Marx's labor theory of value was not essential to his diagnosis of the capitalist ills.[5] At the core of the problem was what Marx had called the "merchandise character" of labor; Karl Polanyi reformulated the problem in modern terms:

> To separate labor from other activities of life and to subject it to the laws of the market was to annihilate all organic forms of existence and to replace them by a different type of organization, an atomistic and individualistic one.[6]

The socialist society which Engels and Bebel expected to become reality around the turn of the last century has receded. Socialism is no longer the vision of a not-too-far off future. Today's steps of reform are still headed in the direction to which the socialists of the 1920s went, or would have liked to go. The difference is that the expectation of an eventual radical change has given way to the ascendance of gradualism. As the 1978 program of the Austrian Socialists put it: the achievement of social democracy is a continuing process.

The issue of radical change versus gradualism had been in the center of the socialist debate in Austria and Germany ever since the first decades of this century. The German socialist Eduard Bernstein was the protagonist of gradualism. He lost the debate, but he seems to have won the argument.[7] The expectation of radical change has receded for two reasons. First, the specter of the Russian revolution has lost its glamour. Our hope for freedom there has borne no fruit. The annihilation of the Prague Spring was the watershed; if allowed to grow, it might have been the first stuttering of a motor about to come to life.

The second reason is that during these last decades the western economies have performed unusually well on the whole. Against a background of substantial general improvement in the standard of living, states have widened access to education and strengthened the social

security system. That there must be a safety net has
become accepted doctrine. The issues that remains are
the density of the net and its institutional permanence.
The difficulties arise from the fact that in times of
economic depression, when the need for the net is greatest, funds are at their lowest.

Still, while things have improved, they are far
from going well. Our capitalist economies, with their
stupendous ability to produce wealth when times are
good, operate poorly when the unavoidable bad times
come. We still have periodic and even long-lasting mass
unemployment.[8] For the underbelly of society, the
uncertainties of existence are still too great. If we
had bought an automobile that ran that poorly, we surely
would ask for a recall and repair. All is not well, and
our tendency to acquiesce is probably part of the trouble. The catalogue of indictments of the capitalist system is still formidable. The distribution of wealth and
income is still too unequal: the poor are too poor, and
the rich too rich. Too large a part of the nation's
wealth is acquired as unearned income, through inheri-
tance and ownership of capital assets. In spite of the
expanded social security system, that maldistribution
still translates itself into shocking differences in
morbidity, mortality, and other aspects of the very
substance of life.[9]

The maldistribution of wealth also translates
itself into a maldistribution of power, which--to quote
the distinguished nonsocialist economist Frank Knight--
"limits the effective freedom of the weaker party and,
if extreme, destroys it...it also corrupts both the
stronger and the weaker."[10] And to quote an eminent
socialist, Kenneth Arrow: "In a system where virtually
all resources are available for a price, economic power
can be translated into political power by channels too
obvious to mention. In a capitalist society, economic
power is very unequally distributed, and hence democratic government is inevitably something of a sham."[11]

There is nevertheless some truth in the free marketers' contentions. If the economy performs at its
peak, when there is only frictional unemployment, the
freedom to choose one's occupation and working place is
great. But at the bottom of the cycle, little is left
of that freedom to accept or refuse, to move or not to
move. In those times, freedom turns into the mockery of
Anatole France's bon mot about the equal freedom of the
rich and the poor to sleep under the bridge. Fortunately, market and planning are not the mortal enemies that
the free marketers make them out to be. As Karl Polanyi
has shown in The Great Transformation, an unfettered
free market has never existed. As Kenneth Arrow explained, it "could not exist for 10 minutes," because,
to cite Frank Knight once more, "intolerable conse-

quences would prevail if society were organized...in the nearest possible approach to the perfectly competitive markets of 'pure' economic theory."[12] It would seem that, for better or worse, all countries aim at some balance between market economy and planning. The western economies have begun to try to tame the free market by a variety of government interventions that increase the security of the individual within the system and move society towards what we have come to call the welfare state. These events have taken place against the background of a sharp rise in the general living standard. As a result, capitalism has regained much of its robustness. The planned economies of the eastern bloc and of China attempt to increase their efficiency by feeding market information back into their plans and even by allowing some private entrepreneurship. However much the ideologues on both sides may protest, the search is for a balance between efficiency and stability, and for greater equity within the system. Wassily Leontief has used the happy metaphor of a sailing vessel: the market economy keeps the vessel moving, and the government at the rudder keeps it on course by its taxes, its expenditures, and its regulative powers. The metaphor continues: a sailboat does not move at all unless somebody holds the rudder.[13]

Yet a just and well functioning economy, however important, was never the sole concern of socialism. Socialism was also to open the way for a new type of man. Allowing the profit motive to be our principal guide may help us to maximize our wealth, but it also tends to maintain a lopsided morality. The profit motive is but a special form of self-interest. If that becomes the religion of a society, if nobody is responsible for anybody but himself, society is in danger. The concern is not a new one. John Stuart Mill feared that the spirit of a commercial people would be "essentially mean and slavish." Max Weber worried over "the pursuit of wealth stripped of its religious and ethical meanings." Yet the share of the pie we can grab is the measure of our success or failure. And when somebody asks us what a man is worth, we are expected to name a figure.

I suspect that it is not only the relative betterment of the economic structure of society that has dampened the socialist zeal but also our reverence for self-interest--the plainer word for which is selfishness. Marx, of course, did not see it that way. In this respect he was a good follower of Adam Smith; he thought the very self-interest of the exploited workers would eventually bring about socialism. Deep down, we have no doubt that selfishness is not a virtue. Our heroes, both the secular and the religious ones, are the men and women who do not seek their own well-being but

that of their fellowmen. The essence of being a socialist is the holding of certain ethical positions about
justice and about duties to our fellowmen. This is not
an original thought. My mother, who never liked the
idea that socialism referred to certain organizational
forms of society, knew that. She once pointed to a man
on the television screen who passionately fought against
some injustice. "This is a socialist," she said.

In this sense, the new men and women of the future
have been around us for a long time, millions of them.
But their morality does not dominate our societies nor,
from all we can learn, the societies of the "socialist"
bloc.

The longing for a socialist society is as much the
longing for the new man as it is the hope for a more
just economy. The profit system does not move us in
that direction.[14] The hope lies beyond it:

> When the accumulation of wealth is no longer of
> high social importance, there will be great changes
> in the codes of morals...I see us free to return to
> some of the most sure and certain principles of
> religion and traditional virtue--that avarice is a
> vice, that the exaction of usury is a misdemeanor,
> and the love of money is detestable. We shall once
> more value ends above means and prefer the good to
> the useful.[15]

We always knew what the new man would look like.
He would be shaped in the image of our beloved friends
in the socialist movement, the men and women who fought
and died for that better world.

NOTES

1. See, for instance, Tom Bottomore and Patrick
Goode, eds., Austro-Marxism (Oxford, 1978).

2. By Otto Leichter, Wirtschaftsrechnung in der
Sozialistischen Gesellschaft (Wien, 1924), and by Oskar
Lange in, for instance, his three essays in Oskar Lange,
ed., Problems of Political Economy of Socialism (Warsaw,
1962). Joseph Schumpeter, although not a socialist, had
little doubt that the accounting problem could be
solved. See an insightful essay about the great economist who expected socialism to win out but had mixed
feelings about the prospect: Gottfried Haberler's
contribution in Arnold Heertje, ed., Schumpeter's
Vision: Capitalism, Socialism and Democracy after 40
years (New York, 1980), p. 2.

3. From an article he wrote for the Vienna news-paper Arbeiter-Zeitung.

4. Karl Polanyi, The Great Transformation (Boston, 1944), p. 288.

5. See H. Zeisel, "Marxism and Subjective Theory," in Problems of the Theory of Value, ed. Ludwig v. Mises and Arthur Spiethoff, Schriften d. Vereins f. Sozial-politik, v. 183/1 (Munich, 1931) p. 177 ff.; H. Zeisel, "An Argument against Marx's Theory of Value," in Der Kampf (Vienna, 1934). See also the revival and summary view of that problem area in Journal of Economic Litera-ture, Vol. 9 (1971), p. 399, stimulated by Paul Samuel-son's article "Understanding the Marxian Notion of Exploitation: A summary of the so-called Transformation Problem between Marxian Values and Competitive Prices." Martin Bronfenbrenner, Abba Lerner, and William Baumol were the discussants.

6. Karl Polanyi, The Great Transformation, p. 163. Cass R. Sunsteini, "Rights, Minimal Terms, and Solidar-ity: A Comment," a contribution to the symposium The Conceptual Foundation of Labor Law, The University of Chicago Law Review, vol. 31 (1984), p. 1041.

7. Even the programs of the European Communists show this shift, with an interesting time lag. The Italian Communists, for instance, with the help of the eminent historian Hobsbawm, have published a detailed statement of their positions. It reads very much like the programs of a socialist party--of the twenties. See The Italian Road to Socialism: an Interview by Eric Hobsbawm with Georgio Napolitano (Westport, Conn., 1977).

8. See Marie Jahoda, Paul F. Lazarsfeld, Hans Zeisel, Die Arbeitslosen von Marienthal (Leipzig, 1933); republished in 1960 in the series Classics of Survey Research (Verlag für Demoskopie). An English translaion is Marienthal, The Sociography of an Unemployed Village (Chicago and New York, 1971). It was no accident that this first systematic study of the devastating effects of extended unemployment grew out of the moral climate of Vienna's socialist movement. When the Austrian trade unions won the eight-hour working day, we thought of studying the use of the newly found leisure time. When the plan was shown to Otto Bauer, he dismissed us angrily. Studying leisure time in a country that has 20 percent unemployment? Go and study unemployment!--which we did.

9. See Evelyn M. Kitagawa and Philip M. Hauser, Differential Motality in the United States: A Study in socioeconomic Epidemiology (Cambridge, Mass., 1973).

10. Frank H. Knight, "Abstract Economics as Absolute Ethics," Ethics, Vol. 76 (1966), pp. 163, 174.

11. Kenneth Arrow, "A Cautious Case for Socialism," Dissent, Vol. 45 (1978), p. 472.

12. See Knight, "Abstract Economics," p. 177.

13. Wassily Leontief, "Sails and Rudder, ships of State," Op-ed page, New York Times, 16 March 1973.

14. John Kenneth Galbraith recently wrote of "The Heartless Society," New York Times Magazine, 8 February, 1984. He was referring to the present-day United States. His point may be a more general one; somewhere I read: "Deep in the heart of capitalism, there is no heart."

15. It is comforting to know that this paragraph was not written by a Marxist socialist but by a bourgeois economist, albeit one who has done a great deal for the betterment of mankind, by John Maynard Keynes. See Essays in Persuasion (London, 1931), p. 371ff.

11. Austromarxism and the Theory of Democracy

Andrew Arato

I'd like to begin my presentation with an apology: these remarks are extremely preliminary and open to correction by experts on Austrian history and Austrian socialism. I don't happen to be an expert in either field. My own interest in Austromarxism has come about in a different way, I suppose, than most of you: I have been for a long time interested in the renewal of Marxian theory in general in the 1920s, in the origins of Western Marxism. Now I am interested in the renewal of democratic theory, especially in our own time but also in the past. In particular I'm interested in a theory of what I would call democratic civil society, and I believe that it is important for social theory to recover the part of the tradition of the left which is relevant to this.

This left tradition is now a longstanding one, and to a certain extent Austromarxism belongs to it. The idea of "a third road" or "the search for a third road" represents something that by now has a rather long history, including not only Austromarxism but also post-World War II developments in France--Sartre's and Merleau-Ponty's early efforts after the war--Eurocommunism, Eurosocialism, the New Left, what is now called the Second Left in France, the East European democratic opposition, and perhaps even the Green Movement in West Germany, which represent, each in its own way, attempts at some kind of "third road." But the words must be put into quotation marks because the question arises: a third road between what and what? In the case of the Austromarxists, the answer to this seems to be rather simple: between communism and social democracy. But I think that by now the issue is not so simple because the road between state socialism and democratic capitalism is not exactly the same thing as that between communism and social democracy, or between democratic capitalism and social democracy. And of course the road between revolution and reform is certainly not the same as between communism and socialism or social democracy, in

a period in which communism has become an extremely
conservative power, on the whole. One might even add
the road between statism and anarchism--that might be
yet another way of raising the question of a third road,
except that it's not exactly parallel to the others. I
believe that even this question belongs to the history
of the topic. Let me first of all anticipate my conclusion: the Austromarxian stress on the first version of
this opposition--that between communism and socialism--
and its identification with primarily this version of
the problem of the third road has led to various difficulties, and from these difficulties we should be able
to learn at least something. But before I argue this, I
would like to turn to Austromarxism as part of a tradition which I believe still has something to contribute
both to the motivation and the formation of political
identities.

Now let me just list some of the crucial elements
of so-called Austromarxism which contribute to a theory
of a third way or, I think more properly, to that of a
democratic postbourgeois civil society. First of all,
there is the critique of nondemocratic forms of industrial social organization, the critique of dictator-
ships--not only of the Soviet Union but also of various
versions of fascism--which is an important aspect of
Austromarxist theoretical history. Obviously the work
of Otto Bauer is the most significant in this respect.
Second, there is the analysis of the form of the state
vis-à-vis the problem of nation and nationality: this
is the federalist conception which is of course as old
as the Brünn Program. It was developed in a most
sophisticated fashion by Renner and Bauer in some of
their early work. Third, there is a theory of democracy
in the strict sense, under the headings of political and
social democracy, or the duality of political and social
democracy. Here again Bauer and Renner and to a certain
extent Adler are the major contributors in the years
after World War I. What is in this context rather
remarkable--and I don't think anyone has yet mentioned
it here--is that by the 1930s the initial conception had
changed. The fourth point is perhaps one of the most
important, namely the theory of law, and respect for the
emancipatory as well as the functional aspects of formal
law. In the history of Austromarxism this was almost
exclusively the contribution of Karl Renner. Of these
four elements, I'd like to focus on only one, primarily
because of time and my own specific interest: the
theory of democracy in the stricter sense. But I would
like to connect it eventually to the critique of dictatorship because the two, I believe, were related.

In the years immediately following the World War I,
in several works under various headings, sometimes under
the same heading ("Rätesystem und Demokratie" was the

favorite title, and perhaps there was even a special
issue of Der Kampf around the topic to which several
people contributed) several Austromarxists worked out a
rather sophisticated conception of the duality of democracy and the duality of revolutions. I won't try to
present the most extended version of this in Adler's
"Die Staatauffassung des Marxismus," first of all because it's the most orthodox, and second because it also
the most complicated, due to its length. Let me begin
with a couple of notions presented by Bauer in two
writings, "Der Weg zum Sozialismus" and "Der Osterreichische Revolution." In both of these, Bauer explains
what constitutes the crucial difference between political and social revolution, and states that Austria, in
his conception, had already completed the former, but
was not ready for and had obviously not completed the
latter. Political democracy, therefore, has been
achieved in the context of the survival of capitalist
property relations which he argued, and I think rightly,
could be abolished only in the context of the double
disaster of, first, a civil war and, second, a drastic
decline of production. The question that arises is
whether he proposed waiting for a future version of the
second revolution, which might happen in some fatalistic
manner. Perhaps his conception later on pointed in this
direction, but what I detect in these early writings is
a crucial difference with all prewar revisionisms, especially those in the German Social Democratic Party:
the idea of a gradual societal democratization is introduced under the headings of selfmanagement, industrial
councils, industrial and economic democracy, which serve
the pedagogical function of preparing workers for a
socialist society. In this respect, his conception was
different from that of Max Adler who believed that the
real pedagogy could begin only after a second revolution.
　　Several aspects of this conception of a transitional development--which is presented under the headings of industrial or economic democracy--are interesting for us. One is that in Bauer's early conception,
only political democracy makes such a development
possible. Second, it is rather clear that democracy in
this conception does not turn out to be merely an instrument for socialism. Rather than democracy being an
instrument for socialism, the very definition of socialization and hence socialism is in fact, in the conception of Bauer, only a more extended system of the same
thing, democracy. He doesn't stress the transformation
of property relations; or rather, to the extent that he
does so, the transformation of property relations must
be seen as the shifting from capitalist property to
versions of group or socialized property which are to be
somehow integrated but certainly not statized. He

stresses the difference between what socialization means
for the bureaucrat and for the worker. Socialism must
be defined as a coordinated system of the units of
industrial democracy which become semisovereign units in
the political sense, he believed. Clearly the influence
of then really-existing socialism is striking in this
work of Bauer and for this reason it could not be proposed today as a useful alternative program of democracy.

At that time, some people, e.g., Max Adler found
the conception attractive precisely because of its
historical reference to the various council experiments.
What is striking, though, is that the conception of
Bauer was, to my mind at least, more compatible with
that of Karl Renner who in other aspects of party history, of course, represents a very different pole of
politics. Renner's own essay "Demokratie und Rätesystem" of 1921 gives a version of the idea of a council
republic. It represents a further refinement of Bauer's
conception and its improvement from the point of view of
constitutional law, but still it is a conception compatible with Bauer's. Of course whereas Bauer relied
mainly on the work of Cole and the guild socialists,
Renner wanted to find an equilibrium between the positions of Cole on the one hand and Sidney and Beatrice
Webb on the other. It is also true that instead of a
monistic conception of democracy Renner offered a
pluralistic one and spoke of democracies, generally in
the plural. But I think that what is deeply compatible
about their conceptions is that an idea of industrial
democracy is introduced in both cases and an end in
itself and not merely as a means or instrument for something else. And in Renner's case there was an even
deeper connection with political democracy: even the
end goal would be a dualistic one.

Let me say just a couple of things about Renner's
conception as I see it. Democratization as far as he is
concerned is not not only a project against the capitalist domination of economic life, even in the social
sense, but also a struggle of democracy even against its
own state, not to speak of someone else's state. The
need for intermediate associations is stressed in the
manner of the philosophical pluralists. The plurality
of the forces of democracy on a total social level is
stressed; for example, he links, on the one hand, functional and territorial democracy, and on the other hand,
local and federal. His conception of the end goal has
room for all of these. He certainly argues beyond a
conception of many democratic theorists of that time
when he points out that there will have to be a need for
new methods of coordination, and when he tentatively
introduces the Webbs' conception of a second chamber,
which had been realized only in some fairly insignifi-

cant form in Germany and in Austria at that time.

Although Renner's conception was by far the most sophisticated of its time, it had some serious difficulties. His democracy, too, excludes conflict and for this reason was open from the outset to a corporatist interpretation. His democracy was also a societal democracy restricted to economic democracy; it was conceived as a project of the working class qua class. All these notions led to the theoretical and political difficulties which people here have mentioned.

I don't know much about Renner's conception from the early 'thirties concerning these matters, but as far as Bauer and Adler are concerned, it's rather clear that both of them gave up the already mentioned duality of democracies. Max Adler in one place in particular defines both democracies as just two forms of equality: political democracy is equality before the law or juridical democracy; economic democracy is substantial equality. The political aspect seems to be missing. I am sure that he went the furthest among all in such a direction, but the trend is nevertheless indicative.

I believe the reason for the trend away from the specifically Austromarxist conception was due to what people have already stressed, namely, the insistence on the unity of the socialist movement at all cost, and the definition of the third road, as a result, as one between communism and social democracy. Such insistence allowed a communist vocabularly and, perforce, orthodox Marxism to dictate also the language of democratic theory. Within the language of orthodox Marxism, the relevant political issues could not, however, be raised; the reason that they could be raised earlier was because, implicitly, there was a break with orthodox Marxism. Second, the third road between social democracy and communism came to mean one between two statist alternatives; hence the whole issue of "against the state" --even one's own state--could not be raised. As a result the idea of societal or economic democracy had to go too.

Thus if we are interested in democratic theory we do have something to learn from this history, something minimal, perhaps, but I think nonetheless significant. Those of us who want to speak about the third road must entirely forget what communists and other authoritarians have in mind. First of all, the question of a third road has to be raised from the point of view of more abstract considerations which are normatively and evaluatively justifiable. And second, one has to see the issue not only as one between reform and revolution but also between statism and anarchism. As opposed to the Austromarxists, any conception of a third road now operates in a continuum in which those considerations--not only reform and revolution but also the relationship to

the state--are included. For this reason I mentioned
the New Left, the French "Second Left," the East European democratic opposition (above all in Poland), and
even the German Greens at the beginning of this talk.
The new conception of the third road I have in mind
applies to them.

Yet each of these movements also has something to
learn from the tradition of left democratic theory of
which Austromarxism was an important part. First of
all, there is the negative lesson: the need for a refusal to allow the authoritarian left to set up the
terms of left discourse. None of the movements mentioned have fully assimilated this lesson, with the
exception (for obvious reasons) of the East Europeans.
But there are also positive lessons to be learned, based
on the richness of a tradition that managed to combine
normative democratic theory with legal theory, with a
conception of nations and nationalism and with a critique of authoritarian formations. None of the movements so far mentioned has matched the Austromarxists
(not to speak of the guild socialists and the English
and French philosophical pluralists) in terms of such
theoretical depth, which is eminently worthy of imitation.

12. Cultural Politics in Austria: From Empire to Republic

William J. McGrath

Although it is valuable to consider the stirring
and fateful events of February 1934 in the light of the
fifty years which have passed, it is also useful to
consider those events from the perspective of the half-
century which preceeded them. My own work on this period leads me to believe that the problems of the First
Austrian Republic were deeply rooted in the earlier
historical context. Therefore, I would like to take up
the invitation of Klemens von Klemperer to examine some
of the ways in which the politics and culture of the
First Republic were warped or distorted by the weight of
the imperial tradition.

In considering the question of the Republic's
alleged Lebensunfähigkeit from a cultural point of view,
our discussion has focused on two issues: the "Lager
mentality" which may have helped point the Republic
toward civil war, and political style and its influence
on the disintegration of political dialogue during the
post-imperial period.' The political tradition which
fostered this twentieth-century political style--
referred to variously as the "politics of illusion,"
"the politics of metaphor," "new-key politics or "metapolitics"[1]--exhibited a contrast between style and
content which also characterized the Social Democratic
Party. It is important to place this particular party
tradition in the larger context of the politics of fantasy, and this reveals a relationship to Freud's theory
of psychoanalysis which demonstrated that fantasy could
exercise a driving force in shaping reality.

William T. Bluhm's book Building an Austrian Nation
provides a valuable starting point for a discussion of
the First Republic's supposed Lebensunfähigkeit. As a
political scientist, Bluhm approaches his topic from a
comparative point of view, and his primary interest lies
in contrasting the success of the Second Republic with
the failure of the First. This comparative dimension
has surfaced frequently in our discussions, but a second
dimension which Bluhm introduces has not and probably

will not again. Bluhm argues that:

> Austria emerging from the ruins of dynastic empire
> in 1918 and the typical post-World War II "devel-
> oping state," rising from the ruins of colonial
> empire, both stood at the beginning of the nation-
> building process. Both had the exterior form, but
> neither had the psychological substance of the
> nation-state (i.e., a spirit of citizenship); nor
> did they have the political and economic institu-
> tions 'which can translate into policy and programs
> the aspirations of nationalism and citizenship.'[2]

Bluhm's unusual comparison of Austria after World
War I with developing states--his examples are largely
African--after World War II has greater plausibility
than it might first appear. He points out a number of
common characteristics: for example, Austria, like many
developing states, lacked firmly accepted borders; the
borders imposed on Austria by the victorious allies
fitted its ethnic realities as poorly as did the borders
imposed on various African states by their departing
colonial masters. In both cases the result was a legacy
of destabilizing nationality problems. Bluhm compares
the attempt of Biafra to secede from Nigeria with the
attempt of the Vorarlberg to join Switzerland in the
aftermath of World War I.
Another point of comparison centers around the un-
wieldy size of Vienna in the post-imperial period. The
economic and social problems posed by a disproportion-
ately large capital city serving a truncated hinterland
also have parallels in developing countries. As Bluhm
notes:

> How like this is to Philips Hauser's description of
> the single sprawling metropolis, swollen with a
> population unjustified by the level of economic
> development of the region, as a chief mark of the
> underdeveloped non-Western state of today.[3]

A third point of comparison involves the cultural
diversity so characteristic of many emerging nations.
This problem also plagued the First Republic. Bluhm
notes the linguistic diveristy even within the German-
speaking population: there were pronounced differences
in dialect between Vienna and the western provinces as
well, as between the middle class and the upper and
lower classes. Turning to religion, he observes that a
nominally universal Catholicism actually dissolved into
a polarity between a large anticlerical component centered in Vienna and a countryside that was predominantly
Catholic but included large islands of once Protestant
and later crypto-Protestant areas. In the nineteenth

and twentieth centuries, these "islands" became areas of
support for the Pan-German and Nazi movements. Bluhm
argues that these linguistic and religious diversities
created centrifugal forces which paralleled those
threatening the coherence of many developing states in
the post-World War II era.

It would be a mistake to assume that Bluhm's comparison fits all the elements of the First Repubiic, because there were certainly many unique problems beset-
ting Austria during this period, but there is one other
area of comparison developed by him which has particular
relevance to the issues under consideration here. Bluhm
points out that:

> ...in the 1930s., the Central European concept of
> 'nation' as 'cultural nation' predominated in
> Austria, and it was assumed on all sides (with a
> few notable exceptions) that polity depended on
> culture. The result was totalitarian warfare, as
> in so many developing states of today. It was only
> after World War II that the Western concept of the
> nation as a preeminently political community gained
> currency, and with it the idea that the 'political
> nation' can have a certain independence of its
> cultural background.[4]

This concept of "cultural nation" and the tradition of
cultural politcs which was closely bound up with it,
have a direct bearing on the development of the armed-
camp (Lager) mentality which proved to be so destructive
to the political life of the First Republic. Mary Mac-
Donald has provided a good description of how the Social
Democratic leaders attempted to implement the ideal of
cultural politics dur'ing this period:

> They labored to build up Social Democratic socie-
> ties which would cover all of a member's activities
> from the cradle to the grave. His intellectual and
> physical needs were all catered for within the par-
> ty. The party provided him with his flat; built
> kindergartens for his children, organized sport
> clubs, literary clubs, political clubs, and social
> clubs for himself and his wife; took charge of his
> economic life...and even provided burial clubs for
> his death.[5]

Although this all-encompassing concern for the whole
life of the individual party member may have had the
effect of isolating him within his class, and may thereby have contributed to the political polarization of the
Republican period, the motives and traditions behind
this policy should be taken into account. In the 1880s
and 1890s when Victor Adler and Engelbert Pernerstorfer

first developed this policy of cultural politics, it
could be seen as a praiseworthy and necessary effort to
overcome the alienation and dehumanization which
impoverished living conditions caused workers to feel.
Adler and Pernerstorfer followed the ideas of Nietzsche
and Richard Wagner in attempting to use art and culture
to uplift the lives of the members of the working class
and provide them with an alternative to widespread
alcoholism and demoralization.[6] They had considerable
success in this effort, and it is not surprising that
those who followed them as party leaders should have
continued this policy into the Republican period--when
its very success became a threat to the nation's social
coherence.

The psychological or artistic style of politics
which was part of this broader tradition of cultural
politics also needs to be approached from a long-range
historical perspective. Unfortunately, Mark Blum fails
to do this in his forthcoming book The Austro-Marxists
and the Politics of Metaphor, 1890-1918: A Psychobiographical Study, to be published by the University of
Kentucky Press. His failure is instructive, however,
because it suggests some common misconceptions about
this important issue. In stressing the contrast between
the highly centralized organization of the Social Democrats and their democratic rhetoric, and more generally
the contrast between pragmatic policies and radical
style, Blum sees this dichotomy primarily as a psychological and moral problem, in other words, as an abuse.
He characterizes the Socialist policy as one of psychological "denial":

It is said that the Viennese painter, Gustav Klimt,
lost his creative spirit when he had to face the
public clamor that surrounded his work, so vocal
and incessant was public discussion of one's vision. A political personality, however, does not
have the luxury of withdrawal from the public....
When a society furthers a politics or science that
relies on principles that cannot be demonstrated
for they are grounded upon metaphor, not concept,
it does so for a reason which may be called flight
from reality....The practitioners of metaphor who
become enchanted by the seeming validity of their
insight, as well as the audience who accepts their
premises, know in the depths of their consciousness
that these so-called objective statements are bear-
ers of multiple meaning which are artfully constructed to hide the painful reality from their
sight, just as a neurotic creates symptoms to hide
from himself and gain an advantage in the environment that health could not achieve.[7]

As Peter Loewenberg has demonstrated, the concept of
psychological denial is relevant to the political problems of the Social Democrats during the First Republic,[8] but Blum's use of it is simplistic and historically naive. It ignores the long tradition of symbolic
or metaphorical politics which preceded the Social Democrats, and it neglects to consider the basic political
reality which fostered that tradition.

The aesthetic political style went far back into
the imperial period. For example, Heinrich Laube, the
director of the Burgtheater practiced a version of it in
1859 when he organized a festival of art and politics to
celebrate the hundredth anniversary of Schiller's birth.
Through stagecraft and metaphor, he managed to advance
liberal political ideals in a repressive political climate.[9] During the 1870s the student groups to which
Pernerstorfer and Adler belonged also pursued a politics
of metaphor, but here it was as much out of necessity as
choice. Because student organizations were forbidden to
participate in political activities, they felt compelled
to cloak their politics in artistic forms and to present
them as part of the intellectual fare of their Leseyer-
ein.[10] Even so, they frequently fell prey to government censorship.

The reality of political censorship, which Blum
largely ignores, not only transformed political activity
by fostering a politics of metaphor; it distorted intellectual and artistic activity in general. Sigmund Freud
understood this point well and used it in developing the
conception of dream consorship which lies at the heart
of his psychoanalytic theory. In comparing dream dis-
tortion to political censorship, he writes:

A similar difficulty confronts the political writer
who has disagreeable truths to tell to those in
authority. If he presents them undisguised, the
authorities will suppress his words--after they
have been spoken, if his pronouncement was an oral
one, but beforehand, if he had intended to make it
in print. A writer must beware of the censorship,
and on its account he must soften and distort the
expression of his opinion. According to the
strength and sensitiveness of the censorship he
finds himself compelled either merely to refrain
from certain forms or attack, or to speak in allu-
sions in place of direct references....The stricter
the censorship, the more far-reaching will be the
disguise and the more ingenious too may be the
means employed for putting the reader on the scent
of the true meaning.[11]

Although the strictness of Austrian censorship was mitigated by Schlamperei, the very fact of its existence

helped to perpetuate and sustain an allusive and allegorical state of mind which had already become deeply ingrained in Austrian culture as a result of various historical factors, not the least of which was the Catholic religious tradition.

Another important dimension of this aesthetic political tradition involves what Carl Schorske calls "politics in a new key." This term, like "metapolitics," was taken from the political vocabulary of the 1880s: both terms describe the conscious attempt to evoke political emotion through symbol, fantasy and art. Drawing on the theories and the artistic examples of that consummate musical psychologist, Richard Wagner, who employed musical symbols to manipulate the emotional reactions of his audience, Adler, Pernerstorfer and many others sought to use similar techniques in the political world. Building on the reality of an expanding franchise, they sought to channel the emotions of the masses to serve their ends.

All of the mass parties which began to emerge in the 1880s employed these new political techniques. Schorske has provided an insightful analysis of how such men as Karl Lueger and Georg von Schönerer put together more or less successful examples of political artwork.[12] The new mass parties were distinguished by the degree to which the artistic political style was guided and held in check by moral values or rational principles. As I have attempted to show elsewhere, Victor Adler demonstrated such a sense of responsibility in his politics in general, and especially in the mass marches which he organized for universal manhood suffrage.[13] To imply, as Blum does, that the politics of metaphor should have been abandoned as a dangerous flight from reality ignores this historical situation. Metaphorical politics was in fact the only game in town, and the Social Democrats under Adler's leadership demonstrated far more integrity in its use than did the other mass parties.

That this aesthetic political tradition was inherently dangerous is undoubtedly true, and even the responsible example set by Adler could evoke unscrupulous imitation. In Mein Kampf, Adolf Hitler refers quite openly to the psychological lessons he learned from the huge demonstrations organized by the Social Democrats. Hitler also noted the political value of the Wagnerian tradition which had influenced other practitioners of "metapolitics." In emphasizing the importance of mood, time and place to the success of a political meeting, he wrote:

No, the time itself exerts a definite effect, just as the hall does on me. There are halls which leave people cold for reasons that are hard to

discern, but which somehow oppose the most violent
resistance to any creation of mood. Traditional
memories and ideas that are present in a man can
also decisively determine an impression. Thus, a
performance of Parsifal in Bayreuth will always
have a different effect than anywhere else in the
world. The mysterious magic of the house on the
Festspielhügel in the old city of the margraves
cannot be replaced or even compensated for by
externals.

In all these cases we have to do with an en-
croachment upon man's freedom of will. This applies, of course, to meetings attended by people
with a contrary attitude of will, who must now be
won over to a new will. In the morning and even
during the day people's will power seems to struggle with the greatest energy against an attempt to
force upon them a strange will and a strange opinion. At night, however, they succumb more easily
to the dominating force of a stronger will.[14]

Whether practiced in a responsible fashion, as in the
case of Adler, or in an utterly unscrupulous manner, as
in the case of Hitler, the politics of fantasy dominated
all aspects of political activity during this period.
If it was a flight from reality it was because the time
as a whole had taken flight.

In that vein, it is instructive to turn to Sigmund
Freud. As Freud's concept of psychological censorship
illustrates, he was able to learn much about the inner
workings of the human psyche from the political history
of his time. His psychological expertise profited as
much from the example of an outer political reality
shaped by the driving forces of fantasy and emotion as
did Hitler's political expertise. Freud's attitude
toward politics underwent a profound change over the
course of his lifetime. From a youthful radicalism
which exalted the benefits of a republic and scorned
monarchichal and aristocratic pretension, he moved to an
increasingly apolitical stance characterized by withdrawal and disillusionment. This is evident in his
reaction to the events of February 1934. In a letter
written on 20 February 1934 to his son Ernst, he
described the situation after the uprising:

But on the whole it was civil war and unpleasant.
The details of it all are not clear; rumor has it
that a certain powerful man insisted on putting an
end at last to the conflict which has been smol-
dering for so long. At some time this was probably
bound to happen. Now of course the victors are the
heroes and the saviors of sacred order, the others
the impudent rebels. Had the latter won, however,

it wouldn't have been much better, for it would
have meant a military invasion of the country. . The
government shouldn't be judged too harshly; after
all, life under the dictatorship of the proletariat, which was the aim of the so-called leaders,
would not have been possible either.

The future is uncertain; either Austrian fascism
or the swastika....Our attitude to the two political possibilities for Austria's future can only be
summed up in Mercutio's line in Romeo and Juliet:
'A plague on both your houses.'

...Just now--Wednesday morning, February 21--
martial law has been repealed. Our government and
our Cardinal expect a great deal from God's
assistance.[15]

Considering the political outlook of his youth, Freud's
attitude of near indifference to the Republic's demise
illustrates one of the negative consequences of the
politics of metaphor. Although the political conditions
of the imperial period made this style of politics almost a necessity, it can be argued that its persistence
into the republican era did indeed help to undermine the
success of the new democracy. With the end of political
censorship, one of the underlying reasons for a metaphorical politics fell away, but since this tradition
was deeply ingrained in political practice and sancti-
fied by party tradition, the possibility of a more open
and less rhetorical political style was not pursued.
The cost of radical rhetoric can be seen in Freud's letter where he rejects the possibility of "life under the
dictatorship of the proletariat." Several speakers at
this conference have suggested that this phrase, which
was used to inspire the uprising, was not meant seriously, but its use had the effect of driving away potential
supporters from the middle classes. To this extent the
practitioners of a politics of fantasy within the Social
Democratic Party may have undermined the possibility of
expanding the party's base of support. This illustrates
one of the ways in which the persistence of the aesthetic political tradition into the changed political context of the Republic may have made it a much more problematic and corrosive force than it was during the Empire when everyone accepted the need to speak in metaphor and adjusted their perceptions accordingly.

Freud's letter and his scientific accomplishments
illustrate both the highly negative and the highly positive results of the politics of fantasy which flourished
during his lifetime. Having expected much of a rational
politics in his youth, he increasingly turned inward to
escape the tensions and pressures generated by the more
and more irrational political climate of his middle and
late years. By comparing the irrational forces within

himself with those at work in the outer world Freud was
helped toward some of his most important discoveries,
[16] and an similar process may have been at work generally in the burst of creative genius and psychological
insight which characterized the culture of Vienna at the
turn of the century. The negative consequences, however, are equally impressive, since the disillusioned
liberals' withdrawal from political engagement left the
field to such practitioners of aesthetic politics as
Hitler. The persistence of the tradition of cultural
politics into the republican period and the use of metaphorical politics by the Social Democrats during this
period only helped to close off the possibility of reconciliation with potentially sympathetic members of the
middle class. It is ironic that the disordered nature
of the times should prove so fruitful in revealing the
power of fantasy within the human psyche and so destructive in revealing its power in the outer world of political reality.

NOTES

1. In this paper I have used these terms, and
others which describe this political style, inter-
changeably. Although distinctions between them could be
developed and might be useful in another context, they
share enough common characteristics to be used synonymously here.

2. William T. Bluhm, Building an Austrian Nation:
The Political Integration of a Western State (New Haven,
1973), p. 1.

3. Ibid., p. 6.

4. Ibid., pp. 9-10.

5. Mary MacDonald, The Republic of Austria, 1918-
1934 (London, 1941), p. 72; cited in Bluhm, p. 21.

6. William J. McGrath, Dionysian Art and Populist
Politics in Austria (New Haven, 1974).

7. Mark E. Blum, The Austro-Marxists and the
Politics of Metaphor, 1890-1918: a Psychobiographical
Study to be published by the University of Kentucky
Press, pp. 3-6.

8. Peter Loewenberg, Decoding the Past: The Psychohistorical Approach (New York, 1983), part III.

150

9. See Richard Charmatz, "Wiens Schillerfeier im Jahre 1859," Neue Bahnen, Vol. V (1905).

10. McGrath, Part I.

11. Sigmund Freud, The Interpretation of Dreams, trans. and ed., James Strachey (New York, 1965), pp. 175-76.

12. Carl E. Schorske, Fin de Siècle Vienna (New York, 1980), pp. 116-180.

13. McGrath, pp. 208-252.

14. Adolf Hitler, Mein Kampf, trans. Ralph Manheim (Cambridge, Mass., 1943), pp. 474-75.

15. Sigmund Freud, The Letters of Sigmund Freud, ed. Ernst L. Freud, trans. Tania and James Stern (New York, 1964), pp. 419-29.

16. I develop this thesis in detail in my forthcoming book, Freud's Discovery of Psychoanalysis: The Politics of Hysteria to be published by Cornell University Press in Winter, 1985.

13. Austrian Intellectuals and the Palace of Justice Fire

David S. Luft

As a point of intersection between the intellectual life of Vienna and the experience of Austrian Social Democracy, I have chosen 15 July 1927, a day that was arguably the most revolutionary moment in Austrian history and perhaps the most significant day of the First Republic. The responses of Austrian intellectuals to 15 July 1927 provide a counterpoint to the day we are commemorating, 12 February 1934.

There is not a massive literature on the relationship between Austrian intellectuals and Austrian Social Democracy, and what does exist is principally from the perspective of Austromarxism.[1] Austrian Socialists were alert to contemporary developments in economics, sociology, and psychology, and Friedrich Stadler's new book emphasizes their connections with the neopositivism of the Vienna Circle.[2] There were points of political contact as well: for example, Sigmund Freud and Robert Musil both signed a statement in April 1927 supporting the Socialist administration of Vienna.[3] But the 1920s leave the impression of a bourgeois intelligentsia that was not very politically involved, if not actually conservative, and Norbert Leser has emphasized the low level of interest on the part of literary intellectuals in Marxist themes and political revolution.[4]

It is precisely in this context that 15 July 1927 is so interesting, not only as a decisive moment for Austrian Socialism and the First Republic, but also because of its powerful impact on Austrian literary intellectuals. I want to comment on three Austrian intellectuals who were born around the turn of the century: Elias Canetti (1905-), Heimito von Doderer (1896-1966), and Ernst Fischer (1899-1972). One might reasonably define these writers as members of the generation of 1927, as a generation whose adult political consciousness was defined in terms of the events of 15 July 1927, when the workers of Vienna marched spontaneously to the center of the city and set fire to the Palace of Justice.

The occasion for these events was, of course, the
killing of a war invalid and an eight-year-old boy by
the Frontkämpfer on 30 January 1927 in Schattendorf in
Burgenland. Six months later, on 14 July 1927, a jury
in Vienna required only three and a half hours to acquit
the killers of all charges against them. Friedrich
Austerlitz's editorial the next morning in the Arbeiter-
Zeitung set the tone for a working class that could only
conclude that class justice was the sole possible kind
of justice in Austria. This was merely the most conspicuous in a series of questionable judicial decisions
involving acts of right-wing violence against socialists, and it contrasted with the increasing electoral
success of Austrian Socialism in 1927 and its control of
municipal institutions in Vienna. All of this made Otto
Bauer reluctant to act, but it made the workers feel
themselves to be on the brink of victory, conscious of
their righteousness. On the morning of 15 July the
workers of Vienna shut down the city and marched down
the Ringstrasse. Police and Socialist leadership alike
were caught off balance, and the chaotic momentum of the
crowd led to the burning of the building with the symbolic name. Before any attempt had been made to allow
the Socialists to control the crowd, Seipel and Schober
ordered the police to open fire. Eighty-five or ninety
workers were killed and many more, perhaps even a thousand, were wounded. I would like to comment briefly on
three intellectuals whose lives and intellectual visions
were transformed by this event.

In the summer of 1927 Canetti was a student of
chemistry at the University of Vienna. He later recalled that his own experience of the day began with his
shock at the headline of the Reichspost, the press organ
of the ruling Christian Social Party: "Ein gerechtes
Urteil" (a just judgment). Canetti argued that it was
"this contempt (Hohn) for any feeling of justice even
more than the acquittal itself" that awakened such rage
in the working class of Vienna. He emphasized the complete spontaneity of this reaction, which was confirmed
by his own response that morning, when he raced into the
city on his bicycle to join the procession. Despite his
extreme individualism and his limited contact with the
political left, he was swept up in the crowd. Forty-six
years later, Canetti still could not get over this experience: "It was the nearest thing to a revolution
that I have experienced in my own flesh." His main memory was of the mass, of being in the mass, of disappear-
ing into the mass, totally and without resistance. Both
his novel Die Blendung and his masterwork Masse und
Macht were decisively shaped by this experience, although the ideas within them had begun to develop during
the early 1920s.[5]

The crowning memory of that occasion for Canetti

was the action of Karl Kraus who, in response to "the
massacre of this day, had posters hung up all over
Vienna in which he demanded that Police President Johann
Schober...step down."[6] The permanent mark of these
experiences is apparent in Canetti's mature work: in
his view of das Feuer, with its power to attract and to
destroy, as the decisive means of the mass, and in his
interpretation of the threat of death as the coin of power.[7] Canetti's discussion of this day in Das Gewissen der Worte is brief but, without being very political, it is dominated by a sympathy for the working
class that recalls Walter Benjamin's advice to historians: "Only that historian will have the gift of fan-
ning the spark of hope in the past who is firmly convinced that even the dead will not be safe from the
enemy if he wins. And this enemy has not ceased to be
victorious."[8]

Doderer was still less political than Canetti and
without ties to the political left, but 1927 seems to
have drawn him into a political vision of the world in a
way that even his experience as a soldier and prisoner
of war in Russia had not. Although he was born in 1896,
he seems to have come to political consciousness not
through war and revolution, but with the collapse of the
Republic after 1927. Initially, July 1927 became the
focus for his anti-Semitism, anti-communism, and Nazism.
But this event gradually became the center of an ideological transformation and maturation, which were apparent first in his attempts during 1936-1937 to revise Die
Dämonen, and then, after 1951, in his introduction of a
working-class figure, Leonhard Kakabsa, and his rewri-
ting of his masterpiece.[9] For Doderer, 15 July became
the climax of his greatest imaginative work and the
point of departure for his eventual conversion from
fascism to an attitude that was more tolerant toward the
working class.

"Das Feuer," the culminating chapter of the novel,
is not a direct description or analysis of the events of
15 July, although it is based on reports in the Neue
Freie Presse, the Arbeiter-Zeitung, and the Reichspost,
as well as the eyewitness account of a friend.[10] For
Doderer, the burning of the Palace of Justice is backdrop and atmosphere, interpreted as the end of freedom
in Austria. The real point of his classic portrayal of
15 July concerns individualism, not world-historical
events.

Originally, the day had turned Doderer toward fascism, as it had the Austrian middle class as a whole.
Even in his final version of these events thirty years
later, Doderer remained somewhat obtuse politically,
emphasizing the random interference of criminal elements
and displaying an uncritical attitude toward the police.
Moreover, his portrayal of the working class, both as a

movement and an ideology, is still unsympathetic.
Leonhard (once a worker and now a scholar) helps to lock
the library doors against the workers; he finds his dead
friend (once a worker, now a policeman, killed by criminal elements); and he turns away from politics to the
private world of his relationship with Mary K. Not only
did Doderer want to show the confusion of these events
as a metaphor for the chaos of life as a whole, but he
also tried to show the failure of world-historical
events to touch the lives of individuals. In this
respect, Die Dämonen is a kind of anti-Hegel (or anti-
Marx). The individual's attempt to come to terms with
reality is always the real point for Doderer; this is an
anti-political novel (the real payoff of the apolitical
turn in Austrian liberalism), and Leonhard Kakabsa is
"the anti-revolutionary figure par excellence."[11]

But Die Dämonen remains one of the great accounts
of 15 July, and, in his commentary on the death of Imre
at the hands of the police, Doderer captured the meaning
of this day for Austrian Socialism: "...every metaphor
that life shatters implies a loss of human freedom. For
freedom can exist only so long as fictions and metaphors
are stronger than crude reality, and thus uphold our
human dignity."[12]

The experience of the young Ernst Fischer, then a
writer for the Arbeiter-Zeitung, shows how the death of
this metaphor was felt inside the Social Democratic
movement. Fischer's account of 15 July in Erinnerungen
und Reflexionen is excellent in the immediacy of its
descriptions, in its thoughtful overview of the day, and
in its analysis of the significance of the event.
Fischer emphasizes the confidence of the workers' party
in the summer of 1927, the righteousness of the workers,
and the extremes of injustice perpetrated by the judicial system (à la Weimar). But he emphasizes above all
the revolutionary spontaneity of these events, in a
situation not unlike the one that confronted Rosa
Luxemburg and the Spartacists in 1918-1919. This was a
case where the party had done nothing at all and, for
Fischer, this was the mistake. Even Austerlitz's editorial seemed to him not the cause of these events; the
cause was rather the inevitable and just outrage of the
workers. Fischer's account makes clear the power of
class perceptions in 1927. Perhaps the most compelling
of his stories relates a scene that took place as workers fled down alleys away from the firing police. One
worker stopped, turned toward the police and opened his
shirt: "Shoot, if you have the guts." They did.[13]

While Schober followed Ignaz Seipel's instructions
to take pitiless revenge on the workers, Fischer begged
his superiors to seize the moment for civil war and to
give weapons to the Schutzbündler and the defenseless
workers. But the killing went on for three hours with-

155

out resistance from the confused and demoralized Socialist leadership. Fischer's summary serves as a reminder
that Otto Bauer's mistakes ought not to obscure the
reality of Austromarxism's lesser power in this situation; but Fischer also makes Seipel look surprisingly
wise and good--the only political figure in Austria who
was up to the occasion. Fischer considered Bauer a hu-
manist who could not act, and not really a revolutionary
at all. To Fischer, the day signalled the failure and
defeat of Austromarxism. For one of the movement's fi-
nest minds, Austromarxism was already over in July 1927,
in a day that displayed so classically both the violence
of the mass and the force of the state.

NOTES

1. See Ernest Glaser, Im Umfeld des Austromarxismus: Ein Beitrag zur Geistesgeschichte des österreichischen Sozialismus (Vienna, 1981); Alfred Pfoser,
Literatur und Austromarxismus (Vienna, 1980); Alfred
Pfabigan, Karl Kraus und der Sozialismus: Eine politische Biographie (Vienna, 1976); Norbert Leser, "Austromarxismus und Literatur," in Franz Kadrnoska, ed., Auf-
bruch und Untergang (Vienna, 1981), pp. 43-68.

2. Friedrich Stadler, Vom Positivismus zur "Wissen-
schaftlichen Weltauffassung" (Vienna, 1982).

3. Glaser, Im Umfeld des Austromarxismus, p. 263.

4. Leser, "Austromarxismus und Literatur," p. 53.

5. Elias Canetti, Das Gewissen der Worte: Essays
(Frankfurt am Main, 1981), pp. 243-246. The actual
headline in the Reichspost on 15 July 1927 was "Ein
klares Urteil" (a clear judgment). For Ernst Fischer's
comments on Canetti's perceptions of the mass, see Ernst
Fischer, "Bemerkungen zu Elias Canettis Masse und
Macht," in Literatur und Kritik, I, H. 7 (1966), pp.
12-20.

6. Canetti, Das Gewissen der Worte, p. 245;
Pfabigan, Karl Kraus, pp. 288-310.

7. Elias Canetti, Masse und Macht (Hamburg, 1960),
pp. 17, 542-43.

8. Walter Benjamin, Illuminations, trans. Harry
Zohn (New York, 1969), p. 255.

156

9. See Elizabeth C. Hesson, <u>Twentieth Century Odyssey: a Study of Heimito von Doderer's "Die Dämonen"</u> (Columbia, South Carolina, 1982), pp. 20-53.

10. Ibid., p. 29.

11. Ibid., pp. 40 and 77.

12. Heimito von Doderer, <u>The Demons</u>, trans. Richard and Clara Winston (New York, 1961), Vol. II, p. 1229.

13. Ernst Fischer, <u>Erinnerungen und Reflexionen</u> (Hamburg, 1959), p. 177.

14. Austrian Social Democracy and the Jewish Question in the First Republic

Jack Jacobs

The Austrian Social Democratic party had an ambivalent position on the Jewish question in the years following World War I.[1] To be sure, the Social Democratic party was far less influenced by anti-Semitism than was any of its major competitors and was a vigorous opponent of anti-Semitic political movements. Social Democrats, moreover, provided both material and moral support for East European Jewish refugees living in Vienna.[2] The Social Democratic party, however, never provided unequivocal support for the Jewish community itself, and publicly claimed that so-called "philo-Semitism" was every bit as noxious to Social Democrats as was anti-Semitism. In so doing, Austrian Social Democracy allowed its enemies to define the field of battle, and, thereby, contributed substantially to its own defeat.

The position on the Jewish question which was accepted by Austrian Social Democracy during the First Republic had been initiated by the party's founders in the Austro-Hungarian Empire. Victor Adler, who later became the dominant figure in the Austrian socialist world, encountered anti-Semitism while a student in Vienna.[3] It was at least in part in order to escape anti-Semitic attacks that Adler, in 1878, converted to Protestantism.[4] However, Adler, while willing to speak out against anti-Semitic political movements, consistently declined opportunities to defend either the Jewish community or individuals persecuted because of their Jewishness during the period in which he was the leader of the Austrian socialist movement. When, in 1891, Abraham Cahan, who represented Jewish workers in the United States, attempted to convince the delegates to the Brussels Congress of the Socialist International to adopt a resolution opposing anti-Semitism, Victor Adler was among those who tried to dissuade Cahan from doing so. Adler believed that Cahan's proposed resolution was tactless, and that it would play into the hands of anti-Semites by giving them an opportunity to identi-

fy the Socialist International with the defense of
Jews.[5] Adler wanted to avoid such an identification
at all costs. He therefore believed that Jewish family
background was an unfortunate burden for a Socialist
leader. "Ich selbst bin schon ein Belastung für die
Partei," Adler used to say.[6]

Unlike other leaders of the Socialist International, Adler defended neither Dreyfus nor Beilis. At the
time of the Beilis case, Adler reportedly exclaimed,
"Jews and more Jews. As if the entire world revolved
around the Jewish question!"[7] Similarly, when asked
by Camille Huysmans for his view of anti-Semitism, Adler
is said to have replied, "My dear comrade! One must have
Jews, but not too many."[8] Adler's stance towards the
Jewish question was thus motivated by fear that Social
Democracy would be identified with Jewry and was characterized by the internalization of anti-Semitic prejudices.

During Adler's lifetime and in the period following
his death, Austrian Social Democrats generally agreed
with his position on the Jewish question. Significantly, Otto Bauer, Adler's political heir, wholeheartedly
accepted this aspect of Adler's legacy. True, anti-
Semitism, which drove Adler to convert to Christianity,
hardened Bauer's resolve to retain his formal membership
in the Jewish community.[9] However, in 1910, Bauer
echoed Victor Adler by arguing that "Marx's 'Judenfrage'
already separated us harshly from liberal philo-Semitism. Social Democracy has never been a 'Jewish protective troop'."[10] Thus it should come as no surprise to
discover that Bauer attacked the anti-Semitic parties as
hypocritical for having taken money from Jewish sources,
but he never published a direct rebuttal of anti-Semitic
arguments during the period of the First Republic. He
was interested in countering the influence of the anti-
Semitic parties, and, if necessary, was willing to use
weapons from the anti-Semite's arsenal in order to do
so. For example, he warded off the charge that Austrian
Social Democracy was "Judaized" by claiming that "the
Jewish capitalist gladly pays the printing costs of
anti-Semitic electoral leaflets in order to weaken
Social Democracy."[11]

Bauer's use of this tactic was by no means an isolated incident. The Social Democrats of the First Republic consistently attempted to protect their party by
drawing attention to "Jewish" influence on other parties. A booklet entitled Der Judenschwindel, published
by the Wiener Volksbuchhandlung in 1923, argued that
"the Christian Socials under Seipel's leadership defended...the citadel of Jewish capital," and that Seipel was
one of "the darlings of the Jewish press."[12] Another
pamphlet published by the Wiener Volksbuchhandlung, Wenn
Judenblut vom Messer spritzt, pointed out that the anti-

Semites "take money from Rothschild," and discussed a
"verjudete Hakenkreuzblatt."[13] A third such work,
which appeared under the title Der Jud ist schuld, tried
to demonstrate the hypocrisy of the anti-Semites by un-
masking a Jewish journalist employed by a pro-Nazi peri-
odical as well as the Jewish origins of a National
Socialist writer.[14]

The best known example of Social Democratic use of
this tactic occurred in July 1926 when Robert Danneberg
--who was himself of Jewish origin--attacked the "Aryan"
banks of Vienna by publicly revealing their economic
ties to individual Jewish businessmen and to "Jewish"
banks. In a speech delivered before Parliament which
was well received by his colleagues, Danneberg provoked
laughter from his audience by commenting, "If I know
these Jewish banks," they did not engage in business
dealings with their Aryan counterparts because of
"Christian charity," but rather for "jingling coins."
[15] The Social Democrats were so pleased with Danneberg's speech that they had it published in pamphlet
form.

The intent of the Social Democrats in pointing to
the "Verjudung" of other parties was to turn the tables
on their opponents. By using such arguments in their
own propaganda, however, the Social Democrats unwittingly helped legitimize a perspective which they hoped to
eradicate.

It is well worth reiterating the fact that Austrian
Social Democracy was officially opposed to political
anti-Semitism. Individuals of Jewish origin, moreover,
held a number of important posts in the Austrian Social
Democratic movement in the years following World War I.
Max Adler, Friedrich Austerlitz, Julius Braunthal,
Julius Deutsch, and Wilhelm Ellenbogen--to name just a
few of the most prominent Austrian Socialists--were all
born into Jewish families. However, the prominence of
Jews within the leadership of the Social Democratic
Party did not immunize the party against anti-Semitic
sentiment. In fact, many of the leading Austrian Socialists of Jewish origin were themselves somewhat prej-
udiced in their view of Jews and Jewry. Stereotypes
with anti-Semitic overtones seem to have been accepted
even in the Socialist ranks. When, in the early 1920s,
Julius Deutsch sued an individual who had slandered him
(by making a claim that was often made by anti-Semites),
the Arbeiter-Zeitung criticized the tactics of the
defendant's attorney by referring to "der jüdische Dreh
eines arischen Advokaten."[16] The Arbeiter-Zeitung
indirectly referred to another stereotype in 1925 when
it published a cartoon with the following caption:

Nach Hitlers Verlobung mit einer Jüdin und nach der
Gründung der jüdisch-hakenkreuzlerischen Wechsel-

160

stube an den Wiener Hochshulen wird ein neues Wappen für die Hakenkreuzpartei geschaffen: eine sin-
nige Verschmelzung von Hakennase und Haken-
kruez.[17]

The use of terms like "der jüdische Dreh" and
"Hakennase" by Socialists almost certainly did more
long-term damage to the Socialists than to those against
whom these terms were directed. Though these terms were
meant by the Socialists who used them to ridicule anti-
Semites, their use in the Austrian context tended to
reinforce widespread prejudices. These terms were
double-edged, but cut the Jews more deeply than the
anti-Semites because of the power dynamics which existed
within the Republic.

Most Austrian Social Democrats believed and hoped
that assimilation (and socialism) would eventually answer the Jewish question. Otto Bauer had delineated the
factors leading towards the assimilation of the Jews before World War I, and he neither retracted nor altered
his stance on this issue between 1918 and 1934. [18]
Friedrich Adler was also a confirmed assimilationist.
Writing for the Swiss Socialist newspaper Volksrecht in
1949, Adler declared:

> I, like my father, always considered the complete
> assimilation of the Jews not only desirable but
> also possible, and even the bestialities of Hitler
> have not shaken my view that Jewish nationalism is
> bound to lead to reactionary tendencies--namely, to
> the resurrection of a language which has been dead
> for almost two thousand years and to the rebirth of
> an antiquated religion.[19]

Friedrich Adler (and most other Austrian Socialists) coupled their pro-assimilationist views with an
anti-Zionist standpoint. Jacques Hannak, writing in Der
Kampf in 1919 (when Zionists were very much in the minority within the Jewish community and were bitterly
opposed by several different tendencies in Jewish political life), characterized Zionism as "not more than an
economic category of specifically Jewish capitalism" and
as a "reactionary phenomenon" which ought to be fought.
[20] Hannak reiterated his charges against Zionism in
another article in Der Kampf which appeared in 1927. In
this latter article, Hannak described Zionism as a
"petty-bourgeois Utopia" and as an "illusion."[21]

Friedrich Adler's hostility towards Zionism led him
to be sympathetic towards the anti-Zionist Jewish Workers' Bund of Poland. In a letter to the Bundist leader
H. Erlich, dated 15 October 1929 Adler urged the Bund to
enter the Labour and Socialist International (LSI),
arguing that "it should be your own special task to rep-

resent in the LSI the interests of the great masses of
the Jewish proletariat outside of Palestine."[22]   F.
Adler also demonstrated his sympathy for the Bund in
1937 by sending it a greeting on the fortieth anniversary of its founding.   Adler's greeting, which was published in the Bundist Naye folkstsaytung, stressed the
"historical merit" of the pioneers of the Bund, and
praised both the fighting spirit of the Jewish organization and its accomplishments.[23]
      However, not all Austrian Socialists of the First
Republic agreed with Bauer's assimilationism and F. Adler's anti-Zionism.   Both Der Kampf and the Arbeiter-
Zeitung occasionally published articles which were sympathetic to labor Zionist efforts.[24]   Max Adler was
the most prominent of the Austrian Socialists who expressed such sympathy.   In 1928 Adler delivered an address on the theme "National and International" before a
meeting of young Jewish socialists.   In the course of
this speech Adler noted:

      Viele meinten früher, dass mit dem Eindringen des
      Kapitalismus in die osteuropäische Wirtschaft das
      Judentum sich assimilieren werde.   Das ist nicht
      eingetreten.   Das Judentum lebt und will nicht
      untergehen; da kann es doch keine Frage sein ob man
      eine jüdischnationale Arbeiterschaft unterstützen
      soll![25]

In that same year, the World Bureau of the Poale Zion
Confederation undertook to organize a conference for the
purpose of creating an international committee which
would support the organized Jewish workers' movement of
Palestine.   Adler expressed his regrets at being unable
to attend this conference, indicating that he was "deeply interested" in the cause.[26]   Two years later, Adler
sent a message to a labor Zionist-oriented conference in
which he expressed his sympathy for and interest in the
efforts made by the socialist Zionists to establish a
Jewish home in Palestine, declaring that he was "filled
with admiration for the idealism and abnegation" of the
labor Zionist pioneers.[27]   Again in 1931 Adler demonstrated his good will by writing a foreward to a work
published by the radical socialist Zionist youth movement Schomer Hazair.   There can be various opinions
within the Socialist International about the necessity
of creating a Jewish national home, and about the necessity of creating such a home precisely in Palestine,
Adler wrote in this foreward:

      ...doch kann man die Tatsache der nationalen
      Wiedergeburt der Juden und ihres Willens zur
      nationalen Konzentration als historische Faktoren
      nicht übersehen.   Man darf sie auch nicht be-

kämpfen. Denn der marxistische Sozialismus ist
absolut kein Gegner des Nationalismus.[28]

Adler's fullest published discussion of his attitude towards Zionism appeared under the title Das Verhältnis der nationalen zur sozialistischen Idee. Bemerkungen zum Poale-Zionismus. It is based on a speech
which he delivered on 22 January 1933 at the twenty-
fifth anniversary celebration of the Poale Zion which
was held in Vienna. In this speech Adler argued that it
was incorrect to consider Zionism only from the West
European assimilationist perspective. The assimilationist point of view, Adler maintained, is actually the
view least capable of comprehending the sociological and
psychological reality of the national problem. According to Adler, the Poale Zion had played an important
role by transforming a sector of the Zionist movement
into a part and means of the Socialist International.
The Poale Zion, Adler believed, had used its influence
to deemphasize the national idea (without, however, excluding it) and to emphasize the socialist idea. It is
because he saw the labor Zionist movement in this way
that Adler referred to the work of the Jewish socialists
in Palestine as one of the few bright spots in the
otherwise dreary situation of contemporary socialism.[29]
Julius Braunthal agreed with M. Adler's view of the
labor Zionist movement. In 1930 he, too, saluted the
work of the "pioneers" in Palestine.[30] After the fall
of the First Republic, Braunthal visited Palestine and
was enormously impressed by the accomplishments of the
labor Zionists with whom he met there.[31] But Braunthal went beyond M. Adler in that he explicitly identified himself with the Jewish community. "I certainly
felt Jewishness," Braunthal once wrote

...and I felt that this added something of an im-
ponderable feature to my individuality which differentiated me slightly from my Gentile comrades.
I also felt a sense of belonging to the Jewish community all over the world....I was never a consci-
entious "assimilationist."[32]

The views of Braunthal, who came from a background which
was markedly different from and more religious than that
of the other prominent Jews in the Austrian Social Democratic Party, were, however, clearly exceptional. Neither Max Adler's views on Zionism nor Braunthal's views
on assimilationism had any noticable impact on the theory, policies, or progaganda of the party.[33] The attitudes towards the Jewish question of Bauer, Danneberg,
and Friedrich Adler, on the other hand, were typical of
those of the party leadership as a whole.

Though this dominant attitude had been initially
adopted partly in order to protect the Austrian Socialist movement from the charges of being "Judaized" and a
"protective troop" for the Jewish community, it did not
succeed in achieving that goal. For despite the attempts made by Bauer, Danneberg, and others to distance
Austrian Social Democracy from the Jewish community in
the minds of the public, Austrian anti-Semites repeatedly attacked the Socialist leaders of Jewish origin
precisely because of their origin. "The brown shirts
bellowed 'Saujud' whenever Danneberg began to
speak."[34] Julius Deutsch was subject to similar
treatment.[35] The term "Judensozi" was widely used
throughout the period of the First Republic.[36]
     It could, conceivably, be argued that the Austrian
Socialists had no feasible alternative to the policy
which they adopted. In the face of overwhelming anti-
Semitism, this argument might run, Austrian Socialists
were forced to dissociate their party from the Jewish
community in order to protect the party itself. Such a
line of reasoning, however, would appear to be undercut
by a comparison of the record of the Austrian Social
Democratic party with that of the German Social Democratic party (SPD). For when faced with a rise of anti-
Semitic sentiment during the Weimar years, the SPD regularly defended Jewish rights to an extent far beyond
that of its sister party in Austria. There were, of
course, lapses even on the part of the German Socialists; yet the SPD cooperated with the Centralverein
deutscher Staatsbürger judischen Glaubens (the most important German-Jewish organization) in order to combat
their common enemy.[37] No comparable examples of cooperation between Austrian Social Democracy and Austrian
Jewry have thus far come to light.
     The Austrian Social Democratic Party had no desire
to cater in any way to Jews, and did not do so. There
were concentrations of Jewish voters, particularly in
Vienna, which were useful to Social Democratic candi-
dates; however, the Social Democrats were well aware
that the collapse of the liberal parties had left an
overwhelming majority of Austrian Jewry with the sense
that it had little choice but to vote Social Democratic.[38] By the final years of the First Republic, the
Social Democrats were receiving approximately three-
quarters of the Viennese Jewish vote.[39] But precisely
because the Social Democrats understood that they could
count on the Jewish vote, the Austrian Social Democratic
party did not engage in strenuous efforts to solicit
Jewish support, nor did it feel a need to adapt its program or propaganda to appeal to the Jewish community.[40] In fact the confidence engendered by the belief
that Jewish voters had nowhere else to turn probably
encouraged the party to continue the policy on the

Jewish question begun by Victor Adler.

There is no doubt that Austrian Social Democracy was less infected by anti-Semitism than was any other major political party in the First Republic. But there can also be no doubt that the anti-Semitic prejudices which were so widespread in Austria at that time had an impact on Austrian Socialists, including Socialist leaders of Jewish origin. By accepting the premise that Jewish origin was a burden to the party, by allowing unflattering stereotypes to be used in Socialist literature, and by refusing to defend the Jewish community, Austrian Social Democrats allowed themselves to be put on the defensive. Precisely because there were so many Jews prominent in Austrian Socialist ranks, the defensive policy on the Jewish question followed by the party ultimately tended to undercut the Party itself.

NOTES

1. There is an extensive literature on the attitude of Austrian Social Democracy towards the Jewish question. See Edmund Silberner, "Austrian Social Democracy and the Jewish Problem," Historia Judaica, 13 (1951), pp. 121-40; "The Jewish Background of Victor and Friedrich Adler. Selected Biographical Notes," Leo Baeck Institute Yearbook, 10 (1965), pp. 266-76; Robert Schwarz, "Antisemitism and Socialism in Austria, 1918-1962," in Josef Fraenkel, ed., The Jews of Austria (London, 1967), pp. 445-66; A. Barkai, "The Austrian Social Democrats and the Jews," The Wiener Library Bulletin, Vol. 24, 1, new series 18 (1970), pp. 31-40; 2, new series 19 (1970), pp. 16-21; J.W. Bruegel, "The Antisemitism of the Austrian Socialists, a Reassessment," The Wiener Library Bulletin, Vol. 25, 3/4, new series 24/25 (1972), pp. 39-45; Robert S. Wistrich, "Victor Adler: A Viennese Socialist against Philosemitism," The Wiener Library Bulletin, Vol. 27, 32 (1974), pp. 26-33; Robert S. Wistrich, "An Austrian variation on socialist antisemitism," Patterns of Prejudice, Vol. 8, 4 (1974), pp. 1-10; Robert S. Wistrich, "Socialism and Antisemitism in Austria before 1914," Jewish Social Studies, Vol. 37, 3/4 (1975), pp. 323-32; Robert S. Wistrich, Revolutionary Jews from Marx to Trotsky (London, 1976), pp. 95-129; John Bunzl, "Arbeiterbewegung und Antisemitismus in Österreich vor und nach dem Ersten Weltkrieg," Zeitgeschichte, Vol. 4, 5 (1977), pp. 161-71; John Bunzl, "Arbeiterbewegung, 'Judenfrage' und Antisemitismus: am Beispiel des Wiener Bezirks Leopoldstadt," in G. Botz, H. Hautmann, H. Konrad, J. Weidenholzer, eds., Bewegung und Klasse (Vienna, 1979), pp.

743-63; Leopold Spira, Feinbild "Jud". 100 Jahre polit-
ischer Antisemitismus in Österreich (Vienna, 1981); and
Robert S. Wistrich, Socialism and the Jews (Rutherford,
N.J., 1982), pp. 175-348.

2. Spira, Feinbild, p. 84.

3. Julius Braunthal, Victor und Friedrich Adler.
Zwei Generationen Arbeiterbewegung (Vienna, 1965), pp.
18-19.

4. Ibid., pp. 19-20.

5. Abraham Cahan, Bleter fun mayn lebn, Vol. III
(New York, 1926), pp. 158-63.

6. Max Ermers, Victor Adler. Aufstieg und Grösse
einer sozialistischen Partei (Vienna, 1932), p. 230.

7. Ber Borochov, Ketavim, Vol. III (Tel Aviv,
1955), p. 265 as translated in Barkai, "The Austrian
Social Democrats," p. 38.

8. C. Huysmans, "Sur le sionisme (réponse à
Kautsky)," Comité socialiste pour la palestine ouvrière.
Bulletin, 4 (1929), p. 10.

9. Ernst Fischer, An Opposing Man, trans. Peter and
Betty Ross (London, 1974), p. 134.

10. Otto Bauer, "Sozialismus und Antisemitismus,"
Der Kampf, 4 (1910), p. 94.

11. Otto Bauer, Der Kampf um die Macht, in Julius
Braunthal, ed., Otto Bauer, Eine Auswahl aus seinem
Lebenswerk (Vienna, 1961), p. 278. It ought to be noted
that Bauer vigorously attacked anti-Semitism after the
fall of the First Republic. See, for example, the manuscript by Otto Bauer entitled "Judenhetze als Herr-
schaftsmittel," Bauer Teilnachlass, Item 30, International Institute of Social History (Amsterdam).

12. Christoph Hinteregger, Der Judenschwindel
(Vienna, 1923), pp. 23, 56. For an example of a similar
claim made in the Socialist daily press see "Die Juden
beim Sepiel," Arbeiter-Zeitung, 3 Dec. 1925, p. 4, col.
3.

13. Wenn Judenblut vom Messer spritzt (Vienna,
[1932?]), pp. 5, 13.

14. Der Jud ist schuld (Vienna, n.d.), p. 11.

15. Robert Danneberg, Die Schiebergeschäfte der Regierungsparteien; der Antisemitismus im Lichte der Tatsachen (Vienna, 1926), p. 11.

16. "Der jüdische Dreh eines arischen Advokaten," Arbeiter-Zeitung, 11 Jun., 1923, p. 2, col. 3.

17. "Das neue Wappen der Hakenkreuzler," Arbeiter-Zeitung, 11 Oct. 1925.

18. Otto Bauer, "Die Bedingungen der nationalen Assimilation," Der Kampf, Jg. 5 (1912), pp. 246-63.

19. Quoted in "The Jewish Background of Victor and Friedrich Adler," p. 275.

20. Jacques Hannak, "Das Judentum am Scheidewege," Der Kampf, 12 (1919), p. 651.

21. Jacques Hannak, "Die Krise des Zionismus," Der Kampf, 20 (1927), pp. 455-56.

22. Labour and Socialist International Archive, 356/25, International Institute of Social History (Amsterdam). On F. Adler's attitide towards Zionism and the Bund see Johannes Glasneck, "Die internationale Sozialdemokratie und die zionistische Palästina-Kolonisation in den Jahren 1929/30," Wissenschaftliche Zeitschrift der Martin-Luther Universität Halle-Wittenberg, Gesellschafts- und Sprachwissenschaftliche Reihe, Vol. 26, 4 (1977), pp. 39-50.

23. F. Adler, "Tsum fertsik-yorikn yoyvl fun 'bund'." Naye folkstsaytung, 19. Nov. 1937, p.10. F. Adler also expressed his support for the Jewish daily Forverts on its fortieth anniversary. See H. Lang, "Der fertsikster geburtstog fun forverts," Forverts, 25 Apr. 1937, section I, p. 17.

24. See, for example, Mendel Singer, "Judenfrage und Zionismus," Der Kampf, 20 (1927), pp. 574-80; Hugo Steiner, "Der Kampf der jüdischen Arbeiter," Der Kampf, 23 (1930), pp. 136-40; Hugo Steiner, Palästina und die Judenfrage," Arbeiter-Zeitung, 2 Sept. 1929, pp. 1-2. The Arbeiter-Zeitung declined to print a rejoinder to Steiner's "Palästina article written from a Bundist perspective by Josef Kissmann. See the letter to Kissmann from the Arbeiter-Zeitung dated 20 Sept. 1929, Kissmann File, Bund Archives of the Jewish Labor Movement (New York). It did, however, print a piece by Karl Kautsky, "Die Aussichten des Zionismus," Arbeiter-Zeitung, 22 Sept. 1929, p. 4, in which he expressed strong doubts as to the viability of a potential Jewish

state in Palestine. See Jack Jacobs, "Kautsky on the Jewish Question," unpublished Ph.D. dissertation, Columbia Univ., 1983, pp. 115-19.

25. "Aus unserem Verbande. Gen. Dr. Max Adlers Stellung zum Zionismus," Jüdische Arbeiter-Jugend, Vol. 2, 2 (March 1928), p. 9.

26. M. Jarblum, The Socialist International and Zionism (New York, 1933), p. 19.

27. Comité socialiste pour la palestine ouvrière. Bulletin, 5 (May 1930), p. 27.

28. Max Adler, "Sozialismus und Zionismus," Der Jüdishe Arbeiter, Vol. 7, 5, 27 Mar. 1931, p. 1, col. 1.

29. Max Adler, Das Verhältnis der nationalen zur sozialistischen Idee. Bemerkungen zum Poale-Zionismus (Vienna, [1933]).

30. Comité socialiste pour la palestine ouvrière. Bulletin, 5 (May 1930), p. 27.

31. Julius Braunthal, In Search of the Millenium (London, 1945), pp. 306-14. See also Brigitte Robach, "Julius Braunthal als politischer Publizist. Ein Leben im dienste des Sozialismus," unpublished dissertation, Universität Wien, 1983, pp. 540-568. My thanks to Dr. Robach for allowing me to see the relevant portions of this work.

32. Braunthal, In Search, p. 298.

33. Barkai, "The Austrian Social Democrats," p. 21.

34. Richard Berczeller, "Robert Danneberg," in Norbert Leser and Richard Berczeller, Als Zaungäste der Politik (Vienna, 1977), p. 185.

35. Walter B. Simon, "The Jewish Vote in Austria," Leo Baeck Institute Yearbook, 16 (1971), p. 110.

36. Classic examples of anti-Socialist propaganda stressing the Jewish origin of some Social Democratic leaders include Karl Paumgartten, Judentum und Sozial-demokratie (Graz, n.d.) and Aurelia Gerlach, Der Ein-fluss der Juden in der österreichischen Sozialdemokratie (Vienna, 1939).

37. Donald L. Niewyk, Socialist, Anti-Semite, and Jew. German Social Democracy Confronts the Problem of Anti-Semitism, 1918-1933 (Baton Rouge, La., 1971), pp.

168

105-106, 190ff. For a somewhat different (and more
critical) view of the record of the SPD see George L.
Mosse, "German Socialists and the Jewish Question in the
Weimar Republic," Leo Baeck Institute Yearbook, 16
(1971), pp. 123-51 and Hans-Helmuth Knütter, Die Juden
und die deutsche Linke in der Weimarer Republik 1918-
1933, Bonner Schriften z. Politik und Zeitgeschichte, 4
(Düsseldorf, 1971).

38. On Jewish voting patterns in the First Republic
see Simon, "The Jewish Vote," pp. 97-121.

39. E. Tramer, "Der republikanische Schutzbund,"
unpublished dissertation, Erlangen, 1969, p. 84ff.,
cited in Bunzl, "Arbeiterbewegung," p. 167.

40. Simon, "The Jewish Vote," p. 121. Robert
Wistrich has expressed an opinion on this point differing from my own: "The antisemitism of the socialists
was inevitably tempered, not so much by their 'Jewish'
leadership as by the importance of the Jewish concentration in Vienna, their main stronghold." See
Wistrich, "An Austrian variation," p. 6.

15. Jura Soyfer's
Death of a Party

Alfred Pfabigan

Those literary works which had their origin in the
writer's confrontation with organized Austromarxism were
not very successful; the works of Alfons Petzold or
Josef Luitpold Stern, for example, are only of regional
significance today. In this respect, there is a great
difference between the Weimar Republic and Austria,
because the latter had no figures like Bertolt Brecht,
Anna Seghers or B. Traven. I cannot discuss all the
reasons for this astonishing gap (astonishing, because
in other literary genres Austria has produced many
famous authors) but I am sure that the early "overcoming" of naturalism was an important factor. The cultural policy of the Social Democratic Party favored a literary style which represented a rebirth of both the
Klassik and the Vormärz, and this bias helped to destroy
the last traces of the oppositional, autonomous Volkskultur which can be found in the work of J.N. Nestroy,
for example.
There is one great exception: the short work of
the satirist Jura Soyfer. The dramas and satirical com-
mentaries of this author--who died at age twenty-seven
in the KZ Buchenwald--illustrate the last years of independent Austria. In particular, he is the author of a
fragmentary novel on the history leading up to 12 February, entitled So starb eine Partei (Death of a Party).[1] We do not know if Soyfer ever finished his
novel since the Viennese police confiscated the manuscript and an important part of the text is lost. But
though we do not know the whole story Soyfer wanted to
tell us, we can say that during the last months of organized Austromarxism Soyfer carried out the kind of
analysis of Austrian society that Heinrich Mann provided
of Wilhelmine German society in Der Untertan and Lion
Feuchtwanger wrote with regard to the period of the
Weimar Republic. In such works, the reader becomes a
witness to historical events, viewing them through the
eyes of people who are both products and producers of a
special sociopolitical situation. Soyfer's characters

169

170

are typical members of the Social Democratic Gegenwelt
(other world) acting under typical conditions. Soyfer
is a realistic writer according to the famous definition
given by Friedrich Engels in his letter to Margaret
Harkness.[2] But I do not want to discuss the aesthetic
conception and merits of Soyfer's novel; rather, I will
focus on its political-ideological content, on the political view of life that Soyfer's figures express.

For Soyfer, a member of the left opposition, the
party had "died." He was not engaged in experiments to
revitalize its dead body; he simply joined the Communist
Party. It was during this transition process that he
started to write, and the novel records the post mortem
examination and his mourning. Because he considered the
party "dead," he had no need to confront it in an aggressive manner. He had a good approach: without de-
tracting from his loyalty to the Communists, he was able
to express his deep feelings about the dead party and to
analyze its last months with both affection and a spirit
of enquiry and criticism. This novel is not an unmask-
ing of the Social Democratic Party by a Communist convert: in his text he never used the word Sozialfaschis-
mus to characterize the political attitude of the Social
Democratic Party.[3] It was Soyfer's opinion that the
defeat of the party was the result of the mistakes and
failures of its leaders, but he did not indulge in the
stereotypical reproach that those leaders betrayed the
masses who wanted to fight. His interest was broader:
the party--its leaders, its functionaries and its mem-
bers--was a complex unity for Soyfer.

Instead of reproaching the leaders, he wrote an
analysis of the organization, the best analysis that
Austromarxism ever produced. The kind of people who are
party members, the rules that organize them, the stratification of power, the question of democracy in the
organization--all these are the classic concerns of an
analysis of a party, but the Austromarxists neglected
them. Soyfer's novel is an exception. He was not a
social scientist so he did not systematize his observa-
tions; however, as a participant he saw more than a
scientific outsider, for he knew the everyday life of
the party.

In his analysis, Soyfer was influenced by two classic approaches: he believed the Social Democratic Party
had turned "oligarchical" and become "bureaucratized."
His novel is one of a broad stream of statements by Austrian and German left-wing socialists on party life before the party became illegal. Some left-wing socialists believed that the reason for the erroneous policy
of Social Democracy was inherent in the very structure
of the organization, but they also opposed the communist
model of organization. Changing the structure of the
workers' parties was, they thought, a prerequisite to

changing the policy of the parties, so they discussed
Robert Michels' thesis of oligarchy and organization[4]
("Wer Organisation sagt, sagt Oligarchie"), the place of
bureaucracy in party life, and the relationship of leadership to bureaucracy. The center of this discussion
was the journal Der Klassenkampf. Two of its editors,
Max Seydewitz and Kurt Rosenfeld, had been excluded from
German Social Democracy and were promoters of the Sozialistische Arbeiterpartei Deutschlands (SAPD). The
Austrian confidant of this group was Max Adler who was
one of the editors of Der Klassenkampf and also one of
the editors of the book Die Organisation im Klassenkampf.[5] Two essays in this book--Helmuth Wagner's
"Organisation und Klasse" and Kurt Laumann's "Organisation und Apparat"--contain political positions we can
also find in Soyfer's novel. But Soyfer did not write a
theoretical article; he wrote a novel. He showed the
structure of the organization through the portrayal of
persons and their behavior.

The novel opens at the main Vienna railway station,
a symbol for Austrian society, at Christmas 1932. Times
are changing: the power of Social Democracy and the
trade unions is diminishing; the balance of forces between the ministry of transport and the workers has come
to an end. Soyfer illustrates this with a significant
detail: Franz Josef Zehetner, a minor civil servant,
starts to play tricks on the powerful leader of the
union of railway station workers, Ferdinand Dworak. The
portrait of Zehetner is one of Soyfer's great accomplishments: he is a petit bourgeois declassé, harrassed
by the fear of sliding down the social scale, a man
whose fear of the Reds turned to hatred after 27 July
when their weakness was exposed, a member of the Heimwehr and also a clandestine member of the Nazi Party.

His counterpart, Ferdinand Dworak, an experienced
and leading functionary, represents a policy comparable
to that of Otto Bauer. This political leader believes
in the existence of a balance of power and a Pause
(interregnum) in the social struggle: "Der Hofrat und
der Lokomotivführer wissen, jeder für sich, Bescheid:
weder--noch. All das sind Geplänkel, die Hauptschlacht
ist vertagt. Man muss bis dahin irgendwie miteinander
auskommen. Grossmacht und Grossmacht."[6] But the
Hauptschlacht had already started and Dworak ignores it,
as did Otto Bauer. Although Soyfer criticizes his private life and his lack of understanding towards his unemployed son, the author depicts him as a man of great
political integrity.

This cannot be said of his partner, deputy Dreher
(the English translation is Turner), whose name conveys
two meanings: his maneuverability and his orientation
towards the politics of Karl Renner. Dreher, the prototype of a so-called Bonze (apparatchik), represents the

proletarian social climber. He is a parvenu who imi-
tates the bourgeoisie, a toady who kowtows to powerful
persons. His son, the bearer of his wish to rise in the
world, is a student and a member of the Nazi SA.
Dreher, as a typical member of the party's New Class,
maintains that his ascent is the ascent of the working
class: "Ich habe lange genug selbstlos dem Proletariat
gedient, jetzt darf ich mit Recht die Früchte
ernten."[7] Soyfer shows that lower functionaries, too,
have this attitude: a comrade named Hadina "[will sich]
net für's Ideal aufopfern wann er keine Anerkennung net
find't."[8] The alliance between Dreher and Dworak
illustrates the thesis that the workers' aristocracy and
the bureaucracy have an identical ideology which holds
the party together. It also illustrates the thesis that
left-wing socialists in the bureaucracy are the root of
revisionism.[9]

While Soyfer portrays these party officials as
strong men, he satirizes the small-time functionary on
whose shoulders the main burden of the humdrum organizational activity rests in the figure of Robert Blum.
Blum is the disfigured heir of a great name, who uses
party life to compensate for his own unhappy life.
Because the Social Democratic Gegenwelt helps him to
forget that he is an underdog, he spends all his time on
the the party, but nevertheless he is an apolitical man.
His one and only concern is that the membership dues are
collected at the right time. This character illustrates
Kurt Laumann's thesis that there is an necessary lack of
political thinking in the group of lower party officials[10] and that this lack is an important factor in
preserving the stability of the party organization.
Between members and leaders lies a large body of functionaries who support the organization's activity while
renouncing critical participation in it. Such stabi-
lity--especially stability in leadership--is a characteristic of oligarchical parties according to Robert
Michels. It was also a characteristic of organized
Austromarxism: leaders were elected without rival can-
didates, their terms lasted for decades, and they took a
hand in nominating their successors.

Soyfer also shows us the way such oligarchs treat
themselves: although the party claims to be an antici-
pation of the "solidarische Gesellschaft" (a term used
by Max Adler) and a "Gemeinschaft der Liebe,"[11] the
oligarchs distrust each other. When Dworak seeks another political position, Dreher starts to calculate
"die Wendigkeit des Rivalen, dessen persönliche Verbindungen zum Parteivortsand, dessen Feinde, die man sich
vielleicht zu Freunden würde machen müssen."[12] Dreher
knows that "...ganz oben, wo man als Fachmann für Eisen-
bahnerfragen sass, war Platz für wenige."[13] But the
competition between oligarchs is governed by rules which

protect the competitors and by mechanisms which protect
the contending parties from each other. One consequence
of the stability of party leadership is a kind of immobility within the whole party. Dreher and Dworak, both
more than fifty years old, experience a life crisis and
a political crisis at the same time, and both men become
weak and tired. We are witnesses to the gradual loss of
Dworak's ability to lead. In his opinion, the strike of
March 1933 is a success--though the despair of a worker
shows him the opposite. This party should change its
leaders, but in an oligarchic organization that is impossible.
     It is the personal and historical duty of these men
to overcome their personal and political crises, and
they choose a comfortable way to do so: they refuse to
face reality. Moreover, the party leaders even misin-
terpret reality:

     Nein, Dworak wusste nichts. Zufällig. Er hatte von
     spät nachmittags bis nachts mit Blum gearbeitet und
     hatte morgens die Zeitung nicht gelesen. Dworak
     seit 25 Jahren Parteimitglied, Ortsgruppenobmann,
     Personalausschussmitglied, Schutzbundkommandant,
     Mitglied des Bezirksvorstandes, hatte seine "Ar-
     beiter-Zeitung" nicht gelesen, ging am 31. Jänner
     durch die menschenerfüllten Strassen seines Be-
     zirkes und wusste nicht, dass am Vortage Hitler
     Reichskanzler geworden war...![14]

And Dreher finds an escape in the stereotypical
statement that there is all the difference in the world
between Austria and Germany. Surrogate activities fill
the lives of the party leaders. If they see the menace
at all, they react with "strong words": "Er wusste,
dass man die Gefahr sehr hoch einschätzte und sich zu
einer äusserst scharfen Sprache entschlossen hatte."[15]
     But the lameness of the party is not only a problem
of the leadership, for the party members, too, misinter-
pret political reality. The paternalistic authoritari-
anism of the oligarchic style has disenfranchised the
members. This is an old criticism of left socialism
which Soyfer tries to illustrate. The members are convinced that their beloved leaders are masters of the
political situation, that they have some hidden trump
cards. Instead of making their own political decisions,
the members deliberate about the intentions of their
leaders. The ambiguous political discourse of Austromarxism promotes such speculations:

     [Man war] schon damals in der Partei gewöhnt,
     hinter den Worten führender Genossen einem Sinn
     nachzuspüren, der aus parlamentarischen, aussen-
     politischen, innerparteilichen oder anderen tak-

174

tischen Rücksichten nur andeutungsweise vorgebracht
werden durfte...gleichzeitig wurde das Gegenteil
gemutmasst. So sassen die ahnungslosen Propheten
von jeher an ihren Sektions--und Wirtshaustischen,
über alles und jedes spekulierend. So sollten sie
noch eine Spanne Zeit sitzen, mit dem Fingernagel
Worte aus der "Arbeiter-Zeitung" unterstreichend,
den erloschenen Virginiastengel zwischen überlegen
gekräuselten Lippen, mit pfiffigem Blick und kurzem
Gedächtnis, streitsüchtig, in ihrer Art glück-
lich.[16]

For all these people the party is a Gegenwelt. But
whereas scholars point out that this Gegenwelt was an
alternative to the hostile institutions of the bourgeois
state, Soyfer shows another dimension of this Gegenwelt:
its "political men" are frustrated in other parts of
their lives, especially in their marriages. Dworak
married an apolitical woman:

Nach der Heirat hatte er versucht, die Bauerntoch-
ter, die ein braves Dienstmädchen gewesen war, in
die Bewegung zu ziehen...von der politischen Katastrophe, die Dworak eben erfahren hatte, verstand
die Frau nicht das geringste....Er war schuld...
aber er bekam nie einen Vorwurf zu hören. Sie war
brav und liebte ihn. Er hatte immerhin einiges an
ihr gut zu machen. Er nahm sich vor, regelmässiger
heimzukommen. Auch sollten sie in Zukunft öfter
wie Mann und Frau zueinander sein. "Ich bin ja
noch lange jung genug, dass ich ihr das bissel
Freud' antu' sagte er sich.[17]

For the functionaries, politics serves as a surrogate
for their dissatisfying lives. The weak garner strength
from the party; the unloved gain something they believe
to be love. But the surrogate is an impediment to living a real life and Soyfer's party officials are hard
men, contemptuous of others, with a strong wish to
assert themselves.
The position from which Soyfer writes is that of
the party youth whose conception of a Neuer Mensch
included all spheres of life. Thus Soyfer's novel is
partly written from a "we" perspective. But the youth
of the left opposition offered no alternative to the
party. Weakened by unemployment, they could not make a
clear choice between their revolutionary wishes and
their loyalty to a mass party. Their position with
regard to the Communist Party was ambiguous; some of
them fled into hysterical activities, oscillating between revolution and loyalty to the mass party:

Nun war Erich Diskussionen mit Kommunisten durchaus
nicht abgeneigt. Aber es mussten ruhige Unter-
haltungen unter vier Augen sein und nicht grob-
schlächtige öffentliche Polemiken. Denn Erichs
keineswegs negative Einstellung zum Leninismus
(wohlgemerkt nicht zur Kommunistischen Partei, hier
musste man Unterschiede wahren) war komplizierter
Natur. Ausserdem war sie mit einer scharfen Kritik
an der SP verbunden, die in vollem Umfang öffent-
lich zu äussern zur Zeit vor der Obmannswahl tak-
tisch unklug gewesen wäre. Hielt man sich aber zu
eng im Rahmen der eigenen Partei, so geriet man in
Gefahr, auf Argumente zu verfallen, die gar nicht
die eigenen waren; Gedankengänge anzuwenden, die
man für gewöhnlich selbst als verbrecherischen
Reformismus brandmarkte. (Ganz abgesehen davon,
dass man vor den provokatorischen Phrasen der Kommunisten oft genug unversehens im seinem Herzen
eine unverantwortliche Liebe zum alterschwachen
Bürgermeister Seitz oder zum fetten Klassenverräter
Renner entdeckte)...Man durfte nicht einfach "nein"
sagen. Man wollte nicht schlechtweg "nein"
lügen.[18]

The "illness" which killed the Social Democratic
Party could be found in all its branches. Soyfer, im-
bued with a love for the dead party (which is reminiscent of Joseph Roth's novels on the decline of the
Habsburg Empire), performed the autopsy.

NOTES

1. Jura Soyfer, "So starb eine Partei," in his Die
Ordnung schuf der liebe Gott (Leipzig, 1979) pp. 225-
376.

2. See Marx-Engels-Werke, (Berlin, DDR, 1972), Vol.
37, p. 42.

3. The Communist Party used this word until 1934.
See Fritz Keller, Gegen den Strom (Vienna, 1978), p.
132.

4. See Robert Michels, Zur Soziologie des Partei-
wesens in der modernen Demokratie (Stuttgart, 1970).

5. Max Adler, Kurt Rosenfeld, Max Seydewitz and
Heinrich Ströbel, eds., Die Organisation im Klassen-
kampf: Die Probleme der politischen Organisation der
Arbeiterklasse (Berlin, 1931).

176

6. Soyfer, "So starb eine Partei," p. 247.

7. Ibid., p. 306.

8. Ibid., p. 297.

9. Max Adler et al., Die Organisation im Klassen-kampf, pp. 94ff.

10. Ibid., p. 135.

11. See Jacques Hannak, Im Sturm eines Jahrhunderts (Vienna, 1952), p. 250.

12. Soyfer, "So starb eine Partei," p. 285.

13. Ibid., p. 284.

14. Ibid., p. 259.

15. Ibid., p. 310.

16. Ibid., p. 255.

17. Ibid., p. 262.

18. Ibid., pp. 271, 274.

16. Austromarxism on the International Scene

Adolf Sturmthal

I should like to address one of the less widely discussed aspects of Austromarxism, namely its international role or impact. Not that this topic has been completely neglected in the literature or in public discussion. It is, among other subjects, part of the three-volume History of the International by Julius Braunthal, one of the post-World War II secretaries of the Socialist International. But in comparison with other aspects of Austromarxism, the topic to which I am referring to has been less intensively studied, in particular with reference to events of the 1930s. It is true, of course, that in the first decade of this century the attention of Austromarxists themselves was directed primarily at the domestic problems of the Austro-Hungarian monarchy. The issue of multi-national co-existence in the empire formed the subject matter of most of the early works of Karl Renner and Otto Bauer. But with the increasing international tensions preceding the outbreak of World War I, the issue of what the International was to do to prevent a war and especially once war had broken out became the most intensely discussed questions within the International. The famous Keir Hardie-Edouard Vaillant amendment was put on the agenda of the International Socialist Congress called for Vienna in 1914. Even prior to this, informal discussions among such figures as Victor Adler, Karl Kautsky and August Bebel had their impact on the thinking of the German party, and Rudolf Hilferding's move to Berlin added to Austrian influence on events and thinking on the German SPD.

Otto Bauer had been assigned the task of preparing a memorandum on the Keir Hardie-Vaillant amendment which proposed the calling of a universal general strike to prevent the outbreak of war. Bauer's paper (which of course never reached the International officially since the Congress did not take place) made two main points in opposition to the amendment. First, given the general mood of super-patriotism created by the impending outbreak of the war, a general strike would have a severely reduced impact on economic life and especially on the mobilization of the armed forces. Second, the influence would be greatest in countries with well-organized labor movements and, therefore, very little impact could be expected in czarist Russia. Organized labor would thus unintentionally contribute to the victory of the most reactionary governments in Europe. This could not be the policy of the Socialist International or of the international trade union movement. Thus only the vague phrase "all appropriate means in opposing the war" could be used in the resolutions of the International. Even the famous last paragraph of the Stuttgart resolution dealt only with action to be taken after the outbreak of the war. (Incidentally, the fact that the assignment of drafting this document went to Bauer made clear what most people in the party knew: namely, that Victor Adler regarded Bauer as his successor in the party leadership. Only caution in the face of Austrian anti-Semitism prevented this fact to be expressed by Bauer's obtaining the presidency of the party.)

Austromarxism, or at least an important section of it, appeared on the international scene during World War I. Friedrich Adler, Therese Schlesinger, and--after his return from prison camp in Russia--Otto Bauer assumed the leadership of a current that was labelled the international pacifists which believed that only the demand for a peace without annexations or tributes could be an internationally acceptable formula. The so-called social patriots who supported the victory of their homeland opposed each other and made the functioning of the Second International impossible during the war. The internationalist-defeatists, whose leader was Lenin, also proposed a solution that was not applicable to both sides of the trenches. That left the current led by Fritz Adler and represented by Therese Schlesinger at the antiwar conferences in Switzerland as the only solution which would make possible the survival of the International. Whether this slogan was realistic was, under the circumstances, a secondary question.

After 1918 Adler and Bauer took over the leadership not only of the party, but also of the international current they had represented. It had grown considerably during the war. The French Socialist Party, the German Independents, the Swiss, a large part of the Italians, and others had joined them. They proceeded to set up the International 2½ whose center was Vienna with Adler as the General Secretary. In spite of the unsuccessful attempt at reunification at the conference of the three executives in Berlin (April 1922), the Viennese did not give up the hope of the ultimate reunification of the international labor movement, now split in three parts. It was only after Zinoviev succeeded in Halle in splitting the German Independents, leaving only a small minority under the intellectual leadership of Hilferding, that reunification turned into a distant goal.

After the merger of the remnants of the Viennese International 2½ and those of the Second International to form the Labor and Socialist International (LSI), Austromarxism became a significant force within the International. At first there were two Secretaries, one from each of the merging organizations: Tom Shaw for the Second International and Friedrich Adler for the Viennese group. But when the first British Labour Government was formed in 1924, Tom Shaw became a minister in the government and Adler remained the sole Secretary General of the LSI. Otto Bauer represented the Austrian party and soon emerged as the leader of a left wing within the executive and the Bureau of the LSI, its two most active and representative organs. He had the support of the French Socialists, particularly of Jean Zyromsky, the main spokesman of the party's left wing at that time; of Alexandre Bracke, one of the old-time French party leaders; of Pietro Nenni of Italy; Jacob Pistiner of Romania; Theodor Dan and Raphael Abramovich, speaking for the Mensheviks; and a minority of the German delegation, led by Arthur Crispien, who was not a powerful personality but one of the three German party chairmen. While working class unity was no longer an immediate objective, it was never rejected. But criticism of the Soviet regime and its show trials was one of the main subjects of LSI proceedings, and Bauer as well as Adler took full part in the anti-Stalin pronouncements.

The left wing was a distinct minority within the councils of the International. The British Labour Party (apart from the small pacifist Independent Labour Party), the great majority of the German SPD, the Scandinavians (except, perhaps, Norway), Belgium and Holland—in other words, the affiliates of the old Second International—controlled the great majority of votes. The Austromarxists influenced the resolutions and communiqués of the LSI mainly by the power of their arguments and the strength of their personalities.

My own role is not easy to describe since Adler did not like to establish clear responsibilities. Moreover, I was a youngster without any standing within the Austrian Party except the support of Helene and Otto Bauer. Only gradually could I win the confidence of Adler to the point that a year or two after I had joined the Secretatiat, I became his principal assistant. Yet the only outward expression of this new role was my official designation as editor of the weekly <u>International Information</u>, the main publication of the LSI.

Bauer's influence is shown most clearly by the fact that most of the draft resolutions of the Executive or

even of the Congresses were produced by him, sometimes
with a small contribution on my part. It was clear.to
him, as it was to the Secretariat, that if the resolutions were not to remain mere paper they had to take
into account where the majority of the votes stood.
Even so, some of the delegates tried to prevent expressions on the part of the LSI that would interfere with
their own policies or, worse still, contradict them.

What separated the left wing from the rest in the
LSI is not always easy to determine. Perhaps the main
issue was that of government participation. Right-
wingers in the LSI regarded Socialist minority representation in parliamentary governments as a more or less
normal occurrence. Bauer and his associates did not reject such participation outright, as a matter of principle, but accepted it only as the result of exceptional
circumstances or what Bauer described as "the balance of
class forces." This concept played an important role in
the theoretical structures of Austromarxism during the
inter-war period. At first, in the years immediately
following the end of World War I, there was an attack on
so-called reformist ministerialism, but that idea was
refined and transformed by the concept of the balance of
class forces.

Such a state of affairs was regarded as fertile
ground for the growth of fascism. Interestingly, the
rise of Italian fascism did not arouse the intense concern of the theoretical heads of Austromarxism. In a
somewhat peculiar fashion, many regarded it as a specific Italian phenomenon with limited significance for the
rest of the European socialist movement. While full
solidarity was extended to the victims of Mussolini's
dictatorship--Giuseppe Saragat travelled on an Austrian
passport to Vienna--those few who looked for an explanation of what had happened in Italy tended to think that
the three-fold split in Italian socialism was the main
cause for its failure to resist fascism in time. It is
significant that, without any official decision having
been made within the LSI, Italian problems became the
domain of a highly respected member of the party Executive, Wilhelm Ellenbogen.

Quite different were the attitude towards and the
concern with the rise of the Nazis. The tendency of
many Socialists in Austria and elsewhere to regard the
Nazis simply as the hired hands and guns of big busi-
ness--an idea which to this day is widely accepted--was
popular at an early stage and fitted well into Communist
propaganda. It seemed to be confirmed by the coalition
that Hitler made with big business as well as with some
parts of the military. The execution of Ernst Roehm and
Gregor Strasser--the latter, at least, could be held responsible for the persistence of semi-socialist ideas in
the Nazi leadership--was further confirmation of this

theory. However, for Bauer and others this offered a satisfactory explanation of only a passing stage in the evolution of German fascism. Very soon they returned to their earlier version of the balance of class forces which permitted the emergence of a ruling Executive above the class struggle and based upon a coalition of the Lumpenproletariat and at least substantial parts of the armed forces. That Hitler's rise to power required his accepting a coalition with the Reichswehr and with a large part of big business was regarded as only a passing stage in the evolution of the fascist movement.

The leading figures of Austromarxism criticized the failure of the SPD to resist the rise of Nazism in time and lambasted subsequent attempts of some individuals in the party and some leaders of the trade union confederation to come to terms with the Nazis; however, soon the internal evolution of Austria absorbed the energies of the Austromarxists. The importance of having forces capable of resisting attempts to destroy the young Austrian democracy was demonstrated by the events of 15 July 1927 and by Theodor Körner's efforts to reorganize the Republican Defense Corps as a guerilla troop supported by the population. But Körner lost out to Alexander Eifler's concept of relying upon the Defense Corps and open battles. In fact, the political and union leaders gave up hope soon after March 1933. The events of February 1934 did not result from a decision on the part of the leadership to resist with armed force, but from the explosion of spontaneous forces outside, indeed against the wishes, of the leadership.

After 1934 the international role of Austromarxism was extremey limited. Whether victorious resistance would have been possible--and I personally doubt it, given the strategic situation of Austria and the unbelievable intensity of class and political hatred in the First Republic--was irrelevant for most outside observers. The main fact was that, just as German reformism had failed, Austromarxism had been defeated--though its end was perhaps a bit more glorious than that of the German party. Otto Bauer and, soon afterwards, Fritz Adler realized that their leadership was at an end. Adler announced to the Executive of the LSI that he was ready to resign so that a representative of a legal party could be elected secretary general of the LSI. No action was taken on this declaration, as will be shown further on in this paper. I resigned from the Secretariat in connection with the nonintervention policy in the Spanish Civil War.

Bauer and Adler clearly felt that their function was to help a new generation take the lead and to assist and perhaps advise their potential successors. Less restrained by "diplomatic" considerations, they now felt the time had come for closer cooperation with the left-

wing opposition within the German labor movement and
primarily with the group known as Neu Beginnen. The
founding manifesto of Walter Loewenheim, who wrote under
the pseudonym Miles, met with the enthusiastic support
of the Austrian leaders in exile, though they had minor
reservations about some aspects of that manifesto. Via
Paul Hertz and the former Austrian Karl Frank, close
contact was established with Neu Beginnen, but it was
impeded by sharp internal and personal quarrels within
that group. Adler, who retained his position as general
secretary of what was left of the Socialist International, attempted to get financial support from the SPD for
the Neu Beginnen group. (I still remember a highly
clandestine meeting at the Secretariat of the LSI--
cleared of all personnel except for Adler and myself--at
which two representatives of Neu Beginnen, Fritz Erler
and Henry Ehrmann, came to plead their cause.)

However, on the European scene, the influence of
the International and even more of Austromarxism declined very rapidly, until, after the fall of Czechoslovakia, it was almost nil. Indeed, for a number of
the surviving parties, the International became a source
of embarrassment and its decisions a danger to those who
hoped somehow to escape the growing threat of Hitler's
Germany. The history of the International in this
period and Adler's role at the center of the dismaying
events that accompanied the end of the International are
less well known, so it seems worthwhile to discuss both
topics briefly.

In approximately the last year of life of the International, a sharp and personal opposition to the
general secretary developed. It was articulated by two
very different groups of parties, which disagreed both
in their motivations for and in the nature of their
attacks. The Scandinavian parties hoped that by disso-
ciating themselves from the International they could
take refuge in their neutrality and escape from the
coming world war. The British considered the rump of
the International useless and their contributions to its
budget a total waste; some of their representatives,
headed by Hugh Dalton, manifested unrestrained disdain
for the representatives of the illegal parties. These
groups combined to attack Adler, but his offer to resign
was rejected, despite a substantial minority which opposed him and a number of abstentions; thus no one
replaced him. The unsuccessful candidate of the opposition was a Norwegian, Bjarne Braatoy, a former employee
of the Secretariat of the LSI who, after World War II,
served for a short time as the secretary of the newly-
reconstituted International. Before the fall of France,
Braatoy's plan was to transform the International into a
mere information agency without any impact on the policies of the affiliated parties. This plan corresponded

to the wishes of the Labour Party as expressed by Hugh
Dalton and the Scandinavians. That Dalton found it necessary to combine his push for a change in the function
--or, better still, a downgrading--of the Socialist International with attacks upon the personal honor of
Adler, added to the feeling of doom that characterized
the end of the International. However, the entire ugly
debate proved useless because the occupation of Paris by
German troops put an end to the activities of the International once and for all.[1]

During the final period of the International, Bauer
(who passed away in 1938) and Adler pursued a policy
they labelled "integral socialism" which was designed to
avoid the errors of both reformism and Bolshevism. Undoubtedly, in the back of their minds was the hope that
the end of World War II--a war which they regarded as
inevitable--would bring about not only the downfall of
Nazism but also of the capitalist system, especially in
Germany. With Germany at its head, "integral socialism"
could form the basis for the reorganization and ultimately the unification of the international labor movement now free of the vices of both reformism and Bolshevism. Bauer did not live to see how far the outcome
of the war fell short of his hopes, nor did Max Adler.
Friedrich Adler retired from political life,[2] and
Robert Danneberg ended his life in a concentration camp.
Otto Leichter's attempt to succeed Otto Bauer in the
Austrian party failed due to resistance on the part of
the entrenched party organization. Julius Deutsch and
Oskar Pollak, both of whom returned to Vienna, accepted
without resistance the leadership of Adolf Schärf and
others who had survived the terror. Karl Renner, unexpectedly the protégé of the Russian occupation troops,
found himself the head of state.

Nevertheless, Austromarxism was not quite dead. It
lived on in the mythology of some Austrian party members; Bruno Kreisky and Herta Firnberg tried to maintain
at least a symbolic connection with the pre-1934 party.
Perhaps more interesting is the fact that, in their
search for an ideology midway between Bolshevism and
reformism, the Eurocommunists rediscovered Austromarxism
and more or less adopted it as their intellectual weapon
against both Moscow and domestic reformists. A new
literature embodying some of the ideas of pre-1934 Austrian socialism emerged, especially in Italy and other
Southern European countries, and a rather lively dialogue existed for a while between Eurocommunists and
left-wing socialists. In addition, in various West
German universities Austromarxism remains an eminently
important subject of research and teaching.

Why did Austromarxism prove incapable of making a
permanent imprint on the policies of the International?
Clearly, this could have occurred only if the affiliated

parties had been willing to consider the authority of
the International superior to that of their own national
executives. This proved impossible after Hitler came to
power in Germany and his aggressive policies accumulated
one success after another; international discipline had
rarely been tested before 1933, and from the mid-1930s
on, European politics was determined by the fear of Nazi
aggression and by desperate attempts to hide from
Hitler's fury. Moreover, the influence of Austromarxism
within the LSI always was based on the intellectual power of Bauer and the moral stature of Adler. The majority of the votes, i.e., the ultimate decision, was in
the hands of British Labour and the German SPD, supported by most of the Scandinavian countries, Belgium
and Holland. From 1933-1934, Great Britain and Scandinavia acquired even more influence because the voting
strength of the illegal parties was twice radically
reduced. Conceivably, if the Independent German Social
Democrats (USPD) had not lost the great majority of
their supporters to the Communists at the Halle Congress, the internal power relationships within the LSI
would have been different and Hilferding could have
aligned himself with Bauer. But when Zinoviev won out
over Hilferding at the Independents' Congress in Halle,
the sphere of Austromarxism was decisively narrowed.
The polarization within the international labor movement
between Bolshevism and reformism did not allow much room
for a center position.

NOTES

1. Lewis J. Edinger, German Exile Politics: the
Social-Democratic Executive Committee in the Nazi Era
(Berkeley, 1956), p. 197, reports that "Adler had to
resign" and was replaced by a "Belgian thought less in
sympathy with the cause of the exiles." This does not
correspond to the official version as presented in the
final "special" issues of International Information, the
newsletter of the Secretariat of the LSI.

2. Friedrich Adler had offered in December 1939 to
stay on in the unpaid position of administrative secretary since he did not wish to accept political responsibility for an International that could not even agree
on whether to report that a meeting had taken place.
This would permit, he said, the orderly election of a
new general gecretary. Adler's candidate for the job
was the Belgian Buset. However, at this point, the
British Labour Party (in the person of George Dallas)
reversed itself, asking that Adler continue as in the

past. The Executive met for the last time in February
1940 in Brussels. Blum proposed the reelection of
Adler. A final decision was postponed pending a meeting
to be held in Paris on May 26. This date proved unac-
ceptable to some members of the Executive. The an-
nouncement that the meeting was postponed was the last
act of the LSI.

17. Red Vienna:
Symbol and Strategy

Anson Rabinbach

Red Vienna between the wars was both a symbol of
the achievements of Austrian Social Democracy, and an
expression of its strategic limits. As early as 1920
its social and cultural accomplishments in the capital
contrasted with the inability of the party to affect the
nature of politics in the First Republic.[1] Interwar
Austrian Social Democracy can be characterized by a
series of striking paradoxes: it was perhaps the most
powerful Social Democratic party in the world--the
largest in per capita terms--and certainly the most innovative. Yet, in its inability to perceive the extent
of the fascist danger, and in its ultimate failure to
defend democratic institutions and the labor movement,
it hardly differed from the German SPD. It too suffered
from the paralysis and what Hans Mommsen called the
"immobilism" characteristic of most Social Democratic
parties in the economic crisis.[2] But it was also the
first party of the European left to take up arms against
fascism. Why then were the architects of Red Vienna--
the boldest and most successful Social Democratic effort
to combine cultural and urban renewal with pedagogical
idealism--so unable to translate their real successes
into political power? And why, given the well-documented fatalism of the party leaders after 1927, did the
Austrian Socialists resist at all?

Red Vienna was a form of compensation for the
powerlessness of the Austrian Socialists in the wider
political arena. The three "camps" that constituted the
political, ideological, and military structure of the
Republic reflected the country's socio-demographic realities and the relentless geopolitical squeeze from Italy, Germany, and Hungary. All parties in the Republic
contributed to its downfall through their inability to
transcend their respective regional, political and ideological ghettos. Power was distributed among these
three hostile camps but ultimately eluded all of them.

For this reason, any explanation of the fate of
Social Democracy in the First Republic has to take into

account the core of its political strategy: the preparation for power in lieu of a clear conception of .
power itself; in short, the idea of a pedagogical politics. Social Democracy was consistently torn between its
radical commitment to a class politics which emphasized
homogeneity or ideological purity, and its faith in
electoral politics which, through the magical 51 percent, would ultimately carry it to power. The dilemma
was misdiagnosed as a purely tactical problem, and the
party believed it could merely balance both of these
commitments. Though it wavered between responsibility
to the Republic and democracy on the one hand and
loyalty to its organizational bastion in Vienna on the
other, it became increasingly inflexible.

The Austrian Socialists regarded Red Vienna in
light of the political situation of 1918-1920 which
froze them out of national power but gave them local
hegemony in the capital (Gemeinderat, Stadt, Land).
They considered municipal socialism a viable political
solution to the limits which they themselves had helped
to impose on the revolution of 1918-1919. As Otto Bauer
explained in his "equilibrium of class forces theory,"
if the party could not rule, it was at least indispen-
sible for rule beause it represented a shadow power that
could exercise tacit if not actual power.[3] In addition, by emphasizing the pedagogical or anticipatory
side of its local hegemony, it could convert control
over Vienna into the active and dynamic element of its
politics. The party regarded the organizational and
electoral growth of its constituency in the capital as a
preparation for power, while placing its ultimate faith
in the eventual conquest of power either--and here the
vagueness of the Linz Program is crucial--through the
ballot or through the disintegration of the ruling class
(the myth of 1918).

After 1920, then, the politics of Austrian Socialism can be characterized as essentially preparatory,
while its conception of power was, as Peter Nettl expressed it, still that of the passive "inheritor party"
typical of the Second International.[4] The party's
housing, health and, above all, pedagogical reforms and
innovations were more than the "model" of a future socialist society. They were the party's central motif:
institutionalism was its real strategy. Institutionalism and education represented the activist side of a
theory that combined pedagogical enthusiasm with a fundamentally pessimistic evolutionism and a passive historical fatalism. It is no accident, therefore, that
the party's left wing was so closely associated with the
educational and youth movement. Max Adler's remark that
the burden of future democracy did not lie in "politics
but in pedagogy" captured this essential truth of the
Austrian Socialists.[5]

Not only was pedagogy the centerpiece of the party's strategy in Red Vienna, it also informed its successes in the realm of urban and social policy. For example, Otto Glöckel's educational reform attempted to abolish clerical and class influences, while the remarkable Vienna housing blocks were intended to create a secular milieu of proletarian socialization which, in turn, would facilitate the formation of neue Menschen. By the late 1920s, however, it became increasingly clear that an ever greater emphasis was being placed on the book as the essential tool of Socialist politics. Political fatalism and a dwindling sense of efficacy in the larger sphere were offset by the institutionalized optimism of the pedagogical movement.[6]

The chief impulse for the construction of Red Vienna came from the limits of the 1918-1919 revolution and the postwar political division of Austria into regional and religious-ideological spheres of power. But the selection of Bildung as the Socialist's chief ideological thrust had prewar roots. The politics of pedagogy was the basis of the Bildungsvereine that had substituted for illicit political organization in the 1870s and 1880s. For Engelbert Pernerstorfer or Victor Adler, the acculturizing role of the party meant "making the advanced culture and civilization created by the German intellectual heroes accessible to the people."[7] Bildung was implicit in the imperial myth of the Erziehungsgemeinschaft which Bauer, for example, hoped would ultimately replace the babel of nationalities in the empire; it was present in the party's acceptance of the mantle of enlightenment, cosmopolitanism, and parliamentarism from the defunct Austrian liberals; and it was present--though always understated--in the crucial fact that, both before and after the war, the party's main ideological enemy was neither the Hapsburg tradition nor bourgeois thought (Kant and Marx were equals in the spiritual pantheon of the Socialists) but clericalism. What else but the promotion of secular, rationalist culture could be the strategy of a party largely led by middle-class Jewish intellectuals in the name of Catholic and German- or Czech-speaking workers?

After 1920 Bildung also became the political core of Austromarxism. The leading Austromarxist theorists (with the possible exception of Renner) saw the educatonal sphere as the only area where they were not on the defensive, and where, as Otto Felix Kanitz, the educational theorist, put it: "we can conquer virgin territory; that is, the territory of revolutionary Socialist education."[8] Kanitz, who was a pupil of Alfred Adler, believed that a new form of education would teach proletarian children to overcome their "social inferiority complex" and would prevent the subsequent formation of a macht lust in a reaction to the ohnmacht of life experi-

ence.[9]   For Max Adler, as Alfred Pfabigan's biography
shows, the goal of socialism was the creation of a
humanized society based on universal socialist ethics.
He did not champion the "proletarian education" advocated by the Communists but "socialist education" in a
universal sense which would undo the effects of proletarian experience.[10]   Socialism was "above all a cultural movement...and only secondarily a political
one."[11]

From this standpoint, the promotion of the virtues
of science and enlightenment, or the establishment of
organized culture to fill the workers' free hours
(workers' leisure time was increasing in the 1920s and
1930s) in no way interfered with the political goals of
the movement, and, in fact, increasingly came to be
identified with them. Bauer himself underscored the
success of this conception of political power at Linz in
1926. The party's double strategy was based "on the one
hand on the concrete recognition of the road to power,
and, on the other, on the great intellectual and moral
educational task involved in creating such a zenith of
class solidarity."[12]

Thus the radicalism of Red Vienna was not simply
the genuinely redistributive justice of its taxation and
housing policies, but its Bildungspolitik, articulated
through the municipality and also through the party's
Vereine, schools, libraries, clubs, lectures, etc. The
actual effect of all this activity is not directly accessible. It is hard to say how much of the new culture
was attributable to Red Vienna and how much to broader
interwar social and cultural changes--for example, the
development of a leisure culture and the emergence of
the "new woman" of the 1920s. How effectively the new
socialist culture acted as a prophylaxis against such
"bourgeois influences" as radio, film, jazz, against
other forms of mass culture, and against clerical
traditions, is even more difficult to answer.

There is no doubt that the culture of Red Vienna
did create a high level of organized political activity,
participation, and solidarity. Whether or not this had
the effect of producing more or less political consciousness is far less clear. In the youth organizations, for example, there was permanent tension between the need for political self-expression and the
party's set of norms and constraints. The Socialists'
pedagogy was generally predicated on traditional literary and aesthetic tastes, and was culturally conservative in some matters, especially on questions of sex,
smoking and alcohol. Women's participation in the cultural sphere was higher than in the political organizations of the party; a 1931 study of working-class women
indicated that only 7 percent of those asked were not
active in political or pedagogical organizations--though

the selection indicates that a particularly socialist
elite was chosen as the sample.[13] There is also little doubt that, through such cultural activities, the
party extended its popularity in non-working-class circles; for example, more white-collar employees, teachers
and students participated in the libraries than were
represented in the party as a whole.[14] Whereas party
membership declined in the provinces, it doubled in
Vienna between 1925 and 1929. In contrast to the SPD,
the SDAP consisted largely of young members (one-third
of its membership was under thirty) and the youth organizations were extremely successful in both membership
and electoral terms.

But the deeper impact of this culture on behavior
is still difficult to assess. Though many workers made
use of the educational facilities, they generally disappointed party functionaries by not meeting their standards and expectations. For the most part, they failed
to respond to the request to read highly promoted
"scientific books" as opposed to novels, nor did they
reflect the party's preference for soziale Romanen over
the ever popular Heimatromanen. Eventually, as Alfred
Pfoser demonstrates, they were directed towards Zola,
Sinclair Lewis, and above all Jack London, but not without considerable coaxing.[15]

The sphere of political organization was still
sharply separated from the private sphere, and as Dieter
Langewiesche has shown, working-class life was only mar-
ginally transformed by the new municipal socialism, and
then far more by its material than its spiritual benefits.[16] On the other hand, within the party organization, the loyalty of party activists and functionaries,
especially at the district level, was extremely high.
With the onset of the economic crisis, and in the aftermath of the party's political humiliation on 15 July
1927, the consequences of the isolation of the party's
preparatory strategy in the institutional sphere became
evident. What Bauer called "the long view" became, in
effect, an illusion of activism, objectified in the
party's infrastructure. It is therefore no accident
that the infrastructure was the first focal point of
discontent within party ranks. If youth groups and
pedagogical agencies constituted the core of the party's
institutionalism, they also were the first to perceive
its weakness as surrogate politics. In the Jungfront
crisis of 1931 and 1932, and in the broader left
opposition that emerged by 1933, discontent with the
fatalism of the party leadership spread throughout the
district organizations of Red Vienna.[17] An extraordinary barometer of the political discontent within
the Vienna party organization are the resolutions and
documents sent to party headquarters from the districts
on the eve of the party's last congress in October 1933.

They reveal profound dissatisfaction with the passivity
and immobility of the leaders and call for an Ausweg
from the crisis. Bauer's attempts to resist the rank
and file's mounting frustration and its radicalism laced
with disillusionment only confirmed Karl Kraus' sardonic
remark that Socialist intellectials were "created by God
in his wrath as politicians in the laborer's cause"
because of their "pathological capacity to see beyond
the immediate."[18]

Throughout the final months of 1933 and in early
1934 the Austrian Socialist Party underwent a profound
inner crisis. The party leadership tacitly accepted the
dissolution of the party as a fait accompli but wavered
between the alternatives of complete capitulation (for
Bauer and the lower Austrians this meant accepting integration in the Fatherland Front, though they hoped to
maintain the trade unions) and combat, which they did
not regard as potentially successful. (Bauer also
unofficially supported the arming of the Schutzbund).
Because it was conceived as a defensive and local compromise with history, Red Vienna became the focus of the
resistance to the party's inner dissolution. This process, which the party crisis of 1932-1934 unleashed,
resulted in a Socialist Party composed of distinct and
independent political groups, each prepared to act on
its own, free from the constraints of party unity. This
is particularly true of the provincial organizations
which regarded the political collapse of Red Vienna as
the affirmation of their own longstanding distrust of
the party center. Because of the growing radicalism of
the party's institutional structure in Red Vienna, and
because of the Schutzbund's unwillingness to accept the
lack of political alternatives, Austrian Social Democracy, unlike the German SPD, succumbed to both immobilism and insurrection.

In the final analysis, the party's Bildungspolitik
mirrored the fate of political liberalism in prewar
Austria. For the Socialists, like the generation of
1848, cultural politics was an alternative to the absence of national power. As the heirs to the liberal
tradition in Austria, the Socialists also received the
minority legacy of liberal ideas, especially rationalism
and positivism. By fusing these traditions with Marxism
and with the progressive urban social policy of Red
Vienna, the Social Democrats hoped to overcome the weaknesses of what they perceived to be a "transitional
phase." In so doing, they contributed to the ideological and political "camp mentality" of the Republic. The
pedagogical triumph of Red Vienna was the reverse side
of the political pessimism which permeated the leadership of Austrian Social Democracy. Though it also gave

rise to the resistance of February 1934, the cultural politics of Red Vienna was far more successful as symbol than as strategy.

NOTES

1. For a clear articulation of this position see Anton Pelinka, "Kommunalpolitik als Gegenmacht: Das 'rote Wien' als Beispiel gesellschaftsverändernder Reformpolitik" in K. H. Nassmacher, ed., Kommunalpolitik und Sozialdemokratie: Der Beitrag des demokratischen Sozialismus zur kommunalen Selbstverwaltung (Bonn, 1977), pp. 63-77.

2. Hans Mommsen, "Die Sozialdemokratie in der Defensive: Der Immobilismus der SPD und der Aufstieg des Faschismus," in Hans Mommsen, ed., Sozialdemokratie zwischen Klassenbewegung und Volkspartei (Frankfurt am Main, 1974), pp. 106-123.

3. See Otto Bauer, "Das Gleichgewicht der Klassen-kräfte," Der Kampf, Jg. 17, No. 2 (February 1924), pp. 56-67.

4. Peter Nettl, "The German Social Democratic Party, 1890-1914 as Political Model," Past and Present, No. 30 (1965), pp. 65-95.

5. Max Adler, Die Staatsauffassung des Marxismus: Ein Beitrag zur Unterscheidung von soziologischen und juristischer Methode (Vienna, 1922), p. 185.

6. Three important recent works on the cultural politics of Red Vienna are: Dieter Langewiesche, Zur Freizeit des Arbeiters; Bildungsbestrebungen und Freizeitgestaltung österreichischer Arbeiter im Kaiserreich und in der Ersten Republik (Stuttgart, 1979); Alfred Pfoser, Literatur und Austromarxismus (Vienna, 1980); Josef Weidenholzer, Auf dem Weg zum "Neuen Menschen": Bildungs- und Kulturarbeit der österreichischen Sozialdemokratie in der Ersten Republik (Vienna, 1981).

7. Karl Renner, An der Wende zweier Zeiten (Vienna, 1946), p. 281.

8. Cited in Weidenholzer, Auf dem Weg, p. 64.

9. Ibid., pp. 78-81.

10. Alfred Pfabigan, Max Adler: Eine politische Biographie (Frankfurt and New York, 1982), p. 204. .

11. Ibid., p. 96.

12. Otto Bauer, Protokolle, Sozialdemokratischer Parteitag 1926 (Vienna, 1926), pp. 276, 277. Cited in Pfoser, Literatur, p. 30.

13. See Käthe Leichter, So leben wir...1320 Industriearbeiterinnen berichten ihr Leben (Vienna, 1932), pp. 116-118.

14. Pfoser, Literatur, p. 109.

15. Ibid.

16. Dieter Langewiesche, "Politische Orientierung und soziales Verhalten: Familienleben und Wohnver-hältnisse von Arbeitern im 'roten' Wien der Ersten Republik," unpublished paper, 1981.

17. On this point see my The Crisis of Austrian Socialism: From Red Vienna to Civil War, 1927-1934 (Chicago, 1983), especially Chapters 5 and 6.

18. Karl Kraus, Die dritte Walpurgisnacht (Munich, 1967), p. 222.

18. Red Vienna:
A New Atlantis?

Josef Weidenholzer

Red Vienna was first and foremost a cultural
achievement. Although it had many connections to
economic and political aspects of Austria in the interwar period, its extraordinary significance--its value
for both supporters and opponents--was a matter of more
than politics or economics. Opponents made it the main
target of their hatred, while enthusiastic supporters
considered it the first step towards the incarnation of
the New Society. Although there are some grains of
truth in such evaluations, there was no soberness in
contemporary judgments, because Red Vienna stood at the
center of a pseudoreligious controversy. To Austromarxists, for example, it could only be represented in
terms of a holistic approach in which all aspects of
life are integrated. Today, the hatred as well as the
enthusiasm for Red Vienna has faded, only to be replaced
by a nostalgia shared, curiously enough, by all political factions in contemporary Austria.

SOME PREREQUISITES FOR THE RISE OF RED VIENNA

Red Vienna came about at a time in Austrian history
when there was a stalemate between the major political
camps. It successfully filled a gap. In analyzing the
prehistory of Red Vienna, three factors have to be mentioned.
1. The central conflicts of modern capitalist and
industrialized Austria were not defined as class conflicts to the same extent as in other Western nations.
From the beginning of industrialization, industrial conflicts had been overshadowed by ethnic and cultural
ones. Because of the dominant role of the German-
speaking bureaucracy, the question of how to gain
access to positions was at least as important as how to
confine the power of entrepreneurs through industrial
struggle. Because of the central role played by the
state and its bureaucrats in the economy, the Social

Democrats have generally pursued the goal of influencing
the state machinery. From its beginnings, Austrian Social Democracy has always been more than a mere labor
movement.

2. Austrian society was never at any stage an indi-
vidualistic society. The extent of institutionalization
was always high compared to that of other nations, and
this was due to Austrian backwardness and not to the influence of reformist forces. Yet the remains of the
feudal past were used by the ruling bureaucratic class
to relieve social tensions. Institutionalizing social
conflicts meant, on the one hand, accepting the serious-
ness of demands and, on the other, taming autonomous
movements and regulating their currents by means of a
state-ordered river bed.

3. The most powerful institution of long standing
was the Catholic Church. Having survived the liberal
challenge of the 1860s and other dangerous situations,
it had achieved considerable influence, sometimes reaching rather remote parts of the population. Due to its
monopoly position, it had developed an organizational
model with which it was possible to hold Catholics in
line. Because of its success, the church became a
prototype for Social Democracy.

More or less unconsciously, the Austromarxists
learned their lessons from this history and organized
their camp along its lines. Instead of counting on the
dynamics of labor conflicts alone, they made the state
the target of their efforts. They knew that all the
social movements which had not established an institutionalized structure had failed in Austria, for this was
the only way to become accepted by the state bureaucracy
and to survive bad times. An institution was regarded
as a house that was necessary in order to weather the
severe gales of reality. As mentioned above, the church
served as the historical example of how to gain and secure legitimacy over a section of the population, and
keep it as long as possible.

Red Vienna came about not by a carefully thought
out scheme but because of the situation of the early
1920s. It was not the first choice of the Austromarxists; it was the only way out of their difficulties.
When the vision of a socialist revolution in a Greater
Germany failed and the historical compromise of 12 November 1918 fell to pieces, only a defensive strategy--
one of organized retreat--remained.

What did this retreat entail? First, securing
positions which were available according to the constitution on the city councils of industrial provincial
towns and in both the city and Land of Vienna, and then
using those positions to create socialist islands in a
capitalist sea. It can also be shown that the threat of
defeat led to the improvement and extension of the par-

ty's educational and cultural programs--retreat more
than attack requires loyalty. And as unity became the
number one goal of the party, a move to the left was
inevitable, at least rhetorically, in order to prevent a
schism. Meanwhile, such areas as industrial relations,
in which the party had been undecided as to its position, were treated defensively, since the Social Democrats lacked appropriate answers to the technological
challenges of the 1920s and 1930s--for example, to the
introduction of new machinery, including conveyor belts.
In summary, the Social Democratic Party was capable of
preventing a disaster from emerging out of defeat. It
was the historic contribution of Austrian Marxists to
have handled the situation to their own advantage,
making a virtue out of necessity.

If we separate the making of Red Vienna--which
includes not only municipal activities but also the
concept of Neuer Mensch (new man)--from this background,
we have to ask who organized the retreat? Who were the
Austrian Marxist leaders? The fact that they were
intellectuals, and not always of proletarian origin, is
not the point. We have to ask why the party rank and
file admired the leaders, why they had legitimacy. As
Tom Bottomore pointed out in his book[1], the significance of Austrian Marxists lies in their educational
approach. Party leaders were accepted because they
explained and interpreted reality to the rank and file.
The leadership of the Austromarxists was rooted not only
in charisma or functionalism, but also in educational
authority, as is illustrated by the fact that Otto Bauer
was treated as the real leader of the party, rather than
the elected leader, Karl Seitz. Philosophy or science--
or whatever you may call it--constituted the core of
Austromarxism and thus of Red Vienna. Although the party organization provided ample facilities for the acquisition of this knowledge, the process of reaching theoretical conclusions was guided by a rather elitist conceptions. We can compare the socialist island of Red
Vienna with Francis Bacon's vision of a New Atlantis,
for both share at least one central institution: Knowledge. Indeed, the Austromarxist theoreticians are
worthy of Solomon's House of New Atlantis.

EVALUATION OF RED VIENNA

Although the result of retreat rather than of strategically planned action, Red Vienna filled gaps which
the conservative camp could not bridge. But it also
promoted the process of fragmentation in Austrian political culture, for the central power which had been
seized by the ruling bourgeois parties found its antithesis in the concept of Red Vienna. Of course, the

socialist antithesis did not provide a totally different
type of political culture or an nonAustrian culture. It
was built on a historical foundation which included
confidence in the possibilities of state machinery (and
not only on the federal level), a tendency to institu-
tionalize social and cultural interests, and the concentration of these institutions in a church-like party
organization. Nevertheless, in ideological terms, Social Democracy stood in sharp contradiction to the official culture for it had adapted Marxism to Austrian soil
and reactivated the streams of oppositional culture
which had emerged from 1848 and from progressive bourgeois culture.

Relatively speaking, the concept of Red Vienna
proved to be the most successful model in overcoming the
crisis of European socialism after World War I. Yet its
vigor was also its weakness. Building a camp also meant
establishing discipline. As long as this discipline was
secure there was no way to defeat the party; however, as
soon as there were signs of weakness--as on 15 July
1927--the other major camp started to challenge Social
Democracy. The events of 1927, which have been clearly
analyzed by Körner, show that the rank and file were not
capable of reacting autonomously without their leaders'
commands. When the situation became serious the party
revealed itself to be a paper tiger. As Körner has
pointed out, the individual partisan lacked the ability
to react on the basis of an autonomous judgment of the
situation, and there was no linkage between the different spheres of working-class life, since the Schutzbund
was very separate from the trade unions.[2] Both disad-
vantages were caused by the concept underlying Red
Vienna. The entire policy of the party was based on
housing programs, rent restrictions, the creation of
leisure facilities, etc.--in short, on the sphere of
reproduction. Private property was challenged mainly
through rent restrictions, and not as successfully
through social legislation. In the period 1920-1933
party membership increased, chiefly in Vienna, but trade
union membership dropped by half. And in February 1934
it was precisely the lack of union support that brought
the fighting to an early end. In many places the
Schutzbund members gave up the fight when they saw the
scheduled trains running.

I have used the terms "Red Vienna," and "Austromarxists" or "Social Democracy" without any distinction,
considering this legitimate given the historical real-
ity--and herein lies another weakness of Austromarxism.
It was mainly a Vienna-based phenomenon. What this implied can again be said with figures: apart from the
special case of Burgenland, only the Viennese party organization could increase its membership. The rising
fascist movement in the agrarian provinces did not meet

enough opposition to stop it from destroying democracy.
     Nevertheless, despite these criticisms, there is no
doubt in my mind that Red Vienna is one of the very few
phenomena in the history of the First Republic of which
democrats in contemporary Austria need not be ashamed.
Although in the long run Red Vienna was doomed to fail
due to the European political and economic crisis of the
1920s and 1930s, it had produced a model, and so could
perish in dignity. Even if what the Austromarxists had
tried to accomplish was to square the circle, utopia
seems to me to be a more humane choice than apathy.
Like many other utopian schemes, it conceived of itself
as an island--islands always attract people. To come
back to the point where I started, "in Zeiten wie die-
sen" it seems to me that it is rather dangerous to look
on Red Vienna only with nostalgia, because to do this
now means simply to escape from reality.

                              NOTES

     1. Tom Bottomore, "Introduction," in Tom Bottomore
and Patrick Goode, eds., Austro-Marxism (Oxford, 1978),
p. 3.

     2. For Körner's assessment, see Eric C. Kollman,
Theodor Körner: Militär und Politik (Munich, 1973), pp.
166-174.

19. The Housing Policy of Social Democracy: Determinants and Consequences

Peter Marcuse

The widely accepted evaluation of Vienna's housing programs under the Social Democrats is typified by A. J. P. Taylor's summary:

> ...in the...years [after 1922], an ambitious program of working-class housing, health schemes and adult education was carried out, giving "Red Vienna" a unique reputation in Europe. These schemes were financed principally by heavy taxes on property in Vienna, which virtually eliminated private income from house rents. House owners and middle-class tenants thus provided the means by which the slums of Vienna were abolished.[1]

Is this description accurate? Why did housing programs play such a central role in the program of the Austrian Social Democrats after World War I, a role unique both in Austrian history and the history of socialism? What were their real accomplishments? Were "the slums of Vienna" really "abolished"? If so, how was this possible? If not, why is Vienna's housing program so widely heralded? This paper addresses itself to these questions.

The discussion will begin with a brief summary of housing conditions in Vienna at the close of World War I, and the history of Austrian socialist positions with regard to housing up to that point. After a very brief summary of what the housing programs actually were and what they did,[2] the paper attempts an explanation of why housing became such a central theme in Viennese politics, and why the Social Democratic government of the city was able to proceed as far as it did in the area. The paper concludes by posing some difficult evaluative questions about Red Vienna's housing accomplishments placed in comparative perspective and suggests some tentative answers.

HOUSING AND POLITICS AFTER WORLD WAR I

Housing was in crisis in what was left of the Austro-Hungarian Empire after World War I. The war had
aggravated, but not caused, the crisis. A housing
shortage existed long before the beginning of the war
and was rather the result of the emergence of capitalism
and industrialization. Philippovich's classic study of
housing in Vienna in 1894 reads much like Engels' description of Manchester in 1845, or Booth's of London in
1889 or Jacob Riis' of New York in 1890.

> ...dark cellar rooms with water-covered walls;
> toilets used by 120 persons, habitations which...
> were scarcely adequate as stalls for domestic ani-
> mals,....The [more] typical apartment of a Viennese
> worker...consisted usually of one room and a kitch-
> en. Opening on a narrow gangway on each floor of
> the court side of the house were ten, fifteen,
> sometimes more, kitchen doors; thus the kitchens
> usually lacked any direct light. From the kitchen
> a door led to a room of about 150-180 square feet.
> Usually two, seldom more, of these apartments per
> floor had an additional narrow room with only one
> window, called in Vienna a Kabinett....Along the
> gangway were a few toilets, each of them used by
> the occupants of two or more apartments. There was
> one water faucet for the common use of all tenants
> of a floor.[3]

Rents were high, taking over 25 percent of a typical worker's wages, and sometimes higher, measured on a
per square foot basis, than for luxury dwellings. [4]
In 1912 according to one estimate, up to 550,000 persons
(one quarter of the population of the city) were at one
time or another in a temporary shelter for the homeless.[5]
The war accentuated the housing crisis and provided
an entirely different political context. There was, of
course, virtually no new housing built in Vienna during
the war: 342 units were built in 1917 compared to an
average of 13,051 per year in the years before the
war.[6] While the population of Vienna shrank slightly
during the war, with residents leaving for army and
government service out of the city, the number of households did not diminish appreciably and other workers
came to the capital because of the expanded needs of the
war. The absolute number of housing units in fact
declined in significant part because of the conversion
of residential units to office use for war- and busi-
ness-related purposes. By 1918 the vacancy rate was
practically zero--the best estimate is that at the
beginning of that year only 254 units were empty and

available for occupancy in the whole city, and in September 1919 only 105 were available and they were not fit for occupancy.[7] The resulting overcrowding is hard to imagine: single-room apartments housed parents, children, grandparents, and often married children with their families, and frequently space was let, not only to subtenants, but also to day lodgers, so that beds might be occupied in shifts by different persons.[8]

Already in January 1917 the Emperor had to impose rent restrictions because the "continued eviction of the families of soldiers might develop into a dangerous situation as well as impair the fighting power of the army." As was pointed out by a Christian Social (Conservative) member of Parliament, if "the prohibition against giving notice had not been introduced...there would have been social disturbances."[9] Two subsequent decrees, still under the monarchy, extended the coverage of controls, prohibited key payments (under the table money passed to get an apartment) and conversions to non-residential uses, and required registration of vacant dwellings. Imperial wartime measures were to bear a close relationship to later ones based on a quite different political philosophy.

The end of the war led to an even worse housing shortage. Returning soldiers and refugees from the former provinces of the Austro-Hungarian Empire swelled the ranks of those seeking shelter in the capital. Family formation, inhibited during the war, shot up, but at the same time the resources necessary for a significant construction program were depleted. The housing crisis deepened.

The factors which led to the particular role of the Social Democrats within the broader context of the times have been well described elsewhere. As Anson Rabinbach summarizes:

> The Socialists emerged as the caretakers of the new Republic because of their unique ability to deal with the returning soldiers, unemployed workers, and radical crowds that voiced revolutionary demands and drew sustenance from the Russian revolution.[10]

It is clear that the Social Democrats, despite their commitment in theory to major social change, saw their role in Austria rather as the stabilization of the new (and still clearly nonsocialist) status quo. The local programs of the Social Democrats in Vienna may only be understood in this context.

> The tasks of the new Socialist administrators of Vienna were to aid the national coalition government (which their party colleagues dominated) in

avoiding a Communist revolution, to reorganize a
practically bankrupt city, and then to rebuild that
city in the literal and the figurative meanings.[11]

For the Social Democrats, "rebuilding the city" meant
first and foremost dealing with its housing problems.
For the conservatives, by the same token, "the substitu-
tion of social policy for social revolution seemed a
small price to pay for maintaining the economic and
social status quo."[12]

THE SOCIAL DEMOCRATIC APPROACH TO HOUSING

With hindsight, the innovative, aggressive, and
widely-heralded housing policies might be viewed as part
of a coherent, explicit, and well-developed theory of
how the housing problem ought to be approached. It was,
in fact, no such thing. Social Democratic theory before
1918 was, if anything, a hindrance to the establishment
of a coherent socialist housing policy.

That theory did not lead to the Viennese initiatives in housing or to the central role housing played
in the Social Democratic Party's overall political
strategy can be seen by a brief look at the theoretical
treatment of housing prior to 1918. In 1872 Engels had
attacked the housing reform proposals of Proudhon and
Sax in which landlord-tenant conflicts were analogized
to shopkeeper-customer, not class, conflict. Socialism
was put forward by Engels as a prerequisite to solving
the housing problem. Consequently, from at least 1872
mainstream Marxists--reformers as well as revolution-
aries--had paid little attention to immediate housing
issues. "Only socialism will dispose of housing misery"
was a phrase still much in use within the Social Democratic Party in Austria well after 1918. To the extent
that the Austrian party had a theoretical position on
housing it was in the revolutionary tradition: housing
comes later.

Yet when the party's actual housing programs were
discussed in general terms after 1918 the approach of
these discussions was hardly very radical by traditional
Marxist standards. Brod's early pamphlet on the housing
question, published under the auspices of the Social
Democratic Party, praised the housing policies of England and Germany (adopted under Conservative and mon-
archic governments, respectively) and assumed public
action within the framework of a private market housing
system. [13] Otto Bauer's first programmatic comments
on the issues, made in 1919, were a somewhat inconsistent collection of policy recommendations. On the one
hand they suggested that rents for small apartments be

set so as to cover only maintenance and administration
(i.e., with no return to capital at all, which practically constitutes expropriation). But on the other hand
Bauer's comments suggested that land or buildings only
be expropriated with full compensation, "naturally."[14]
Expropriation would be undertaken only where advanta-
geous, primarily in areas of growth. The federal role
was only to provide appropriate powers to municipalities, and the "right to a dwelling" which Bauer saw as
a necessary part of any socialist program--but in the
context of a continuing private market in housing, with
ownership rights legally respected.

In today's terms, the Austrian Social Democratic
Party prior to 1918 was "work place oriented" in both
theory and practice. Gulick recounts only two prior
actions of party affiliates relating to housing, one a
resolution at a conference of workers' sickness funds in
1904, the other a motion at a city council meeting in
1911 that dealt with housing. Its shift to essentially
"consumption-oriented" issues, housing prominent among
them, came as an adaptation to its post-1918 situation,
and, while radical within a traditional capitalist context, was hardly at the revolutionary edge of socialist
theory.[15]

THE IMMEDIATE POLITICAL AND ECONOMIC SETTING

The pressures that impelled the Austrian Social
Democratic Party to make housing a central concern of
its program came from three sources: the impact of the
housing situation on the party's natural constituency,
the direct extraparliamentary demands of the ill-housed,
and the electoral situation. The extent of the housing
shortage--the "housing misery"--that afflicted Vienna at
the end of the war has been described above. It was the
subject of constant discussion in the press and dominated everyday life for many. Of course, it dispropor-
tionately affected Social Democratic Party members and
their natural constituency which was overwhelmingly
tenant. Even before the party developed its own active
program for housing construction, its energetic espousal
and promotion of rent control and requisitioning policies provides evidence of its sensitivity to the critical role that the housing shortage played in the lives
of its natural constituency. It simply had no choice in
the matter; anything of such immediate and major concern
to its constituency had to be dealt with by the party.

Those in need of housing did not wait until leadership initiatives or electoral results pushed the governing party of the city of Vienna to take action on housing. They expressed their demands directly, concretely,
and with increasing militance. Massive demonstrations

in front of city hall by the ill-housed, self-help initiatives by large numbers of families who squatted on
empty land in the green belt surrounding Vienna, and
constant pressure at public meetings and from veterans'
groups, reinforced the critical nature of the housing
issue.

The electoral situation confirmed the Social Democrats in their decision to make housing a central and
long-term theme of their policy. Neither the Social
Democrats nor their conservative opposition, the Christian Social Party, initially gauged the electoral reactions to the housing crisis properly. Victims of their
own very different ideologies, both were inclined to
underestimate it. The right believed that the sanctity
of private property would appeal even to those suffering
from its adverse consequences in their day-to-day lives;
the left at first believed that traditional work place
issues and the appeal of socialism as a goal were the
best bases on which they could increase their vote. But
election result after election result showed the Social
Democratic Party that they had a winning issue in a
strong protenant stand on housing. When the right
finally chose to make rent control a major issue in the
national electoral campaign of 1923, it helped contribute to the largest vote for the Social Democrats to
that date.[16] So central did housing issues become to
the party that it was a joke of the times that it should
change its name from Social Democratic Party to Tenants'
Party. Had the Social Democrats no other reason to see
housing reform as a main strategic goal, simple electoral opportunism would have pushed them in this direction.

Thus the choice of housing as an issue was dictated
to the Social Democratic Party by the direct interests
of its own constituency, the pressures of those most
affected by the housing crisis, and the obvious popularity of the issue with the voters to whom the party
looked for support. The direction of its actions was
likewise dictated to it, in this case by the economic
and political situation in which Vienna found itself.

The inflation that was rampant throughout central
Europe immediately after the war set the immediate context for the early actions of the Viennese council. The
council had to deal immediately with events in the private housing market; programs of new construction did
not seem conceivable under the circumstances. The inflation had two asymmetrical effects on housing. For
landlords and property owners, mortgages and other debts
were effectively wiped out: with an inflation rate to-
talling around 10,000 percent over the four-year period,
a debt of 10,000 schillings could be paid off in 1923
with paper having a real value of only one prewar schil-
ling.[17] Since mortgages covered an estimated two-

thirds of the value of Vienna housing[18], property owners in effect found the value of their property tripled by inflation. For tenants, their real rents, if held to the levels of 1914, would be reduced to virtually zero. Inflation thus provided direct benefits to both landlords and tenants and mitigated the sharp level of conflict that the early rent regulation and requisitioning policies of the Vienna council had produced. It is to a brief summary of these policies that we now turn.

THE HOUSING PROGRAMS AND THEIR RESULTS

The story of Viennese housing policy between 1918 and 1934, in the period of Social Democratic control of the city, may be summarized under three headings, which also roughly parallel the order of evolution of the programs.

1. There was control over the private housing market. For example, rent and eviction controls fixed rents under a formula which based returns to landlords on prewar rents not adjusted for inflation (thus virtually nil), plus costs of operation, maintenance, and taxes. In addition, private housing that had been determined to be underutilized or unnecessarily vacant was requisitioned and reallocated according to a complex but objective formula in which housing need was the main component.

2. There was city support for self-help activities. Squatters in the green belt around Vienna--the so-called "wild settlements"--were awarded legal status and provided with architectural services, materials, transportation, and utilities. The city also supported the cooperative housing activities which developed out of and parallel to the squatters' movement and were based largely on guild socialist ideas. Title and control of housing built with public resources was transferred by the city to the cooperatives. Garden-city type developments were also built and assistance in construction and financing was provided, permitting individual ownership of units in some of the developments, although on a quite limited basis.

3. There was direct municipal construction and ownership of housing. A tax on housing occupancy, strikingly progressive in its rates and impact, was earmarked entirely for housing construction, and new construction of social housing was paid for in full (without borrowing) out of the proceeds of this housing occupancy tax. Much of the construction took the form of large Höfe built around inner courtyards and provided with extensive community facilities. Public land banking bought up land ahead of need, on a large scale and at reduced

cost in the absence of a viable private market. Public
enterprises established by the city itself, in some
cases with the direct involvement of the construction
unions and consumers, provided building materials and
construction services.

What were the results of these programs? The city
built over 60,000 units of housing over a period of less
than ten years. All of its housing construction was
fully paid for out of current revenues derived primarily
from a steeply progressive, productive, and stable tax,
levied within the housing system itself and earmarked
solely for housing use. Rents both in municipally owned
and private housing were kept very low, amounting to
less than 5 percent of income for most workers. ecuri-
ty of occupancy was given in all accommodations, public
and private. Social services and community facilities--
in short, the infrastructure of neighborhood life--were
all built into the planning and construction process
from the outset and were provided at a very high level
of quality and quantity. Special attention was given to
the situation of women within the typical working person's family and efforts were made to rationalize housework and provide collective facilities to relieve individual work. Architectural design and planning arrangements were thoughtful, innovative, and very highly regarded throughout Europe, and the cooperative, collective, and self-help involvement of residents was pioneering and attracted international interest [18].

These accomplishments were hailed all over the
world. Both their direct beneficiaries and the international housing community--architects, planners, housing theorists, political leaders, and sociologists--saw
these housing programs as one of the most promising
social phenomena of the times, indeed as evidence that
Red Vienna might be a harbinger of a better world.
Building for a new humanity was seen as the essence of
what was happening; WITH US, A NEW AGE ARRIVES ("Mit uns
zieht die Neue Zeit") was the slogan, and the housing
developments of Red Vienna were its symbol. Delegations
came from all over the world to see what the housers of
Vienna had achieved and World Congresses analyzed how it
was done. No one doubted that the housing program would
remain one of Viennese Social Democracy's most enduring
memorials.

Thus the Social Democratic Party, for a period of a
decade and a half, substantially abrogated the private
housing market in Vienna. Not entirely, of course: the
substantially better-off still were able to use their
resources to get better than average housing for themselves, and the expectation of profit, if not its current realization, still dictated the actions of many
private interests in the housing field. But, by and
large, public priorities, not private profit, estab-

lished the policies that dominated housing construction, occupancy, and use. It was almost as if an entire sector of the economy--and a powerful one indeed on the local level--had been removed from the operation of the normal laws of the private market system in the midst of a city, and a nation, that remained, in every important sense, firmly capitalist in its economic structure.

THE DETERMINANTS OF HOUSING POLICY IN VIENNA: THEORETICAL FRAMEWORK

I have tried elsewhere to suggest the framework for a theory of the determinants of housing policy.[19] The theory traces the roots of state housing policies to conflicts among major social and economic groupings, from interest groups to classes.[20] Part (and it is important to remember that it is only a part, and a small one at that) of the way in which the changing outcomes of these conflicts are reflected--and, rarely, resolved--is in policies affecting housing. The issues around which these conflicts center, to the extent that they involve housing policy, might be defined as follows: (a) political power (stability of the political system, hegemony, legitimacy of the established order); (b) profitability in the economy as a whole (national economic prosperity and growth, the long-term accumulation of capital); (c) housing-sector profitability (profit from the construction, financing, ownership, and management of housing); (d) residential use (the individual and collective enjoyment and consumption of housing).

The priority of concerns of the predominant interests in society, are hypothesized as follows: (1) In periods of crisis, and as an underlying long-term thrust, the need for political stability and legitimation will take priority. (2) The maximization of profits in the overall economy--the guarantee of maximum accumulation--will under normal circumstance be the most important general determinant.[21] (3) The maximization of profits within the housing sector, the distribution of profits among its components, and the arrangements for the residential use and enjoyment of housing as a consumption good will, subject to the above priorities, generally determine short-term housing policy.

Using this framework, what factors accounted for Viennese housing policy in the 1920s?

THE HISTORICAL SITUATION IN AUSTRIA

Vienna in 1918 was in the midst of a world in revolution. The tsar had been overthrown in Russia, and a

communist government established. Béla Kun, under the
communist banner, was attempting to establish a revolutionary regime in Hungary. Workers and soldiers councils were seizing--or threatening to seize--power in
many cities in Germany, and the threat existed in Austria as well. With the collapse of the Hapsburg monarchy, the threat of a communist revolution appeared
imminent to most in Austria.

The Social Democratic Party of Austria, long in the
reformist camp of the socialist parties of Europe and an
experienced participant in electoral campaigns, wished a
full-scale revolution as little as did the conservative
successors to the monarchy's powers. They acted accordingly.

> ...[Austrian] social democracy succeeded in the
> critical months from May 1917 to June 1919 in re-
> moving the revolutionary edge from the movement and
> in supporting bourgeois democracy, inclusive of the
> capitalistic economic system. The price which it
> demanded for this conservative position was higher
> than in any other European country outside of Rus-
> sia.[22]

Control over the municipal government in Vienna--includ-
ing the right to establish progressive housing policies
there, and the ability to negotiate with some power at
the national level--was a part of that original price.
Therefore, in the early years of the First Republic, the
Social Democrats were much better able to push through
radical changes in private housing arrangements (requisitioning and tough rent control, for instance), even
though their apparent electoral strength was greater
later.

It was the first determinant of housing policy
suggested above, the stability of the established order
--the top priority in times of crisis--that led to this
initial set of housing policies. Yet in the early 1920s
national economic forces, the second and normally predominant determinant of housing policies, helped create
a favorable position for certain aspects of Social Democratic housing policy. In order to end rampant inflation in Austria and integrate the nation with the economic system of the Allied powers (predominantly the
United States), Austria's conservative national leadership agreed in 1923 to a wide-ranging set of monetary
reforms and received substantial loans from the U.S.
under terms of repayment which were considered onerous
at the time. Partly as a result, Austrian industry was
forced to become heavily export-oriented. Its ability
to be competitive on the international market, in turn,
depended significantly on the level of wages paid workers inside Austria. In the United States in the early

1920s the political and social repression of the Red
Scare and the Palmer Raids was used to keep cash wages
low. But in the Austrian political context at that
time, pressure on militant labor activity was not necessary, given the alternative of cooperation with the
Social Democrats to achieve the same results.

One way of achieving those results--keeping cash
wages low--was housing policy. The impact of rent control has already been discussed; the figures show that
controls lowered the proportion of the average worker's
pay which went to housing from something over 20 percent
before the war to under 5 percent in the 1920s. The direct relationship between housing policy and wage levels, on the one hand, and the competitiveness of the
Austrian economy, on the other, was noted by Gulick, who
came to this conclusion without having drawn any precon-
ceptions from housing theory:

> The real wages of Austrian workers were extremely
> low....This enabled Austrian industry to maintain a
> certain position as exporter on the world market
> ....Austrian industry could successfully compete on
> the world market...only because of the export pre-
> mium industry received in the form of tenants' pro-
> tection. Abolition of tenants' protection would
> have made increases in wages unavoidable...further-
> more, a rise in wages would involve, for some time
> at least, an appreciable increase in a large part
> of the social burdens such as social insurance
> contributions...[23]

In a fascinating footnote, Gulick explores the availability of direct evidence to prove this contention, and
finds it lacking. Indeed, some manufacturers opposed
rent controls vigorously. This Gulick explains in part
by the availability of company-owned (and thus price-
controlled) housing outside of Vienna, in part by the
political and ideological conservatism of some of the
manufacturers. Neither the conceptualization nor the
evidence are conclusive at this point, although before
the war the Chamber of Commerce of Vienna clearly was
directly concerned with ensuring that there was adequate
reasonably priced housing for workers.[24] Kainrath
also supports the hypothesis about the influence of
rents on wages, arguing that the monarchy in 1917 and
the bourgeoisie in 1922 both understood the relevance of
low housing costs to low wages. The city of Vienna made
the same point in defense of its policies in 1929, Kainrath observes.[25]

Friedrich Hayek, who attacked rent control from an
ultra-conservative viewpoint in 1930 in Vienna, seems to
take a different point of view, but in fact also supports the hypothesis. He contends that rent controls

may force up wages because they reduce living costs
during the period of a strike and thus encourage militancy. Whatever the merits of that argument, he con-
cedes that lifting rent controls would increase the
pressure on wages. Hayek directs his argument against
"the generally accepted view that rent controls help to
keep production costs down."[26] He thus supports the
point made here that the desire to hold wages down was a
major factor permitting rent controls in Austria.
Robert Danneberg, too, indirectly corroborates it: he
suggests there was only limited new construction because
in Vienna "ordinary incomes are determined by such factors as the lowness of rents."[27] As was pointed out
earlier, the Nazis in Germany adopted rent controls for
a similar purpose. Another way to think of the relationship between wage demands and rents is to consider
it as part of a general Social Democratic shift in
strategy from direct confrontation at the factory to
political combat at the polls and in the legisla-
ture.[28]

Because of these critical aspects of the political
and economic situation, the lesser and more parochial
interests of the housing industry had to play a more
subordinate role, at least temporarily. In a crisis,
real estate interests are expendable. (Certainly the
limitation of their interests is negotiable.) It was
Lord Keynes, after all, and not Karl Marx who spoke of
the "euthanasia of the rentier."[29] Social Democracy
in Austria was able to seize on the vulnerability of the
real estate industry under particular historical circumstances to forge a housing program at the progressive
edge of anything that was seen up to that time and perhaps even up to the present.

In summary, the two major factors which permitted
the Social Democratic housing policy to go as far as it
did in Vienna were the threat of political instability
and the concern of export-oriented economic interests
with reducing the pressure on wages. Both of these
vanished at the end of the decade. The threat of basic
political change ended with the failure of the 1927
general strike, while the possibility of normal profits
from export was cut short by the international economic
crisis. With them went that balance of forces that
permitted the programs of Red Vienna. Thus those programs came to an abrupt and ultimately bloody end.

COMPARATIVE PERSPECTIVE

Yet there is a puzzle in the story about housing
which we have recounted. The picture presented has
internal coherence, but on comparative examination the
conclusions about the achievements of Viennese housing

policy appear strange. For, if the truth be told, while each of the individual accomplishments is remarkable, none is unique, none is without its critics, and none could not, individually, find its parallel in other countries. As an example: the volume of housing construction was substantial, but it was not more substantial (proportionately) than that of the city of Frankfurt in an even shorter time, and it was substantially less than that of the United States in the same time period. In terms of the percent of the housing stock built in the years shown, the figures are:[30]

TABLE 19.1
Percentage of housing stock built

	U.S.	Frankfurt	Vienna
1926-1930	18%	11%	5%
1924-1933	28%		11%
1931-1940	11%		

To interpret these figures, a number of other factors must of course be taken into account: the relative prosperity of the countries involved (Austria's lower per capita national income, which even today is only two-thirds of that of the U.S.); prices paid for housing; the economic difficulties faced by Austria in the 1920s, which were much more akin to the 1930s in the U.S. than to the 1920s (a comparison with the U.S. in the 1930s shows much greater equality of production). U.S. population growth was substantially greater, so that the improvement in units per household might show much less of a difference than the proportional numbers built. Yet the situation in Frankfurt was probably closer than that of most U.S. towns to the situation in Vienna. In any event, no one at the time, and certainly not the residents of the new developments, doubted that Vienna's achievement was a giant step forward, in comparison to elsewhere.

And there is another example of the gap between the general commendation and the objective fact. According to a few sceptics, the municipal developments had entirely inadequate interior space, were badly located in terms of transportation, of inferior and unimaginative design, and technologically backward in their architecture and construction. Defenders referred to limited resources, to differences in taste, and to differences in social philosophy, e.g., the positive preference for providing amenities communally rather than privately. But that the units were small--almost tiny--even by contemporary standards is hard to deny. In the first municipal building program adopted in 1923 only two sizes of units were provided: one of 38 square meters (about 414 square feet), the other with 48 square meters (about 520 square feet). With the new building program adopted in 1926 a larger unit of 57 square meters (about 630 square feet) was also provided, but this was the maximum amount of space available even for the largest of families. In the earlier units, the kitchen also generally served as living room; after 1926 kitchens were deliberately made smaller as a result of the desire to rationalize housework. Private baths were not provided; the minimum kitchen facilities were only a water faucet and a gas cooking stove (or plate).[31]

This then is the puzzle: neither the absolute quantity nor even the physical quality of housing in Vienna in the period in question came anywhere near to justifying the near-euphoria pervading the citizenry about the city's housing accomplishments. That euphoria is all the more remarkable given the fact that, even in Vienna itself, the level of housing construction in the years immediately preceding the war was more than twice as high as the average for the best years of the Social Democratic administration. The idea of comparative improvement does not hold in absolute numbers. Certainly A. J. P. Taylor's comment that "the slums of Vienna were abolished" is an overstatement. At its party congress in 1928 the Social Democratic leadership admitted frankly that they had been unable to overcome the housing shortage in Vienna. Danneberg publicly acknowledged dissatisfaction with the building rate by pointing out that it only served 40 percent of new marriages in the 1920s, compared to 50 percent before the war. The large majority of Viennese workers lived in older and overcrowded housing, primarily the Zinskasernen (literally, "rental barracks") before, during, and after the Social Democratic administration of Vienna.[32]

EVALUATION: THE PERMANENT CONTRIBUTION

Given these real limitations, the glowing tributes paid to Red Vienna's housing appear to be something of a puzzle. But perhaps that is because we misjudge (as contemporary participants also misjudged) the nature of the contribution that was made to the residential life of the majority of Viennese. The real contribution of Red Vienna's housing policies lies, I believe, in an aspect of housing policy which it is difficult to name--

in part because it is so rarely considered a "real" aspect of housing. Of the accepted terms used in housing
policy, perhaps "fairness" or "equity" are closest.
"Symbolic" might also be appropriate, except that it
suggests appearance rather than reality, and this aspect
of housing was a very real part of a real social rear-
rangement which worked to the benefit of working people
in Vienna. "Democratic" might be the best word, if it
is clear that substantive democracy, not merely a set of
formal procedures, is meant. It was what the city's
housing policy said to the people of Vienna about their
own lives, their roles in society, the respect to which
they were entitled, the importance of their welfare, and
their ultimate control over the conditions of their
lives that made the difference--even if at that particular time they could not provide for themselves that
ultimate level of housing which they wanted and which
they believed they would ultimately obtain.

Several examples illustrate the point. The first
is price. For the average Viennese worker, the figures
given above suggest that rent constituted less than 5
percent of income in 1928. The roughly comparable U.S.
figure in 1929 was 26.1 percent.[33] If the quantity
and quality of housing available to the average Viennese
was substantially less than that available to his or her
U.S. counterpart, the amount paid was far less. And the
reason seemed clear: a general shortage, not the fact
that someone was making an undue profit or holding back
on supply until a profit could be made. One person's
hardship was not another person's gain.

A second example involves the allocation of housing. In Vienna, virtually all housing constructed during the period in question was publicly built. Both
this new housing and much of the older housing coming
vacant was allocated on a publicly established point
system based on current conceptions of need. A low
income, to the extent it was relevant, might well lead
to priority in assignment, since it would generally
correspond to housing need. Furthermore, rent controls
guaranteed that there would be no regressive reshuffling
of occupancy in existing housing by income. In the U.S.
during the same period, by contrast, there was no publicly built housing whatsoever and only a trifling
amount was publicly assisted in any way. Both in existing and in newly built housing, the ability to pay--
income and wealth--determined occupancy patterns, the
best off receiving the best housing, the worst off the
worst. It might be expected that the Social Democratic
system of Vienna in the 1920s would strike those affected by it as vastly fairer than the U.S. system at the
corresponding time, even if statistically the U.S. system provided physically superior housing.

The collective features of Viennese housing policy

216

provide another example of its equitable and democratic
character. Community facilities, libraries, schools,
health centers, meeting halls, and recreation spaces
were provided as part of a comprehensive and long-range
housing program. Its stated aim was to help achieve a
good and fruitful life for all people. Thus current
facilities could be taken as an indicator of the overall
goals of society and government and also as an indicator
of the value attached to each individual, regardless of
birth or wealth, and perhaps to the value attached to
working people in particular.

It is also significant that these aspects of housing were not granted by the state as the result of a
top-down choice. Vienna's housing policies had been
fought for from the bottom in election campaigns, in
street demonstrations, in organizations and in every
aspect of daily life, sometimes against the city government's own immediate wishes. It was consistent with
this reality that the workers who lived in Vienna's
proud new projects felt that they were theirs, built by
them, fought for by them, and worth defending by whatever means were at their command. Vienna's housing
policies were part of a whole political and social program, and not a product of technical sophistication or
benevolent government.[34]

Perhaps the real achievement of Social Democratic
housing policy in Vienna during the 1920s is the improvement of housing as part of the total social life of
the individual, including political life in the broadest
sense of the term. What was involved was not only the
improvement of the physical quality of the private dwelling, but, perhaps even more important, political control over its shape and use, and the consequent social
improvement in the quality of residential life. Residential life was affected in terms of the price paid for
it, the distribution of its benefits, the control of its
direction, the provision of neighborhood facilities and
services necessary for its enjoyment, and the collective
and community-building nature of that enjoyment. These
were what made Viennese housing policy a great achievement in the eyes of participants.

Yet even from this perspective, there were limitations. The policies of rent control, of the construction of large developments, and of the allocation of
private rented housing on the basis of need, had nothing
to offer homeowners, whether rich, middle-class, or
poor--and there were, indeed, many poor homeowners in
the countryside all around Vienna.[35] This limitation
had serious political consequences; if the Social Democratic Party could be labeled the Tenants' Party of
Vienna, this was both a strength and a weakness. Homeowners represented a fertile area for recruitment by the
forces opposed to democracy in Austria. To what extent

a different housing policy might have retarded this development is an open question, for it was not tried.

The impact of Vienna's housing policies on women is as yet too little explored, but the indications are that they were quite different from the impact on the average man. The very recent discussion by Pirhofer and Seidel on this issue is provocative; relying largely on current interviews with women who lived in the municipal developments in the 1920s, Pirhofer and Seidel conclude that the petit bourgeois family among workers' households was in fact reinforced by the city's housing policies: the father's patriarchal role was reinforced; women were less employed outside the house (because extended-family child care was less possible); the day-to-day management (of the collective laundries, for instance) remained in the hands of men, with conventional sexist results. It may well be that the contribution of municipal housing was in direct proportion to the nonhousing-based social, economic, and political position of the individual, with politically active men being at one end of the spectrum and isolated women with small children at the other end.

To complete the list of major shortcomings presented above, then, we would have to add that there were substantial limitations in physical quantity and quality in the municipal construction program; that homeowners obtained no direct benefits from housing policies; and that women were less positively affected than men, and major changes in the structure of family life were not accomplished. But we would also have to note the accomplishments, such as the fact that equity and fairness in the housing system as a whole--in allocation, rent levels, security of tenure, and taxation--were accepted by virtually the entire population. In addition, housing contributed to a sense of dignity and of the democratic nature of the society as a whole for workers and poor people, thereby reversing the previous pattern of housing as a badge of inferior political, social and economic status.

An evaluation of Red Vienna's housing policies must report shortcomings as well as accomplishments. Some of the shortcomings are more evident with hindsight than they could have been then. For example, issues related to the status of women and the role of the family are more apparent and better understood today. Furthermore, the importance of dealing with the desire for home ownership is a lesson learned from painful experience over the last decades. Other shortcomings, such as those of physical quality and quantity, are more relative, and far outweighed by what were then perceived to be more important factors.

The successes of the Social Democratic housing policies in Vienna in the 1920s, then, lay as much in their social as in their physical character, and as much

in the totality of the approach they represented as in
their individual components. Tax policy, planning, ·
architecture, construction, administration, control of
the private market, collective and cooperative facilities, and housing-based political and social organization all played key roles. Housing was not seen as
shelter alone, but rather as part of an overall reconstruction of life around goals of human dignity and
public responsibility. There was pride in Red Vienna's
improvement of the physical quality of the city's housing because this accomplishment was seen not as an end
in itself but as the beginning of an effort to build a
better, fairer, more democratic life.

NOTES

1. Encyclopedia Britannica, Vol. 2 (1959), p. 747.
Underlining added.

2. A fuller description is provided in Peter
Marcuse, "A Useful Installment of Socialist Work," in
Rachel Bratt, Chester Hartman and Ann Meyerson, eds.,
Critical Perspectives on Housing, forthcoming from
Temple Univ. Press.

3. Eugen von Philippovich, "Wiener Wohnungsverhält-
nisse," Archiv für Soziale Gesetzgebung und Statistik,
Vol. 7 (1894), p. 40, quoted in Charles A. Gulick,
Austria: From Habsburg to Hitler (Berkeley, 1948), p.
409.

4. Philippovich, "Wiener," p. 239, quoted in
Gulick, p. 411.

5. Wilhelm Kainrath, "Die gesellschaftspolitische
Bedeutung des kommunalen Wohnbaus im Wien der Zwischen-
kriegszeit," in City of Vienna, Kommunaler Wohnungsbau
in Wien (Vienna, 1978), p. 1.

6. C. O. Hardy, The Housing Program of the City of
Vienna, (Washington, D.C., 1934), p. 42.

7. Ibid., p. 46. Gulick refers to a slightly higher estimate for Dec. 1918, 315 units, and calculates the
vacancy rate at .056% (5% being generally taken as "normal"). Gulick, Austria, p. 428.

8. Gottfried Pirhofer and Reinhard Sieder, "Zur
Konstitution der Arbeiterfamilie im Roten Wien: Familienpolitik, Kulturreform, Alltag und Ästhetik," in

Michael Mitterauer and Reinhard Sieder, Historische
Familienforschung (Frankfurt, 1982), p. 352.

9. Gulick, Austria, p. 423.

10. Otto Bauer, Der Weg zum Sozialismus (Vienna,
1919), p. 95, quoted in Anson Rabinbach, The Crisis of
Austrian Socialism: From Red Vienna to Civil War, 1927-
1934 (Chicago, 1983), p. 20.

11. Gulick, Austria, p. 356.

12. Rabinbach, The Crisis, p. 24.

13. J. Brod, Die Wohnungsnot und ihre Bekämpfung
(Vienna, 1919), Pt. I, pp. 4 and 8; see Gulick, Austria,
p. 430.

14. Bauer, Der Weg, pp. 22-24. Bauer later (in
1921) referred to these comments as having been "thrown
together in haste," but did not change them. Gulick,
Austria, pp. 437-8.

15. Gulick, Austria, p. 436. Housing is not only a
"consumption" issue, and consumption, production, and
reproduction of the labor force are initially related.
For a fuller discussion, see Peter Marcuse, "The Determinants of Housing Policy," Columbia Univ., Division of
Urban Planning, Papers in Planning 21a, 1980. In the
context of Austrian politics, however, consumption
issues predominated.

16. The account by Gulick is both detailed and
accurate; see Gulick, Austria, especially Chapter XIV.
He considers the choice of campaign issues to have been
one of the few major blunders of the shrewd leader of
the Christian Social Party, Ignatz Seipel.

17. Paper crowns (the basic unit of currency) were
stabilized at 14,400 to 11 (pre-war) gold crowns. The
general cost of living did not keep pace with the inflation; Gulick gives a figure of 9,601 for the cost of
living index in February 1923, with 1914=1. See Gulick,
Austria, pp. 442-3.

18. The additional aspects necessary to complete
the picture are listed at the end of this paper.

19. See Peter Marcuse, "The Determinants of State
Housing Policies: West Germany and the United States,"
in Norman and Susan Fainstein, eds., Urban Policy Under
Capitalism (Beverly Hills, 1982) and, for an earlier and
more tentative but fuller discussion, Marcuse, "The

Determinants." See also Emily Achtenberg and Peter
Marcuse, "Toward the Decommodification of Housing" in
Chester Hartman, ed., America's Housing Crisis: What Is
To Be Done (Boston, 1983).

20. The word is used here synonymously with "frac-
tions" in Marxist terminology.

21. Here are included most considerations of macro-
economic policy, as well as arrangements for what Marxists call, in a phrase jarringly inconsistent with
every-day usage, the "reproduction of the labor force."

22. Kainrath, "Die gesellschaftspolitische." My
translation is from the German. The statement, which
reflects what is by now a prevailing understanding of
the period, was written by an active participant in the
present Social Democratic Party in Vienna and published
in its official catalogue of housing in that city.

23. Gulick, Austria, pp. 483-4.

24. Felix Czeike, "Wiener Wohnbau vom Vormärz bis
1923" in City of Vienna, Kommunaler Wohnungsbau in Wien
(Vienna, 1978), fn. 9.

25. Kainrath, "Die gesellschaftspolitsche."

26. Friedrich A. Hayek, "Austria: The Repercussions
of Rent Restrictions," in F. A. Hayek, Milton Friedman,
et al., Rent Control: A Popular Paradox (Vancouver,
1975), p. 76. This article by Hayek was adapted from an
article by him in Schriften des Vereins für Sozialpoli-
tik, 182 (1930).

27. Robert Danneberg, Zehn Jahre neues Wien
(Vienna, 1929),p. 59.

28. Mary Nolan describes a similar process in Germany during the same period: "The Social Democrats
attempted to redress the loss of power on the shop floor
and in the labor market by political means, by reliance
on the state and a center-right government in which they
did not participate. They sought social welfare reforms
in return for their economic concessions...." See Mary
Nolan, "Capital, Labor and the State: The Politics of
Rationalization in the Weimar Republic," paper delivered
at Davis Center Seminar, 22 January 1982, p. 5.

29. Although Marx would also agree: "Landed property is different from other types of property in that,
at a given level of development, it appears as superfluous and harmful even from the standpoint of the capi-

talist mode of production." See Karl Marx, Das Kapital, (Chicago, 1909), Vol. 3, p. 635.

30. Figures are inclusive of the years shown. Vienna figures are from Gulick, Austria, pp. 450 and 457; there is a slight discrepancy between the figures given for housing construction by the city by year, and the total owned by it at the end of the period, but it is of an order of magnitude that does not affect the picture presented. U.S. figures are from Historical Statistics of the United States, 1975, pp. 639-40. The Frankfurt figure is from Ferdinand and Lore Kramer, "Sozialer Wohnbau der Stadt Frankfurt am Main in den 20er Jahren," in Kommunaler Wohnungsbau in Wien (Vienna, 1978).

31. For an interesting discussion of the consequences of the reduction in kitchen space, see Pirhofer and Sieder, "Zur Konstitution," p. 352ff. It must also be said that these space standards, while low, were a substantial improvement over those prevailing earlier and the average density per unit was reduced from 4.0 in 1910 to 2.9 in 1934. See City of Vienna, Low Cost Housing in Vienna, Catalogue for an Exhibition in New Delhi, India (1954), p. 30. With the reduction of the quantitative shortage of housing, a single unit was generally used by only one family; yet the result was still that in most units children and parents had to share a bedroom. See Pirhofer and Sieder, "Zur Konstitution," loc. cit. On kitchen and bathroom facilities, see Gulick, Austria, pp. 450-1.

32. Parteitag, Reports of the Congress of the Social Democratic Party, Sept. 1928, pp. 18-27; Gulick, Austria, pp. 493-4; Danneberg, Zehn Jahre, p. 72.

33. Calculated from U.S. Bureau of the Census, Historical Statistics of the United States, Series G-846 (Washington, D.C., 1975), p. 327.

34. The architectural achievements of German progressive architects during the same period, more striking in some ways, may perhaps be distinguished from the Viennese by these essentially political differences, and even the role of the architects in the two situations seems to have been very different, as their results certainly were.

35. For one of the best current discussions of the issue, see Damaris Rose's article in "Housing," Political Economy of Housing Workshop, Conference of Socialist Economists, London, 1981.

20. Socialist Party Culture and the Realities of Working-Class Life in Red Vienna

Helmut Gruber

PAST AND PRESENT APPROACHES TO AUSTRIAN WORKING-CLASS CULTURE AND MUNICIPAL SOCIALISM

The institutional cultural efforts of the Austrian Social Democratic Party (SDAP) and Viennese municipality have largely become accepted as <u>the</u> culture of the workers. This is due in no small part to the sense of nostalgia encouraged during the Kreisky era, when the postwar Sozialistische Partei Österreichs attempted to create a heroic past.[1] The ennobling of the party's history resembles in many ways the transformation of Antonio Gramsci into an icon, which was carried out by the Italian Communist Party over the past three decades. While not denying the genuine and unique contributions of Austrian socialist party culture or Gramscian theory, we must demystify such reconstructions of the past, in order to attain a better understanding of the relationship between culture and politics, and theory and politics.

The institutional efforts of the SDAP in the sphere of culture were mainly directed at the workers' domestic life and leisure. The factory or workplace, so central to the cultural life of workers, remained largely untouched by official cultural programs. Nor has the unofficial culture of the workplace been studied since that time. In its institutional efforts, the SDAP treated the workers as one undifferentiated mass and paid little attention to existing substructures. Cultural programs showed little awareness of ethnic minorities--Czech, Jewish, Croatian, Slovak--within the workforce. The existing monographs, by John Bunzel on the Jews and by Karl Brousek on the Czechs, fall far short of probing the cultural configuration of these two subcultures within the Viennese working class.[2] Similarly, regional comparisons of the Viennese working class to that in small provincial towns and cities are only at the beginning stage.[3] Insufficient attention was paid by the Social Democrats to the distinct difference in

life-condition and mentalité between men and women and
between married and single members of each gender. The
profound differences in the experiences, needs, and
expectations of young adult and more mature workers was
generally neglected, except for the most superficial and
obvious references in the Socialists' cultural program.
As a rule, the party's cultural reformers deni-
grated the existing cultural forms and lifestyles found
among the workers, characterizing them as barbaric and/
or reactionary.[4] They were determined to create a
tight network of institutions which would produce a
"higher" socialist workers' culture composed of transformed humans--the "neue Menschen." To this task the
reformers brought little understanding of indigenous
worker cultures and important social networks in working-class communities. Historians will have to learn a
great deal more about these communities if the problems
and consequences of attempting to implant a new culture,
created and directed by the party, are to be understood.
This will necessitate a careful study of the rural origins of the working class and an analysis of the social
and cultural adaptation of two generational waves in
working-class formation.[5]
Recent studies of working-class culture have quite
naturally--given the nature of the sources--dealt exclusively with the organizations of the SDAP and Viennese
municipality.[6] In so doing, they have failed to distinguish clearly between the impact of party culture on
party and trade union functionaries on the one hand and
on the mass of the workers on the other. Weidenholzer
cites the figure of 40,000 functionaries in Austria, of
whom 18,700 were in Vienna alone. It is therefore very
tempting to hypothesize that Socialist culture reached
mainly the party cadres and failed to reach the rank and
file. The monographs by Reinhard Krammer on Arbeitersport[7] and Reinhard Kannonier on the Arbeitermusikbewegung[8] suggest that these two party organizations,
with their emphasis on drill, discipline, and structure
or on high culture, were resisted at the grass roots.
In short, scholars have been looking through the
wrong end of the telescope, hoping that by examining
(and enumerating) the cultural programs and organizations of the Socialists and the municipalities, they
could discover how Viennese workers spent their leisure.
From time to time, party spokesmen sniped at "uncivi-
lized" and "unsocialist" expressions of the workers'
older indigenous culture and warned about the dangers of
embourgeoisement. These outbursts showed little understanding of the practical difficulties experienced by
workers living in a metropolis in which a developing
"culture industry" proffered enticing products to fill
their sparse hours of leisure and recreation. In a significant sample of female industrial workers studied in

1931, for instance, the preferred form of leisure activity was listening to the radio (generally coupled with housework). As for recreation outside the home, this same group showed a decided preference for the cinema.[9] Film and radio were the great bastions of manufactured mass entertainment through which the dominant culture exercised its influence over the workers' world. We cannot hope to understand the latter in all its complexity without evaluating the impact of mass culture.

The view from below--the reaction of those for whom the cultural programs and reforms of the party were intended--has only begun to be studied. To date, the most important attempt to probe the everyday reality of worker life is the study of Viennese working-class women during the First Republic. Through "oral history," in-depth interviews of fifty-one subjects, Gerhard Sieder and Gottfried Pirhofer have unearthed considerable detail about the worker family: the perception and division of gender roles; the workings of extended-family and neighbor networks; and the persistence of older local or regional cultural forms and symbols.[10] Three highly original surveys of female workers by Käthe Leichter dating from the First Republic are extremely useful, especially if the nature of the sample she selected is kept in mind and the author's uplifting conclusions are measured against the data presented.[11] Equally important for insights into the everyday and family life of workers is the ground-breaking study of the experiences and perceptions of the unemployed by Marie Jahoda, Paul Lazersfeld, and Hans Zeisel, which uses new methods of social and social psychological analysis.[12]

But the real work of unearthing the sources of everyday life still needs to be done. The model for this should be the urban archaeology carried out quite successfully by English and French historians. In the case of Red Vienna one would hope to consult court records and search for household accounts and diaries; to peruse the collections of Bezirksmuseumen for traces of the family, marriage, and sexual consultation clinics; to unearth school records and certificates; and to examine diocesian entries of birth, confirmation, marriage, and death. The Beisel--a combination of working-man's café and restaurant--should yield information about the rich social life of which it was a center.

By focusing our attention on institutional attempts to create a new socialist workers' subculture, we have neglected the role of the dominant culture in the lives of the workers. The atavistic remains of the old regime, particularly its emphasis on hierarchy and authoritarian practices, appear to have been ubiquitous. In the First Republic, the use of titles (for example: Magister, Doktor, Professor, Direktor, Diplomingenieur,

Hofrat, Kommerzialrat, Chirurg. These represent but the
tip of the iceberg.), though often honorific, continued
to mark the boundaries of social deference and distance.
Socialist leaders were by no means immune to this mania
for titles, allowing themselves to be addressed as "Comrade Dr." The infantilizing authority experienced by
male workers at their workplace was similarly exercised
by them in a paternalistic manner in their domestic
sphere where antiquated laws still on the statute books
made them masters of their realm. During the 1920s, for
instance, cases still appeared before the courts in
which husbands were charged with having "excessively"
physically chastized their wives.[13]

Little as yet is known about the extent to which
the Catholic Church continued to play a role in the
daily lives of workers. As an institution, it published
newspapers and journals, conducted its own cultural
program,[14] administered the sacraments that marked the
rites of passage, and continued to exercise considerable
influence on the public schools through weekly release
time for religious instruction. But the Church also
exerted its influence as an informal cultural institution, since holidays and associated ritual practices
(Lent, Corpus Christi, etc.) continued to find popular
acceptance. We know that religious pictures still frequently decorated the walls in workers' apartments. To
what extent this indicates that the Church's teachings
on morality, the function of marriage, abstinence, and
sexuality played a role in workers' lives remains to be
ascertained.

The one force in the dominant culture which was
probably most proximate to the everyday lives of workers
and, therefore, most readily lent itself to imitation
was the world-view and everyday norms of the petty bourgeoisie. We must discover the extent to which its values with respect to individual and family accumulation
and success, comportment, and domesticity penetrated
indigenous worker cultures and competed with party-
sponsored socialist aspirations in what took the form of
a latter-day Kulturkampf.

WORKING-CLASS CULTURE IN RED VIENNA
AS PARADIGM FOR INTERWAR SOCIAL DEMOCRACY

Otto Bauer and other Socialist leaders understood
the inherent contradiction in the two constellations:
power without culture, and culture without power. After
the Linz Congress of 1926, they opted decisively for the
second course, but failed squarely to face the fact that
the party's extensive cultural program rested on its
inability to alter the balance of political power. In
practice, the growth of the cultural program correspond-

ed to the diminution of political power. Despite this
contradiction or, perhaps, because it was understood,
the SDAP went further than any other party in developing
a comprehensive socialist cultural program. The socialist and laborist parties in France, England, and Belgium, for instance, never went further than electoral
politics. Though the Labour Party and the Section française de l'internationale ouvrière (SFIO) briefly gained
a very contingent poltical power (under MacDonald and
Blum), a cultural program aimed at creating a worker or
socialist subculture was never on their agendas. It
would have involved the kind of mass mobilization from
below which both the Labour Party and the SFIO feared.
The cultural animation of the workers in both England
and France fell to their respective communist parties in
the 1930s.

Even the most successful post-World War II experi-
ment--Italian municipal communism--has come up against
the same contradictions as those faced by Red Vienna.
Moreover, the "red" Italian cities have lacked one important advantage enjoyed by interwar Vienna: an independent power of taxation which made public housing and
other social welfare measures possible, despite the
hostility to such reforms evinced by a national government controlled by the political opposition. In Red
Vienna those contradictions were revealed, for example,
by the defeat of the party's Mittelschule reform (a
first step in providing equality of opportunity in higher education) in 1927 and by breaches in the rent control law, a bastion of municipal socialism, in 1929.
After 1930 the independent taxation powers of the Viennese municipality and province were vitiated by the central government, which returned a diminished portion of
general tax income to the municipality, forcing it to
sharply curtail its social program.

In the "cultural laboratory" of Red Vienna, a fun-
damental and perhaps unbridgable distance between leaders and masses came into being. It expressed itself in
their two worlds of socialization, their distinct and
separate spheres of everyday existence, and their opposing cultural experiences and expectations. Put another way, the average worker and the typical higher
functionary inhabited two different worlds: their
clothes, speech, physical care, comportment, interper-
sonal relations, health, and daily motivations were so
different as to afford few points of comparison or contact. There is a crying need for a collective biography
of the Socialist leaders and the functionaries of the
party's institutions and trade unions. Only then can we
speak more precisely about this social and cultural distance. In the absence of such a valuable tool of analysis, the following biographical sketches are offered for
comparison. Admittedly, the method of selection is

impressionistic.
Käthe Leichter:[15]   functionary in the Vienna.
Chamber of Labor and member of the central committee of
the Socialists' women's section; descended in grandparents' generation from Bohemian textile industrialists
and Romanian bankers; Jewish; rich and class-segregated
childhood (nannies, summer villas, birthday presents of
1,000 kronen) in six room apartment on the fashionable
Rudolfsplatz; Ph.D. in economics from Heidelberg; later
adult life in comfortable suburb with one or two servants.
Ernst Fischer:[16]   journalist for Grazer socialist
press; after 1927, editor of Vienna Arbeiter-Zeitung;
father was a major in the imperial army and an instruc-
tor at the military academy; mother an aristocrat, her
father a general; father an anti-Semite and anti-socialist; family experiencing financial difficulties in order
to maintain expected social standard; adult life in Graz
and Vienna; bohemian and self-centered.
Joseph Buttinger:[17]   leader of party youth group
(Kinderfreunde) in Carinthian small city; later party
secretary in the same town; mother was an orphaned farm
maid, father a roadworker; childhood of poverty, hunger,
migrations, interrupted schooling; employed as a cowherd
and factory worker; read his first real book at age fifteen; self-taught, later educated in party Arbeiter-
hochschule.
Three Viennese Female Workers.[18] Mrs. Kle: born
1913; father a wood turner, died 1918; mother Polish,
worked as a domestic; five siblings; vocational school
for dressmaking, apprenticeship, then unemployed; entered workclothes factory; leisure time in Socialist
Turnverein and Kinderfreunde. Mrs. Seb: born 1902;
father a teamster; two brothers; in school till age
fourteen, then worked in factory, one year as domestic;
1921 marriage to streetcar worker, living with parents
in three room apartment till 1927; moved to municipal
Sandleitenhof, gave up employment at husband's request.
Mrs. Stu: born 1903; father a silversmith's helper;
five siblings; in school until age fourteen, then an
untrained seamstress in uniform factory (doing piece-
work); took over household after mother's illness; first
child illegitimate, married the following year, lived
for four years with parents and siblings; moved to municipal Karl Marx Hof in 1929.
One need not invoke the "iron law of oligarchy" to
be reminded that such a distance between leaders and
masses is a chronic malady of social democracy, recognized long ago. One is reminded of the dirigiste nature
of socialist party leadership in most countries during
the interwar years. Federation secretaries in the SFIO
were referred to as the "prefects of Monsieur Faure"
(the party secretary), because of the parallel to Napo-

leonic structure of the French administration. The situation in the German SPD was a virtual parody of hierarchy and of the isolation of leadership. But Austrian
socialism represented a heightened and exemplary form of
this malady, because it attempted to go beyond the at-
tainment of a 51 percent electoral majority--which had,
anyhow, become hopeless after 1926--and because it invested so much in its cultural mission. Those "elected"
to carry it out acted as the "chosen leaders" of what
became at times a part-socialist and part-spiritual
quest. The paternalistic relations between socialist
leaders and masses, which seems to arise quite normally
in the political activity of socialist parties, grew
stronger and became more apparent as Socialist functionaries attempted to act as cultural tutors to their less
fortunate brethren.

One need not be surprised, therefore, that no
evidence has appeared which would indicate that Socialist leaders and cultural directors encouraged workers to
take the initiative in shaping or controlling their own
cultural enrichment. The squatters' and settlers' movement on the outskirts of Vienna after World War I, for
instance, was greeted by the party with suspicion because it was spontaneous and outside the party structure.[19] Eventually, the SDAP gained control of this
"garden city" movement and killed it. The reasons which
it gave for doing so--the fact that the cost of superblock municipal housing was considerably lower than that
of one-family houses, and that the superblocks served
larger numbers--can not be controverted. But one senses
that the reasons were more complicated and that self-
management in the garden city enclaves was a contributing cause; it was seen almost as a kind of anarchism
which was disruptive to the customary channels of party
activity and control.

The further we probe into the Socialists' cultural
institutions--whether the "social uplift" implicit in
the exposure to high culture (Bildung) or the "ornamental quality" of party-organized proletarian festivals
[20]--the more apparent the distance of the leaders from
the realities of working-class life becomes. The Socialists had the grand vision of liberating the workers
from capitalism by developing for them a culture of
their own, which would have the moral content of socialism even though socialism had not yet been attained
politically.[21] Since the party could do little to
alter the dominant position of capitalism at the work
place, it concentrated its efforts on the workers' private sphere. But the architects of party culture
avoided confronting the powerful indirect means by which
capitalism had permeated the workers' private lives--the
cultural restraints which enthralled workers and prevented them from attaining the selfhood and powers of

self-management which were a prerequisite for the party's socialist culture of neue Menschen. The most powerful and pervasive of these restraints was the authoritarian structure of the male-dominated worker family and
its corollary, the servile place of women in gender
relations.[22] Even less recognized was the pitifully
impoverished sexuality of workers, which tended to grav-
itate between the extremes of abstinence and brutali-
ty.[23] When the party did not avoid these sensitive
subjects altogether, it addressed them in an ennobling
and uplifting tone that had little relation to their
limiting, if not crippling, effect on workers'
lives.[24]

WORKING-CLASS CULTURE, EVERYDAY LIFE, AND POLITICS

Recently the branch of social history concerned
with culture and everyday life has been accused (with
some justice) of a particularism bordering on antiquar-
ianism.[25] More specifically, these charges have centered on the remoteness of life as seen from below from
arenas of power and politics in the world of institutions. It remains, therefore, for this writer to re-
insert his musings about culture in Red Vienna into the
larger historical framework from which it was extracted
in the search for special insights.
Since the publication of Carl Schorske's Fin-de
Siècle Vienna[26] in 1981, it has become fashionable to
view art and culture in Vienna as a metaphor for politics. The application of this paradigm to the municipal
socialism of the First Republic, however, can at best
lead only to a half truth. As Max Adler insisted in
1924, Austromarxism viewed culture as a weapon of the
class struggle.[27] The Socialists' cultural activities
and pronouncements left no doubt that culture was considered the continuation of politics by other means. We
might now judge them naive for having thought so, but
that is beside the point. Historically, it is their
conviction which counts.
The socialist attempt to create a party culture in
Red Vienna and the impact of this experiment on existing
worker subcultures tell us a great deal about the politics of the Socialists. In both political and cultural
work, party leaders assumed a tutelary attitude toward
the workers. They assumed the mission of bringing about
socialism through political means (electoral politics)
and when these lines were blocked, they turned to the
cultural realm. But in neither case were they concerned
with fostering the kind of self-consciousness that would
have led to self-direction and creativity from below.
That would have required a kind of familiarity with and
sensitivity to the actual lives of workers which the

leaders, despite their sympathies for "the proletarian
condition," were incapable of. In both cases, the rank
and file was relegated to the role of consumers of party
programs and shut out from their creation or management.
The relationship of socialist party culture to working-
class reality in Red Vienna may well lead us to the
deeper dimensions of Austromarxist politics. An understanding of the strengths and weaknesses of that "socialism in one city," as one critic called it,[28] may
yield important clues to the general malaise and deterioration of social democracy in the interwar years.

SOCIALIST PATERNALISM IN CREATING NEUE MENSCHEN

No one can doubt the unique achievement of the
socialist-dominated Viennese city council between 1919
and 1934. Its housing and social welfare programs were
all the more remarkable because socialists elsewhere in
Europe neither achieved so much nor aimed so high.
Moreover, Social Democratic leaders viewed these
achievements in municipal socialism as the cornerstone
of a far greater and more comprehensive cultural program, expressing the meaning of Austromarxism as the
blending of politics and culture in the struggle toward
socialism. Unfortunately, almost from the beginning,
the genuine attainments of municipal socialism were
mythologized by the Social Democratic Party as a major
social and structural transformation--something which
the reality could not support.[29] This historical
obfuscation has continued down to the present day in the
work of otherwise exemplary historians who tend to make
heroic precisely what they have set out to analyze and
evaluate.[30] The following attempt to examine aspects
of the Social Democrats' reform program should serve as
an antidote to such myth-making and allow the true nature of the Viennese experiment to emerge, with all its
strengths and weaknesses.

Between 1919 and 1934 the municipality build some
63,000 apartments concentrated in sizable housing projects to alleviate the dire housing needs of Vienna's
working population.[31] But this admirable program was
not the outgrowth of long-standing socialist social
policy. It was a response to the housing crisis in the
immediate postwar years which had been brought on by the
rent control laws of 1917-1918 combined with galloping
inflation.[32] Their effect was to reduce rents virtually to zero and to bring all housing construction to a
standstill.[33] The municipal council responded to the
emergency by successfully extending rent controls in the
Rent Law of 1922. At the same time, it became apparent
that the municipality would have to replace the private
sector in carrying out a building program.

The municipal housing program came into being in
1923 because the housing market had collapsed and not
because a longstanding socialist strategy had been moved
to the top of the Socialist Party agenda.[34] In fact,
the party was largely unprepared for the role which the
municipal government had to play. Before the war,
socialist theorists had paid little attention to
piecemeal reforms in the expectation that housing and
other social needs would be satisfied by a general social transformation.[35] But between 1870 and the turn
of the century, the housing question had been widely
discussed by liberal reformers, who had put forward
various schemes for improving the living conditions of
the lower classes. One proposal of 1874 called for the
construction of "worker barracks" including communal
facilities such as laundries, bath houses, clinics, central heating, and common dining rooms.[36] The Stif-
tungshof and Lobmeyerhof, two housing complexes for the
lower classes created by a private foundation in 1900,
were even more exemplary for the Socialists as they
devised their housing plans in 1922-1923. These two
projects occupied only 45 percent of their allotted land
(instead of the usual 85 percent), and the remainder was
used as an interior courtyard of greenery and gardens.
In this interior courtyard, various common facilities
were grouped, including communal kitchens, central bath
houses, a medical dispensary, a library, a lecture hall,
free enterprise shops, and a male and female old age
home.[37] Two-thirds of the 383 apartments consisted of
a kitchen and a single room; rents were about 10 percent
below the market price; and subtenants were prohibited.
Thus, we can see that the municipal housing of the
interwar years was not an original socialist conception
or demand but rested on liberal reform ideas and
experiments of the late nineteenth century.
    Socialist originality lay elsewhere: in the means
of financing the building program and in the potential
power of the municipality, now the sole builder, over
the entire building industry. The creative financial
plan of municipal councillor Hugo Breitner rejected the
traditional method of mortgages and relied on an annual
housing tax borne by all but heavily dependent on the
contributions of wealthier residents.[38] The resulting
building fund was supplemented by luxury taxes levied
against all objects and means of entertainment associated with middle-class conspicuous consumption. This
scheme was made possible when Vienna became a federal
state (as well as the capital) on 1 January 1922, with
the power to levy taxes for state purposes.
    With the inauguration of the first building plan in
1923 the municipal government faced important decisions
which affected the building industry and work force. By
rejecting the most modern and sophisticated methods of

construction (molded and prefabricated structural sections) in favor of brick and mortar, it was able to increase employment in the building trades by 12,000 workers a year, and this figure would be considerably larger
if the mobilization of the building materials sector
were taken into account.[39] The need for more employment was a powerful argument used by Social Democrats
against modernist architectural critics. More difficult
to explain is the limited perspective of the Socialists
regarding the monopolistic control of the municipality
over the entire real estate and housing industry. There
is remarkable silence in party literature on the potential restructuring of that industry away from the market, a restructuring made possible by the controlling
position of the municipality.[40] Surely, such a partial redirection of the economy would have been at least
as important a socialist accomplishment as the 63,000
apartments which were built by 1934, if the long-range
implications for housing are considered. But here, too,
the Socialists appear to have been unprepared to consider a question that went to the heart of any effort to
create, expand, and maintain a socialist Vienna. The
housing program remained largely an improvised affair,
part of the mechanism for justifying rent control and a
temporary substitute for the depressed market forces in
housing.
    Spokesmen for the SDAP hailed Vienna as a "Mecca"
because of its accomplishments in housing. At the
least, they claimed that the municipality's housing
policies signalled the beginning of the long march
toward socialism.[41] To what extent were such claims
justified? It is true that the Socialists' maintenance
of rent control, which went far beyond the efforts of
any other major municipality in Europe,[42] created a
sense of security for those who resided in Vienna before
1918. Moreover, the law for requisitioning apartments
(Wohnungsaufforderungsgesetz) which was in effect until
1925 made available 44,838 domiciles otherwise free or
under-utilized.[43] But the enforcement of rent control, which guaranteed cheap rents in the worker tenements, led to the expulsion of subtenants and bed
renters who had been needed to sustain working-class
households. These subtenants, who were not covered by
rent control laws, were compelled to seek housing in
apartments of the middle class. The marriage rate increased sharply in the postwar years, and young couples
found themselves forced to live with parents and in-laws
in the same crowded conditions as before.[44]
    In practical terms, the Socialists' municipal hous-
ing program did little to alleviate the dire needs of
the working population. The 63,000 apartments which
were built by 1934 accounted for 10 percent of all domiciles. But nearly half of these fell into the construc-

tion program of 1928-1933, so that for most of the period the impact of new housing was much smaller. Most of
the Viennese population continued to live much as they
had before, under conditions which the Socialists repeatedly described as less than human.[45] A clear sign
of the limited impact of municipal housing on living
conditions within the city is the catastrophic growth of
the population of homeless persons by 1934 (three times
the number of 1924).[46]

Were there other measures the Socialists might have
taken? Hindsight dictates caution, yet it does seem
remarkable that there was no discussion within the
Social Democratic Party of socializing at least part of
the private housing stock.[47] Part of the housing
problem arose from the bad distribution of domiciles due
to the existence of a black market in rent-controlled
apartments and a free market in sub-tenancies. The
quality of the existing housing stock continued to
deteriorate greatly because of the limited maintenance
allowances included in rents. Landlords on the whole
were unhappy with what they considered to be worthless
investments, and felt trapped. It is difficult to imagine that a significant number of worker tenements could
not have been socialized and managed by the municipality. Such a step might have created better living conditions for many more than 10 percent and given claims
about the "road to socialism" more substance. An explanation for Socialist inaction on this matter may lie
in the fact that renovations rarely carry the symbolic
impact of massive new construction.

It is useful to enumerate in what ways the municipal housing projects were improvements over the typical
worker tenements: there were light and airy apartments
facing interior courtyards of greenery; basic facilities
such as gas stoves, cold running water, and toilets in
each apartment; communal facilities such as mechanized
laundry facilities, bathhouses, kindergardens, play-
grounds and wading pools, medical and dental clinics,
libraries and lecture halls, shops of the consumer association, and youth and mothers' consultation bureaus.
[48] Yet it is important to be aware of the danger of
viewing these rationalized dwelling units and their
related communal facilities uncritically as many contemporary and latter-day sympathizers have done.[49] It
is worthwhile to recall the important amenities left out
by the city fathers and their planners. These include
private bathrooms, central heating, and hot water. Of
these, the first was probably unrealizable given the
small size of apartments (until 1927 they were 38 or 48
square meters; thereafter some larger units of 57 square
meters were built), but central heating and hot water
are another matter. The maintenance of stoves for heating and the procurement of the necessary coke were left

to the individual household, and there was a constant
need to boil water (colored wash, for instance, could
not be done in the communal facilities and had to be
done by hand at home). All this contributed greatly to
the burden of housework for women, much as it had in the
tenements.[50]
     There is no concrete substantiation for the reason
which was given at the time for the lack of these ameni-
ties--their excessive cost--especially since the socialist city fathers insisted on putting hard wooden parquet
flooring in the rooms (other than kitchens and toilets).
On the basis of the available building techniques, one
might argue that the collective cost of the installation
and operation of these facilities, when added to the
minimal rent, would have been supportable. There is
another danger in the practice of simply enumerating the
improvements made in the municipal housing projects. A
full array of communal facilities was available only in
the largest projects. Central laundry facilities and
bathhouses, where they existed, tended to be overtaxed
with use.[51] Many municipal housing tenants were
forced to seek communal facilities (public showers,
swimming pools) quite some distance from their homes.
     The very small size of apartments and the prohibi-
tion of subtenancies revolutionized the family structure
in these new dwellings. The open family of the
tenements had consisted of diverse relatives, subtenants, and bed renters, in cheek-by-jowl proximity.
They had comprised an intricate network of social relationships and had given mutual aid. The nuclear family
of the municipal houses--parents and one or two chil-
dren--experienced an unaccustomed privacy which alter-
nated with necessary participation in highly controlled
public facilities.[52] This transformation corresponded
closely to the Social Democrats' aim of creating municipal socialism. The cornerstone of the party's vision
was the ordentliche worker family, a term connoting not
only orderliness but also decency and respectabil-
ity.[53] The municipal "people's palaces," as they were
popularly called, were considered a laboratory and
learning environment in which the party could socialize
the worker family and provide it with a new socialist
culture. The "humanizing" of worker life may have ema-
nated from the highest ethical motives; in practice it
had pronounced coercive connotations.[54]
     The management of any public facility requires
certain rules and regulations but, in the municipal
houses, life outside the cell-like apartments was regi-
mented beyond reasonable limits. The paternal managerial structure,[55] which drew its authority directly
from the housing bureau of the municipal council, included a concièrge charged with the power to prescribe
and enforce building rules (the time and place to beat

rugs and deposit refuse; the nature and location of
child play in the courtyard; the appearance of hallways,
cellars, and balconies, etc.). There was also a laundry
supervisor who scheduled the monthly wash days of each
family, kept all but the women out of the washing facility (on the prudish grounds of protecting female modes-
ty), and supervised the use of machinery; an apartment
inspector who made monthly visits to all domiciles to
ascertain their state of maintenance and to receive
reports on infractions of the rules from the concièrge
(children playing on the grass in the courtyard were
duly marked down in a book of infractions); and an array
of "experts" in the clinics, consultation centers, kindergardens, and libraries, whose function was tutelary
above all. Private initiatives by tenants to regulate
and control their collective living spaces were discouraged. Tenants' committees were elected in each of the
housing projects, but they were limited to a purely
advisory function. The arbitrary and invidious power of
the slum landlord was a thing of the past; however, the
regulations of the municipal projects--all in the spirit
of creating the ordentliche Familie--still left the
worker-tenants the objects of superior (but wiser?)
forces.

The paternalist tendencies in the housing policy of
the municipal council were even more pronounced in its
extensive welfare system. Under the guidance of the
famous anatomist Julius Tandler who headed the Public
Welfare Office, the community assumed the responsibility
for raising the "moral climate" of the Viennese family.
[56] The justification for extensive intervention into
the lives of families was the strongly eugenic view that
the health and nurturance of future generations demanded
the intervention of experts. Using the dispensation of
welfare aid as a legal wedge, the Public Welfare Office
set out to determine whether parents were capable of
raising their children "properly." Female welfare officers made regular compulsory visits to families who were
receiving public assistance and to the homes of foster
and illegitimate children (the latter were made legal
wards of the city).

If, in the course of such surveillance, the welfare
officer found the conditions for child-rearing to be
physically or psychologically damaging, the children
were remanded to a child observation center. There, it
was determined whether they should be consigned to foster care, to a children's home or to a correctional
institution, or returned to their parents. That this
interventionist system functioned with considerable bru-
tality is attested to by former welfare officers who
were interviewed by Sieder. The removal of children had
all the features of a police raid; it involved the
courts and youth bureau, and it cast the welfare officer

in the role of a hostile government agent. Consequently, she was feared in working-class communities.[57]
Sectors of the working class which deviated from the
norm of the orderly and respectable worker family desired by the Socialist city fathers were subjected to
the aforementioned social controls that were also reinforced by modernized kindergardens and day nurseries.[58] In 1927 the Public Welfare Office initiated
the distribution of layettes to the mothers of all the
newborn, regardless of need. This allowed welfare workers to visit homes to which they would otherwise not
have had access. Thus they were able to observe and
report on the standard of family life and to set in
motion the machinery of intervention if in their judgment conditions were "abnormal."[59]
     The municipality's rather simplistic approach to
complex social structures and problems and its reliance
on so-called "experts"[60] to bring about a "better"
working-class family was based on a disregard for the
subjects' own framework of experience.[61] Small wonder, then, that municipal socialism was often viewed as
regimentation from the top, a condition to which workers
were already subjected in full measure at the workplace.
In short, municipal socialism, in its propensity to act
in loco parentis, reinforced the paternalist/authoritar-
ian tendencies present in the socialization of working-
class families in the pre-republican era and in the
later dominant culture.
     It is necessary to return for a moment to the role
of municipal housing to dispel the negative bias which
may have been suggested by my critical examination.
Despite the fact that the municipal housing program
failed to affect the living conditions of the Viennese
working class in significant, practical ways, it had a
powerful symbolic effect. The momumental, palace-like
and superblock architecture of many of the projects
(Karl Seitz Hof and Karl Marx Hof, for example) suggested a power and protectedness readily appreciated by
the Viennese workers.[62] The apparent force of a
working-class presence, and even predominance, in the
city--though that force was directly experienced by only
a few--contributed to a sense of rising expectations
among the workers, which the political realities in
Austria could hardly justify.
     The Socialist leaders themselves appear to have
been deceived by the powerful symbols they created and
to have believed that the reforms of Red Vienna could
take the place of political struggles in the national
arena against an opponent prepared to use not only the
conventional weapons of politics but terror as well.[63]
But the socialists surely saw the straws in the wind:
in 1929 the political opposition undermined rent control
and began to reduce the apportionment of the national

238

tax to the province of Vienna.[64] Quite clearly, the
expansion of social programs (not only in building) was
dead before February 1934.[65]

In looking back on the socialist reforms dealing
with habitation and welfare, one should see them in the
context of both the cultural possibilities and political
realities of the time. In the realm of culture, the
reforms were often modest in substance and/or paternalist in form, largely because the Social Democratic leaders had little knowledge of the workers as they really
were and refused to accept their indigenous subcultures
as points of departure.[66] In directly political
terms, the notion that the cultural enclave of Red
Vienna could act as a countervailing force against reaction on the national scene was continually challenged
and finally (from 1933 to 1934) shown to be an illusion.
And, yet, this incomplete experiment in municipal socialism has much to teach us about the very nature of
reform, about the relationship of leaders to masses, and
about the complicated social structure of contending
classes in which changes in perception and in lifestyle
are shaped. The housing and welfare reforms of the
Socialist city fathers may have been shortsighted and
heavy handed. But they were only a part--the external
structure--of an envisaged cultural transformation that
was both grand and naive, somber and heroic.[67]

NOTES

1. For an excellent illustration of this tendency
to view past accomplishments uncritically, see Mit uns
zieht die neue Zeit: Arbeiterkultur in Osterreich 1918-
1934 (Vienna, 1981), which is the catalogue of an impressive public exhibition of working-class culture in
the First Republic, held in Vienna in 1981.

2. John Bunzel, Klassenkampf in der Diaspora: Zur
Geschichte der jüdischen Arbeiterbewegung (Vienna,
1975), and Karl Brousek, Wien und seine Tschechen
(Vienna, 1980). More promising is John Bunzel, "Ar-
beiterbewegung, 'Judenfrage' und Antisemitismus: Am
Beispiel des Wiener Bezirks Leopoldstadt," in Gerhardt
Botz et al., eds., Bewegung und Klasse: Studien zur
österreichischen Arbeitergeschichte (Vienna, 1978).

3. See Helmut Konrad, "Zur Regionalbeschreibung der
Arbeiterbewegung in Osterreich," ITH Tagungsbericht, No.
17 (Vienna, 1983). The number of workers outside Vienna
still remains a matter of conjecture. My estimate is
that they equalled those in the capital.

4. With irony bordering on contempt, Richard
Wagner, editor of a trade union newspaper and head of
the trade union school in Vienna, attacked the symbolic
representation of "vassalage to capitalism" in workers'
homes: holy pictures, pictures of royalty, postcards and
artistically vulgar reproductions, and particularly the
homemade antimacassars used to prettify the furniture
(Deckerln). "Klassenkampf im Proletarierheim," Blätter
für sozialistisches Bildungswesen, Vol. XIII, No. 7-8
(1926).

5. An important beginning has been made in tracing
the preurban roots of successive waves of worker families. See Michael Mitterauer and Reinhard Sieder, Vom
Patriarchat zur Partnerschaft: Strukturwandel der Familie (Munich, 1977-1980) and Joseph Ehmer, Familienstruk-
tur und Arbeitsorganisation im frühindustriellen Wien
(Vienna, 1980).

6. Most important of these are: Joseph Weidenholzer, Auf den Weg zum "Neuen Menschen": Bildungs-
und Kulturarbeit der SDAP in der Ersten Republik
(Vienna, 1981), especially p. 35; Dieter Langewiesche,
Zur Freizeit des Arbeiters: Bildungsbestrebungen und
Freizeitgestaltungen österreichischer Arbeiter im
Kaiserreich und in der Ersten Republik (Stuttgart,
1979); and Alfred Pfoser, Literatur und Austromarxismus
(Vienna, 1980). These works represent a great step
forward in developing the institutional history of
socialist party culture.

7. Reinhard Krammer, Arbeitersport in Österreich:
Ein Beitrag zur Geschichte der Arbeiterkultur in
Österreich bis 1938 (Vienna, 1981).

8. Reinhard Kannonier, Zwischen Beethoven und
Eisler: Zur Arbeitermusikbewegung in Österreich (Vienna,
1981). For the most interesting recent use of oral
histories in writing the history of the working class,
see Gerhard Botz and Josef Weidenholzer, eds., Mündliche
Geschichte und Arbeiterbewegung (Vienna, 1984) and Irene
Etzersdorfer and Hans Schafranek, eds., Der Februar 1934
in Wien: Erzählte Geschichte (Vienna, 1984).

9. Käthe Leichter, So leben wir...1320 Industriearbeiterinnen berichten über ihr Leben (Vienna, 1932),
p. 114.

10. Gottfried Pirhofer and Gerhard Sieder, "Zur
Konstitution der Arbeiterfamilie im Roten Wien:
Familienpolitik, Kulturreform, Altag und Ästhetik," in
Michael Mitterauer and Reinhard Sieder, eds., Hi-

240

storische Familienforschung (Frankfurt am Main, 1982).

11. Käthe Leichter, Wie leben die Wiener Hausgehilfinnen? (Vienna, 1926); Käthe Leichter, Wie leben die Wiener Heimarbeiter?: Eine Erhebung über die Arbeits und Lebenverhältnisse von tausend wiener Heimarbeitern (Vienna, 1928); and Käthe Leichter, So leben wir.... Leichter also edited the very useful reference work, Handbuch der Frauenarbeit in Österreich (Vienna, 1930). All of these studies were sponsored and financed by the Wiener Arbeitkammer of which Leichter was a functionary.

12. Marie Jahoda, Paul Lazarsfeld and Hans Zeisel, Die Arbeitslosen von Marienthal (Vienna, 1933). Although this work is important in the development of modern social science because of its innovations such as the sociogram, it does not provide a picture of unemployment in Austria in general. Its findings are based on an atypical locale of unemployment--an industrial small town in which the single source of employment has collapsed--which does not compare to larger and more complex socio-economic settings.

13. Between 1923 and 1926 such cases were reported with some regularity in the pages of Die Unzufriedene: Eine unabhängige Wochenschrift für alle Frauen.

14. See Alois Hudal, ed., Der Katholizismus in Osterrich: Sein Wirken, Werden, und Hoffen (Innsbruck, 1931).

15. Herbert Steiner, ed., Käthe Leichter: Leben und Werk (Vienna, 1973).

16. Ernst Fischer, Erinnerungen und Reflexionen (Hamburg, 1969).

17. Joseph Buttinger, Ortswechsel: Die Geschichte meiner Jugend (Frankfurt am Main, 1979).

18. Pihofer and Sieder, "Zur Konstitution der Arbeiterfamilie."

19. See Wilfred Posch, Die Wiener Gartenstadt Bewegung: Reformversuch zwischen Erster und Zweiter Gründerzeit (Vienna, 1981) and Klaus Novy, "Selbsthilfe als Reformbewegung: Der Kampf der Wiener Siedler nach dem 1. Weltkrieg," ARCH: Zeitschrift für Architekten, Sozialarbeiter und kommunalpolitische Gruppen, 55 (March 1981).

20. Proletarian festivals of the time are a particularly fruitful area for the study of the relations

between party culture and rank and file consciousness.
See Roberto Cazzola, "Die proletarischen Feste: Zwischen
revolutionärer Propädeutik und ästhetischem Ritualis-
mus," Wiener Tagebuch, No. 4 (Apr. 1981). See also,
Alfred Pfoser, "Massenästhetik und Massenspiel," ITH
Tagungsbericht, No. 16 (Vienna, 1981) and the much ear-
lier exploration of the subject by the German critic
Siegfried Kracauer, Das Ornament der Masse (Frankfurt am
Main, 1965).

21. The extent to which the SDAP's efforts in
practice resembled Antonio Gramsci's theory of egemonia
awaits its analyst. Since the completion of this article such a beginning has been made. See Alfred Georg
Frei, Rotes Wien: Austromarxismus und Arbeiterkultur
(Berlin, 1984), pp. 46-48.

22. A recent controversial article traces this
servility to Marx's "idealization of men's economic
providership." See Harold Benenson, "Victorian Sexual
Ideology and Marx's Theory of the Working Class,"
International Labor and Working Class History, No. 25
(Spring 1984).

23. See, for instance, the clinical cases reported
and the conclusions drawn in Wilhelm Reich, Sexualer-
regung und Sexualbetriedigung (Vienna, 1930).

24. In studying some of the major party journals--
Die Arbeiterinnen-Zeitung/Die Frau, Die Unzufriedene,
Die Mutter, Die Sozialistische Erziehung, Der Jugenliche
Arbeiter, Der Vertrauensmann--one is overwhelmed by the
level of obfuscation on these subjects.

25. See especially the controversy between Jürgen
Kocka and Martin Broszat in Merkur: Deutsche Zeitschrift
für europäisches Denken, Nos. 10 and 12 (Oct. and Dec.
1982).

26. Carl Schorske, Fin-de-Siècle Vienna: Politics
and Culture (New York, 1981).

27. Max Adler, Neue Menschen: Gedanken über
Sozialistische Erziehung (Berlin, 1924), pp. 170-81.

28. See Jill Lewis, "Red Vienna: Socialism in One
City," European Studies Review, XIII, No. 3 (July 1983).

29. Otto Bauer's address Mieterschutz, Volkskultur
und Alkoholismus (Vienna, 1929) is typical of the vulgar
comparisons of workers' living conditions during the
monarchy and republic which simplify and overstate the
party's reforms. Glowing reports of the new housing

242

projects, lacking an ounce of analysis, can be found in
virtually all the party literature but especially in Die
Arbeiter-Zeitung, Die Unzufriedene and Die Frau.

30. See, for instance, Klaus Novy, "Der Wiener
Gemeindewohnungsbau: 'Sozialisierung von unten'," ARCH,
45 (July 1979); Hans Hautmann and Rudolf Hautmann,
"Hubert Gessner und das Konzept des Volkswohnungs-
palasts," Austriaca: Cahiers universitaires d'information sur l'Austriche, 12 (May 1981); Wolfgang Speiser,
Paul Speiser und das rote Wien (Munich, 1979), pp.
50-52; Hans Hautmann and Rudolf Kropf, Die österreichische Arbeiterbewegung vom Vormärz bis 1945 (Vienna,
1974), pp. 146-48.

31. For the best analysis of socialist communal
policies and accomplishments, see Rainer Bauböck, Wohnungspolitik im sozialdemokratie Wien 1919-1934 (Salzburg, 1979) and Maren Seliger, Sozialdemokratie und
Kommunalpolitik in Wien: Zu einigen Aspekten sozialdemokratischer Politik in der Vor- und Zwischenkriegskeit
(Vienna, 1980).

32. The imperial government had introduced laws
fixing rents and rent increases and prohibiting evic-
tions as a means of social pacification in wartime.

33. Die Wohnungspolitik der Gemeinde Wien (Vienna,
1926), p. 30.

34. Seliger, Sozialdemokratie und Kommunalpolitik,
pp. 137-39.

35. Bauböck, Wohnungspolitik, pp. 108-14.

36. Peter Feldbauer and Wolfgand Hösl, "Die
Wohungsverhältnisse der Wiener Unterschichten und die
Anfänge des genossenschaftlichen Wohn- und Siedlungs-
wesens," in Botz et al., eds., Bewegung, pp. 690-91.
This plan of E.H. Aigde was rejected by industrialists
who feared that such concentrated housing would lead to
worker solidarity and radicalism.

37. Ibid., pp. 698-99.

38. An indispenable source on the mechanics of
social policy is Felix Czeike, Wirtschafts- und Sozial-
politik der Gemeinde Wien (Vienna, 1959), 2 vols.

39. Novy, "Wiener Gemeindewohnungsbau," pp. 17-18;
Bauböck, Wohnungspolitik, pp. 147-148. Indeed, both
employment and wages in the building trades in Vienna
remained relatively high throughout the period.

40. Ibid., pp. 146-147. The municipality con-
tracted the building to private firms which otherwise
would simply have disappeared.

41. For instance, Robert Danneberg, Zehn Jahre
neues Wien (Vienna, 1929), pp. 50-56; Karl Honay, "Auf-
bauarbeit in Krisenzeiten. Der Wiener Stadthaushalt im
Jahre 1932," Der Sozialdemokrat, 1 (1932), pp. 6-8; and
Otto Leichter, Glanz und Elend der Ersten Republik
(Vienna, 1964), p. 26.

42. Charles A. Gulick, Austria trom Habsburg to
Hitler (Berkeley, 1948), I, p. 445.

43. Bauböck, Wohnungspolitik, pp. 91-108.

44. Ibid., pp. 87-91; Gulick, p. 424.

45. Of the industrial female workers responding to
Leichter's questionnaire (and they were clearly above
the norm) 17.9 per cent had gas, running cold water, and
electric light in their apartments; 17.9 per cent had
none of these. Leichter, So leben wir..., p. 84.

46. Bauböck, Wohnungspolitik, pp. 153-54, cites
302,735 nights in municipal shelters for 1924 and
929,062 for 1934. These were facts which Social
Democratic publicists attempted to disguise.

47. Seliger, Sozialdemokratie und Kommunalpolitik,
pp. 137-38.

48. Hautmann and Hautmann, "Hubert Gessner," pp.
118-19; Hans Hautmann and Rudolf Hautmann, Die Gemein-
debauten des roten Wien 1919 bis 1934 (Vienna, 1980).

49. For instance, Richard Wagner, Der Klassenkampf
um den Menschen (Berlin, 1927); Robert Danneberg, Das
neue Wien (Vienna, 1930); Karl Honay, "Sozialistische
Arbeit in der kapitalistischen Gesellshaft," Der Kampf,
V (1929); Gulick, Austria from Habsburg, pp. 503-04;
Austellung Kommunaler Wohnbau in Wien (Vienna, 1977).

50. Reinhard J. Sieder, "Housing Policy, Social
Welfare and Family Life in 'Red Vienna', 1919-1934,"
Journal of the Oral History Society, forthcoming.

51. Hautmann and Hautmann, "Hubert Gessner," p.
118, lists 33 central laundries with a total of 830
workplaces. That allows for 302,950 washdays for 63,000
tenants or 4.8 washdays per tenant per year. Sieder,
"Housing Policy," pp. 10-11, cites 5,032,847 baths taken

in municipal bathhouses (other than the three in the projects) as a sign of increased cleanliness. But even a conservative estimate of use works out to one bath in two weeks per person.

52. Reinhard J. Sieder, "The Daily Life of Viennese Working-Class Families during World War I," Conference on the European Family in the Period of the First World War, Pembroke College, Cambridge, 11-14 Sept. 1983, p. 26.

53. For the origins and development of the concept ordentliche Familie, see Joseph Ehmer, "Familie und Klasse: Zur Entstehung der Arbeiterfamilie in Wien," in Michael Mitterauer and Reinhard Sieder, eds., Historische Familienforschung (Frankfurt am Main, 1982).

54. Sieder, Housing Policy," pp. 9-10. Sieder and Gottfried Pirhofer have collected fifty-one oral history biographies of Viennese working-class women. The feeling of pressure from the building management, complaints about the strict regimentation, and the desire to escape from the controls of municipal housing are constant refrains among these women.

55. Pirhofer and Sieder, "Familie und Wohnen," pp. 190-91.

56. Sieder, "Housing Policy," pp. 12-21.

57. "It was also the worst punishment," one former welfare officer recalled. She concluded that only those parents who really could not cope with their children or did not want them surrendered them, to the public authority voluntarily. Ibid., p. 17.

58. On the potentiality for public intervention in the private lives of workers which was created by marriage consultation centers and those for mothers, see Pirhofer and Sieder, "Konstitution Arbeiterfamilie," pp. 328-31.

59. Ibid., p. 332.

60. There was nothing socialist about calling for experts to improve the quality and management of families and childrearing. Liberal reformers and statist interventionists have made such calls for over a century, and these demands have, by now, been largely fulfilled. See Christopher Lasch, Haven in a Heartless World: The Family Besieged (New York, 1976). In the Social Democratic Party, the first order of experts were the functionaries themselves. See Peter Kuhlmann, Am

Beispiel des Austromarxismus (Hamburg, 1979), pp.
313-24.

61. Julius Tandler equated sexual problems among
workers with sexual disease and blamed them on overcrowding in the tenements. That the worker's repressed
sexuality might not be "healed" by having a room of his
own did not occur to him. See "Wohungsnot und Sexualreform," Weltliga für Sexualreform, Sexualnot und Sexualreform: Verhandlungen, IV. Kongress abgehalten zu
Wien von 16. bis 23. September 1930 (Vienna, 1931), pp.
5-14.

62. For Hautmann and Hautmann, "Hubert Gessner," p.
124, the architecture of the structures embodied "the
ethical-moral norms of the working class"; for Pirhofer
they "represented an erotic which was only partly
'human'." See "Ansichten zum Wiener kommunalen Wohnbau
der zwanziger und frühen dreissiger Jahre," in Helmut
Fielhauer and Olaf Bockhorn, eds., Die Andere Kultur.
Volkskunde, Sozialwissenschaften und Arbeiterkultur
(Vienna, 1982), pp. 233-34.

63. See Anton Pelinka, "Kommunalpolitik als
Gegenmacht. Das 'rote Wien' als beispiel gesellschaftsverändernder Reformpolitk," in K.-H. Nassmacher, ed.,
Kommunalpolitik und Sozialdemokratie: Der Beitrag des
demokratischen Sozialismus zur kommunalen Selbstverwaltung (Bonn, 1977), pp. 63-77.

64. Gulick, Austria from Hapsburg, p. 499, points
out that the breach in the rent law led to an
increase in rents by
servative estimate, the proportion of a workers' budget
which went towards rent increased from 3.4 percent in
1928 to 5.4 percent in 1932. The combination of
increased unemployment and welfare payments plus the tax
starvation of Vienna by the national government tended
to vitiate the Breitner municipal taxes.

65. For an excellent recent analysis of the contradiction between the Socialists' perception and understanding, on the one hand, and their immobility on the
other, see Anson Rabinbach, The Crisis of Austrian Socialism: From Red Vienna to Civil War 1927-1934
(Chicago, 1983), especially Chapter 4.

66. Demystifying the Socialists' attempt to
"create" a working-class culture should not imply
falling into the opposite trap of glamorizing "life from
below," the horrors and poverty of which must also be
exposed and understood.

67. Having dealt with the Socialists' attempts to define the space of workers (their private sphere), I am currently examining the SDAP's plans and programs to define the sexual roles of workers. With the aid of monographs by my active and energetic Austrian colleagues, I intend to write a comprehensive history of Austrian working-class culture--one that will strive to overcome the problems and limitations outlined in the earlier part of this essay.

21. The Weaknesses of the Socialist Strategy: A Comparative Perspective

Charles S. Maier

Although the position of Austria and of the Austrian Socialists was very difficult in this period, and most alternatives were virtually foreclosed, still I think that a comparative perspective may help us to discern what possibilities there may have been for historical action and to look at roads not taken that may have made some difference. May I say in passing that, for Americans concerned with civil war, 12 February 1984 is also an important date: Abraham Lincoln's one hundred and seventy-fifth birthday.

The first comparative aspect I would cite is the fact that the Austrian reliance on Vienna--the policy of constructing a local bulwark--was not unique in Europe at this time. Other socialist parties followed it at various times, but I believe that at each juncture it had deficiencies. The most obvious parallel would be that of the German Social Democrats' reliance on their hold in Prussia during the Weimar Republic--what has been termed the Prussian strategy. Even when excluded from power in the Reich, the SPD kept a share of power in the state of Prussia and tried to control the interior ministry and the police. They also used Prussia as an arena in which to enact some of the same social-welfare, educational, and other reformist policies that the Austrian Socialists inaugurated. Obviously in contrast with Austria, Prussia's Social Democrats were not prepared to defend their bastion by force. It might well have been hopeless; in any case the SPD regime was terminated by Papen's Staatsstreich of 20 July 1932.

Italian Maximalist Socialists in 1920 attempted a similar strategy, believing that they could build a revolutionary movement on the basis of controlling the Chambers of Labor and the city halls in the Po Valley of northern Italy. The Maximalists made this area a center of socialist companionship, sociability, agrarian policies, and apparently imposing strength. Yet these local strongholds, too, fell like houses of cards before the assault of fascist squads from the fall of 1920 through

247

1922.

So we can see situations which if not exactly parallel were still somewhat similar, and they force us to
ask what were the virtues and what were the defects of
this type of local strategy. The virtue obviously was
that the party achieved a great sense of morale within
its enclosures. Nonetheless, the strategy of the bastion also produced extreme vulnerability and often led
to insufficient strategic thinking about how to relate
the local stronghold to the larger society. There was
often a failure to coordinate with potential democratic
allies, whether (as in the interwar years) those outside
Bologna, outside Berlin, or outside Vienna. The leadership often overestimated the strength that could be
drawn upon.

A second parallel can certainly be seen between the
Austrian and the German parties. This was what might be
termed a crisis of youth or activism which emerged in
the 1920s and 1930s and was perhaps inevitable in the
bureacratic party. If we look at Weimar Germany, there
were young leaders, some of whom then perished in the
Resistance, such as Julius Leber or Carlo Mierendorf,
who were impatient with the tone of constrained compromise set by the party leadership. These men were not
necessarily more socialist in any programmatic way, but
they were more activist. What one might have wished for
would have been a sort of "premature" Popular Front,
that is, a mobilization of democratic energies around a
program that would have been minimalist in its specific
calls for nationalization but maximalist in its commitment to the defense of democracy.

Instead the thrust of the party may have actually
undercut this sort of broad mobilization. (I do not
wish to be unfair; the Austrian Socialists faced excru-
ciating choices and every alternative might have been
doomed.) Still, the party emphasized mobilizing its
loyal adherents more than broadening its base. It
stressed: apartments now, inevitable socialism la-
ter--an ideological combination that may have led to a
tendency toward immobilism in the crisis. To point this
out, again, is not necessarily to say that the other
tactic would have worked, or that these are not all hard
choices made under some of the worst of times.

If Austria's divided society did not permit a
catch-all party to prosper, might not a more consistent
search for coalition possibilibies have been appropriate? Should not coalition invitations have been weighed
more seriously during the crisis even if they would have
limited the party's economic and social goals? If a
party is not prepared to, or cannot, woo voters across
basic social and cultural cleavages, then power-sharing
must be thought about much more constantly.

In this regard, Otto Bauer's whole notion of the

"51 percent" is worth rethinking. The idea that winning 51 percent at the polls would be the prelude to a thoroughgoing socialist transformation was not the same as Leon Blum's distinction between the exercise of power and the mandate of power. Blum accepted that even if the Socialists had a meager electoral majority, they could not go ahead with changing the social order. The majority of French people might vote the Socialists into power to govern on a day-to-day basis without voting for a social revolution. The French had no notion that any majority whatsoever would mandate a transition to socialism. Bauer's idea of the 51 percent was thus not a programmatic view analogous to the "exercise of power"; indeed it was, I think, a disastrous type of programmatic concept, especially in a society largely composed of peasants and small holders. So I believe that the socialist vision of Hans Zeisel's mother--she had a good sense of the unity of theory and practice at least--of socialism and justice, is precisely the one that Blum came to during the war years when he wrote A l'Echelle Humaine. Such a vision may have indeed motivated many Austrian party members, but I'm not sure that party ideology really allowed it to be used to best advantage. The Austrian Party could not draw upon its appeal to appeal for broad mobilization.

As in Germany, the Socialist Party in Austria achieved power by virtue of the collapse of a regime in the wake of a disastrous military defeat. They were not brought into power by electoral mobilization alone. People voted for the Socialists afterward because they voted for the gradualists against the revolutionaries; and there was, to be sure, a certain wave of enthusiasm. Nonetheless, both the Austrian party and the German party really were the legates of empire. And, as the legates of empire, they achieved their moment of greatest power in 1918 and 1919. Thereafter the electoral results were disappointing, except for some revival in the late 1920s, and I don't think the Socialists came to terms with that. The lessons they were starting to learn before the war in Germany--and perhaps in Austria under Victor Adler--were how to adjust to the situation of being a strong party, but a party that must also think about coalition behavior. The revolutions of 1918 allowed them, to a degree, to forget these lessons for a heady year or two, but openly at their peril. I don't think the Socialists ever really came to terms with the accidental nature of their hold on power as the result of defeat in World War I.

Let me say briefly, in regard to the comparison of national fascisms, that the Catholic countries--at least Austria and Spain--are different from Germany. Fascism arises in Austria and Spain out of a bipolarity engendered by the Church's alliance with traditional social

strata. If we look at Spain, for instance, in the wake
of the defeat of the Austrian left in February 1934, we
see the meteoric rise of the CEDA, the Spanish clerical
conservative party, potentially fascistic according to
Gil Robles's ambiguous pronouncements. The CEDA became
ever more menacing through October 1934 and was invited
to join the new right-wing government. This provoked
the left's effort at a general strike. In fact there
was a defensive civil uprising patronized by the Socialist left under Largo Caballero and then a disastrous and
cruel suppression. Thereafter followed the waning of
the CEDA and the rise of the Falange in 1936, which resembled the two-step sequence on the Austrian right,
with the Nazi's displacement of the Heimwehr.

Now Spain was obviously a much larger society with
all sorts of regional differences. It had a much more
difficult land problem to solve than did Austria and it
probably had more agonizing church-state problems to
solve than Austria. It did have a more supportive international context for its left--the ambiance of the
Popular Front. The Spanish left drew on the slogan
"Better Vienna than Berlin" when it offered militant
resistance to the right. The difficulty with that slogan was that both Vienna and Berlin had been disastrous
for the Socialists. Still, when the Austrian Socialists
faced a right wing based upon the entrenched Church,
they may well have dealt with a fascism that was in some
sense less brutal than a fully developed national socialism. At the same time, however, the emergence of a
fascism rooted in the Catholic right may well have been
almost more inevitable because of the alignment of
traditionalist classes with the conservative forces.

Finally, let me return to the question of Austria's
international orientation during this period. The issue
is not whether Anschluss before 1933 would not have comprised a nice development. Anschluss, after all, might
have brought stability to an enlarged German Republic.
It might even have brought an alternation of Catholics
and Socialists before the postwar period. (The numerical balance of the parties is about the same in both
Austrian republics.) But Anschluss was just not in the
cards--France had not fought World War I to consent to
an enlarged Germany of 85 million. That the Socialists
persisted in the dream of Anschluss was unfortunate.

And the preoccupation with Anschluss was unfortunate in another way. Although the Austrians were the
most cultivated of socialists, aware of developments in
British labor and in France, their strategic thinking
was so oriented towards the SPD that obviously the German events from 1930 through 1934 were a disaster for
them as well as for the SPD. The defeat of Germany's
Socialists gravely undermined the position of Austria's
Socialists--all the more since the SDAP was so spiritu-

ally oriented toward Berlin. Would it not have been healthier to have encouraged a less German-centered type of socialist internationalism (looking more toward Paris, less toward Berlin) with a different texture of international support and one that might also have helped to reorient Austrian socialism's internal thinking about domestic politics?

Obviously such possibilities might not have been in the cards; however I do believe that, in trying to assess Austria's dilemmas, we must at least canvass them. What is interesting about Austria--as the Austrians themselves insist, whether they are on the right or the left--is that their land is one of the most European of countries, in that it absorbs political vibrations from elsewhere and adds its own Viennese "genius." Austrian Socialists, however, were not playing upon those European possibilities to the most imaginative degree in this period.

Comparative history can thus help us place the sad developments in this country of 6.5 million in the context of Europe's wider tragedies and it can reveal the Austrians' historical options in the light of those that were and were not chosen by others during this interwar period.

Abbreviations

AZ   _Arbeiter-Zeitung_ (Social Democratic daily paper)

CEDA   Confederacion Espanola de Derechas Autonomas
        (Spanish Confederation of Autonomous Rightist
        Groups)

FPO   Freiheitliche Partei Osterreichs (Austrian Free-
        dom Party)

KZ   Konzentrationslager (Concenration Camp)

LSI   Labor and Socialist International

NSDAP   Nationalsozialistische Deutsche Arbeiterpartei
        (National Socialist Party)

OVP   Osterreichische Volkspartei (Austrian People's
        Party)

RS   Revolutionäre Sozialisten (Revolutionary Social-
        ists)

SAPD   Sozialistische Arbeiterpartei Deutschlands
        (Socialist Workers Party of Germany)

SDAP   Sozialdemokratische Arbeiterpartei (Social Demo-
        cratic Workers Party)

SFIO   Section française de l'internationale ouvrière
        (French Section of the Workers' International)

SPD   Sozialdemokratische Partei Deutschlands (German
        Social Democratic Party)

SPO   Sozialistische Partei Osterreichs (Socialist
        Party of Austria)

USPD   Unabhängige Sozialdemokratische Partei
        Deutschlands (German Independent Social Demo-
        cratic Party)

Contributors

ANDREW ARATO is Associate Professor of Sociology at the Graduate Faculty of the New School for Social Research in New York. He is the coauthor of The Young Lukács and the Origins of Western Marxism (1979) and coeditor of The Essential Frankfurt School Reader (1978). He has also published articles on the democratic movement in Eastern Europe and on the theory of Soviet-type societies.

C. EARL EDMONDSON is Associate Professor of History at Davidson College, North Carolina. He is the author of The Heimwehr and Austrian Politics, 1918-1936 (1978) and of reviews published in the American Historical Review, the Journal of Modern History, and the Austrian History Yearbook.

HELMUT GRUBER is Charles S. Baylis Professor of History at the Polytechnic Institute of New York. His publications include Léon Blum: French Socialism and the Popular Front; A Case of Internal Contradictions (forthcoming), International Communism in the Era of Lenin (1973), Soviet Russia Masters the Comintern (1974) and numerous articles on the socialist and communist movements. He is editor of Labor and Working Class History and chairman of the University Seminar in History of the Working Class at Columbia University. His current research is on "Working Class Culture in Red Vienna."

JACK JACOBS is an Assistant Professor in the Department of Political Science at Columbia University. He is currently completing a book on "Marxism and the Jewish Question after Marx."

KLEMENS VON KLEMPERER is L. Clark Seelye Professor of History at Smith College. His many publications in German and Austrian history include Germany's New Conservatism; Its History and Dilemma in the Twentieth Century (1957; German translation 1964), Ignaz Seipel;

Christian Statesman in Time of Crisis (1972; German
translation 1976), _Mandate for Resistance: The Case of
the German Opposition to Hitler_ (1969), and numerous
articles. His forthcoming books are _The German Resistance against National Socialism; Foreign Relations
1933-1945_ (Oxford University Press) and an edition of
the Correspondence of Shiela Grang Duff and Adam von
Trott zu Solz, 1932-1939 (Oxford University Press).

PETER LOEWENBERG is Professor of History at the University of California, Los Angeles and faculty member of
the Southern California Psychoanalytic Institute. He is
author of _Decoding the Past: The Psychohistorical
Approach_ (1983), which includes treatments of the Austromarxists.

DAVID S. LUFT is Associate Professor of European History
at the University of California, San Diego. He is the
author of _Robert Musil and the Crisis of European
Culture 1880-1942_ (1980). His recent publications
include "Schopenhauer, Austria and the Generation of
1905," _Central European History_ (March 1983) and "Otto
Weininger als Figur des fin de siècle," in _Otto
Weininger: Werk und Wirkung_ (1985).

CHARLES S. MAIER is Professor of History and a Research
Associate of the Harvard Center for European Studies.
He is the author of _Recasting Bourgeois Europe; Stabili-
zation in France, Germany and Italy in the Decade After
World War I_ (1975) and is currently working on a study
of political and economic reconstruction in Europe after
World War II.

PETER MARCUSE is Professor of Urban Planning at Columbia
University. He has written widely on housing policy,
city planning and urban history, including "The Myth of
the Benevolent State," "Gentrification, Abandonment and
Displacement in New York City," "Housing in City Planning History," "Towards the Decommodification of
Housing," and other works. A more detailed description
of the housing program of the Austrian Socialists,
incorporating the present article, will appear in Rachel
Bratt, Chester Hartman and Ann Meyerson, eds., _Critical
Perspectives on Housing_, forthcoming from Temple University Press.

WILLIAM J. McGRATH is Professor of History at the University of Rochester. He is the author of _Dionysian Art
and Populist Politics in Austria_ (1974), and a forthcoming book, _Freud's Discovery of Psychoanalysis: The
Politics of Hysteria_, to be published by Cornell University Press this year.

BRUCE F. PAULEY is Professor of History at the University of Central Florida. He is the author of The Habsburg Legacy, 1867-1939 (1972), Hahnenschwanz und Hakenkreuz: Steirischer Heimatschutz und österreichischer Nationalsozialismus, 1918-1934 (1972) and, most recently, Hitler and the Forgotten Nazis: A History of Austrian National Socialism (1981). His articles and reviews have appeared in the Austrian History Yearbook, German Studies Review, Central European History, and the American Historical Review. He is currently completing a study entitled In the Shadow of Death: Austria's Jews, 1914-1938.

ANTON PELINKA is Professor of Political Science and Director of the Institut für Politikwissenschaft at the University of Innsbruck. His books include Stand oder Klasse? Die Christliche Arbeiterbewegung Österreichs 1933-1938 (1972), Die Grundsatzprogramme der österreichischen Parteien. Dokumentations und Analyse (1979), and Bürgerkrieg - Sozialpartnerschaft. Das politische System der 1. and 2. Republic Österreich. Ein Vergleich (1983).

ALFRED PFABIGAN is Assistant at the Institut für Philosophie, University of Vienna. He is the author of Karl Kraus und der Sozialismus (1976), Max Adler: Eine Politische Biographie (1982), Ausgewählte Werke von Max Adler (1982), and studies of Hans Kelsen and B. Traven.

ANSON RABINBACH is Assistant Professor of History at The Cooper Union for the Advancement of Science and Art. He is the author of The Crisis of Austrian Socialism: From Red Vienna to Civil War 1927-1934 and articles on modern European history. He has been an editor of New German Critique: An Interdisciplinary Journal of German Studies since 1974. His current research is on the problem of fatigue and energy in the perception of work at the end of the nineteenth century.

R. JOHN RATH has been Professor of History at the University of Minnesota since 1980. His works include The Fall of the Napoleonic Kingdom of Italy (1941), The Viennese Revolution of 1848 (1957), The Provisional Austrian Regime in Lombardy-Venetia (1969), and numerous articles and reviews published in U.S., Canadian, Italian, Austrian, German, and Norwegian journals. He is the founder and former editor of the Austrian History Yearbook. Professor Rath received the Austrian Honor Cross in Arts and Sciences in 1963.

KARL R. STADLER is Professor of History at the Institut für Neuere Geschichte und Zeitgeschichte at the University of Linz and Director of the Ludwig-Boltzmann-

Institut für Geschichte der Arbeiterbewegung in Linz.
His numerous publications include Hypothek der Zukunft.
Entstehung der österreichischen Republik 1918-1921
(1968), Opfer verlorene Zeiten. Die Geschichte der
Schutzbund-Emigranten (1974) and Adolf Schärf: Mensch,
Politiker, Staatsmann (1982).

ADOLF STURMTHAL is Emeritus Professor of Labor and
Industrial Relations at the University of Illinois, and
formerly Philip Murray Professor at Roosevelt University, Chicago. He is a leading authority on problems of
economic development and the international labor movement and the author of numerous studies including The
Tragedy of European Labor (1942; 2nd ed. 1951), Worker's
Councils: A Study of Workplace Organizations on Both
Sides of the Iron Curtain (1964), White Collar Trade
Unions (1966), and, most recently, Left of Center:
European Labor since World War II (1983). Before
emigrating to the United States he was editor in chief
of International Information (1926-1936) and assistant
to Friedrich Adler at the LSI.

MELANIE SULLY is a Senior Lecturer in History at North
Staffordshire Polytechnic, England. Her books on Aus-
tria are Political Parties and Elections in Austria
(1981) and Continuity and Change in Austrian Socialism
(1982). Dr. Sully has written widely on contemporary
Austrian politics for Political Quarterly, The World
Today, Parliamentary Affairs, and West European
Politics.

JOSEF WEIDENHOLZER is Professor of History at the
Institut für Gesellschaftspolitik at the University of
Linz and at the Ludwig-Boltzmann-Institut für Geschichte
der Arbeiterbewegung, Linz. He is the author of Neuen
Menschen: Bildungs- und Kulturarbeit der österreichischen Sozialdemokratie in der 1. Republik (1981) and is
currently completing a study of social policy in Austria
from Josef II to Ferdinand Hanusch.

HANS ZEISEL is Professor of Law and Sociology Emeritus,
The University of Chicago. He was an active member of
the Austrian Social Democratic party before 1934 and a
frequent contributor to its theoretical journal, Der
Kampf. After 1945 he contributed to its successor, Die
Zukunft, maintaining his ties with Austrian Socialism.
With Paul Lazarsfeld and Marie Jahoda he coauthored the
classic first study of the psychology of unemployment,
Die Arbeitslosen von Marienthal (1933). Since emigrating to the United States he has been a leading expert on the sociology of law and the jury system. His
works include Say it With Figures (1946) and, with Harry
Kalven Jr., the standard text on the American jury sys-

259

tem, The American Jury (1956). He has been awarded the
Grosse Goldene Ehrenkreuz, Austria's highest civilian
honor.

A Nature Guide to
Boundary Bay

A Nature Guide to
Boundary Bay

Anne Murray
with photographs by
David Blevins

Nature Guides B.C.
Delta

Nature Guides B.C.
PO Box 18170, 1215c - 56 Street Delta, B.C
Canada V4L 2M4
www.natureguidesbc.com

Library and Archives Canada Cataloguing in Publication

Murray, Anne, 1952 Feb.16-

A Nature Guide to Boundary Bay / Anne Murray; with photographs by David Blevins

Includes Index.
ISBN 0 - 9780088 - 0 - 4

1. Natural history --Boundary Bay Region (B.C. and Wash.)

1. Blevins, David Preston, 1967- 11.Title.

QH106.2B7M87 2006   508.711'3   C2006-900583-4

Printed by Friesens in Canada, on recycled paper.

Disclaimer: While every effort has been made to make the information in this guide accurate and up to date, the author and publisher take no responsibility for problems arising as a result of readers' nature viewing activities or use of this guide.

CONTENTS

MAP OF BOUNDARY BAY
and surrounding areas

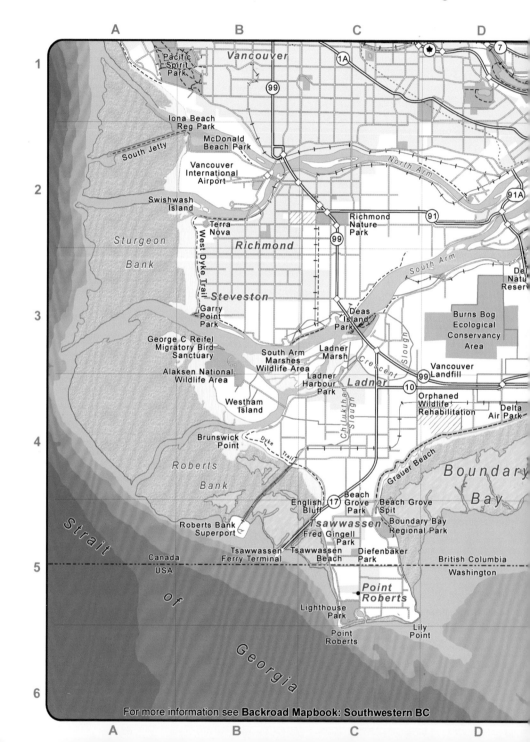

For more information see **Backroad Mapbook: Southwestern BC**

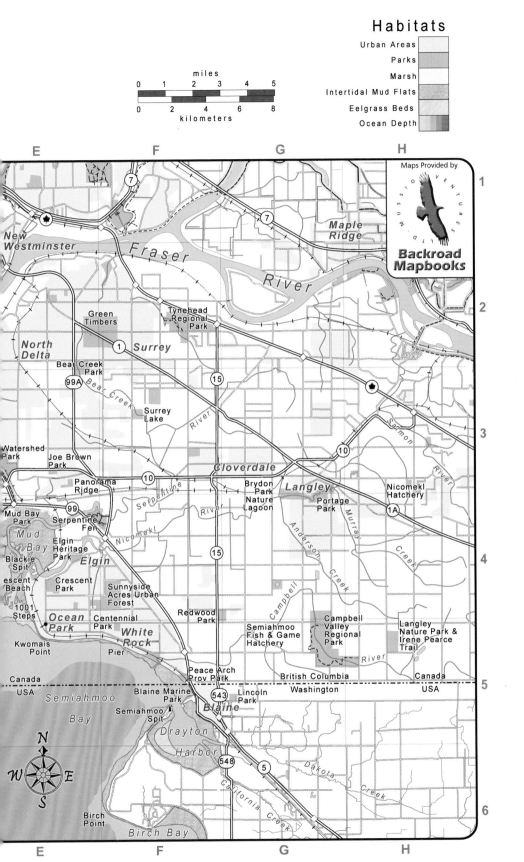

Habitats

Urban Areas	
Parks	
Marsh	
Intertidal Mud Flats	
Eelgrass Beds	
Ocean Depth	

miles
0 1 2 3 4 5

0 2 4 6 8
kilometers

Maps Provided by

MUSSIO VENTURES LTD.

Backroad Mapbooks

New Westminster

Maple Ridge

Fraser River

7

7

North Delta

Green Timbers

Tynehead Regional Park

Surrey

1

Bear Creek Park

99A

Bear Creek

Surrey Lake

15

Sermon River

Watershed Park

Joe Brown Park

Cloverdale

River

10

10

Panorama Ridge

Brydon Park Nature Lagoon

Langley

Nicomekl Hatchery

Serpentine

Portage Park

1A

Mud Bay Park

99

Serpentine Fen

River

Anderson Creek

Murray Creek

Blackie Spit

Elgin Heritage Park

Nicomekl

Elgin

Crescent Beach

Crescent Park

Sunnyside Acres Urban Forest

1001 Steps

Ocean Park

Centennial Park

Redwood Park

Campbell

Semiahmoo Fish & Game Hatchery

Campbell Valley Regional Park

Langley Nature Park & Irene Pearce Trail

Mud Bay

White Rock

Kwomais Point

Pier

Peace Arch Prov Park

British Columbia

River

Canada

Canada USA

USA

Semiahmoo Bay

Blaine Marine Park

543

Lincoln Park

Washington

Semiahmoo Spit

Blaine

Drayton Harbor

548

5

Dakota Creek

N W E S

Birch Point

California Creek

Birch Bay

Acknowledgements

I would like to thank all the people who made this book possible. I am indebted to Dr Mary Taitt and John Ireland for sharing their expertise on mammals, birds and ecology, and to the late Dr Jamie Smith, who generously gave his time, enthusiasm and knowledge. Rob Rithaler and Laura Friis were very helpful with amphibian information and Terry Taylor helped me learn about the fascinating world of fungi. Many thanks to Don Munro for providing reminiscences of natural history in the White Rock area, dating back to the 1930s and to Joan Wilmshurst for her guided tour of Langley. Many other people helped me in various ways including Bert Brink, Sean Boyd, Rob Butler, Richard Cannings, Marg Cuthbert, Dick Dekker, Kyle Elliott, Lanny Englund, Jude and Al Grass, Louise Gratton, Felicity and Mike Jenkins, Susan Jones, David Nagorsen, Margaret and W. J. O'Hara, Mike Price, Bev Ramey, David Riley, Rob Rithaler, Jorge Rocha, Glenn Ryder, Joan Snyder, Rick Swanston, Rosemary Taylor, Ken Thorpe, Duanne Vandenberg and Kathy Wilkinson. Thank you all.

Thank you to the kind people at Backroad Mapbooks who helped us create the Boundary Bay map. For detailed maps and listings of places to view wildlife, both locally and around the province or country, be sure to look for the relevant Backroad Mapbook title. Thanks also to Chris Hutton at Nature Canada for supplying the Pacific Flyway map. Special thanks to Ellie Murray, for her advice on biological and ecological topics, and to Catherine Murray for introducing me to the complicated world of viruses. I am very grateful to Sarah Murray, who supplied professional editing and proof-reading services; any errors remaining in the manuscript are entirely my fault. Finally, this book would never have been produced without the constant support and encouragement of my husband, Len.

~ Anne Murray

I find it easier to get close enough to photograph wildlife by allowing them to approach me rather than trying to get close to them. As a result, I am deeply appreciative of each of the animals pictured in this book that chose to spend part of their day with me. I am also grateful for the help I received from humans while creating images for this book. Don Benson, Geoff Clayton, Hugh Griffith, Brian and Rose Klinkenburg, Susan Leach, Eliza Olson, Doug Ransome, Candi and Jeff Staley, Russ Weisner and Lisa Zabek each helped make some of the images possible. Most of all I would like to thank my wife, Leandra, who accompanied me on many walks in and around Boundary Bay, helped me create some of the images, and without whose love and support this would not have been possible.

~ David Blevins

Left: A cedar waxwing perched in a western redcedar at Serpentine Fen in Surrey.

Hundreds of thousands of ducks and geese gather on migration on the calm waters of Boundary Bay. The bay's dramatic and diverse coastline connects southern British Columbia with the northern state of Washington.

A SENSE OF PLACE

"Boundary Bay is the most important coastal bay for shorebirds and waterfowl on the coast of British Columbia"

~ Robert Butler & Wayne Campbell - The Birds of the Fraser River Delta

When I first moved here twenty years ago, the incredible wealth of bird life found around Boundary Bay came as a complete surprise. This wonderful wildlife destination seemed to be virtually unknown outside the Pacific Northwest! Searching around for a nature guide book, I soon realised that a whole library of field guides was necessary to learn about the birds, animals, fish, plants and intertidal life of the area, and that no one had written one complete guide.

In the intervening years, conservation groups have highlighted the ecological importance of Boundary Bay and the Fraser River estuary. Not only is this area a crucial resting place for migrating and wintering birds, but it is also a rich habitat for salmon, crustaceans and marine mammals. As a consequence, residents strongly supported the public purchase of Boundary Bay parks and Burns Bog, and the designation of Wildlife Management Areas at the mouth of the Fraser River and on the intertidal banks. International recognition has come in the form of designations: the Fraser River estuary, including Boundary Bay, was recognised as the top Important Bird Area in Canada and a Western Hemispheric Site for migrating shorebirds. It also meets the criteria for a UNESCO Ramsar Site.

As interest has grown, residents and visitors want to learn more about nature in the region: where to go and what to see. The purpose of this comprehensive guide book is therefore to provide a convenient and accessible introduction to Boundary Bay's remarkable nature.

A Nature Guide to Boundary Bay covers the whole watershed of Boundary Bay, including the river valleys and uplands from which freshwater flows into the bay. This geographic area encompasses both sides of the international border, from Langley, Surrey, White Rock, Delta and Richmond, B.C., to Point Roberts, Blaine and Birch Bay, Washington.

Wildlife viewing

Nature follows a seasonal cycle: learning about the behavior patterns of birds and animals helps you to see them. Sitting quietly, waiting and watching is often the most rewarding activity for successful wildlife viewing.

- **Know where to look.** Every animal and plant has a specific habitat where it thrives best. Habitats around Boundary Bay include sand flats, bogs, marshes, wet meadows, and the rivers and forests of the watershed.

- **Visit the right habitat at the right time of year.** This will increase your chance of wildlife viewing success. Many birds are migratory and only visit at certain seasons. Some animals hibernate. The best times of day for seeing and hearing wildlife are early morning and late afternoon.

- **Consult tide tables before planning a trip to the beach or dyke.** View shorebirds as the tide comes in, waterfowl at winter high tide, and intertidal life in summer at the lowest tide of the month (full moon).

- **Take proper equipment.** Binoculars help to observe wildlife at a distance, and a telescope is useful for watching water birds from the shore. Botanists use a pocket magnifier to get a closer look at plants.

- **Take a personal guide.** Field guides are a great help for identifying different species of mammals, birds, plants, insects, etc. Look for guide books to the Pacific Northwest, British Columbia or Washington.

- **Watch and photograph from a distance and restrain your dog, so that both you and other people can enjoy the sight of wild animals and birds.** Animals with young, and nesting or migrating birds, are easily disturbed by people and dogs approaching too closely. This is especially important at high tide when birds are crowded close to the shore.

- **Let the animals be wild!** Wild animals remain healthy by eating natural food that they find themselves. Feeding them is not necessary and fed animals can become pests, especially such species as coyotes, raccoons and Canada geese. Coyote attacks around Vancouver have all been by animals that were regularly fed or that ate garbage.

- **Keep records.** It's a great help in learning about local nature and it contributes to the body of biological and ecological knowledge that is gradually being collected for this region.

- **Join a local naturalist group for a field trip.** You will learn more about Boundary Bay's wildlife and habitats, meet enthusiasts and have fun!

WILDLIFE HABITATS

" I have spent many happy times birdwatching ...."

~ Robert Bateman in An Artist in Nature

This chapter describes the habitats found around Boundary Bay and where to go to enjoy them. We move from the deep waters of the Strait of Georgia through to Burns Bog, the Fraser River and the forested parks of the uplands.

STRAIT OF GEORGIA

The deep waters of the Strait begin where the sea floor drops down at the delta face, to a depth of about 150 m (480 ft) near Birch Point and Point Roberts. This is where the strong winds and surf thunder onto pebble beaches in winter, stirring up the kelp forests along the shore. These waters are home to many animals, including killer whales (or orcas), harbour seals, California and Steller sea lions and harbour porpoises, as well as fish such as herring, hake and Pacific salmon. Look here for groups of colourful male harlequin ducks swimming

A horned grebe in winter plumage.

with their plain brown females in the turbulent water. They dive down to look for crabs and other crustaceans on the sea floor. Other exciting birds include three species of scoters, long-tailed ducks, horned grebes, pigeon guillemots, rhinoceros auklets and marbled murrelets. Dense groves of spectacular orange sea pens grow in the fast current off Roberts Bank. Dungeness crabs gather to rear their young and sea squirts, scallops, sea stars, green and plumose anemones and tube worms are other inhabitants of this rich marine setting.

Further out in the Strait, the sea floor plunges to over 400 m (1360 ft). At these depths, red and yellow light wavelengths fail to penetrate the water. The specialized species of this marine zone, such as red algae and certain species of rockfish, must survive by absorbing cold blue or green light. Storms stir up even the deepest waters and rough weather washes many fronds of red algae onto Boundary Bay beaches.

BEACHES & SANDFLATS

Boundary Bay is a shallow marine bay, less than 30 m (98 ft) deep and awash in saltwater during high tide. At low water, vast sand flats are exposed to the air. Hidden beneath the sand are millions of tiny plant-eaters, as well as filter feeders such as lugworms, burrowing shrimps, clams and cockles. These provide food for many other species, including migrating shorebirds. Marine mammals also visit beaches, including harbour seals, river otters, mink, and more rarely, harbour porpoises and grey whales. Summertime beaches are used by many types of gull, mostly non-breeders slowly moulting into mature plumage, and by large groups of great blue herons. In winter, bald eagles are common and flocks of dunlin twist and turn over the bay.

Many intertidal creatures were introduced either accidentally or intentionally from other countries.

Mudflat snails

The little mudflat snail crawls in the shallows, far from its original home in Japan, and shiny, purple varnish clams have spread rapidly since their first appearance in 1980.

EELGRASS MEADOWS

Eelgrass, a type of bright green sea grass, is the predominant vegetation growing on the intertidal flats. It provides critical habitat for many different kinds of animal, from bubble snails to brant, and from herring to herons. The dense fronds provide both food and shelter for wildlife.

Eelgrass is a type of sea grass, related to the lily family.

The eelgrass meadows of Boundary Bay and Roberts Bank are the most extensive in the Strait of Georgia, covering thousands of hectares.

Eelgrass meadows are extremely rich in marine life of all kinds. In studies of Pacific Northwest eelgrass ecosystems, over 120 species of invertebrates, 350 species of seaweed, 90 species of microscopic algae, and numerous vertebrate species have been recorded. Most commercially taken fish and shellfish spend at least part of their lives among eelgrass.

The eelgrass meadows of Boundary Bay are the most extensive in the Strait of Georgia

There are two species of eelgrass growing in the Boundary Bay area, both of the *Zostera* genus. The native, perennial, common eelgrass generally flourishes in deep waters, while the smaller Japanese eelgrass occurs in shallow water and can tolerate greater exposure to sun and air. The perennial plant makes most of its growth by means of shoots arising from rhizomes, or underground stems. The introduced species is an annual and dies back in winter.

For more about eelgrass meadows, see Life in the Intertidal page 47.

SPITS & SAND DUNES

The cliffs at Point Roberts, Ocean Park and Birch Point are eroding. Longshore drift currents transport sand and gravel along the shoreline into the bay. The sediments settle out in elongated spits, or bars, aligned roughly parallel with the east and west shores of the bay. Semiahmoo Spit, Blackie Spit and the sand bars at Beach Grove and Boundary Bay Regional Park were all formed in this way. In each case they shelter lagoons of quiet, shallow water that are used by birds much of the year. Similar bars are found along the banks of the lower Fraser River.

Dune grass, silver burweed, entire-leaved gumweed, vetches and beach pea will grow on the poor soil of sand and gravel spits and are tolerant of salt spray and seaside conditions. Eastern cottontails scamper at dusk from the shelter of bramble bushes, and birds such as American pipits, horned larks and Lapland longspurs visit on migration.

Bent-nose clam shell and gull track on the sandy beach of Boundary Bay Regional Park.

Savannah sparrows nest on the ground under clumps of grass, gulls and waterfowl gather here to sleep and moult, and the extended, gently sloping shorelines are good feeding areas for shorebirds, such as dowitchers, sandpipers and yellowlegs. Brant come ashore on gravel beaches to search for grit for their gizzards. Grauer Beach, just north of the Beach Grove lagoon, is one habitual place for this activity.

Artificial spits can be good habitat. Blaine Marine Park was created from an old landfill in Semiahmoo Bay and a compensation lagoon has attracted Caspian terns to Roberts Bank. The pebbly edge of the ferry causeway unexpectedly created the right conditions for nesting black oystercatchers, just a few metres from heavy traffic.

Old sand bars and dunes from prehistoric beaches are set back from the current shoreline by as much as 0.75 km (0.47 mi). They are the site of shell middens, remains from the homes of ancestors of the Coast Salish, some up to 5000 years old! Relict dunes, such as those in Boundary Bay Regional Park, have interesting plant communities, with big-headed sedge and blue-eyed mary.

The sand spits of Boundary Bay are affected by dredging, dumping and by general pressure from crowds of people out admiring the view or walking the dog. The spits' unique and attractive natural attributes are being increasingly recognized, and some efforts are being made to restore vegetation. Ideally, humans and wildlife will continue to enjoy these special shoreline areas as they have for thousands of years.

POSTS, PILINGS & PIERS

Even artificial constructions are not devoid of life. In the marine environment, they quickly become part of the habitat, with barnacles, mussels, limpets and different sea weeds (red, green and brown algae) competing for anchorage space. Concrete reefs at the Roberts Bank terminals have lingcod, copper and black rockfish and blackeye goby, as well as mottled stars, hermit crabs and whelks. Some areas are heavily grazed by green sea urchins, preventing colonization by a wider variety of animals and plants.

Pilings and posts left over from the old canneries provide nesting sites for glaucous-winged gulls, double-crested and pelagic cormorants. These birds are often seen standing around on pilings, as are herons and eagles. At Blackie Spit, purple martins use nestboxes on posts over the water. Glaucous-winged gulls and ring-billed gulls sit or stand on the piers at White Rock and Blaine, waiting for snacks. A very rare ivory gull made a surprise visit to Roberts Bank in winter 2001, where it spent several weeks sitting on a barge.

Glaucous-winged gull on pilings.

SALT MARSH

Salt marsh is a tremendously important and rich habitat that occurs along select shorelines of Boundary and Semiahmoo Bays, in Drayton Harbor and close to the dyke on Roberts Bank. It needs a predominantly marine environment to flourish and differs ecologically from the estuarine marshes that line the mouth of the Fraser River.

Salt marshes are enormously fertile, in terms of primary production

Prior to dyke construction in the late 1800s, salt marshes were much more widespread across the delta. In the northwest corner of Boundary Bay, for example, the fringe of intertidal salt marsh once covered the area where fields now lie. Migrating and wintering waterfowl still visit the marshes in the tens of thousands. Salt marsh plants typically have thick rubbery leaves with special pores through which they release excess

salt. The most familiar is a spiky, low-growing sea asparagus, also known as salicornia, pickleweed or American glasswort; other common plants are sea arrow-grass, seashore saltgrass and (in summer) the bright orange tangles of salt marsh dodder.

In terms of primary production, which is the growth of plants by photosynthesis, salt marshes are enormously fertile. However, the first impressions of the marsh can be uninviting: the mud is thick, black and oozy with a thin pale crust and thre is a strong smell, caused by anaerobic bacteria. Hordes of little flies are attracted in summer to the decaying piles of eelgrass leaves. The tide brings in oxygen and nutrients and flushes out waste, or detritus, driving the productivity of this strange maritime habitat.

Primary production is a key measure of the fertility of land or ocean. The tidal flats of Boundary Bay, rich in eelgrass, average more than 400 gC/sq m/year productivity, ranging

---

Saltmarsh loss

University of B.C. geographer, Margaret North, has compiled a map of historic vegetation in the Fraser River Estuary that shows the total salt marsh was 2230 ha (5575 ac) in 1858. By 1984, salt marsh was down to 380 ha (950 ac), a loss of 83%. Today the loss is believed to be close to 99%.

to around 200 gC/sq m/year at the mouth of the Fraser River. This compares very favourably with the best farmland on the continent. Salt marshes measure even higher in primary productivity. Despite this, salt marshes have been consistently dismissed as wastelands and many have been filled or drained.

Salicornia marshes are home to salmon fry and other young fish. Dabbling ducks, such as mallard and gadwall, loaf and sleep in the marsh during summer. Winter high tides bring in big flocks of northern pintail and green-winged teal, that feed on seeds, leaves and invertebrates. The higher ground of the marsh is covered with logs thrown up by the tide, between which grow a mass of dune grass, sea rocket, gumweed and Pacific silverweed. Clumps of cow-parsnip and sea-watch provide food for anise swallowtail caterpillars. Coyotes, Townsend's voles, northern harriers, savannah sparrows and Puget Sound garter snakes are all common in this habitat.

A gadwall taking flight: note its pale underwing linings.

ESTUARINE MARSH

Estuaries, where the river meets the sea, are full of life, particularly in the spring and summer. Their driving force is the mixing of fresh and salt water, sustaining a complex food web of plants and animals.

The Fraser River estuary is one of the richest habitats on the Pacific Northwest coast and the largest marshes are at the mouth of the Fraser River. Smaller ones are found throughout the Boundary Bay watershed, wherever rivers and creeks flow into the sea.

Estuaries sustain a complex food web of plants & animals

Estuarine marshes are important wetlands for migrating salmon and eulachon, and the wildlife that prey on them. Typical marsh plants, like tule, American bulrush and Lyngby's sedge, are able to tolerate brackish water, and tend to slow its flow, while cattails prefer locations with a greater percentage of freshwater.

Snow geese and trumpeter swans make a fine sight in winter as they come in to graze on rhizomes and shoots. Their presence actually ensures the future growth of the marsh. As they grub, they make puddles and troughs that fill with tidal waters and attract yet more fish and waterfowl, increasing

Large stands of tule flourish at the mouth of the Fraser.

the diversity of the marsh. Their droppings fertilize the mud, and tough sheaths of bulrush rejected by the birds gather in strands along the tideline, collecting sediment and debris around them and building up dry land. In these ways, the life and structure of the marsh is intimately connected with the geese.

Estuary marshes are the place to see Puget Sound garter snakes, mink, ermines and cottontails. Cattails are home to red-winged blackbirds, marsh wrens, Virginia rails, soras and American bittern.

For more about rivers, sloughs and streams, see Nature Destinations, pages 165 - 204.

RIVERS

Boundary Bay is a landscape created by the mightiest river in British Columbia, the Fraser. A handful of other small rivers drain into the eastern side of the bay.

The most famous river inhabitants are the seven species of salmon that use the rivers as spawning areas, juvenile rearing grounds and corridors to the sea. In historical times, beavers, otters and muskrats were very abundant, and some still live along the rivers and sloughs. Here, spotted sandpiper and killdeer nest on shorelines, belted kingfishers call from overhanging branches, swallows dart and swoop over the water and great blue herons stalk the shallows.

THE FRASER RIVER & ITS PLUME

The Fraser River is the fifth longest river in Canada; its watershed covers over 234,000 sq km (90,000 sq mi), a quarter of the province. From its headwaters near Jasper in the Rocky Mountains the river flows for a distance of 1378 km (856 mi), in a great S-shaped curve through the dry interior and lush lower valley, finally reaching the shoreline marshes on the Strait of Georgia. By the time it reaches the delta, the river is a murky grey brown and flows at about 3.5 knots. Transported sediments drop to the sea floor, creating sand banks and shoals at the river mouth, and helping the delta build outwards at the rate of 3 m (10 ft) a year.

From mid-May to mid-July, the mountain snow melt pours into the river. This is called the "freshet". The flow through the delta increases to 5.5 knots, carrying huge logs in the powerful current. The immense volume of freshwater transported, and the high level of dissolved oxygen, have major impacts on the Strait of Georgia and the whole delta.

The river is the main migration corridor for salmon, with an annual average of 800 million out-migrating juvenile salmonids (*for more about salmon, see pages 130-131*). The delta reaches are also the home of giant white sturgeon and a migration corridor for eulachon in spring.

Freshwater from the river pours into the strait's salt water in a trailing plume, reaching almost as far as the shores of Galiano Island and with a strong northward flow. This freshwater plume, between one and four metres deep, full of nutrients and suspended sands and silts, surges into the strait at ebb tide. This creates strong currents at the river's mouth. The tide pulls the salt water southwards, allowing freshwater to dominate the estuary. When the tide races back into the Strait, the northbound current surges past Point Roberts, backing up the Fraser River and filling the marshes with salt water at high tide. The salt water is dense and forms a wedge underneath the freshwater, which rides buoyantly on top.

The **plume** is a distinctive ecosystem. Its salinity is half that of the Strait

Dawn on the water-logged marshes at the mouth of the Fraser River; Swishwash Island, Richmond is seen in the distance.

of Georgia, about 15 psu to 30 psu respectively (a psu is the "practical salinity unit", equivalent to parts per thousand). Turbulent waters at its edge attract copepods, microscopic animals less than 2 mm (1/13 in) long, that graze on phytoplankton. Shoals of fish eat the copepods, preyed on by hordes of seabirds, diving ducks and loons. As the freshet builds to a peak through May and June, the plume becomes full of sediment and very turbid, so plankton, copepod and fish numbers fall. A few species, such as lampreys, lurk in salt water under the plume.

Eighty percent of the river's flow is through the main arm, also known as the South Arm. With dyking and training, the active front of the Fraser River delta is no longer contoured by the braiding action of a free river, but constrained into a fixed path. This creates instability by increasing flow rates and piling all the sediment into only a few locations; slumping and settling are common.

Further constraints come from the twin causeways for the B.C. ferry terminal and the Roberts Bank port complex, both of which stretch out across the flats between Tsawwassen bluffs and Brunswick Point. Built in 1960 and 1962 respectively, and enlarged upon ever since, they have dramatically altered how the river plume interacts with the tide. (*For more about tides around Boundary Bay see page 47.*)

The Serpentine River near its source at Tynehead.

SERPENTINE & NICOMEKL RIVERS

These two rivers flow into Mud Bay just a couple of kilometres apart, having slowly wound their way for 35 km (22 mi) across the flood plain. At one time they must have shared a large estuary, awash at every high tide and rich in marsh vegetation. The rivers are now dyked, and their mouths barred by sea dams, so only the lowest reaches are tidal. The intervening drained grasslands and marshes are mostly farmed, but the Serpentine Wildlife Area has big flocks of wintering waterfowl and migrating shorebirds.

The **Serpentine River** rises in Surrey, with its source in streams near Tynehead Park, where there is a hatchery for coho and chum salmon. The river winds through cedar hemlock forests before entering the farmland of the upper valley. For the first few kilometres it makes a circuitous journey, giving credit to its name, and is eventually joined by

A saltmarsh at the mouth of the Nicomekl River, Surrey.

several salmon-bearing tributaries, including Latimer Creek, Bear Creek (Mahood River), and Hyland Creek.

Glacial gravels provide good spawning habitat for coho, chinook and chum

Further downstream the river has been dyked and straightened, its banks reinforced with concrete and pump stations spaced at regular intervals to drain the farmland. Altogether the Serpentine River drains 116 sq km (45 sq mi) of upland and valley, including the city of Surrey. The area drained is often referred to as a "watershed".

The **Nicomekl River** rises in Langley, as a thin stream, choked with aquatic vegetation and beaver-worked logs. The Nicomekl watershed drains 149 sq km (58 sq mi), incorporating the tributaries Anderson, Murray, Best, Logan, Erickson, McLellan and

McInnes creeks, several of which cut through deep, forested ravines, before joining the main river.

The upper reaches of the Nicomekl watershed are rural. Small ponds and wetlands throughout the area attract amphibians and wintering waterfowl. An occasional black bear roams these woodlands and coyotes run in the fields. An Ecological Reserve in the Murray - Anderson Creek uplands, managed by the Wild Bird Trust of B.C., is typical alder - maple woodland, with ruffed grouse, western screech owl and songbirds.

On the floodplain, the narrow river slowly flows through parks, then farm fields. Lower reaches have been dyked, and the estuary's muddy tidal banks are the haunt of waterfowl, shorebirds, and herons. Coho and chum salmon runs occur during the autumn rains and the Nicomekl Enhancement Society maintains a salmon hatchery on the river. Together, the Serpentine and Nicomekl flow into the eastern side of Boundary Bay, at Mud Bay.

Coho salmon.

LITTLE CAMPBELL RIVER

For nearly 30 km (19 mi) the **Little Campbell River** winds through the countryside near the Canada - US border, flowing with a gentle gradient past fields, forests and golf courses, draining 74 sq km of land (29 sq mi).

It is gazetted as the Campbell River, but known locally as the Little Campbell. Uncommon mountain beaver and green heron have been seen near the headwaters in south Langley, where alder, cedar and maples shade the water, and the banks are lined with cattails, hardhack, red osier dogwood and clumps of reed canary grass. The upper valley is less developed than the Serpentine and Nicomekl valleys, and the abundant wildlife includes great blue herons, American beavers, mink, muskrats, deer and a variety of waterfowl.

Still little more than a stream, the river makes a large loop north-south through Douglas-fir forest and wetlands in Campbell Valley Park. It flows down a valley carved from the melt waters of the Sumas glacier, the last of the great Fraser Valley ice sheets. The glacial gravels provide good spawning and rearing habitat for coho, chinook and chum salmon, steelhead and cutthroat trout and a number of smaller fish. Dragonflies dart around and wild flowers line the banks.

The river has a host of little side streams: Jacobsen and Jenkins Creek, then Little Brook, and Annie's, Sam Hill, Fergus and McNalley Creeks. Fergus Creek may still have locally rare marsh (Pacific water) shrew and Trowbridge's shrew; both were seen

A view of shrub meadows in Campbell Valley Park

here in 1992. The stretch of river flowing through the Semiahmoo First Nations's land remains quite idyllic, with great blue herons fishing the shallows, shorebirds probing the mud and flocks of ducks in winter. The river then turns suddenly and flows into Semiahmoo Bay under a railway bridge.

DAKOTA & CALIFORNIA CREEKS

The watershed of the two forks of **Dakota Creek**, and its tributaries, is a rural area of second growth forest, small farms and acreages. The North Fork emerges on a ridge of upland, about 14 km (9 mi) from the ocean shore, in an open pastoral landscape that has magnificent views across to Mount Baker and the North Cascades. From here the river cuts narrow ravines through birch and alder woodlands, joined by smaller creeks along its length and by the South Fork near Custer Road.

Columbian black-tailed deer, bald eagles and red-tailed hawks are common in the valley, and the river is home to beavers, mink, spotted sandpipers, great blue herons and belted kingfishers. Occasionally a black bear roams down from the wilder country eastward.

The lower, tidal, reaches of the river flow through acreages, farmland and woodlots before entering Drayton Harbor.

California Creek

California Creek and its tributaries are about the same length as Dakota Creek, and they run roughly parallel, flowing in a northwesterly direction through open farmland and small communities. Streams fan out through the grass pastures. Altogether the watershed of Dakota and California Creeks covers 14,040 ha (34,690 ac).

SLOUGHS, STREAMS & DITCHES

Historically, the lowlands around the bay were riddled with sloughs and streams, winding through marshes to the sea. Some have since been lost to culverting and drainage schemes, but those that remain are important fish and wildlife habitat.

Sloughs are tidal creeks that were important transportation routes, prior to dyking of the delta. They once carried canoes, skiffs, scows, gillnetters, steamers and ferries, but as their tidal flow was restricted, many eventually silted up.

Sloughs are home to a wide range of species, from beavers and muskrats to nesting wood ducks, herons and garter snakes.

Artesian springs in the uplands are the source of many freshwater **streams**. Cool, shaded streams are habitat for aquatic salamanders and breeding red-legged frogs, while rare marsh shrews (Pacific water shrews) inhabit slow-moving streams in forests. Streams gradually flow downhill towards the main valleys, and together all these little tributaries form the watershed of the river. When we look at the health of a river, the whole, interconnected watershed must be considered.

Ditches are used to drain the agricultural land, particularly on the delta. Farm ditches are regularly dredged and some are brackish. Ones with open, grassy banks have introduced green frogs and American bullfrogs, rather than native species. Some ditches, however, are good fish habitat. Cattails crowd into even the smallest water courses, and are quickly adopted by nesting blackbirds and marsh wrens.

Juvenile great blue herons hunt voles along the banks, green herons lurk in shady backwaters and dabbling ducks shelter there from winter storms. Stinging nettles, sea-watch and cow-parsnip provide essential food for anise swallowtail and red admiral caterpillars (*for more about butterflies, see pages 134 - 135*).

FARMED FIELDS, OLD FIELDS & SHRUB MEADOWS

Working farms around Boundary Bay grow dozens of different crops in summer and rear a variety of livestock. Farming has been a major occupation for a hundred and forty years and small family-run farms in the watershed raise everything from Chinese geese to grapes, llamas and loganberries.

At the same time, intensive farming occupies an increasing part of the agricultural land base, especially in the flat, lowland valleys and around the bay, where enormous greenhouses have been constructed. Open farmland is a very important environment for many kinds of wildlife in the watershed, where it substitutes for the wet prairies of days gone by.

Lowland fields, especially those that are muddy or flood easily, are essential habitat for many birds and animals. Flooded farm fields mimic the original marshes that once existed across the delta.

Hawks, harriers, bald eagles and falcons hunt for prey across the farmland. Flocks of geese, swans and dabbling ducks descend to feed. Pastures are good habitat for black-tailed deer, coyotes, shorebird flocks, northern harriers, red-tailed hawks and other wildlife.

A northern harrier hovers as it seaches for voles.

Old fields are mature pastures which have lain fallow for a few years, growing thick, untidy grass and patches of sedges, rushes and wild flowers. The highest diversity of wintering raptors in Canada, at some of the highest densities, occurs on old field habitats in Delta. These fields provide food and shelter for huge numbers of voles and mice, many raptors' primary food source.

The large Townsend's vole is the principal food for resident northern harriers, red-tailed hawks and barn owls, wintering short-eared owls and rough-legged hawks and juvenile great blue herons (*see page 76*).

Wintering songbirds, such as house finches, American pipits, Lapland longspurs and western meadowlarks are attracted to open prairie areas. In summer, savannah sparrows build their nests on the ground among the clumps of grass. Fallow fields and field margins are used by many animals, including voles, coyotes and ermines (short-tailed weasels).

The highest diversity of wintering raptors in Canada occurs on old field habitats in Delta.

As they age, old fields become covered with long grasses, crimson-flowered hardhack, small birch trees, rowan, Pacific crab apple and Himalayan blackberry. This "red top prairie" resembles the original shrub meadows that covered much of the delta prior to dyking, and it can provide excellent habitat for wintering sparrows, finches and other small birds, as well as hawks, owls and northern shrikes.

Savannah sparrow

FENCES, HEDGEROWS & BARNS

Birds and animals can find many places to live within the farming landscape. Raptors use fence posts as hunting lookouts, feeding places or resting spots. Red-tailed hawks, northern harriers and wintering rough-legged hawks are often seen sitting on fence posts along highways, such as Highway 17 towards the Tsawwassen Ferry terminal. Fences are sometimes lined with mature trees, such as horse chestnuts and bigleaf maples.

Flocks of northwestern crows, starlings, Brewer's blackbirds and wintering red-winged blackbirds congregate on fences, hydro and telephone lines, and noisy groups of swallows gather on overhead wires before migration in late summer. Peregrine falcons and bald eagles are among the birds that perch on power poles, risking electrocution.

Hedgerows are very rich bird habitat, used by dozens of different species. Together with uncut, natural field margins, hedgerows can create miniature wildlife sanctuaries. Black hawthorn, red elder and Pacific crabapple provide good forage and nesting cover for Cooper's and sharp-shinned hawks, songbirds and roosting long-eared owls. Coyotes raise pups in dens beneath them and voles abound in the grass margins.

Golden-crowned sparrows are often found in hedgerows and field margins in winter.

Many studies have shown that hedges and field margins promote beneficial insects and pest predators, dispelling concerns that they might harbour agricultural pests. The Delta Farmland and Wildlife Trust is actively planting both hedgerows and field margins across the delta, and some farmers elsewhere in the watershed are working to save established hedges, especially those with mature trees.

The picturesque old **barns** of the Boundary Bay farmland are slowly sliding into ruin and being replaced with modern structures. Barns are used by barn owls and swallows for nesting and roosting, and by maternal colonies of yuma myotis and little brown myotis, two similar types of small bat. Old barns can be seen at Alaksen, Campbell Valley Park, Elgin Heritage Park and Deas Island; others are on private property.

For more about the Delta Farmland & Wildlife Trust see page 105.

BOGS & FENS

The beautiful wetland world of Burns Bog, the largest bog remaining in the Lower Mainland, lies between the Fraser River and Boundary Bay. Many parts of Richmond are also underlain by peat soils, composed of partially decomposed vegetation.

Burns Bog is the most southerly, west coast bog in Canada, and home to plants more typical of the cool north. Flowering plants and shrubs such as bog St. John's-wort, northern star flower, cloudberry, crowberry, Labrador tea, bog blueberry and velvet blueberry are characteristic of the damp, acid, nutrient-poor soils.

Western bog laurel is just one of many beautiful flowering plants found in Burns Bog.

Aquatic and terrestrial insects are abundant and at least four rare species of these occur. Many insects are restricted locally to Burns Bog, such as the zigzag darner and subarctic darner dragonflies, and an endemic waterbug.

A handful of greater sandhill cranes arrive to nest each year, Columbian black-tailed deer are common and a few black bear still roam in the wooded margins. Large numbers of nesting, migrating and wintering waterfowl visit the bog. A presumed extinct subspecies of the southern red-backed vole was discovered here during an extensive ecological review in 1999, along with numerous other small mammals, reptiles and amphibians.

Typical of bogs, rainfall is the source of incoming water; the Fraser River bypasses the bog to the north and Boundary Bay has receded to the south. Water from one third of the bog drains into the bay and many of the birds which use the bay fly into the bog at high tide or in stormy weather. In the evening, vast flocks of gulls leave the Vancouver landfill on the southwest corner and fly out to sea across Boundary Bay.

Burns Bog is a domed bog, created by an accumulation of organic soils, peat and sphagnum moss over the course of five thousand years. The acidic nature of the wetlands, the distinctive vegetation and its wild

Stunted shore pine in Burns Bog.

untamed terrain in the heart of the lower Fraser Valley, make the bog a unique and special place. The wettest areas consist of pools left from peat digging, which are in the process of reverting to nature.

Plants such as cloudberry, sedges and the carnivorous sundew grow on the margins of these ponds, which are attractive nesting areas and winter refuges for waterfowl. Yellow pond-lily bloom here in summer. Across the damp centre of the bog, sphagnum moss and reindeer lichen dominate, with blueberry and bog laurel abundant throughout. The wetlands of the bog merge into a slightly drier heathland of Labrador tea, hardhack, salal, bracken and mosses, grading into a forest of stunted lodgepole pines.

The Delta Nature Reserve, in the northeast corner of the bog, is a coniferous swamp. The ground here is spongy and damp, and thick with salmonberry, thimbleberry and the giant growths of skunk cabbage. The bog is bordered by woodlands of paper birch, western hemlock and spruce, and dense hardhack brushland, where land cleared for agriculture has been left fallow.

For more about Burns Bog see page 195.

For more about the Burns Bog Ecosystem Review 1999-2000 see www.eao.gov.bc.ca

Across the Fraser River, Richmond Nature Park is almost the last, natural area of the once extensive Richmond bogs, most of which have been drained and developed. The park vegetation is characterised by sphagnum mosses, dense clumps of blueberry, Labrador tea and salal, and stands of birch and pine. Pools of water are good amphibian and waterfowl habitat.

Fens are acidic peatlands with inflowing water, sedges, shrubs and willows. Fens once lay around the lower reaches of the Serpentine and Nicomekl Rivers, near Mud Bay, where soils are peaty and periodically washed by river flood waters. Wild cranberry and blueberry bushes grew here in historical times. In the late 1800s the fens were dyked and drained for pasture and arable land. The Serpentine Wildlife Area (Serpentine Fen) was also once part of this marshland, drained for farming in 1900 and now managed for wildlife. Ponds were excavated to encourage ducks and geese to winter in the fen. Hedgerows are alive with blackbirds, finches and juncos. Great blue heron fish along the banks of the ditches and dragonflies skim the sloughs. A few other patches of fen still occur next to the northeast corner of Burns Bog, at the foot of the North Delta escarpment.

For more on Richmond Nature Park see page 196; Serpentine Fen page 187.

FORESTS

Beautiful coniferous forests can be found in the Boundary Bay watershed, remnants of the dense and inpenetrable forests that once covered all the coastal hillsides. The original oldgrowth was logged out by the start of the twentieth century, yet second growth forests, up to a hundred years old, survive in many parks. Even in residential suburbs, small woodlands, ravines and escarpment slopes have huge Douglas-fir, grand fir, western redcedars, bigleaf maples and red alders. Shrubs, ferns, wild flowers and many different fungi grow beneath the trees.

These forests hold many interesting animals: northern flying squirrels, Douglas's squirrels, Pacific treefrogs, Hutton's vireo, band-tailed pigeon and great horned owl all call the forest home. Pileated woodpeckers can still be spotted in coniferous forests on the east side of the bay, but have disappeared from former habitat in Tsawwassen. Mountain beaver, porcupine, bobcat and Townsend's chipmunk, that used to live in the oldgrowth forests, are now found in only a very few locations in Langley and Whatcom County, Washington.

There are several types of forest around Boundary Bay, each with a different community of shrubs and flowering plants in the understorey.

FLOOD PLAIN FORESTS: BLACK COTTONWOOD & RED ALDER

Flood plain forests of red alder and black cottonwood, also known as swamp forests, can withstand seasonal inundation by fresh water from rivers and streams. The groves of tall, fragrant trees cling to river banks and valley bottoms in areas with mineral soils. Beneath them grow willows, hardhack, vine maple and skunk cabbage, all tolerant of the damp conditions.

This is the place to look for great horned owls, bald eagles, red-tailed hawks, wood ducks and great blue herons.

Colourful songbirds like western tanager and black-headed grosbeak nest here and you might catch a glimpse of river otters or mink. Salamanders and frogs need the wet vegetation and seasonal pools to complete their life cycles.

Cottonwood trees are notorious for suddenly shedding branches and have abundant fluffy seeds, that can cause allergies. Consequently, cottonwoods are often cut down, yet they are a vital part of the ecosystem. Flood plain forests still exist in a few low-lying areas in the Nicomekl, California Creek and Dakota Creek watersheds, Ladner Marsh, Burns Bog, below the Watershed Park escarpment and on Deas Island.

Moss-covered black cottonwood roots and damp forest floor in a small low-lying floodplain in Green Timbers.

CEDAR HEMLOCK FOREST

Where the annual rainfall is higher and the slopes have a good supply of moisture, western redcedar and western hemlock dominate the forest. Maples and alder grow among them, together with Sitka spruce in wetter areas. This is the common coniferous forest growing on the hills east of Boundary Bay.

Carpets of Oregon beaked moss, lady fern and sword fern cover the ground, mingling with clumps of fringecup, herb robert, vanilla leaf and bleeding heart. Spotted towhees and Douglas's squirrels forage noisily in the undergrowth, and American robins sing melodiously from tree tops. Varied thrushes use the dark shade beneath western redcedar to search for insects. Northern flying squirrel, raccoons, striped skunks, Douglas's squirrel and Columbian black-tailed deer are other residents.

Damp, low lying areas have clumps of large-leaved avens, horsetails, creeping buttercup, skunk cabbage and mosses. Slugs thrive in this environment, and both banana slugs and introduced black slugs are very common. Pacific tree frogs and terrestrial salamanders may be found around puddles or damp rotting logs. Cedar hemlock forests are found in many upland parks (*see Nature Destinations page 165 onwards*).

PAPER BIRCH FOREST

Birch trees can tolerate cool, damp conditions and are almost the last of the deciduous trees to turn yellow in the fall. Depending on the moisture level of the soil, birches grow together with red elder, snowberry, salmonberry, salal, ferns, horsetails or skunk cabbage. Creeping voles and other small mammals live on the numerous seeds and fungi that are found on the forest floor.

Typical birds are downy and hairy woodpeckers, bushtits, kinglets, Bewick's wren, chickadees, and migratory warblers. Western screech owl and ruffed grouse are scarce residents of some local birch forests.

Paper birch on the edge of Burns Bog.

Paper birch trees grow well on the fringes of Burns Bog, in the Drayton Harbor watershed and in parts of Langley. Birches are also commonly planted in suburban areas.

SHORE PINE FOREST

Shore pine is a type of lodgepole pine and was one of the first trees to grow when the glaciers of the Ice Age retreated. Bracken, hardhack, Labrador tea and salal are the commonest shrubs in the undergrowth. Shore pines grow in abundance around Burns Bog, becoming stunted in the centre where the soil is peatier. They are also found along the coast.

COASTAL DOUGLAS-FIR FOREST

More typical of the sunny San Juan and Gulf Islands, Douglas-fir grow on well-drained slopes on the west side of the Boundary Bay watershed. Tall secondary growth trees mingle with maples and western redcedar. Shrubs like salal, red huckleberry and dull Oregon grape grow beneath the trees, and in fall thousands of fungi emerge. The forest is home to birds such as the tiny winter wren. As night falls, Swainson's thrushes start to sing and nocturnal bats and northern flying squirrels emerge.

There are coastal Douglas-fir forests in Ocean Park and Sunnyside Acres, Surrey, Watershed Park and English Bluff, Delta, and Lincoln Park in

Large Douglas-fir and sword fern in Watershed Park.

Blaine. Large Douglas-fir also grow along the dykes at Reifel Migratory Bird Sanctuary and Alaksen.

BLUFFS, ESCARPMENTS & RAVINES

The hills surrounding Boundary Bay end abruptly in steep, wooded bluffs, carved with deep ravines and lush with ferns and shade trees. Where trees have fallen, the ground is crowded with salal, blackberry tangles and flowering salmonberry, and sword ferns flourish in the dappled light. Bluffs and ravines are used by raccoons, coyotes and deer

For more about Trees see pages 147 -151.

for denning and movement corridors and sometimes a black bear will wander up those connecting Burns Bog to North Delta.

Bald eagles nest in Douglas-fir on the top of bluffs, where they get a good view of the landscape. Ravine creeks are cool and sheltered for fish and amphibians, and the surrounding woodlands have warblers, winter wrens and thrushes. Ravines in White Rock are a good place to look for Anna's hummingbird.

SUBURBAN & URBAN NEIGHBOURHOODS

Suburban gardens are regularly visited by raccoons, striped skunks, opossums and squirrels. Small myotis bats live in trees around houses, particularly if there are nearby ponds or streams. Songbirds benefit from birdfeeders and berry-bearing shrubs and crows seem to thrive on human association.

Ornamental trees and shrubs give a beautiful year-round display. Rhododendrons, azalea, cherry trees and spirea are spectacular in spring, and palms, eucalyptus and yuccas flourish in the mild coastal climate. Exotic plants are not generally good habitat for native birds or butterflies.

More people are now becoming interested in wildlife gardening. We can all enjoy the sights and sounds of wild birds and animals by keeping natural habitat around our homes.

Flowering cherries are spectacular in the spring.

Town centres have very few natural spaces, but even in these sterile environments a few wild creatures manage to survive. They are mostly introduced ones, like starlings, house sparrows or rock doves, but also include such highly adaptable species as gulls, Canada geese, peregrine falcons and crows. Geese nest on flat roofs in coastal areas and crows roost in Burnaby town centre (*see page 57*). Little white-crowned sparrows take up residence on spindly ornamental trees in shopping malls, surprising the passerby with a melodious burst of song. Nature can be found in the most unexpected places!

For Wildlife Gardening see page 162.

SEASONS, SIGHTS & SOUNDS

"Immense flocks of plover were observed flying about the sand"

~ John Work,   Hudson Bay Company, 1824.

Typical of temperate climate zones, Boundary Bay has four seasons. Shielded by north-south mountain ranges and washed by the Pacific Ocean, the weather on the coast is far less extreme than most of the continent and is certainly not the "frozen north" of Canadian reputation. Summer is seldom oppressively hot, since cool sea breezes blow in at night, and winter is never very cold, because northern air currents are held at bay by prevailing southwesterly winds. Spring comes early, and autumn months are misty and mild. Showery weather in early fall turns to winter rains through November and December. Some snow usually falls in January or February. More severe winters, when rivers and bays freeze and snow lingers several weeks, occur only periodically. This four season climate cycle has been in place for thousands of years, tempered by long term variations generated by the neighbouring Pacific Ocean.

WHAT TO LOOK FOR IN SPRING

February 2 may be Groundhog Day, but Boundary Bay does not have groundhogs to forecast the coming of spring. Residents of the warm west coast must start counting snowdrops and crocuses instead! While most of the northern half of the continent fends off Arctic outflows and shovels snow, residents of the Boundary Bay watershed are admiring the fresh green leaves of Indian plum and the russet glow of swelling alder catkins.

Salmonberry blooms early in the spring; flowers appear by late February in sheltered locations.

One sign of spring we could look for on Groundhog Day is the arrival of early swallows, whisked up the coast by southerly winds. A few have been recorded as early as late January. Or should we listen for the tentative spring song of the red-winged blackbird, calling from the marsh, the cascading notes of an optimistic house finch or the territorial "fee-bee" call of the male black-capped chickadee? All are indicators that spring will soon be here.

By February, bald eagles have repaired winter damage to their nests and started laying eggs, which will hatch out in thirty six days time. Great horned owls are also nesting and with an unmistakable resonating hoot, call loudly every night.

Around this time, tiny migrants are heading northwards. Rufous hummingbirds travel thousands of kilometres from Central America and southern California, following the blooming of red nectar-bearing flowers. They arrive in the Fraser estuary just as the first salmonberry and red-flowering currant blossoms appear.

... tiny migrants are heading northwards

Spectacular yellow cowls, the flower of the skunk cabbage, push through the dark marshland mud along slough and river banks, while pussy willow and beaked hazelnut catkins brighten the hedgerows.

A few insects that have spent the winter in hibernation wake and spread their wings in the warmth of the spring sun, just as the early flowering plants present their blossoms for pollination.

Plankton blooms and fish spawn

Boaters out in Boundary Bay or the Strait of Georgia may notice more colour in the surface waters. This is due to clouds of phytoplankton, microscopic marine plants that

Skunk cabbage cowls push through the damp mud in March.

multiply rapidly in spring, an event known as a "bloom", although no flowers are involved. The bloom provides food for equally tiny animals, the zooplankton, along with a host of larger marine life. Zooplankton rise up from deeper water where they have spent the winter, and are eaten by fish, squids, crustaceans and birds. Sometimes the bloom is so colourful and bright, it can be seen from the air.

Fish spawning is a dramatic spring time event. Herring move inshore in March, to deposit eggs and spawn in favourable locations. Milky white herring roe covers long stretches of coastline in a good year. The spawn was once a regular event in Boundary Bay, but has been less intense in recent years. Most spawning now takes place further up the Strait. Eulachon come into the Fraser River in April looking for suitable gravel spawning beds; the location varies from year to year. California and Steller sea lions which have been wintering in the Strait of Georgia, follow the fish into the estuary.

In April, curious little fish, called plainfin midshipmen, move inshore to spawn in shallow water at Crescent Beach, on the east side of Boundary Bay. Gulls and bald eagles gather for the feast. Other marine fish, like shiner perch and starry flounder, also come closer to shore. Prickly sculpin swim downstream to lay eggs on estuarine sand bars.

Red-flowering currant is another early spring flower.

The influx of fish into the shallows is the signal for great blue herons to begin their nesting cycle in early March. The heronry becomes a noisy place as these giant birds manoeuvre sticks into place at the top of trees to build their large, flimsy nests. As eggs are laid and young reared, the herons line up along the tide line, sometimes a hundred or more together, stalking fish.

Chum, coho, and chinook salmon and trout fingerlings hatch out in shallow streams and tributaries that feed into the Fraser River. The young fry swim down to the estuary. Throughout spring in the estuary, chinook are active at dusk and dawn, resting in quiet back eddies or in deeper water during the day.

Deep in the intertidal sand and mud, as the shallow sea warms up, clams and snails start to move closer to the surface.

For more about Life in the Intertidal see pages 47 - 51.

Bird migrations

Hundreds of thousands of shorebirds and waterfowl migrate through the bay between March and May. Some will stay only a few days on their way north, the sheltered waters providing one more refueling stop as the birds fatten up ready for breeding. Those which are plump and strong will do the best job of raising healthy young ones in the northern tundra.

The commonest shorebirds are members of the sandpiper family, including dunlin, western sandpipers and least sandpipers. As the tide rises, the shorebird flocks move onto neighbouring fields, particularly ones that have been freshly ploughed. Brant, small, dark sea geese, come through in March and April. They have flown from their wintering grounds in Baja California and descend hungrily to graze in Boundary Bay's eelgrass meadows. Snow geese return to the mouth of the Fraser on their way north to Russia and their white v-shaped skeins against a blue sky are one of the most spectacular sights of spring.

For more about Bird Migration see pages 41 - 45.

In April, the flocks of wintering and migrant ducks prepare to depart for northern and inland nesting areas. Elaborate courtship rituals take place with much bowing and turning of heads, and pattering flights across the water. Finally one evening at dusk, skein after skein rises into the darkening sky and heads north. By the end of April, all the flocks are gone.

Mallards have been feeding and loafing in pairs for several months

Sanderling probe the mud for food. These small shorebirds are very sensitive to disturbance or harassment while resting and feeding on migration.

A marsh wren proclaims his territory.

Marsh wrens have a whole hectare of cattail marsh to defend, together with a harem of four or five females. The staccato burst of the male's song sounds from every cattail bed and clump of reed canary grass.

A drawn out wheezy call and flashing red shoulder markings announce the presence of the red-winged blackbird. His group of brown females will be nearby, each building a cup-shaped nest, wrapped around the stalks of the cattails. The female defends her nest, rather unusually, with a song of her own.

Marsh wrens have a whole hectare of cattail marsh to defend

already, the green head of the male becoming glossier as spring progresses. Pair bonds for ducks and geese are established and reinforced in spring; these bonds can last a lifetime (up to 28 years for a wild Canada goose). Resident mallard, along with cinnamon and blue-winged teal from California, search the wetlands for good nest sites and settle into the breeding season. The duckweed they love to eat floats to the surface, buoyed by little air pockets in the leaves. Aquatic larvae and insects hatch out, providing a steady source of food for ducklings.

Wetlands in spring

Wetlands are lively places in spring. Common yellowthroats, marsh wrens and red-winged blackbirds proclaim territorial boundaries by singing from conspicuous perches.

Frogs also become vocal in early spring. In many parts of Boundary Bay, the commonest species is now the introduced bullfrog. In some remaining freshwater wetlands and damp woodlands, groups of Pacific tree frogs chorus from dusk long into the night. Garter snakes living on the shore warm themselves in the April sunshine.

Insects begin their annual cycle as the weather improves. Mourning cloak and satyr comma butterflies spend the winter as hibernating adults, yet they have to warm up before they can fly. The first ones can be seen in flight by the second week of April, together with cabbage whites, spring blues and anise swallowtails. Western tiger swallowtails emerge from cocoons in which they have passed the winter, metamorphosing into their final adult form. These beautiful butterflies are a common sight from May through July.

Carnivorous larvae of dragonflies hatch from eggs in freshwater pools and streams, and spend this major stage underwater, for up to five years. Queen bees and queen wasps that have survived the winter emerge to establish new colonies of workers. Aphid eggs hatch out in time to feed hoards of hungry young songbirds.

This is the time of year, children find "lost" birds

By early May, blossom-covered trees and fresh leaves have transformed the landscape. Wildflowers are blooming along dykes and verges, hedgerows and woodlands are suddenly green and lush with dense vegetation and gardens are at their best. Farm fields are ploughed and planted, the fresh green crops growing rapidly as the soil warms.

At dawn, the forest rings with birdsong. Warblers and vireos are passing through, and finches, sparrows, thrushes and chickadees are proclaiming their breeding territories. Many of the resident

Shore pine catkins almost ready to release their pollen in May.

birds have already hatched their first brood, and the fussing calls of young ones become very noticeable.

This is the time of year, children find "lost" birds and attempt to rescue them. Most of the downy nestlings will have a mother bird nearby ready to feed them, so it is best to just lift the youngster onto a nearby branch and let nature takes its course.

As the leaves open on the trees, the main wave of warblers arrives from the south. The small greenish birds are well camouflaged in the leafy canopy of alder, birch and maple through which they move, feeding on insects. Some warblers stay to nest in woodlands near Boundary Bay and Burns Bog, where their melodious songs join those of the vireos, flycatchers, black-headed grosbeaks and American robins. Most of them fly on to nesting sites elsewhere in British Columbia.

For more about Warblers see pages 114 - 115.

WHAT TO LOOK FOR IN SUMMER

Summer begins in June, a month often marked by cloudy, wet weather in Boundary Bay. Depressions move in from the south, bringing warm Pacific air laden with rain. Foliage and flowers become luxuriant in the mild, moist climate and insects abound. Strawberries ripen and potato fields flower in acres of lilac and white. This is the time to visit the pick-your-own fruit farms and enjoy the bounty of the land. The last of the bird migrants arrive: listen for the thin high calls of cedar waxwings from the tree tops and watch for an occasional nighthawk, hawking for insects on a warm summer evening.

Black swifts can suddenly appear in their hundreds around Boundary Bay during stormy weather. These scimitar-winged birds circle in flocks around atmospheric depressions, Forever on the wing, they make looping journeys of hundreds of miles, feeding on clouds of insects that are prevalent in low pressure zones. They hardly perch even to

One of the best wildflower displays in the area can be found in the gumweed meadows near 64 Street Delta in early August.

raise young, and will sometimes leave nestlings unfed for several days. The young must fall into a deep torpor to survive. Where all the swifts nest is a mystery, as only a few remote mountain cliff locations have ever been found.

High summer is a quiet period for birds as they retire to moult their feathers and recover from the rigours of raising young. Songbirds stop singing and skulk around in dense vegetation, trying to stay cool and hiding from predators as they lose vital flight feathers. Waterfowl, which lose all their flight feathers at once, take refuge in favourite moulting sites around the estuary, where they are safe and well fed.

Hot, dry weather in July coincides with daytime low tides. The warm sandy beaches are perfect places for flocks of non-breeding and post-breeding gulls of various kinds to hang out together, to moult, preen and practice their clam-breaking skills. It is common to see a gull pick up a clam, fly into the air and drop it onto the pebbles of the beach, hoping to crack it open. Some succeed, others try unsuccessfully above soft mud. Northwestern crows, which spend a lot of time scavenging along the shoreline, will also try this trick.

Double-crested cormorants breed in Drayton Harbor and near the B.C. Ferry terminal. They fish in open water. Afterwards they stand around on old cannery pilings, with their wings stretched out. Why exactly cormorants assume this pose is a mystery. It is unlikely to dry the wings, the commonest explanation, because they do it even in the rain. Other theories include restoring trapped air to the feathers, helping digest fish, keeping the birds warm or signalling to other cormorants that fishing has been successful.

Double-crested cormorants resting on a floating log at high tide.

Pine white butterflies emerge in July.

Salmon and sandpipers

At the end of June, early runs of sockeye enter the Fraser estuary, the first of several summer runs. Out at sea, terns and seabirds dive for shrimp, crab larvae and baitfish, and ocean watchers have a good chance of spotting killer whales. Kayakers and boaters encounter harbour seals bobbing in the water, accompanied later in the month by their pups, and sometimes porpoises roll into view.

Grasses, sedges and flowers grow lush in the shoreline marshes. Their pollination is performed by insects, which in turn provide food for birds, bats and shrews. Pine whites hatch out in July and flutter amid the conifers. Lorquin's admiral, painted ladies and western swallowtails are other conspicuous butterflies seen in summer. Shimmering red, blue and green dragonflies and damselflies emerge from the larval stage to dart over wetlands. The commonest large dragonfly, the blue-eyed darner, is everywhere in August, even far from water.

On hot days, sometimes the only creatures stirring are the noisy field crickets chirring from the edge of the dyke, perfectly camouflaged among the grasses.

As summer progresses, the bay basks in the long hours of daylight, the delta fields are dry and golden in the summer sun. The mountains rimming the valley fade to a hazy blue. Upland forests and shoreline meadows fall quiet, birds no longer sing, the vegetation grows tired and dusty along the trails, with the flowers of spring all gone to seed. Fireweed and thistle plumes, beloved by goldfinches, decorate the dyke sides. Ocean beaches are warm and inviting.

Warm summer evenings around twilight are the time to look for bats, and late on August nights shooting stars pass overhead. The big dipper rides high in the sky. Across in the east, three brilliant stars, Deneb, Vega and Altair, compose the summer triangle in the constellations of Cygnus, Lyra and Aquila.

Ochre star, Ocean Park, Surrey.

In mid-summer, some migrant birds are already returning. The numbers of small sandpipers build steadily throughout July and early August, and most will have already moved on by the time the larger shorebirds migrate through in September.

Young birds feel the urge to scatter after they leave the nest, and some of them immediately disperse quite long distances. Normally they regroup with other birds, forming roaming flocks in the late summer, and gradually moulting into adult plumage. Sometimes birds become disoriented, so the post-breeding season is the time that keen birders look for accidental occurrences of birds far from their usual locations.

Boundary Bay often has rare visits from shorebirds blown adrift from Asia (*see pages 89 - 91*). Small mammals breed prolifically in the fine weather and their young also disperse around the countryside. Juvenile coast moles often come above ground and get eaten by barn owls or caught by domestic cats.

During the last week of August, as holiday crowds still linger on the beach, the first small groups of ducks begin to fly in at dusk. Swallows gather on wires, and the northern flicker, a colourful, noisy woodpecker, arrives in suburban gardens giving its distinctive, end of summer call. Fall is on its way.

An August evening at Point Roberts.

WHAT TO LOOK FOR IN FALL

Gradually the trees change colour, the mornings are heavy with dew and spiders' webs appear suddenly throughout the garden. Sunny days at this time of year are some of the nicest times for a walk along the bay or through the woods. There is once again a bustle of activity among birds and animals, fungi are sprouting up everywhere in all their wonderful variety of form and colour, and berry bushes are heavy with fruit.

The leaves of deciduous trees turn from green to yellow, gold, red and brown, before falling to the ground. Chlorophyll production, a process which accounts for the green colour, is reduced as a response to cooler temperatures and shorter daylight hours, and the underlying yellow pigment then becomes visible. Trees stressed by drought, pollution or low levels of nitrogen produce the glorious red colouration as a "sunscreen" so that leaves can linger longer, helping the tree survive.

Season of fruitfulness

Out in the farmland, sweet corn ripens and pumpkins swell orange in the field. Rolls of hay and silage in white plastic rolls stand around like a giant marshmallow harvest, and

October is pumpkin month in the delta.

flocks of Canada geese fly in to feed on the stubble. Waterfowl numbers build steadily in September as skeins of ducks fly in from northern and interior regions.

A succession of shorebirds arrive on mudflats, shores and upland fields around Boundary Bay, including unusual visitors, like sharp-tailed, stilt and buff-breasted sandpipers. Warblers pass through quickly, difficult to spot in their drab non-breeding plumage. Finches and sparrows gather into flocks to spend the winter roaming hedgerows and weedy fields. Squirrels can be seen everywhere, preparing for winter by searching for nuts and finding dens. Garter snakes become torpid and retreat to hibernacula.

Fungi are vital components of forests

Warm, misty September days merge into October and a sudden fruiting of fungi takes place. Thin white fungal strands, or mycelia, lie hidden underground and in rotting wood all year, and colourful mushrooms and toadstools appear overnight in clumps and masses on lawns and gardens and all over the forest floor. Fungi are vital components of forests and an amazing number and variety exist, including many that are poisonous and difficult to identify. Wet weather produces the greatest diversity; however, even in a dry fall, dozens of species can easily be seen in a short woodland stroll.

Fall is berry season, with all kinds of soft fruits ripening at this time. Wild crabapples, hawthorns and rose hips festoon the hedgerows. Blueberries and cranberries flourish in Burns Bog, and succulent blackberries fruit in the bramble bushes. Yellowjackets buzz around the berry bushes and seem to sting more at this time of year. By early November most of them have died off, as have the majority of other insects.

Climate & Weather

Weather in the Strait of Georgia and surrounding areas is governed by two major climate regimes.

The **Aleutian Low** is a low pressure system over the Gulf of Alaska that predominates throughout fall and winter. Its counterclockwise air flow brings rain-bearing westerly winds to the Pacific Northwest coast. The Low breaks down when the sun warms the Arctic, beginning soon after the spring equinox on March 21, the day that the sun is directly over the equator at noon.

The **North Pacific High** is a high pressure system centred further south, that expands in summer, displacing the Aleutian Low and bringing warm sunny weather. Fine summer weather frequently lasts until the fall equinox on September 22, when the Aleutian Low rebuilds once more.

Even when one system or another is dominant, the combination pattern of air flow can create unusual weather patterns. The "Pineapple Express" is a strong, warm wind that brings sudden, extremely wet, sub-tropical air to the region, while Arctic outflows may occur in winter when winds shift to the northeast.

Arrival of the snow geese

For spectacular sights, it is hard to beat the annual autumn gathering of lesser snow geese on Westham Island. Late in October, long white skeins suddenly apppear, drifting across the sky, and we hear their distinctive cries, so evocative of the north country and wide Arctic skies. Thousands upon thousands gradually descend onto the fields of Alaksen National Wildlife Area, Reifel Migratory Bird Sanctuary and Westham Island farms, reaching a peak of 80,000 birds or more in a good breeding year. They have come from Wrangel Island, off the northeastern coast of Russia, high above the Arctic Circle at 74 degrees north. The geese are present in the western delta through October and November, but in December they move on south to the Skagit Valley in Washington, where they remain until March.

Snow geese

Winter rains fill the creeks and rivers

The heavy winter rains usually arrive in late October or November, in time to fill the creeks and rivers for the return of chum and coho salmon to their spawning grounds upstream. Annual rainfall around Boundary Bay averages 1150 mm (45 in), with a higher precipitation on the uplands to the east of the bay than on the west side. The change in weather often comes suddenly with wild storms, leading to downed trees, power outages and localised flooding. Strong winds bring down the last of the deciduous leaves and cedar droppings, preparing the trees for their winter rest.

Wildfowl flocks build up as the rains arrive, until between 100,000 and 200,000 ducks are gathered in the sheltered waters of the bay. Migrating brant rest on the shoreline as they make their return flight to Mexico. Swans arrive during the wet days of November, as winter gales lash the delta and flood the fields. The huge trumpeters settle in big flocks on fields around Westham Island and near the Fraser River, looking for unharvested potato tubers and roots.

For more about snow geese, brant & swans see pages 102 - 105.

WHAT TO LOOK FOR IN WINTER

Regular frosts by early December and the short daylight hours mark the beginning of winter. Big flocks of dunlin, a type of sandpiper, pass through the bay; tens of thousands of them stay, the highest number wintering anywhere in Canada (*see pages 87 - 90*). It is an awesome sight to see the swirling smoke-like flocks of thousands of dunlin, flashing across the bay in perfect synchrony. They fly in these clouds to escape the ever-present peregrine falcons and merlins, predators which follow sandpiper flocks from the north.

Rough-legged hawks arrive from the Arctic, to spend the winter around Boundary Bay.

Falcons, hawks and eagles are a common sight around Boundary Bay

Falcons, hawks and eagles are a common sight around Boundary Bay, the best location in Canada for winter bird of prey diversity. The bay is also the best place near Vancouver to see wintering sanderling, a small sandpiper that skitters along the waves at the edge of the tide.

The delta loses colour in winter, becoming a landscape of grey, brown and ochre. The wind blows bleakly across the wide open countryside, permanently bending trees and bushes along the dykes. Ditches and fields become waterlogged. Coniferous woodlands retain their colour but seem silent and somber until a Douglas's squirrel chatters indignantly from an overhead branch or a noisy flock of chickadees and kinglets passes through.

Hibernation time

Many plants and animals become dormant or hibernate in winter, even in the temperate conditions experienced most years on the coast. By the end of fall there is a marked decrease in the number of insects around, most of the adults having died. They leave behind eggs, larvae or pupae which will hatch out or metamorphose into adults in the spring. Some beetles, a few butterflies and the queen wasps and bees, hibernate through the winter in sheltered locations. Ladybird beetles seem to have an uncanny ability to predict a cold winter. Long before a severe freeze-up they will seek out secure and sheltered hibernation spots, whereas prior to mild winters they congregate in more exposed locations.

Christmas bird counts regularly find 140 to 150 bird species

Larger animals also hibernate. Frogs and salamanders wait out the cold weather in a torpid state, in damp mud, leaf mould or undergrowth. Occasionally a Pacific tree frog will wake in mid-winter, and call briefly. Garter snakes hibernate deep under rock piles from about November to February, and turtles lie dormant at the bottom of ponds. Most bats sleep through the winter in holes in trees or attics, although a couple of species migrate south. Even raccoons and squirrels retire to winter dens or nests if the weather turns extremely cold; however, on the mild days of a typical coastal winter they remain up and about.

Winter birding: eagles and owls

Winter birding can be excellent on Boundary Bay, with thousands of waterfowl feeding on the water and in the fields, raptors patrolling the dykes and all kinds of sparrows and finches

Boardwalk through a wintry Delta Nature Reserve.

roaming the shorelines. December to February is the time to see many Arctic birds, including northern shrikes and snowy owls, during "invasion years". The woods are full of mixed feeding flocks of dark-eyed juncos, chickadees, nuthatches and pine siskins. When the snow flies in the mountains, the flocks are joined by thrushes, sapsuckers and woodpeckers. The annual Christmas bird counts regularly find 140 to 150 bird species within a 12 km (7.5 mi) radius around Ladner and White Rock, often the highest counts in Canada.

Annual snowfall in the Boundary Bay area averages 45 cm (18 in). Snow seldom stays for more than a couple of weeks and some years there is hardly any snow at all. Every seven years or so, there is a much colder spell, when the bay freezes up and temperatures plummet. Frosty winter nights are the time for star gazing, as the constellation Orion the Hunter rises above the horizon. The bright planets Venus and Jupiter are clearly visible, and shooting stars split the sky.

High tides occur in the daytime in winter, so waterfowl are often seen loafing, preening, feeding and sleeping close to the dyke. They are easily disturbed when bald eagles and other birds of prey fly over or when a dog or coyote runs along the

The tidal mudflats of Boundary Bay frozen over.

shoreline. Then the flocks rise with a great clatter of wings and cacophony of calls, circling around until things quieten down and it is safe to land again. A combination of high tides, rain and wind sends ducks and geese into the surrounding fields to feed, especially at night. Muddy, undrained fields with lots of puddles are highly prized by many ducks and shorebirds, but the American wigeon loves short green grass. A flock of these hungry birds will decimate a farmer's winter forage crop overnight.

Bald eagle numbers mount in January. Early in the winter they feed on salmon at Squamish and the Harrison River. As the salmon supply runs out, they come down to Boundary Bay to hunt and scavenge for ducks and shorebirds. Adult eagles make a spectacular sight as they perch in tall cottonwoods, their white heads gleaming against a blue winter sky. January is also a good month to listen for owls calling in the woods, signalling the start of their nesting season.

Even when the winter is cold, it does not last too long around the bay. Soon the first yellow hazel catkins have begun to flower and red alder catkins swell once more. Spring is returning.

Join in a Christmas Bird Count at Ladner or White Rock: contact Federation of B.C. Naturalists at www.naturalists.bc.ca

THE MYSTERY OF MIGRATION

"The more research that is completed, the more we realize how little we know" ~ Dr James Tansey, Univerity of British Columbia

Boundary Bay, in the heart of the Fraser River estuary, is a major hotspot for migrating birds. It is one of a handful of stopovers for several million shorebirds and waterfowl as they travel up and down the west coast of North America. Birds are very vulnerable on migration: if they fail to find a safe place to rest and feed, they are forced to keep flying until they do. Good habitats are essential *en route*; without them, exhausted birds drop into the sea and perish. Boundary Bay and the estuary provide irreplaceable habitat for migrating flocks, as well as spectacular viewing opportunities.

Not only birds migrate: whales, butterflies, bats and fish all make phenomenal journeys at certain times. There have been exciting developments in our understanding of migration, but many aspects remain a complete mystery.

Thousands of dunlin feeding on the mud flats of Boundary Bay, just behind the falling tide.

The Pacific Flyway

An incredible impulse drives tens of millions of birds, all over the world, to perform the seasonal commute between wintering grounds and nesting areas. The migration routes up and down the west coast of America are often referred to as the **Pacific Flyway**, a broad corridor followed by millions of shorebirds, waterfowl and songbirds. At "staging areas", like Boundary Bay and other parts of the Fraser River estuary, birds interrupt their journey to rest, sleep and forage, thereby gaining the fat and energy they need to fly to the next stopping point, which may be several thousand kilometres away.

Every spring, migrating birds depart from Central and South America, Mexico and California, and head to cooler northern lands in British Columbia, the Yukon and Alaska. The vast Arctic tundra has plenty of space for establishing nesting territories, and the long hours of daylight in the northern summer allow time to lay eggs and raise young. Clouds of Arctic insects provide abundant food for nestlings. Birds have been migrating north to breed in this way for thousands of years, for even during the Pleistocene glaciation the northwest Alaskan tundra remained ice free.

Shorebirds start their return trip early in summer. By fall, thousands of ducks, geese, songbirds and birds of prey are on the move. Some will remain for the winter, while others will travel on and on, a few going as far south as Tierra del Fuego, on the southern tip of South America.

Dunlin in flight

Migrating birds can fly incredible distances in a very short time. A semipalmated sandpiper, that was banded on the Fraser delta on 16 August 1987, was found just two months later in Guyana, South America, 23,000 km (14,300 mi) to the southeast. Neotropical migrants, such as warblers, can travel 100 km per day (60 mi per day) for thousands of kilometres, between the cool north and warm equatorial latitudes. For other birds, migration may be just a short hop, from the Interior valleys and mountains to the open waters and snow-free fields of the coast.

The Pacific Flyway is not the narrow highway that the name might suggest, but rather a broad front used in different ways by different species. Many birds travel one route going north and another going south. There are flyways favoured by hawks: cliffs and bluffs help them spiral and soar on thermals, then glide to the next landmark. Swallows swoop low over the dykes as they follow sky trails along the coast. Northern hawks and owls congregate near the bay in winter, their numbers cycling according to available rodent prey in the tundra. Peregrine falcons and merlins follow the flocks of shorebirds from the Arctic, preying on them as they go.

Migration routes do not always lie in a north-south direction. They can be east to west, for birds breeding inland and wintering at the coast, or down slope from mountain tops to sea level. For example, western grebes that breed in Alberta or the

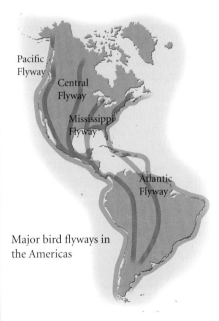

Major bird flyways in the Americas

Map courtesy of Nature Canada
www.naturecanada.ca

Shuswap Lakes of British Columbia fly to Boundary Bay in late summer and stay for the winter.

Harlequin ducks nest on mountain streams but spend the rest of the year searching for crabs in the Strait of Georgia. Heavy snowfalls force juncos, red-breasted sapsuckers and varied thrushes down from forests in the mountains, to join roaming flocks of kinglets, siskins and robins.

How do birds migrate?

About three-quarters of all North American birds make some sort of migratory journey. It is awe-inspiring to think of the distance they travel, their navigation skills and the speed with which they cover unknown or hostile lands. Numerous theories and many experiments have been proposed to explain these feats. Modern tracking technologies are filling the picture, but much is still a mystery; for instance, how do birds navigate so well across continents?

Birders know to expect migrants at precise dates: birds often reappear annually almost to the day at nesting areas or migration stopovers. Partly explaining this remarkable consistency is a combination of physical traits used to time their journey and find the way.

Most birds have good sight, excellent visual memories and can see the full colour spectrum, as well as some ultraviolet and polarized light, invisible to our human unaided eye. Generally speaking, the faster a bird's flight speed, the sharper its vision. Hawks and falcons have large fields of view and good depth perception, as do many shorebirds. Conversely, nocturnal birds see colour poorly, but have extremely acute hearing.

Birds hear a broad range of sounds, including low frequency infrasounds below 20 Hertz. They may even be able to detect slight differences in barometric pressure, allowing them to take advantage of weather patterns, such as a following wind. Birds orient to the correct direction by the position of the sun or the pattern of stars around the north star, which they learn as nestlings, combined with their sense of the earth's magnetic field, which they are somehow able to detect. Adult birds are able to follow known landmarks, like coastlines and mountain ranges.

An internal biological clock sets a period of migratory restlessness that keeps them flying for the correct length of time, very important for first time migrants. Any deviation from the route could mean flying exhausted into the sea or getting hopelessly lost. Every fall, some juveniles turn up in strange places.

For more about shorebird migration see page 87 & Fraser River estuary Important Bird Area www.ibacanada.ca

The Amazing Western Sandpiper

A western sandpiper measures barely 17 cm and weighs less than a granola bar.

A western sandpiper was clocked flying from California to Alaska, a distance of 3000 km (1900 mi), in less than 48 hours! It probably paused briefly at Boundary Bay, one of the few foraging stops along the way. Twice a year, these tiny shorebirds make an 11,000 km (6800 mi) journey between the Yukon or Kuskokwim River deltas in Alaska, and their wintering homes on the sub-tropical mud flats and mangrove swamps of Panama, Ecuador or Suriname. They normally average about 200 km (124 mi) per day. From 500,000 to 1.2 million sandpipers have been recorded on Boundary Bay and Roberts Bank during peak migrations, a quarter of the world's population on a single day!

The breeding season for western sandpipers is very short. Arriving in the Arctic in May, the female builds a skimpy nest on the ground and lays four eggs. Her chicks hatch fully-feathered, able to run and to feed themselves. With a job well-done, she heads south in late June or early July. The male stays a couple of weeks longer before heading south, leaving the juveniles to follow later, totally unguided by their parents. Those young that make the trip land briefly at Boundary Bay a month or so later, then fly on to the wintering areas. It is one of the great natural mysteries of the world as to how tiny birds, barely four months old, can navigate from the Arctic to Central America, without adults to lead them.

Flocking allows birds to benefit from group knowledge and safety. They often call to each other while they fly, especially at night. The leader of the v-shaped skeins and lines constantly changes, providing each bird the chance to slipstream, which saves considerable amounts of energy. Many migrants fly at night and most fly high up, particularly in the dark and over the ocean, to take advantage of tailwinds and cooler temperatures, and to avoid hazards. Swallows and pipits prefer to migrate in daylight, as do hawks, eagles, vultures and sandhill cranes, for these birds need strong daytime thermals for soaring.

The waves have left their pattern on the Boundary Bay intertidal mud flats.

LIFE IN THE INTERTIDAL

"Take time to enjoy the colours and patterns of the seaweeds."

~ Gloria Snively, Exploring the Seashore

Boundary Bay tides

Boundary Bay has an amazing tidal range. The sea disappears to the far horizon on summer days, becoming a thin glistening band between sky and sand. In the late afternoon the sea oozes back across the flats at a walking pace, to lap at the shoreline just in time for an evening swim before the sun goes down.

In winter, waves crash in from the southwest, ripping up eelgrass by its roots and throwing it onto the shore. Huge logs brought in by the tide grind up the mud and sand as they toss and roll. The tide stays high through much of the day, bringing ducks and loons close to shore and keeping the shorebirds on the move between elusive patches of mud, before ebbing away in the middle of the night.

People familiar with tides elsewhere in the world may be surprised by the pattern of those in Boundary Bay, which is known as a "mixed semidiurnal" system. Typically, it has two high tides and two low tides in each twenty-four hour period, with one fluctuation often much larger than the other. The pattern is caused by gravitational forces modified by the complex coastline of the Pacific Northwest. Boaters, fishers and naturalists always check tide tables before heading out. It is amazing how much the beach changes under different tidal conditions.

Intertidal animals and plants that live between the highest and lowest tidal limits have to withstand the force of water and the predation of other creatures at high tide, and survive the sun's heat and desiccation at low tide. Many of them have evolved highly specialised lives.

Tidal Ranges

Average tidal range in Boundary Bay is 2.7 m (8.86 ft).
Extremely high and low tides occur near winter and summer solstices: December 21, June 21.

Moderate fluctuations occur when the sun is over the equator, at the spring and fall equinoxes: March 22, Sept. 22.

Tides and their causes

Gravitational forces between the earth, moon and sun translate into the ebbs and flows experienced by the world's oceans.

While gravity pulls the moon and earth together, centrifugal force keeps the moon in orbit. These forces are felt by both land and water, but the response of the mobile ocean is much more noticeable. As the earth spins on its axis, the ocean water bulges outwards in line with the moon, pulled by both the forces, twice in each twenty four hour rotation. This creates a wave of ocean water around the earth. The situation is complicated by factors such as the tilt of the earth's axis to the vertical, the inclination of the moon's orbital plane and the influence of the sun's gravitational force.

In practice, the presence of large land masses disrupts the path of this wave, and sets up standing waves in the major oceans of the world. These standing waves are reflected, refracted and diffracted as they meet the edge of continental shelves, narrow gaps between land or changing water depths. In the northeast Pacific Ocean, these effects create rotary standing waves, with the high tide moving up the coast as the water rotates in two unequal circular motions. The resulting tidal pattern in the Strait of Georgia is, not surprisingly, very complex and highly irregular.

Tides are also affected by weather and climate. Strong winds drive ocean waters onto land, so that winter high tides are often much higher than those in summer. Very low-lying parts of the coastline are at risk from unexpected storm surges, tidal waves generated by earthquakes and flooding from rising sea levels.

The incoming tide up the Strait of Georgia flows strongly northward, generating rips and eddies as it rounds headlands, islands and bays. Boundary Bay faces south towards the oncoming current, but is sheltered by the Point Roberts peninsula. As the tide flows in, sea water comes past Bellingham Bay and Birch Point, into Boundary Bay on the east side. It swirls counter-clockwise across the mouth of the bay before funneling south around the reefs below Lily Point and west around Point Roberts. For thousands of years, salmon fishers set up reef nets here to catch homecoming sockeye as the current carried the fish towards the Fraser river. More ominously, this tidal pattern means that a spill from an oil tanker or the refineries in Washington would immediately send oil northward on the current to Boundary Bay's beaches.

At the southwestern corner of Point Roberts, the tide does battle with the Fraser River's current, and standing at Lighthouse Park one can see the distinct line of pale, muddy river plume pushing south as dark ocean water confronts it heading north.

Outflow from the Serpentine and Nicomekl rivers creates a strong soutward current in a channel through the mud flats along the east shore of the bay. The spits and causeways across Drayton Harbor keep that bay calm and sheltered.

Life in the intertidal zone

The smallest plants and animals occur in the greatest numbers. Millions of simple, microscopic plants, called phytoplankton, float and bloom on the ocean's surface, while others live on the sea floor, between the sand grains. They stick the grains together with slimy mucus, creating a base for larger plants to take root. Phytoplankton are consumed at the surface of the ocean by tiny, free-floating animals,

Spring Tides

The sun's gravitational pull is strongly felt when the sun and moon are directly in line. This happens every month of the year during new and full moons. Tides at this time are much stronger and are known rather confusingly as "spring" tides, (but are nothing to do with the season).

During spring tides, the highest high tide and the lowest low tide differ by up to 4.1 m (13 ft), the other pair of tides having a moderate to small range.

At neap tides, during first and third quarter moons, both pairs of high and low tides vary little, falling in the minimum range of about 1.5 m (5 ft).

such as euphausiids and copepods, collectively known as zooplankton. Other species of zooplankton live within the sand and mud flats. The warm, shallow water of Boundary Bay is particularly rich in these

The Nicomekl River estuary at low and high tide.

micro-organisms: the mud flats are estimated to contain at least 130 different kinds. Crustaceans, burrowing worms, mud shrimps and snails prey on the tiny animals and in turn are eaten by larger marine animals.

Tiny but abundant insect-like creatures, called amphipods and isopods, swarm and scavenge for waste matter on the sea floor. Clams, mussels and oysters sift sea water for edible matter, and fish and jellyfish larvae, opalescent squid, brooding anemones, crabs and barnacles scan the water for edible plankton.

In the mud, one can find elusive, pale pink ghost shrimps

Marine invertebrates move nearer the surface as the sand warms up in spring. A stroll across the beach will reveal the shells and spoutings of heart cockles, butter clams and bent-nose clams and the whitened remains of sand dollars. Tidal pools have tiny juvenile fish, the fry of sculpin and sole.

Little tubular sand grain towers are evidence of aptly-named, segmented bamboo worms. Digging in the mud, one can find elusive, pale pink ghost shrimps. They are strange bleached creatures, living in deep, branching burrows. Steelhead anglers dig them for bait.

At low tide, you can sometimes find the mud tube homes of bamboo worms.

Transparent moon jellyfish grow up to 10 cm long (4 in), and are common and harmless. Looking like nothing more than a transparent blob they float in tidepools and become stranded on the mud. Sometimes in late summer, flotillas of a much larger, deep red jellyfish come ashore. This is the lion's mane jellyfish, or sea nettle, a very common jelly off the outer Pacific Northwest coast. Its sting can be painful, particularly for children, who may touch it as it floats inertly in the shallows or lies in a jellied blob on the beach.

Seaweeds

Most marine plants are in the green, brown and red algae families, collectively known as "seaweeds". They are very primitive plants, with tough, rubbery, slippery leaves that can stand the severity of intertidal life. They have no roots, but attach to cobbles and rocks with a finger-like "holdfast". Seaweeeds have strange reproductive systems, first producing spores and then two generations of thin, sheet-like or branched plants.

The most diverse range of seaweed shapes, colours and textures occur on outer shores, where the water is cold and full of oxygen. However, a search along the Boundary Bay tide line will reveal tangled ropes of bull kelp, smooth green leaves of sea lettuce, rough brown fronds of sea brush and pieces of nobbly, dark red turkish towel. The bull kelp and red algae grow in deep water around Point Roberts and Birch Point. Green seaweeds are prevalent in shallow water and coat the mud flats in summer. Common brown rockweed, its forked blades tipped with rounded, yellow bladders, clings to old piling posts and boulders.

Eelgrass meadows

Eelgrass is neither a grass nor a seaweed, but a member of the lily family. It likes warm shallow water and a gentle salt water current, the exact conditions found within the intertidal flats of Boundary Bay, Drayton Harbor and Roberts Bank. Eelgrass meadows make habitat as they grow. Dense tangles of floating

Eelgrass with sand dollar

leaves slow the water current, and encourage the deposition of sand and mud, which are then held in place by the plants' roots and rhizomes (underground stems). The waving leaves and network of rhizomes prevent predators from reaching juvenile fish, crabs, nudibranchs and jellyfish. Transparent eelgrass isopods, stripy sea slugs and slender, green, bay pipefish, which are members of the seahorse family, blend perfectly as they move around the plants. Stable mud around the roots provides a home for prized Dungeness crab.

Eelgrass leaves are coated with a brown scum of plankton and bacteria, that is eaten by crab larvae, juvenile fish, shrimp, snails and waterfowl. Pacific herring and opalescent squid eggs are laid on the leaves. Adult squid are an important food of salmon, and herring roe are relished by many animals in the food chain. Young fish are prey for salmon, Pacific cod and harbour seals. Tiny copepods living in the eelgrass are a key food of chum, and the meadows are an important rearing area for juvenile chinook and coho.

Striped sea perch, starry flounder, staghorn sculpin, three-spined stickleback and coastal cut-throat trout are among many other fish using this habitat, where they are stalked by great blue herons.

For more about eelgrass see pages 4 - 5.

CYCLES OF LIFE

"Only a few.... understood how nonlinear nature is in its soul."
~ James Gleick in Chaos

The world of nature is dynamic, cyclical and inter-connected, quite different from industrial processes based on steady conversion of resources to single products. The complexity of nature is on a very large scale of space and time.

Nature's destructive power can be massive: erupting volcanoes shower the landscape with ash, storm surges wash away huge sections of shoreline, glaciers grind the landscape into gravel, beetle infestations decimate forests, that in turn succumb to raging fires.

On the other hand, the abundance of nature is far more than enough to feed its flocks and shoals. Plants produce billions of spores and seeds, fish produce millions of eggs, many times in excess of reproductive needs. It is estimated that a single bull kelp sheds four trillion spores a season and an alder tree three million seeds. A hundred million *Callianassa* burrowing shrimp turn over two hundred thousand cubic metres of sand every summer on Roberts Bank. This wealth feeds thousands of forms of life, creating a network of interdependent living

The complex shoreline of intertidal mud flats and tidal marshes in Mud Bay.

creatures. Although humans are part of this web of life, all too often we remove ourselves from the picture.

A single bull kelp sheds four trillion spores a season

Many animals exhibit cycles in their population, because of the complex relationship between climate, food availability and predation. Rising and falling numbers of voles and mice (small mammals that have prolific breeding habits,) dictate the abundance and distribution of predators, such as owls and hawks. Some voles have peak populations in fall or winter and rapid declines in spring.

Pacific tent caterpillars build up to peak populations every eight to eleven years, and painted lady

Kelp washed onto a rocky beach at Point Roberts.

butterflies are on a ten year cycle. Salmon have perhaps the best known population cycles of all the local species, occurring in peak abundance every two to six years, depending on the species. Pink salmon runs occur every odd year up the Fraser River, while sockeye peak on average every four years.

Animal population cycles are not well understood. Small disturbances can have large effects on non-linear systems, the proverbial flutter of a butterfly's wings causing a tornado. Scientists concerned with climate change and biodiversity protection are exploring the many cyclical patterns present in the environment, looking for correlations.

The earth moves through three very long term cycles, known after their discoverer as *Milankovitch cycles*, lasting 105,000, 41,000 and 21,000 years. They are caused by the shape of the earth's orbit, the tilt of its axis and the precession of the equinoxes respectively. Solar cycles of 180 and 80 years and an eleven year sunspot cycle also occur. Sunspots are huge, dark, relatively cooler patches that intermittently arise on the surface of the sun. They are associated with strong magnetic fields and generally last about a week. Sunspot cycles are thought to correlate with northern precipitation levels, glaciation patterns and also perhaps such animal cycles as the well-documented snowshoe hare, owl and lynx cycle.

Climate Change

In recent years, more attention has been paid to major climatic effects around the Pacific Ocean, including the phenomena of *El Niño* and *La Niña*. These warming and cooling events in the ocean off Peru, may be part of a forty to fifty year cyclical climate pattern, the Pacific Decadal Oscillation (PDO). The cumulative impact of such cyclical patterns, and human-caused carbon emissions, is driving climate change.

Sea surface temperature rose three times higher than the global average

Cool surface waters, associated with *La Niña* years and a negative PDO index, are more productive for northern marine life than warm ones. If the top layer of the ocean is cold, convection currents will gradually overturn it, essentially stirring the water from bottom to

El Niño

El Niño is a recurrent, localized warming of the ocean off the shore of Peru, that occurs around Christmas time every three to seven years and lasts for six to eighteen months. It alternates irregularly with *La Niña* years, in which the offshore ocean is cooler than average.

top. The currents bring mineral-rich water up from the deep into the sunlit realm of the phytoplankton, creating a fertile environment for plankton clouds and all the marine life that feeds on them.

In contrast, warm water in the upper layers tends to be rather stable. Its presence reduces convection stirring and nutrient replenishment, lessens the duration and quantity of the plankton clouds and diminishes the food supply for large fish, shellfish, birds and mammals. Warm waters increase the risk of a timing mismatch between prey abundance and seabird hatching, as well as being more inviting for predatory southern fish, such as mackerel. As environmental stress on the cold water fish increases, shoals become smaller or disperse.

In the Georgia Basin, between the mainland and Vancouver Island, sea surface temperature rose three

CYCLES OF LIFE · 55

times higher than the global average between 1914 and 2001 (1.8°C or 3.2°F compared to 0.6°C or 1.1°F; all figures from B.C. government). One contributing factor is decreased glaciation on upstream mountains, leading to a reduction in cooling run off from snow and ice.

Climate change also affects plants and wildlife on land. In order for pollination to occur, spring blooms must coincide with the emergence of insects from winter dormancy. Songbirds feed their chicks on the insects that hatch when flowers and foliage are at their most luxuriant. A cool spring can delay breeding or prevent young being reared.

During this century, the annual air temperature rose 0.5 - 0.6°C (1°F) in the Georgia Basin, equal to the global average rise. Interior temperature rise has been higher, leading to a ten percent reduction in snow pack in the western mountain ranges. Shrinking glaciers contribute less run off and snow melts earlier; the river discharges more of its total flow earlier in the year and the water is warmer in the summer.

Between 1953 and 1998, the Fraser River warmed at a rate of 2.2°C (3.9°F) per century, an increase that cannot fail to affect fish and other river wildlife, sensitive to water temperatures. For example, sockeye salmon need an ambient temperature between 12 to 15°C (53 to 59°F) for basic survival.

The air temperature rise is not evenly spread across the year, and the increase is actually due to the climate becoming less cold rather than more hot. There are higher day temperatures in spring and fall, and fewer frosty nights in winter and spring. The growing season has lengthened with the increase in number of frost-free nights and spring arrives earlier.

Unfortunately, pest insects and microbes survive better too, so it is not all good news for farmers and gardeners. More importantly, this shift in the seasons will have many unpredictable effects on the environment, as natural partnerships get out of step and even break down.

Red tide

"Red tide" is a common name for paralytic shellfish poisoning (PSP). Clams and mussels siphon in toxic algae, which accumulate up the food chain, affecting fish, birds, marine mammals and humans.

Two algae responsible for PSP in the Strait of Georgia are *Alexandrium catanella* and *A. acatenella* (previously *Gonyaulax*).

Global incidences of red tides have risen in the last twenty five years, a phenomenon that may be linked with climate change.

NOCTURNAL NATURE

"For I ne'er saw true beauty till this night" ~ William Shakespeare

Driving home late at night, we sometimes see the ghostly shade of a barn owl fly silently past, or catch a quick glimpse of a raccoon family lurking in the shadows. Most of the time, though, the light-loving modern human is unaware of the natural life of the night.

By being diurnal, the interested observer misses many interesting animals in the Boundary Bay area, those which are most active in darkness. Yet, despite the pervasive presence of human noises, lights and activity, strolling the dyke or wandering down a woodland path at dusk still allows us to enter this secret nocturnal world.

Take advantage of winter nights to look up at the stars. The night sky is often bright and clear over Boundary Bay, well removed from the city, and affords an opportunity to see many natural wonders of the cosmos.

Dusk view across Boundary Bay to the North Shore mountains and Burnaby: glare from city lights can be both an ecological and social problem.

Roosting flights

Dusk and dawn are the time to see roosting flights of birds that spend the night in large congregations. All the crows around the Fraser estuary roost from late summer to early spring in central Burnaby, where over 11, 000 huddle together on roof tops and ledges. They fly together in long straggling lines across the darkening sky to arrive at the roost just before nightfall. The crows are back in their usual neighbourhood at dawn.

European starlings and glaucous-winged gulls are also congregational roosters. The gulls fly out from the Burns Bog landfill in long skeins at dusk every winter evening, headed for a roost on Mandarte Island in the Strait of Georgia. They also gather in large mixed flocks in fields. In spring, great blue herons return at dusk to their nesting colonies, the last daytime birds to be flying as night falls.

Creatures of the night

Owls and bats are famously active at night, but many other local animals are also nocturnal, such as skunks, flying squirrels, opossums, raccoons, Pacific jumping mice, frogs, salamanders and moths. Deer, rabbits and coyotes are often seen at dusk or dawn.

Mysterious creatures of the night, bats are the subject of myths and

Great blue herons roost in trees for the night.

misconceptions. Despite common fears, bats will not fly into your hair, since they have a precise echolocation system and can pinpoint flying insects with great accuracy. Bats are seldom active in the winter, for they den up in attics or hollow trees to stay warm. The best time to look for them is on summer evenings. Many bats emerge just after sunset, where open meadows and ponds meet the forest edge. Parks organize bat walks to visit maternal colonies and use bat detectors to hear the bats' usually inaudible, high frequency calls.

Greater Vancouver Regional District Parks' bat watches: 604 432 6359
www.gvrd.bc.ca
See page 81 for more about bats.

The Boundary Bay watershed is one of the best places in Canada for owl watching, with a great variety of resident and visiting species. Some can be seen during the late afternoon or early morning, but for others a night walk in the woods is necessary. Local naturalist clubs organize guided owl walks, so you do not have to stumble around in the dark on your own. Evenings in winter are the best time to look for them, although chance sightings of roosting owls often occur in late summer when juvenile dispersal is taking place. (For more on owls *see pages 96 - 98*).

Raccoons are frequently seen at night, crossing suburban roads or prowling around yards. Striped skunks and flying squirrels may be seen at night near forested areas. Listen for the nocturnal peeping of Pacific tree frogs, chorusing on spring nights in freshwater wetlands.

The night sky

Despite a steady increase in artificial light threatening to engulf a view of the night sky, there are still places around Boundary Bay where one can observe shining stars, planets, meteor showers, comets and other astronomical delights. Moon rise on a clear night, as it lifts from behind Mount Baker and the Cascade Mountains, is a breathtaking sight. Cold, crisp winter nights are often the best times for star-gazing.

A moonlit night begins in Boundary Bay as the l...

Comets & meteor showers

A few times in every lifetime, a comet makes an appearance, looking like a bright star with a characteristic plume streaming behind. Comets are nothing more substantial than balls of deeply-frozen space dust, with two tails, a white feathery trail of dust and a less visible blue tail of gas, streaming away from the sun. Although comets are only periodically close enough to be seen, their long tails lie hundreds of thousands of kilometres through space. Some comet tails intercept the path of the earth's orbit, resulting in a series of annual meteor showers.

The Perseid meteor shower is a spectacular cosmic event not to be missed. It can be seen every summer, as the earth passes through a region of space full of dust from the Swift-Tuttle comet. This comet has a 130 year orbit around the sun and is due to return to our skies in 2126. The meteors or shooting stars, are just tiny particles of this dust, melting from the comet.

the sun paint the summit of Mount Baker.

During the Perseid shower, shooting stars streak across the sky, crossing from northeast to southwest in a steady stream, at a peak rate of 80 per hour. They are visible for a couple of weeks every year in mid-summer, but the best views are obtained after midnight around August 11 - 13, when the earth heads directly into the stream.

The earth passes through the Swift-Tuttle dust trail again in October, producing the less dramatic Orionid meteor shower. Meteor showers from other comets include the Leonids, that can produce dramatic storms of activity on November 17 and 18 and the Geminids, with a high peak stream around December 13.

Rest assured that meteor showers do not result in meteorites coming to earth. However, rare, large, very bright sporadic meteors, known as "fireballs", may signal the fall of rocky debris.

Planets & stars

The planet Venus is often noticed as the very bright "evening star" conspicuous just after sunset. At other times of year, it makes its appearance shortly before sunrise, as the "morning star". It is not seen in the middle of the night. This planet's orbit lies closer to the sun than the Earth's. Another planet, Mercury, orbits the sun even closer than Venus but is seldom noticed by casual observers. It is only visible from Earth for a few weeks a year, at dusk or dawn.

Stars appear to twirl overhead in a slow dance through the cosmos, producing star trails on a time-lapse photograph. It is actually the earth's rotation on its axis, not the movement of the stars, that produces this effect. The stars are so far removed in space that their actual motions are barely perceptible over millennia.

Jupiter is the brightest planet visible in the middle of the night. It has four moons, visible through a telescope when conditions are favourable. The planet is far distant from the sun; its trajectory through space lies between that of Saturn and Mars, the small red planet lying closest to Earth. The other planets, Uranus, Neptune and Pluto, are not visible with the naked eye. All of the planets are confined to orbits within the plane of the solar system, in a region of the night sky defined by the star constellations known as the zodiac.

Identifying stars can be quite daunting. Simple groups to pick out are Orion, a constellation that rides high in the winter sky, and the big dipper, in Ursa Major. Look towards the big dipper for a view of Deep Space, an exciting region to explore with binoculars or telescopes.

The constellations of Cassiopeia and Perseus photographed from Lighthouse Park, Point Roberts.

Further information

The Night Sky Month by Month
by Jean-Louis Heudier
Nightwatch ~ A Practical Guide to Viewing the Universe
by Terence Dickinson

The Royal Astronomical Society of Canada www.rasc.ca

Macmillan Planetarium, www.hrmacmillanspacecentre. com 604 738 7827

Whatcom Association of Celestial Observers www.whatcomastronomy.org

The big dipper also leads the way to Polaris, the north star, and three bright stars, Sirius, Arcturus and Spica. Look also for Betelgeuse and Rigel, two supergiant stars in Orion, the twin stars of Castor and Pollux and the Summer Triangle, a trio of stars whose arrival heralds warm weather.

The Milky Way, millions of stars forming a pale white cloud across the sky, is the home galaxy of planet Earth. It is a spiral galaxy, consisting of about 100 billion stars. It is just one of the thousands of galaxies so far identified, a tiny speck in the vast infinity of space.

Dawn chorus

As night draws to a close, the eastern horizon glows brightly, ushering in the new day. During the songbird breeding season, from early April through May, a chorus of bird song greets the first light.

The sweet full-throated warbling of American robins is our introduction, accompanied by the melodies of the song sparrow. They are followed by the deep "coo coo" of band-tailed pigeons, the cascades of house finches and the trills of spotted towhees. Marsh wrens, yellowthroats and red-winged blackbirds sing vigorously in wetlands, where the strange, braying calls of Virginia rail can also be heard.

A male red-winged blackbird singing and displaying near his nest site.

Birds sing at dawn when the air is clear so that their voices carry well, up to twenty times further than at midday. There are far fewer competing noises, such as insect hum, at this time and other activities, such as feeding, are not an immediate priority.

Mostly male birds do the singing, announcing their breeding territory to potential mates and rivals. They may choose a conspicuous perch and show off ornamental feathers, such as the vermilion red epaulettes of the red-winged blackbird. Others have a display flight; for example, the male rufous hummingbird calls as it performs a dive-bombing loop over its territory, while the Wilson's snipe drums with its tail feathers as it flies a circuit.

A few female birds also sing, such as song sparrows and red-winged blackbirds. They probably use this as a way of announcing a nesting territory, especially to other females.

Keen birders always try to be out in the field in time to catch the dawn chorus, when many elusive species can be identified by sound alone. After singing, birds feed for another hour or two. This makes them easy to see and identify.

Further information
The Singing Life of Birds by Donald Kroodsma

Lily Point cliffs are a spiritually significant site for the Coast Salish people (including the Lummi, Semiahmoo, Saanich and members of the SencoT'en Alliance) and the site of First Salmon ceremonies through the ages.

THE DYNAMIC EARTH

"Our landscape is active - the earth movements that created it continue today!" ~ John Clague and Bob Turner in Vancouver, City on the Edge

From almost anywhere around Boundary Bay, there are excellent views of the geologically-active landscape, from the sharp peaks of the North Shore Mountains, to the deep rift of the Strait of Georgia and the snow-capped peak of Mount Baker.

The Ring of Fire

Nothing seems as solid and unmoving as a rock, but even the ground itself is always slowly in motion. Plates of continental crust glide over the surface of the hot, liquid centre of the earth, like skin on boiling milk. The plates bump and grind into and under each other, lifting and eroding mountain ranges. The various movements in different dimensions at differing speeds can generate an earthquake, a sudden release of energy that transmits in seismic waves through the ground.

The earth's interior is made up of concentric layers: a dense, innermost core, a hot and liquid mantle, and a relatively thin layer of crust. Magma, the liquid rock from the mantle, is oozing up through the Pacific Ocean floor, pushing the crust apart and creating an underwater mountain ridge as it cools.

The crust is forced towards the North American plate, at a rate of 5 cm per year.

The crust, known in this area as the Juan de Fuca plate, is forced towards the larger, more stable North American continental plate, at a rate of 5 cm (2 in) per year. This hectic pace is about half the speed at which human fingernails grow!

The crust plate is then sucked below the continent into a hot, molten region, known as the Cascadia subduction zone. Many geologists believe that a high magnitude earthquake, the 'Big One', measuring M8 or more, is likely to originate in this subduction zone. Volcanic and earthquake activity along unstable plate margins all around the Pacific Ocean, create the famous "Ring of Fire".

Over millions of years, as plates moving east under the Pacific have met the continental mass, the rocks have been crumpled and pushed upwards. This creates rows of geologically young mountains and deep valleys, running north-south, including the Coastal Mountains and the Cascades Range. Within these ranges, over 200 volcanoes mark where hot, molten rock from the mantle is moving to the surface. A wonderful view of five or six of the solitary volcanic peaks can be seen from the air on certain approaches to the Fraser Valley.

Earthquakes

Boundary Bay is in one of the most seismically active regions of Canada, shaken almost every day by an earthquake! Most are much too small to be felt: the odd jolting sensation of a minor earthquake happens only once every few years.

The intensity of the tremor depends on the ground below; seismic waves are amplified by soft sands in the delta floodplain. In the case of a severe earthquake, magnitude M7 or more, liquefaction of the ground could occur as water-filled sands became mobile. This effect would be most likely in areas of recent sedimentation, such as river islands.

Unless one is close to the epicentre, earthquakes are not readily felt on the glacial gravel hills around the bay.

Liquefaction is unlikely there, but land slides can be triggered on steep bluffs. While earthquakes could cause extensive damage, remedial engineering work, such as has been carried out around the foundations of Fraser delta bridges, helps to limit the risk.

Most earthquakes experienced in Boundary Bay originate over 20 km (12 mi) down in the continental plate. Catastrophic, subduction earthquakes occur every 500 years or so. An M8 took place in January 1700 off the West Coast and caused a tsunami that went right across the Pacific Ocean to Japan. Subduction earthquakes are marked by large magnitude, prolonged shaking (1-3 minutes) and repeated aftershocks.

Moment Magnitude

Moment Magnitude (M) scale measures earthquake strength based on seismic moment, the amount of energy released by the quake.

This scale has now replaced the similar, Richter Scale, a logarithmic scale based on seismic wave amplitudes.

For the latest tectonic and seismic events, check out the Pacific Northwest Seismograph Network at www.geophys.washington.edu/SEIS/PNSN/BAKER/

A view of Mt. Baker from Roberts Bank.

Mount Baker ~ our local volcano

Mount Baker is the beautiful snow-capped peak in the Cascade Mountains, southeast of Boundary Bay. This young, moderately active volcano rises to 3285 m (10,778 ft). It has erupted several times in the last ten thousand years.

Mount Baker is known as a stratovolcano, a steep-sided cone built up by lava deposits, flowing from magma deep underground. It is unusual in being so heavily glaciated. The present cone developed 30,000 to 10,000 years ago during the glacial period, and glaciers eroded the flanks of the mountain, leaving the sharp peaks and summit protruding. A notable eruption occurred around 6600 years ago, throwing ash and rock into the air and precipitating a vast debris flow of mud, ice, rocks and trees down the Nooksack River.

More recent events occurred in 1792 (witnessed by Galiano and Valdes, the Spanish explorers) and in the 1800s. Sulphur gas and steam rising from Sherman Crater in 1975, excited concerns that more eruptions were imminent, but the volcano stabilized again two years later. Nowadays, the peak is monitored on a daily basis for any seismic activity or the deep harmonic tremors that would precede an eruption.

George Vancouver named it Mount Baker after his third lieutenant, Joseph Baker, who was the first of his crew to spot the peak. The Lummi name is *Kul-shan*, meaning bleeding wound or scar, a reflection of its eruptive history. The Nooksack who lived beneath its peak, named it "the white mountain", *Quck-sman-ik*.

Glaciers

The landscape of Boundary Bay was carved by prehistoric glaciers that pushed down the valleys, grinding and pulverising the earth beneath. These glaciers were part of the vast Cordilleran ice sheet that covered a large portion of the northwestern continent during Pleistocene times, between 2 million and 11,000 years ago.

At its peak, the ice above the international boundary was nearly 2 km thick

The Ice Ages, as they are popularly called, were marked by a cycle of glacier advances and retreats, right across the northern hemisphere. Surprisingly, the air was only an average 3 to 5°C (6 to 10°F) colder than it is today, yet this difference was sufficient to cause the drastic change in climate.

Further information

Vancouver, City on the Edge by John Clague and Bob Turner.

British Columbia: A Natural History by Richard and Sydney Cannings.

The United States Geological Survey: http://vulcan.wr.usgs.gov

Once started the glaciation was self-perpetuating. Regular, heavy snowfalls built up alpine glaciers that clung to the mountain sides, expanding and joining one another to become ice sheets that filled the valleys. The maximum extent of the Fraser Glaciation, the last glacial episode, 14,500 years ago, took glaciers down to the ocean mouth of the Juan de Fuca Strait and to the southern end of Puget Sound.

At its peak, the ice above the international boundary was nearly 2 km (1.2 mi) thick. All but the very highest peaks were covered. Once melting began, it was fairly rapid, at more than 100 metres (300 ft) a year, leaving most of the Boundary Bay watershed ice clear by 12,500 years ago. The ocean stretched across the Lower Mainland to the North Shore mountains and Point Roberts was an island. The earth slowly rebounded from the weight of the ice and the sea retreated once more.

Standing on the shores of Boundary Bay today, one can recognise many signs of the last Ice Age. Sharp mountain peaks of the highest North Shore, Cascade and Olympic mountains were above the ice sheet, but their flanks were draped with alpine glaciers like those on Mount Baker. The surrounding lower hills have rounded, eroded tops and U-shaped valleys, showing they were buried beneath the ice sheets. Large glacial "erratics", blocks of igneous and metamorphic rocks from the Fraser Canyon, are scattered across the landscape. Drayton Harbor has a particularly noticeable collection of erratics in the shallow water and the giant glacial boulder at White Rock gave the city its name.

The gravels and erratics deposited by the glaciers form a thick layer, reaching to depths of 200 m (650 ft) below North Delta and Surrey, up to 330 m (1100 ft) under White Rock and up to 800 m (2600 ft) below the Fraser delta. These unconsolidated materials overlie Tertiary sandstones and conglomerates which form the base rock far below.

The Sumas glacier blocked the Fraser Valley near Langley and was the last to go. Meltwater carved the valley of the Little Campbell and built a delta into the sea just northwest of where the regional park now lies. "Kame and kettle landscape" is the geological name given to the hummocky countryside visible in this part of Langley, where lumps of ice calved from the glacier and slowly melted in place.

Fossil shells from cockles, mussels and clams that lived in the ocean thousands of years ago were found in tills exposed in cliffs around the uplands.

Erratics scatter the sand of Drayton Harbor. These giant boulders were carried in the glaciers that once covered this whole area.

WILDLIFE PROFILES

"The marine life of British Columbia is among the most diverse in the world" ~ Richard & Sydney Cannings in British Columbia: A Natural History

This part of the book gives a broad overview of the different animals that can be found around Boundary Bay, from enormous whales to microscopic bacteria. To learn more about individual wildlife species and their habitats, consult a field guide or take a guided walk with local naturalists.

WHALES & PORPOISES

Humpback whales may be returning to the Strait of Georgia.

The unmistakable **killer whale** or orca is the most spectacular of the local whales. This large black and white whale has three distinct races in the Pacific Northwest: residents, transients and offshores. They have different languages, lifestyles and eating habits and do not interbreed.

There are fewer than a hundred resident killer whales roaming the southern Strait of Georgia, Juan de Fuca Strait and Puget Sound. They travel in three groups, called J, K and L Pods. They are fish eaters, and depend heavily on salmon, particularly chinook, which they track down using echolocation. J Pod are sighted year round, but K and L Pod visit from June to October, perhaps spending the winter as far south as California. Transient whales sometimes come by, traveling alone or in small groups, and hunting seals and sea lions in shallow water along the coast. Offshore killer whales, as their name suggests, stay in deep ocean waters, seldom venturing into the Strait of Georgia.

Resident killer whale populations are in decline. The chinook salmon

Further Information

Whales of the West Coast by David Spalding

Whales and other Marine Mammals of British Columbia and Alaska by Tamara Eder

Vancouver Aquarium, Stanley Park, www.vanaqua.org

they eat are in short supply, they are susceptible to toxins concentrated in the food chain, and there was a gap in the breeding demographic because of aquarium captures in the 1960s and 70s. Killer whales can live between 50 to 80 years, the females generally living much longer than the males, but they breed slowly. By 2005, the southern resident population was 87 whales, down from 98 in the mid 1990s.

Good places to see killer whales locally are from the west shore of Point Roberts or from the B.C. ferry.

In 1993, a small **false killer whale** arrived off Roberts Bank and stayed until 2004, following small boats. It was affectionately known as "Willy". Sometimes wrongly identified as a pilot whale, false killer whales are normally found in the warm waters of Central America, and are identifiable by their smaller size.

The **minke** or piked whale is a rare visitor to the waters off Point Roberts, although it is not uncommon in the neighbouring Gulf Islands. It is long, dark and sleek, with a small fin.

Humpback whales were historically abundant in the Strait of Georgia; however, they were locally extirpated by aggressive whaling operations in the early 1900s. Although none had been seen for many years in Boundary Bay, one was sighted by Vancouver Whale Watch in April 2004 off Saturna Island, just south

Whale Watching

Going out in a boat is a fun way to get close to whales, as long as the animals themselves are not disturbed. Whales and porpoises can often seem very comfortable around boats, but the constant noise and excitement can disrupt their lives, and even cause injuries or death.

The following guidelines are recommended by the Marine Mammal Monitoring Project:
• Slow down to under 5 knots.
• Reduce wake and noise.
• Maintain a couple of hundred metres distance. Sometimes the animals will come closer to you when you do this.
• Never chase or feed them, avoid crossing their path or approaching from behind.
• Stay offshore of animals traveling close to shore.

Reputable whale watching groups will observe the standard guidelines and ensure a good viewing experience, without harassing the whales.

of the bay. **Grey whales** have huge mouths equipped with special filters or baleens, which strain out tiny shrimps, fish, crabs and krill from the water. Even though they eat such small food, grey whales are enormous, measuring fourteen metres (46 ft) in length. They are occasionally seen blowing offshore, especially in spring, and sometimes get stranded in Boundary Bay.

Two species of porpoise occur in the area and can sometimes be seen off Point Roberts, Birch Point or in the Strait of Georgia. Traveling alone or in small groups, **harbour porpoises** prefer shallow bays and inshore waters. They are about 1.8 m (6 ft) long, dark above and pale below. Their inshore feeding habits make them susceptible to water pollution and collisions with water craft, and their numbers have declined in the past decade. Groups of the slightly bigger **Dall's porpoise** love to play in the wake of boats. Close up the white mark on the dorsal fin distinguishes them from the darker harbour porpoise. Dall's porpoises live in deep water and are more common in the Strait of Georgia than the bay.

Stranded whales?

Report strandings to Fisheries and Oceans Canada at 1 800 465 4336 or to the Marine Mammal Research Group Stranding Hotline 1 800 665 5939

In the US, call the National Marine Fisheries Service 1 800 853 1964.

Report whale sightings

B.C. Cetacean Sightings Network www.wildwhales.org

Orca Network www.orcanetwork.org

SEALS & SEA LIONS

Seals and sea lions are more often encountered than whales. **Harbour seals** (harbor seals) can be virtually guaranteed on any trip to the beach or Fraser River mouth at high tide. The round bobbing head, large dark eyes and calm demeanor of this common seal are quite distinctive. They like the warm shallow waters of the bays and rivers and up to two hundred have been counted hauled out on sand bars in Mud Bay.

Seals mate in the water through late spring and summer and the pups are born ten months later, mostly in July and August. Male seals are territorial in summer, and approach each other closely, putting their heads side by side and uttering sounds. This determines the dominant male. If the sound test is inconclusive then they fight, biting each other on the skin of the neck and becoming quite aggressive. The splashing and noise of these displays can be heard at a distance.

Harbour seals are not confined to marine waters but swim upriver with the tide as far as the Pitt valley. They are reputed to know when a freeze-up is likely, descending to the sea coast just before it occurs.

A sighting of the **northern fur seal** is a rare event. Solitary individuals of this dark seal have been recorded from Roberts Bank.

Sea lions may superficially resemble seals, but they are not the same family and they have different physique and behaviour. Harbour seals have pale, greyish, spotted fur and round heads, and are less than 1.8 m (6 ft) long. Sea lions are brown, have strongly shaped heads with a high brow, and are over 2 m (7 ft) long. In contrast to the leisurely swimming seals, sea lions move fast through the water, humping their backs. They are able to rotate their flippers and have loud, barking calls.

California sea lions are relatively new arrivals to the British Columbia coast, spreading up from the south in increasing numbers since 1980. Females and young sea lions leave California in the fall and go south to Baja, but males disperse up the coast to British Columbia. Large numbers gather in the Strait of Georgia, where they make a noisy scene around the mouth of the Fraser River, especially during herring spawn in March and April. Boat charters head out from Steveston to view them gathered along the jetty, while Point Roberts and Blaine pier are good places to spot them from shore. Most leave by the end of May.

Large numbers of California sea lions gather in the Strait of Georgia

The enormous **Steller sea lion**, the bulls weighing about 600 kg (1323 lb) and measuring 3 m (10 ft), used to be the only sea lion found in the Strait of Georgia. Anthropologist Wayne Suttles related how every March large herds of sea lions passed through Porlier Pass in the

Harbour seal resting on a rock off Lily Point in Boundary Bay.

Strait, where they were hunted by the Kuper Islanders, with mussel shell and antler harpoons. In the 1920s, sea lions were culled on the west coast almost to the point of extinction, but they have made a come back in British Columbia since 1972, protected by the Fisheries Act.

Steller sea lions have a breeding colony in the Scott Islands, off the northwest coast of Vancouver Island, and several hundred winter on islets adjacent to Saturna Island, immediately south of Boundary Bay. They are sometimes seen cruising the waters of the Strait of Georgia, or hauled out with California sea lions on Steveston jetty in Richmond. On land, male Steller sea lions can be distinguished by their thick golden brown fur manes, enormous size and raucous grunting.

Seals and sea lions tend to be less disturbed by boat traffic than whales, but should still be given full respect. Sea lions are very large and potentially dangerous animals. Maintain several hundred metres distance from haul-outs, colonies or individual animals and keep disturbance to a minimum.

Further Information

Mammals of British Columbia by Tamara Eder and Don Pattie

Coast Salish Essays by Wayne Suttles

BIG MAMMALS: DEER & BEARS

Boundary Bay is no longer the wilderness of prairie, marshes and giant conifers that so astounded early European explorers and gave haven to Roosevelt elk, mule deer, grizzly and black bears. The grizzly bear and elk are now gone, but surprisingly for such a developed region, a few black bear survive and deer are still common in rural areas.

Local deer are a small subspecies of mule deer, known as **Columbian black-tailed deer**. They are generally shy and cautious, and can best be observed at dusk or dawn, when they browse at the edge of woodlands or

Columbian black-tailed deer

wander along the shore. In some rural areas, they come boldly into gardens, even in the daytime, and can be quite a nuisance.

Deer rely on corridors of habitat provided by power lines, railway tracks and river valleys. These corridors link feeding areas and also create opportunities for deer to connect with others, especially at night. In spring and summer, deer feed out in the open, in fields and brushy areas and in Burns Bog. They need dense woodlands to survive the winter, though, and to provide secure sleeping sites.

Once abundant throughout the watershed, deer have been reduced by land development, habitat loss, traffic fatalities and harassment.

About five black bears are believed to still live in Burns Bog

Black bears are not an animal often encountered in the Boundary Bay watershed. About five bears are believed to still live in Burns Bog and its immediate surroundings, despite its increasing isolation from other suitable habitat. There are occasional reports of bears seen at dusk or dawn, sometimes beside Highway 91, in the northeast corner of the bog. Rare sightings of bears plodding down the hydro easement

Black bear

through North Delta and Surrey suggest that they might still try to make their way from the wooded uplands to the berry patches of the bog, as they did for thousands of years. Bears also occur in the Dakota Creek and California Creek valleys and sporadically in the Nicomekl and Little Campbell watersheds, probably wandering down from forested areas among the foothills of the North Cascades. Their presence is generally discouraged by farmers and other landowners.

Further Information

Status of Black Bears in Burns Bog, by K.Anre McIntosh & Ian Robertson. Discovery, Vol. 29, No.1: 26-31, 2000. Vancouver NHS

The native Douglas's squirrel, also called chickaree.

SQUIRRELS

Many people enjoy watching the lively activity of squirrels, and often try to tame and feed them.

The **Douglas's squirrel** is the native red squirrel of mainland coastal forests. These little squirrels have a noisy chattering call and defend their territory pugnaciously. Young ones stay with their mother for a few months after birth, and the grown males are generally solitary. The Douglas's squirrel relies on dense ground cover and thick conifer stands to provide nesting sites and protection from predators, so it is vulnerable to forest loss. These attractive native animals have declined as forests in the Boundary Bay uplands have been logged. The best places to see them are forest parks, such as Tynehead, Campbell Valley or Green Timbers.

Everyone is familiar with the lively squirrels that run around suburban parks and gardens, scampering up trees and jumping between branches. These are **eastern grey squirrels**, native to the broadleaf woodlands of Northeast America. They dispersed from a small group that was introduced into Stanley Park, Vancouver, sometime before 1914. For many years they stayed inside the park boundaries, but as their population grew they gradually escaped, or were removed. Biologist Emily Gonzales found that between 1970 and 1995 grey squirrels spread

The introduced eastern grey squirrel.

at a rate of 3.64 km (2.26 mi) a year, arriving in the Boundary Bay area between 1989 (Surrey) and 1993 (Tsawwassen). By the late 1990s they were in Langley, at the head of the watershed. They prospered wherever there were open lawns and mature trees. Grey squirrel fur can be either black or grey. Black morphs are typical of northern squirrels, but are also the most prevalent locally since the Stanley Park population held more blacks than greys.

Eastern grey squirrels can live alongside Douglas's squirrels, and while grey squirrels have a notorious reputation for ousting the smaller native species, this hostility is unproven. Possibly habitat loss is a greater factor in the Douglas's local decline, than competition. The grey squirrel mates earlier in the year, and its young are born in February. A second brood is born in summer, at which time squirrels are noisy, making harsh scolding calls from the branches. While a grey squirrel needs up to two hectares (5 ac) for foraging, an individual's range will overlap with several others.

During the fall "reshuffle", all the young squirrels and adults disperse to find winter homes. This gives the appearance of there being more squirrels in the neighbourhood than usual. Grey squirrels can live up to ten years; however, cold winters, predators and mange mite parasites kill many, particularly the more vulnerable young.

Most people never see our third squirrel, the nocturnal **northern flying squirrel**. A resident of forested uplands, this little animal does not really fly. It got its name by gliding between trees on extensions of skin between its front and hind legs, like a small furry cape. During the day they hide in old woodpecker holes. Flying squirrels are not uncommon in the forest, but only a chance encounter at night will reveal their presence. Sadly, they are more often seen when injured ones are brought into animal shelters.

The coniferous forests in which flying squirrels make their home are also habitat for a wide variety of mycorrhizal fungi *(see page 160)*. The fruiting bodies of these fungi, either above or below ground, are a favourite food of the northern flying squirrel. Squirrel droppings, containing both nutrients and fungal spores, spread fungi throughout the forest. In this way, the flying squirrel contributes to the health and life of other forest species, while supporting itself.

The **Townsend's chipmunk** looks like a small stripy squirrel. It only occurs in the highest reaches of the Boundary Bay watershed.

Further Information

Eastern Grey Squirrels - An Introduction to an Introduction Emily Gonzales, Discovery Vol.28 No.1: 22-25. Vancouver NHS.

SMALL MAMMALS: VOLES, MOLES & SHREWS

Small mammals play an important role in local forest and grassland ecosystems. Some of them dig and burrow, thus turning over the soil, and allowing seeds to germinate. Others chew and snap plant stems and leaves into organic mulches. Small mammal droppings fertilize the soil and propagate seeds that are too hard to be digested. Furthermore, these abundant little animals aid in the spread of mycorrhizal fungi, which can help the growth of trees and other plants, by providing them with nutrients from the soil.

Small mammals are an integral part of the food chain, and are the reason that so many different types of birds of prey can be found around Boundary Bay. Other than dangling from some bird's beak or brought in by the cat, it is unusual to see a wild vole, mole or shrew. It is quite easy, however, to find signs of their presence, such as burrows, earth mounds or gnawed grass stems.

The largest member of the vole family in North America is the **Townsend's vole**. It is the dominant prey item around Boundary Bay for wintering rough-legged hawks, resident and wintering northern harriers, barn owls and both adult and juvenile great blue herons. Three quarters of the food eaten by young barn owls are voles. Townsend's voles are the ultimate grassland animal, burrowing into the grass for their homes and eating grass leaves, stems and roots. Signs of their extensive burrows and surface runways are found on the foreshore and in fields left fallow for a few years or managed as grassland "set-asides".

Townsend's voles are the dominant prey item for wintering hawks and owls

Young voles are small and dark, a quarter the size of adults, but they quickly grow to their full weight: 75 to 100 g (2.3 to 3.5 oz). Mary Taitt has studied voles on and off for 34 years, and suggests that winter rains flood the grasslands forcing voles to the surface, where they cluster in patches of grass above the water table. As they eat the grass cover they become vulnerable to predators. She notes that rather than regular 2 to 5 year cycles in numbers, Townsend's voles appear to fluctuate annually and outbreak occasionally, reaching up to 1200 per hectare in ideal old field grassland habitat.

The smaller **creeping vole** is also a common inhabitant of the Boundary Bay watershed, usually in more wooded areas. Typical of many voles, it is subject to strong cyclical population changes, being very

Pellets

The presence of small animals can be confirmed by skulls and bones found in owl pellets. When owls eat prey, they regurgitate feathers, bones and fur in greyish pellets, 2 - 4 cm long (1 - 1.5 in). These can be found under owl roost trees or along dykes.

By separating out the constituents, much can be told about what the owl was feasting on. Care should be taken with pellets: they could be confused with coyote scat, which can harbour pathogens.

abundant every four years or so, and scarce in intervening years. Their numbers also fluctuate seasonally through the year, characteristically falling to their lowest level just before breeding in the spring and then peaking again in fall.

A subspecies of the **southern red-backed vole**, *Clethrionomys gapperi occidentalis*, was discovered in a Burns Bog pine forest in 1999 and is the only known population of this subspecies in British Columbia. **Long-tailed voles** are occasionally found in the Fraser delta by specialist researchers.

Shrews are small, aggressive animals living a fast-paced lifestyle that lasts less than 18 months. They forage much of the day and night and can sometimes be seen scuttling across a footpath. Thousands are caught by domestic cats every year. Most mammals, including cats, prefer not to eat them because they have an unpleasant smell, but they are a common prey of owls.

Shrews do not hibernate but are active year round.

The tiny **vagrant shrew** is the most common shrew in coast marshes, delta old field habitat and moist western redcedar forests. It has three litters a year. Other shrews are found only in forests. The **cinereus shrew** likes moist undergrowth and is resident in the uplands, as is the **montane shrew**, which is found in western hemlock forests and acidic soils, usually near water. **Trowbridge's shrew** has a limited distribution, favouring creekside clumps of damp grasses, ferns, shrubs and other plants in mature, undisturbed forest.

The **marsh shrew** (often known by its old name of Pacific water shrew) is listed as "Threatened" in Canada, where it is confined to the Lower Fraser valley of British Columbia. It has been found locally only in Burns Bog, the Surrey uplands and a few tributaries of the watershed. It is always associated with water, as this large shrew is a strong swimmer and feeds on aquatic larvae, as well as slugs, snails and spiders.

Moles are sometimes confused with voles, but differ in shape and habits. **Coast moles** seldom emerge from their underground burrows, being vigorous excavators. They dig up huge piles of dirt to create the ubiquitous mole hills found on lawns, fields and verges.

The industrious mole is active day and night, year round. Tunnel building peaks during autumn and winter when frequent rains make the soil more workable. Their burrows are typically up to one or two metres (3 to 7 ft) deep, and can be many metres long, with hundreds of mole hills thrown out by a single animal. Each hill averages 30 cm diameter and 15 cm high (1 ft x 0.5 ft).

At the end of the summer, young moles disperse to find new burrows, and as they travel briefly above ground they are at risk from barn owls and short-eared owls.

Many gardeners wage constant war on moles because they spoil the look of manicured lawns. However, mole

---

Further information

Opossums, shrews and moles of British Columbia by David Nagorsen

Rodents and Lagomorphs of British Columbia by David Nagorsen

The Natural History of Shrews by Sara Churchfield.

burrowing aerates the soil and does no real harm to garden plants, so nature enthusiasts will tolerate their activities.

At the end of the summer, young moles disperse to find new burrows

The coast mole's smaller cousin, the **American shrew-mole**, has a western continental distribution yet is only found in the Lower Mainland within British Columbia. It lives above ground in moist, shady upland habitats and Burns Bog. These little moles are said to be sociable, traveling together in small bands.

Deer mice are small native rodents, that weigh on average 18 g (0.6 oz), and are common throughout the region's salt marshes, old fields, hedgerows and woodlands. They are highly nocturnal, consuming a wide variety of foods and being eaten in turn by bird and mammal predators, including the delta's resident barn owls. Deer mice breed prolifically through the spring and summer.

Deer mice are known to be carriers of hanta virus, a very contagious disease, that occurred as a serious outbreak in 1993 in southwestern US (*see page 143*). They are also hosts for *Ixodes* ticks that spread lyme disease. Mice droppings or nests should be avoided.

THE WEASEL FAMILY

Weasels are carnivorous animals with long slim bodies and short legs. While reasonably common and widespread, they are most active at dawn and dusk and can be easily missed. **Ermines** (short-tailed weasels) live along hedges and ditch margins in farmland, hunting small animals. The lowlands of the Serpentine and Nicomekl valleys and around Boundary Bay are good locations to look for them. An ermine is about 25 cm (10 in) long, with a brown back and white belly, and a black tip to its tail. Unlike animals in colder regions that turn pure white, Boundary Bay animals do not change colour in winter.

The **American mink** is a larger, darker member of the weasel family that roams coastal wetland areas and river valleys. In the 1850s, wild mink were very common in the marshes of the western delta, but numbers plummeted as demand for fur coats rose. Eventually, mink farms were set up in the Fraser Valley and near Boundary Bay. Some animals were able to escape and formed feral populations in the area. Since trapping in the region ended, mink are holding their own and can even be a nuisance at fish hatcheries.

The sleek, elegant **northern river otter** is another inhabitant of the Boundary Bay wetlands and can be looked for along beaches, ponds and ditches in quieter areas. It is still sometimes shot at and is often wary, diving for cover under water at the slightest disturbance. Otters live in holes in slough banks and, despite their name, are often seen in the ocean as well as in rivers.

Muskrats live in farm ditches and sloughs.

River otters are often seen in the ocean, as well as in rivers

Two species of skunk are known from Boundary Bay, but there have been no recorded sightings of the **western spotted skunk** in the last ten years. It used to be common in agricultural areas of the delta.

The **striped skunk** is still regularly seen, but this once abundant animal also declined when the upland forests were logged. Both skunks are nocturnal, the spotted preferring brushy areas near streams and the striped living in thick woodland. Long-time resident Don Munro remembers the White Rock area being "loaded with striped skunks" in the 1920s, one particularly large tree stump yielding eleven animals!

Everyone is familiar with the bad reputation of skunks as foul-smelling, due to a spray they emit when cornered or stressed. The smell is quite overwhelming; it is best to keep one's distance.

MUSKRAT & BEAVERS

Industrious little **muskrats** can be seen on summer evenings swimming in quiet backwaters, where they are sometimes mistaken for baby beavers. They burrow nest holes into the slough bank or build a conspicuous nest of cattail stalks and reeds.

During the nineteenth century, muskrats were extremely common and most unpopular with delta homesteaders, who tried to stop them digging into the banks of newly erected flood-control dykes. A bounty was put on the muskrats and many were killed, yet today they are still quite a common sight in Boundary Bay's wetlands. Some are occasionally trapped by farmers, looking to protect their ditches, but the pelts are not highly valued.

The beaver, officially now called the **American beaver** despite its scientific name of *Castor canadensis*, is a much larger animal and its activities can have a profound effect on wetland environments. Beavers were historically abundant in the watershed and their dams, pools and debris from log felling activities were a major influence on river flows. In the 1800s beavers were the target of trappers and fur traders. At the end of the century, loggers moved in, clearing the dense timber in the valley bottoms before heading up the slopes. With forests and beaver diminished, water flow increased and many of the low lying areas consequently flooded at spring freshet. Today, beavers are still a factor in controlling water levels, particularly in Burns Bog. These busy animals can be seen in rivers and streams, and signs of their tree felling activities are very common on river banks.

Sightings of the **mountain beaver** are most unusual, and confined to a very small range within the upper Boundary Bay watershed. This large, primitive rodent is an inhabitant of old growth temperate rainforests, where it lives in holes under mossy stumps.

An unusual sighting of mountain beaver.

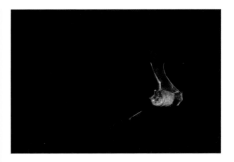

This small bat was photographed near a maternity colony in White Rock.

BATS

Very little is known about local bats. They have been recorded from many locations in the watershed but hardly any studies have been done of their populations, winter roosts or behaviour.

Bats navigate in the dark by using echolocation, emitting high-pitched sound waves and then detecting the echoes. Long-lived and slow to reproduce, they are vulnerable to extinction, especially if their insect prey is eliminated with pesticides or their roosts are destroyed. Four out of ten American bat species are in decline, and many forest bats have disappeared from the Fraser Valley.

Bats are a difficult group to identify on the wing, especially since they are nocturnal. The best way to decide which of nine possible bats they could be is to find a colony or a roosting animal. Sometimes this happens most unexpectedly. Once I came home to find a **little brown myotis** asleep in my kitchen sink! This little myotis bat spends much of its life asleep. Roosting all day in summer in trees or attics, it emerges about half an hour after sunset for a short, erratic feeding flight lasting about 15 minutes. After that it is time for another doze, followed eventually by a few short flights before dawn. No wonder bats live a long life: up to 32 years in the wild! The little brown myotis has been demonstrated to eat up to 600 mosquitoes in an hour, and up to 1700 insects a night, making it a vital part of the environment.

Yuma myotis are small fast-flying bats, that emerge after sunset and fly around near water. Two important maternity colonies of mother and baby Yuma myotis have been found in Delta: at Deas Island, in the attic of one of the old buildings, and in a barn at Alaksen National Wildlife Area. There were several hundred at Alaksen in 1996 and about a thousand females at Deas Island in recent summers. Each mother bat has one baby a year, so in September double the number of bats leaves the

> Be extremely careful if you have to handle a bat, as they can carry parasites, and in very rare cases, the bat rabies virus; it is wise to wear thick gloves. Bats behaving normally, flying overhead, are absolutely no danger to humans.

colony and seeks out a winter roost. Where Boundary Bay area bats go in winter to hibernate is unknown, although typically bats use caves or mines where the temperature is stable.

The tiny **California myotis** is almost impossible to distinguish in the field from other small bats. The slightly larger, **big brown bats** emerge at twilight, about twenty minutes after sunset, and fly around buildings, open grassy areas and woodlands. **Long-eared myotis**, a late flyer around buildings in thinly forested areas, and **long-legged myotis**, a colonial bat, may occur in the area. Specimens were collected in the 1940s and 50s from the Lower Fraser valley, but none have been collected recently. The **Townsend's big-eared bat** is a rarer species, perhaps found in wooded regions of the watershed.

Two bats may migrate south in winter. The very large **hoary bat** and the slightly smaller **silver-haired bat** are both solitary fliers, that have been seen in the Boundary Bay area.

Further information

Bats of British Columbia by David Nagorsen and Mark Brigham.

For information on building bat boxes for roosting bats, or for cruelty-free ways of excluding bats from your attic, contact Bat Conservation International www.batcon.org

COYOTES & FOXES

The **coyote** has truly earned its reputation as a survivor. Unpopular with many ranchers and farmers, it is frequently shot at, trapped and poisoned. This versatile and intelligent predator has over the years not only outwitted its persecutors, but has spread throughout the North American continent, from Central America, northeast to Quebec and northwest to Alaska.

Coyotes arrived in Whatcom County, WA and the lower Fraser valley after the grey wolf was hunted out around 1900. They soon learned that towns and cities were safe havens from the bounty hunting which took place in rural areas. Tolerating traffic and city streets, their numbers have steadily increased in the last few decades. Around Boundary Bay, they live in fields and hedgerows, and will come into residential areas, especially at night.

Coyotes adapt well to many habitats, hunting voles and deer mice in fields, squirrels, rats and pet food in suburban yards, and foraging for fallen fruit in orchards. They occasionally snatch small dogs and cats, and have been seen far out on the mud flats, prowling

A coyote watches intently, as it searches for voles in the long grass of a field. Coyote populations have increased around Boundary Bay in the last twenty years, but the numbers of red foxes have declined during the same period.

the tide line for duck carcasses. Coyotes are much smaller than wolves, weighing on average only 12 kg (26 lb), and measuring about 1.2 m (4 ft). They have erect ears, bushy tails and a loping gait, and are leaner and sharper-featured than domestic dogs.

Coyotes are versatile and intelligent predators

Coyotes live alone or in family groups, and communicate with each other by howling, yapping or barking. Their dens are built under a fallen tree or in a hedge bank. Pups are born in early spring, staying with their parents from April to October.

Population numbers are not known for the Boundary Bay watershed, but there are about 200 coyotes in the Vancouver area and an estimated

Further information

Coexisting with Coyotes program, Stanley Park Ecology Society; http://Stanley.server309.com

To report aggressive wildlife in British Columbia, call Wildlife Branch 1 800 663 WILD

Washington Department of Fish and Wildlife has information on wildlife viewing and tips for "Living with Wildlife" www.wdfw.wa.gov

two to three thousand more up the Fraser Valley. When coyotes are fed they lose their fear of humans and can become troublesome. While they rarely attack people, there have been several cases of children being bitten in the Vancouver area. It is wise to keep a safe distance. If one comes too close, scare it away with very loud, determined shouting.

Red foxes were still regulars in the Boundary Bay countryside until about twenty years ago. Today, sightings are rare and usually at night. As coyotes increased, the red fox disappeared. The fox may have been displaced by the larger dog, although the two animals have been known to coexist elsewhere.

Foxes also suffered from the loss of hedgerows and other denning and hunting sites, as well as increased disturbance from dogs. Ground-nesting birds on which foxes prey have also declined, due to wetland drainage, intensification of agriculture and loss of marginal habitats.

A recent review of red fox sightings showed reports from Burns Bog, Drayton Harbor watershed, Point Roberts and the upper Little Campbell and Nicomekl valleys. Naturalist Glenn Ryder found a den in Campbell Valley Park in 1976, and Don de Mille found 4 pups near the old peatmoss plant in Burns Bog in 1991.

The raccoon lives in a grey world, unable to distinguish colours, but it has good night vision.

RACCOONS

Raccoons are woodland animals which have been squeezed by urbanisation. They survive by their adaptability. These entertaining creatures remind one of small bears as they stroll across the garden or nimbly climb a tree, stopping to peer down curiously, bright eyes shining from the black face mask.

Raccoons require large coniferous trees for denning, but they are not fussy about what they eat. Slugs, young birds, eggs, seafood and fruit are all on the menu, and they pick at their food with mobile little hands, occasionally dipping it in water. They visit garden ponds and will pull at pool covers or hot tub lids to get at water.

Mother raccoons will defend their pups vigorously

In January or February the male and female den together, before the male wanders off on his own. The young from the previous year stay in the den until spring, when the new season's brood of three to five babies are born. Survivors stay with the mother and sometimes other family members, roaming around gardens and woodlands through the summer. During this time the young learn valuable life skills. Sadly many young raccoons are killed on roads.

Mother raccoons will defend their pups vigorously, and summer is the time of year that complaints of aggressive raccoons and injured pets are most frequent. In the autumn, raccoons are on the search for any food they can find, preparing to den up for the winter. During mid-winter months, they become lethargic but do not actually hibernate. They can often be seen up and about on mild days, often in the middle of the day.

Raccoons make strange noises and calls, including churring sounds, snarling and growls, all of which can sound eerie in the night. They tip over garbage bins and claw open plastic bags; make sure bins are secured with tight-fitting lids, or you will be picking up a mess!

Raccoons cause few problems if they are treated with a normal respect

Raccoons may prey on rats, and thus naturally control these pests. Local zoologist Dr Mary Taitt noticed that black rats became established at Reifel Migratory Bird Sanctuary when a distemper epidemic wiped out many of the local raccoons.

Do not feed or approach raccoons; they do not make good pets and can be aggressive to dogs and cats if cornered. In rare cases, they have been known to carry rabies. Discourage unwelcome incidents by keeping pet food out of reach, and roofs, walls and sheds free of entry holes.

These native animals are a natural part of the ecosystem, and watching their interesting behaviour from a respectful distance can be a great source of enjoyment.

Further information

A Natural History of Raccoons by Dorcas MacClintock.

NEW ARRIVALS: RABBITS, RATS & OPOSSUMS

Several animals were introduced to the area, either deliberately or accidentally. **Eastern cottontails** are small brown rabbits with white powder-puff tails, originally from eastern Canada. They were brought from Washington to Langley Prairie and Cloverdale about 1950, when hunters temporarily introduced a number of game species, such as ring-necked pheasants, California quail and grey partridge.

Cottontails now live all along dykes, hedgerows and field margins. Within the past thirty years, they seem to have totally displaced the native **snowshoe hare** or varying hare. Like most rabbits, cottontails are crepuscular, or most active at dawn and dusk. These countryside rabbits are different from the pet rabbits sometimes seen hopping around industrial areas or park entrances. Pet rabbits do not usually survive long in the wild.

The **black rat** (roof rat) and **Norway rat** were brought unwittingly ashore by the first sailors to arrive from Mexico and Europe, and have become established in the watershed. The black rat is more common and is likely the one you hear scratching in attics or behind walls. They also live in the countryside where they make round nests of twigs and leaves

During the day, eastern cottontails hide under blackberry tangles, where the only signs of their presence are narrow trails leading into the bushes.

in small trees, and eat young birds and eggs. Large, brown Norway rats burrow around buildings, especially along the water's edge. They have been reported less frequently at the port now that containers are sealed. The introduced **house mouse** is much smaller than either rat. It can be a nuisance if it gets into storage areas.

The **North American opossum** is a strange, nocturnal resident. It is the only marsupial or pouched mammal found on the continent. It spread north from the southern states early in the twentieth century, helped by purposeful introductions into Washington State in 1925. The first official opossum records for British Columbia were at Crescent Beach, where two were killed in 1949. Opossums are now very common south of the Fraser. They thrive despite the number killed on roads, because they eat anything, have large broods, and are aggressive, adaptable and tolerant of humans.

SHOREBIRDS

The Fraser River estuary is the top site in Canada for the diversity and number of migrating and wintering shorebirds. It is also among the world's top locations for shorebirds. Boundary Bay is the largest undeveloped part of the estuary and provides excellent viewing opportunities at numerous locations. Fifty shorebird species have been recorded, almost a quarter of the 212 different shorebirds found worldwide. They include many that are rare in the Pacific Northwest.

Fifty shorebird species have been recorded

Good times of year for observing shorebirds are from late April to the first week of May for sandpipers and plovers heading north, July and August for southbound sandpipers, and late August to September for the larger shorebirds. September is often the best month for rare species, which are usually juvenile birds gone astray.

Dyke walkers often see big swirling flocks of **dunlin**, the commonest wintering sandpiper. Winter dunlin numbers are the highest for Canada.

For more about Bird Migration see pages 41 - 45.

Dunlin congregate in the thousands on Boundary Bay.

Total numbers in the bay average between 30,000 and 60,000, from October to March, peaking in November and December. Many others just migrate through, heading south to Grays Harbor, WA, the Columbia River estuary or Tillamook Bay, OR. Up to 92,000 have been counted on a single day in Boundary Bay during migration.

Low tide in winter is at night, so the dunlins feed in the dark, along the tide line and out across the mud flats, avoiding falcons which prey constantly on the flocks. In stormy weather, heavy rain moves the food organisms deeper into the mud. This forces dunlins to fly over the dykes to feed on farm field invertebrates, which conversely come closer to the surface in wet weather. Some dunlin roost at high tide in ploughed fields, and many more fly around in flocks far offshore while the mud is covered. When they are hunted by peregrines, dunlins fly in tight formation, twisting and weaving in the air in perfect unison, like a cloud of drifting smoke or a shimmering shoal of fish.

Tall, slim waders with yellow legs are either **greater** or **lesser yellowlegs,** both of which are migrants. A few greater yellowlegs also spend the winter in the bay (they are pictured on page iv).

The wide beaches of Roberts Bank and Boundary Bay attract hundreds of thousands of **western sandpipers,** along with several other very similar species, which birders collectively call "peeps". The numbers of these shorebirds vary from year to year,

Unusual Shorebirds

One or two of each of these shorebirds are spotted most years. Listening to the Vancouver Natural History Society Bird Alert Hotline (604 737 3074) can help you locate them in season.

Black-necked Stilt - spring, Blackie Spit.

American Avocet - any time, Beach Grove lagoon, Blackie Spit, Roberts Bank.

Willet - rare summer, very rare winter at Blaine, Blackie Spit, ferry lagoon.

Wandering Tattler - mostly Aug, Sept. at Roberts Bank, Point Roberts. One at Blackie Spit was very rare for this sandy location.

Long-billed Curlew - rare spring and fall migrant; Boundary Bay, Roberts Bank. Has stayed for the summer at Blackie Spit.

Hudsonian Godwit - rare fall migrant, Blackie Spit, Beach Grove, Mud Bay.

Bar-tailed Godwit - late summer and early fall, in fields, mud flats around Boundary Bay.

Marbled Godwit - a rare summer migrant, recorded from shoreline lagoon areas.

Red Knot - very rare in spring, regular in fall; Mud Bay or nearby fields, Blaine area.

Sharp-tailed Sandpiper - mid-September to mid-October. Reifel Migratory Bird Sanctuary is reputedly the best spot in North America south of Alaska to see this species, also Boundary Bay shoreline between 84 and 104 Streets.

Stilt Sandpiper - August and September, in lagoons and shallow shoreline areas.

Buff-breasted Sandpiper - August and September, grass and turf farm fields north of the bay.

Ruff - a few juveniles visit every fall, since the first record in 1971; Blackie Spit, Reifel Migratory Bird Sanctuary, Serpentine Fen.

Red Phalarope - a pelagic, very late migrant, Oct. - Nov., more abundant in invasion years: 1982 Blackie Spit, 112 St., 1995 Crescent Beach; also Point Roberts, Beach Grove.

Snowy Plover - rare in June, some years only; Boundary Bay, Roberts Bank.

Note: *As can be seen from this list, and the one on page 91, the Boundary Bay foreshore near the dyke at the south end of 112 Street is a hot spot for shorebird observation. However, there is absolutely no public parking on this road. The nearest public car park is at 104 Street at the GVRD Delta Air Park, about 2 km (1.2 mi) west of 112 St. (see Nature Destinations pages 174 - 176 & page 182).*

according to climate, weather and the presence of predators. The entire world population of western sandpipers migrates in spring and fall through the Pacific Northwest. A large percentage stop to rest and forage for a few days in the Fraser River estuary. In their lifetime, these tiny birds travel a distance equivalent to four times round the world, as they fly between Arctic breeding grounds and their winter homes, in the tropics. During the 1980s and 1990s, over 1.2 million western sandpipers passed through the Fraser estuary during their annual migration. These numbers have dropped suddenly in the last five years. In fact, most shorebirds populations across the continent are declining. The reasons for this are unknown, although the loss and degradation of habitat probably plays a key role.

Migrating **dowitchers** occur in the hundreds in Boundary Bay, especially at freshwater inlets. They feed in tight flocks, jabbing the mud with a repetitive, "sewing machine"

Migrating dowitchers can occur in the hundreds

movement. **Sanderling** are tiny, silvery-white fall and winter visitors that run to and fro along the tide line. Boundary Bay Regional Park is a good place to see them. Tens of thousands of **least sandpipers**, the tiniest native "peep", pass through in mid-April with even greater numbers (50,000) returning in fall. They feed on the tide line among the salt marsh plants. **Baird's sandpiper** are regular late summer visitors to the wrack line of eelgrass and algae.

Three percent of North America's black-bellied plovers come through the estuary

Wary and with good eyesight, beautiful **black-bellied plovers** are often the first to take flight when a falcon or eagle appears. Like many of the shorebirds feeding on the tidal flats, they roost on newly ploughed fields come high tide. On a single day in spring, three percent of North America's entire population of black-bellied plovers can come through the estuary. They are heading for nesting grounds in the high Arctic tundra. In August, the flocks return and some birds fly on as far as South America. A few plovers stay in Boundary Bay for the winter: up to two thousand can be seen on a mid-winter day.

Whimbrels are mostly spring migrants, passing through quickly

Ones to watch for

These are "accidental" shorebirds, rare visitors with fewer than three records in the last thirty years: all records should be sent for verification to the Vancouver Natural History Society, Bird Records Committee, PO Box 3021, Vancouver, B.C. V6B 3X5.

Far Eastern Curlew - one record, a juvenile, on September 24 1984 at Boundary Bay, near 112 St. was Canada's first and only, and the first North American record south of Alaska.

Bristle-thighed Curlew - a sight record at Blackie Spit, May 13/14 1983, was listed as the second Canadian Record but is disputed by some authorities.

Great Knot - the first report of this species in Canada was from Boundary Bay in May 1987 but has not been confirmed.

Little Stint - British Columbia's second sighting was at Boundary Bay, near 112 St. on 10 July 1988.

Red-necked Stint - 2 on July 13 1992 at Boundary Bay near 112 St; 2 other records for Fraser River delta.

Temminck's Stint - a juvenile present at Reifel Migratory Bird Sanctuary, from September 1 - 4, 1982 was the first Pacific Northwest record.

White-rumped Sandpiper - one in September 1978 at Blackie Spit and several records from Iona Island, Richmond.

Spotted Redshank - 1 record from Serpentine Fen, 3 records from Reifel.

between late April and May. Up to fifty have been recorded at Cain Creek, Blaine and on the mud flats of Drayton Harbor. **Black turnstones** gather in flocks to winter on pebble shores at Point Roberts, Roberts Bank, Semiahmoo Bay and Blaine. **Wilson's phalarope** and **red-necked phalarope** are uncommon visitors, instantly recognisable by their habit of swimming in tight circles.

The majority of shorebirds migrate through the bay and some remain for winter. Only a handful stay to nest around Boundary Bay. Of these, the **killdeer** is the most familiar. Its plaintive cries echo from fields and beaches at all times of the year. The female killdeer lays her eggs on the ground. If you approach her chicks too closely, she will distract you by trailing her wings and displaying the orange on her back, feigning injury. **Spotted sandpipers** draw attention to themselves as they bob up and down on slough banks, calling repeatedly. In contrast, the cryptic plumage of the **Wilson's snipe** keeps it well hidden in the long grass and marsh habitat where it lives.

Only a handful of shorebirds stay to nest around Boundary Bay

Black oystercatchers have regularly nested on a pebble beach at Roberts Bank; they were the first breeding record of this bird for the British Columbia mainland. The colourful **American avocet** has tried to nest on several occasions around Boundary Bay, notably at Blackie Spit and Serpentine Fen. This very attractive shorebird is more commonly seen as a transient on migration.

Further information

Shorebirds of the Pacific Northwest by Dennis Paulson

The Birders Guide to Vancouver and the Lower Mainland, edited by Catherine Aitchison, Vancouver Natural History Soc.

Shorebirds of Boundary Bay, a checklist by Michael Price, Discovery 1990, 19(4) VNHS www.naturalhistory.bc.ca/VNHS

EAGLES, HAWKS, FALCONS & HARRIERS

Boundary Bay has the greatest diversity of birds of prey wintering anywhere in Canada. Birds of prey include eagles, hawks, falcons, harriers, accipiters and owls (see next section). Also known as raptors, these birds are carnivorous, possess hooked beaks and sharp talons for catching and tearing at food and have remarkably sharp eyesight. Typically, female raptors are larger than males.

The most spectacular of our birds of prey is the magnificent **bald eagle**. Its brilliant white head and tail, on both male and female mature adults, contrasts with a dark brown body. It takes over four years to achieve this plumage, and immatures are dark with varying amounts of white on their bodies and wings, depending on their age.

Soaring against a blue sky or enthroned on a bare tree branch, bald eagles look every inch the noble predator; however in reality they are scavengers and opportunists, harassing other birds and taking their kill.

January and February are the best months to see eagles around Boundary Bay. Look for them soaring overhead, congregating out on the tidal flats, in trees or on the ground in muddy farm fields.

An immature bald eagle greets the dawn in Boundary Bay Regional Park.

Up to 25 eagles have gathered at the black cottonwood stand in Beach Grove, and as many as 200 eagles have been seen at the Burns Bog landfill.

January and February are the best months to see eagles around Boundary Bay

Large cottonwoods and Douglas-fir along the Fraser River, in the South Arm Marshes and at Deas Island, are important nesting and roosting sites. David Hancock has studied local eagles for nearly five decades, tracking their recovery from bounty hunting and the grim pesticide years

of the 1960s and 70s. In 2002, he recorded 75 nests south of the Fraser, a remarkable comeback for this once endangered bird.

Sometimes confused with eagles, **turkey vultures** are large dark birds of prey that fly with their wings in a v-position. Their plumage is almost uniformly black, their wings are translucent and they have bare red facial skin, the head looking small in comparison to an eagle. Turkey vultures have large nostrils and an unusual ability to smell; they can detect carcasses from many miles away. They watch each other circling, and when one starts to descend, the others home in on the same spot.

Turkey vultures migrate through Boundary Bay in May and September, and are generally only seen in ones or twos flying above the uplands or along bluffs. Sometimes a group will gather to soar on thermals above the Point Roberts peninsula, in an activity known as "kettling". The other large bird of prey very occasionally seen around Boundary Bay is the beautiful white and black **osprey**; one pair nests near the Roberts Bank port.

The commonest local member of the hawk family is the **red-tailed hawk**. This is the oval-winged hawk that you can see circling high in the sky, or perched on fence posts along the highway. Many red-taileds move to the coast for the winter, where they find plenty to eat in snow-free woodland and open country with long grass. Large coniferous trees serve as roosting areas and nest sites.

A related bird, the **rough-legged hawk**, nests on the Arctic tundra and ventures south to the Fraser delta in winter, where it feeds on Townsend's voles in old fields and marshes. Boundary Bay is one of the best places in the lower mainland to observe this hawk. Watch for its characteristic hovering flight as it searches for prey. Like the red-tailed hawk, it roosts in coniferous trees in Burns Bog or on upland bluffs.

Hawks of forest and hedgerow, the accipiters, have rounded wings and long tails. This allows them to chase down songbirds through foliage. Both the **sharp-shinned hawk** and the similar, larger, **Cooper's hawk**, are quite common year-round in the region. Cooper's hawks are more abundant in winter, when snow brings them down from nearby mountains. The sharp-shinned preys on juncos and chickadees attracted to bird feeders, darting from the shelter of a conifer to strike at unsuspecting birds.

The third member of this family, the **northern goshawk**, is an exciting winter find. This large accipiter of the deep forest has been spotted in such places as Point Roberts, Alaksen and Campbell Valley Park. They are superb hunters, chasing down

Cooper's hawks are fast-flying, agile hawks of forest and hedgerow that prey on songbirds.

large birds, rabbits and other game with great efficiency. John Ireland, Manager of the Reifel Migratory Bird Sanctuary, where goshawks sometimes overwinter, has noticed how most other birds fall silent when the goshawk is around. Moreover, lesser predators, such as long-eared owls, move out of the area or become prey.

The "poster bird" for Boundary Bay, the **northern harrier**, is a common resident of grasslands, hardhack clumps and marshes. It flies low over the ground, searching for voles, wings held in a wide v shape. The male is a beautiful pale grey while the larger females are streaked brown and juveniles are rust brown. All have broad white patches on the rump where the tail joins the body, making them easy to identify in flight. Curiously, rough-legged hawks share the same habitat in winter and also have white on the upper tail. However, the harrier has longer, narrower wings, and their flight styles are quite different.

Peregrine falcons follow the shorebirds south in July and August

Falcons are designed for fast flight, with sharp pointed wings and streamlined bodies. The most spectacular is the **peregrine falcon**, a supreme hunter which preys on the vast flocks of wintering shorebirds. Dick Dekker has spent a lifetime studying peregrines, including many hours on the Boundary Bay dyke watching them hunt. He observed how the male, or "tiercel", is a fast-flying, formidable hunter, stooping from great heights at 200 kph (125 mph) or flying in fast and low across the mud flats to knock a dunlin from the flock and scoop it as it falls into the sea. The female is larger and slower than the male, but stronger, able to bring down and transport birds as heavy as mallards.

In August, the peregrine falcons follow the shorebirds south and are even believed to stimulate the sandpiper migration. As peregrines recovered from pesticide poisonings of the 1960s and 70s, their numbers increased, enhancing the effect on shorebirds. Some biologists think that the lower sandpiper numbers recorded in some localities may be due to peregrine harassment moving them on.

Other local falcons include the merlin, American kestrel, prairie falcon and gyrfalcon. Boundary Bay is the most important wintering habitat in the Fraser Valley for **merlins,** small falcons that hunt songbirds and dunlin. **American kestrels** are quite common during spring and fall passage, and some stay for winter. Individuals sit on roadside wires, watching for shrews and crickets. A **prairie falcon** was a rare winter visitor to Roberts Bank for several consecutive years from 1988 onwards. Furthermore, about half the Fraser lowland sightings of wintering **gyrfalcon,** a northern visitor, are from Boundary Bay.

Further information

The Bald Eagle of Alaska, BC and Washington by David Hancock

Bolt from the Blue by Dick Dekker

Raptors ~ The Birds of Prey by Scott Weidensaul

To see raptors close up, visit O.W.L, orphaned wildlife rehabilitation centre, *see page 177.*

A barred owl roosting in the Reifel Migratory Bird Sanctuary

OWLS

Boundary Bay is a great place to see owls, with thirteen species on the area checklist. Nowhere else in Canada is there such a number and variety in winter, and both sides of the bay have excellent owling locations.

The river valleys and Burns Bog are home to great horned owl and western screech owl, while barn owls and short-eared owls inhabit the open fields of the western delta. Northern sawhet owls and barred owls live in coniferous forests.

The **great horned owl** is a widespread resident, that is found even in small woodlots. An early nester, this owl is at its most vocal between November and February. Bay residents familiar with the owl's location annually enjoy the sight of large downy young being fed by their parents.

Barred owls are expanding their range south and west and are now regularly seen in local forests. Opportunistic feeders on mice, squirrels, birds and frogs, their numbers probably fluctuate with rodent populations. Good locations to see and hear this owl are Point Roberts, Campbell Valley and Delta Nature Reserve.

The **western screech owl** is a much scarcer bird, preferring open moist woodland to dense forest. Numbers have declined in recent years, probably from predation by barred owls and loss of lowland trees.

Barn owls are at the northern limit of their range in the Lower Mainland, where they were first recorded in 1909. They nest in old barns around the farmland, one of the few regions in Canada where there is a resident population of this cosmopolitan species. In the early 1990s, there were as many as 1000 birds, or 250 to 300 breeding pairs. Sadly, loss of habitat and road deaths may have reduced numbers since then.

Barn owls regurgitate pellets of rodent bones and fur, making a mess of barn floors but providing masses of interesting information for the biologist. Barn owls have the keenest sense of hearing of all birds and can capture their prey in total darkness.

The short-eared owl is suffering a long-term decline in numbers

The beautiful, daytime-flying **short-eared owl** arrives in the Fraser delta for the winter, where it lives in the long grass and shrubs of old fields, a habitat it shares with the northern harrier. On late winter afternoons, short-eared owls and northern harriers can be seen together, both hunting for Townsend's voles.

Though its hearing is acute, the soft, pale brown short-eared owl has no visible ears, short or otherwise. It roosts communally on the ground or in low shrubs, and twenty eight were once found together in Boundary Bay Regional Park.

Owl numbers fluctuate with rodent populations, but the short-eared owl is suffering a long-term decline as well, probably as a result of habitat loss and disturbance. They once commonly nested in old field habitat around the delta, but are now hardly ever spotted in summer, and winter populations are also down.

Fifteen years ago, twenty or more short-eared owls could regularly be seen near Centennial Beach

A short eared owl hunting a farm field on Westham Island in the late afternoon.

and Boundary Bay. Today one is lucky to see one or two. Hundreds were shot adjacent to Vancouver International Airport in 2000 and 2001, apparently as a transportation safety measure. The cull may have affected regional populations. The best places to see this beautiful bird are old field habitats near the coast. The foreshore and dykes around Boundary Bay, Brunswick Point and Serpentine Fen are especially good viewing locations.

Huge **snowy owls** occur irregularly in winter and are easily seen since they sit out in the open on fence posts and foreshore logs, even in the day time. They fly south from the Arctic and once at the coast they prey on buffleheads and other waterfowl, rather than voles. Adults are a pure snowy white, while younger birds are spotted grey. In a good year, ten or twenty of these magnificent large white owls can be seen along the foreshore and they wander as far south as Bellingham, where as many as 32 were counted in 1973. They invade about one year in every six; the last time was winter 2005/06.

Other owls are infrequently spotted. **Long-eared owls** roost in winter in mature hedgerows. They are very difficult to see, their brown mottled plumage blending superbly with the branches and dead leaves of their surroundings. The **burrowing owl**, a dry country species, used to breed in the delta but was extirpated in 1976. A captive breeding program has since taken place near Mud Bay, with birds being released in the Nicola Valley. Rarely, one will stop by Boundary Bay, turning up in odd locations.

The long-eared owl is extremely well-camouflaged when roosting in hedgerows.

The **northern pygmy-owl** is a rare resident of coniferous forests, where it calls on moonlit nights. The **northern saw-whet owl** is a locally uncommon resident and winter visitor, preferring young evergreen trees near water for its daytime roost.

Three northern owls are seen on rare occasions in winter. The **northern hawk owl** has been recorded from Dakota Creek, Point Roberts, Beach Grove and Campbell Valley Park, where the impressive **great grey owl** has also been seen. A very rare **boreal owl** arrived in winter 1995 at Reifel Migratory Bird Sanctuary and again at Ladner in 1997, the first live records for the checklist area.

Further information

Reifel Migratory Bird Sanctuary sometimes offers the opportunity to see wild owls - *see page 169.*

To see owls close up, visit O.W.L, orphaned wildlife rehabilitation centre, *see page 177.*

Bird Studies Canada Nocturnal Owl Survey www.bsc-eoc.org/regional/bcowls.html

The Birds of British Columbia by R. Wayne Campbell et al.

DUCKS, GEESE & SWANS

Waterfowl are the quintessential birds of Boundary Bay. The whistle of their wings, their gentle calls, and the sight of skein upon skein drifting across the evening sky, are reminiscent of a wilderness and time that is lost to the modern world.

The lure of the flocks has always drawn hunters to the bay, from the early Coast Salish, their canoes slipping in darkness through the water, to the market hunters of the early 1900s, blasting with shotguns from the dyke. Today there are fewer hunters, but plenty of people who appreciate the sight and sound of ducks, geese and swans.

Ducks, geese and swans have been migrating through the estuary ever since its formation, 9000 years ago. The flocks pause here on migration or linger for the winter, benefitting from the ice-free waters. The agricultural fields behind the bay

Diving ducks, like this surf scoter, patter along the water to take off, and fly in long lines close to the ocean's surface.

are welcoming haunts on stormy days, when choppy waters and high winds send large numbers of ducks over the dyke.

There are three main types of ducks: diving ducks, dabbling ducks and mergansers. All three are found throughout the year in Boundary Bay, but the largest flocks and greatest diversity are present in winter.

Diving Ducks

Diving ducks nest inland in early summer, but spend the rest of the year on the coast. For this reason they are also known as "sea ducks" and some brave the deepest, roughest ocean waters. All submerge completely to feed, finding small fish, invertebrates, crabs and molluscs. Huge flocks or "rafts" of diving ducks winter in the bay, including **greater** and **lesser scaup**, **surf scoters** and **white-winged scoters**, **common** and **Barrow's goldeneye** and **buffleheads.** They can regularly be seen floating above the deep water near Point Roberts, Kwomais Point, Blaine Harbor and Birch Point. The ducks bob together, loafing, sleeping and preening, secure in a group from marauding eagles and peregrines.

Harlequin ducks nest on fast-flowing streams in the Rockies and Cascades and winter on the coast. The males come down to the bay as soon as breeding is completed, and join lively bachelor parties

American wigeon lifting off. Dabbling ducks can lift straight off the water, in contrast to diving ducks. Two percent of the world's population of American wigeon descend on the bay in winter.

for the summer. The females and young arrive in late summer, at which time the mated pairs become reacquainted for the winter, staying paired throughout their lifetimes. Male harlequins are most attractive ducks, with glowing patches of red and white, brilliant in the sunshine.

Dabbling Ducks

Dabblers, or puddle ducks, tip up to feed on grasses, seeds, and invertebrates in shallow inshore waters, or come on land to graze. When taking flight, they rise straight up. In contrast, diving ducks need to run along the surface of the water before becoming airborne. The majority of the huge wintering waterfowl flocks in Boundary Bay are made up of four common dabbling ducks: **mallard**, **American wigeon**, **northern pintail** and the diminutive, fast-flying **green-winged teal**. Tens of thousands of these ducks winter in the bay, tens of thousands more pass through on migration and a smaller number are resident year round. Two species of duck migrate here for the summer: **blue-winged teal** and **cinnamon teal** both breed in quiet pools and sloughs near the bay and in Burns Bog.

Mallards are common throughout the year, and are often rather tame.

These are the ducks that crowd around the gate at Reifel Migratory Bird Sanctuary, waiting for handouts of grain. The male has a glossy green head, the female is streaked brown and has a yellow bill. In spring pairs explore the wetlands together. They aim to find a suitable nest site on the ground near water. Soon groups of ten or twelve fluffy ducklings are following the mother duck, although many ducklings do not survive the first few days. Later in the year, mallards gather in large flocks for the moulting season. The moult includes all their flight feathers and flocking helps protect them from predators.

The colourful **wood duck** nests in holes in trees, from which the fluffy young have to jump down and head for the water with their mother. The ducklings have a special temporary hook on each foot, that enables them to accomplish this dangerous feat. Wood ducks nearly died out in the Lower Mainland when trees

The male wood duck is a beautiful bird with colourful, iridescent plumage and a dramatic crest.

along the sloughs were felled for housing developments, but thanks to conservationists who started a nest box program in the 1960s, the wood duck made a successful comeback.

The plain brown **gadwall** is another common breeding duck, which began nesting in the 1960s after being introduced at Serpentine Fen by duck enthusiasts. A pair of **ring-necked ducks** was found nesting in Burns Bog, the first breeding record for the Vancouver checklist area.

A few **American wigeon** nest each year at Reifel Bird Sanctuary and in Burns Bog. This common duck is at its most abundant in winter, when two percent of the world's population descend on the bay and surrounding fields. This presents a problem for farmers, because wigeon love to graze on winter wheat and other young grasses. They can wipe out a whole field in one night! The Delta Farmland and Wildlife Trust was set up to address this type of problem between bird conservation and agriculture (*see page 105*). Look among the flocks for one or two **Eurasian wigeon** from Siberia, which have red, not green heads, and are increasingly being seen.

Northern pintail and **northern shoveler** are mostly winter visitors. Male pintail have exquisite plumage (*photo: see page ii*). This beautiful species is in decline across some of its range. Pintail eat a higher proportion of animal matter than some of the other dabblers. They can often be seen flying between the bay and Roberts Bank on winter days. Shovelers occur in smaller numbers and prefer mud flats on the western bay to the sandier shores of Blackie Spit or Crescent Beach.

Three vagrant duck species have been locally recorded: the only B.C. record of **Baikal teal**, one shot November 1957 in Ladner; **smew** recorded at Reifel Bird Sanctuary in 1974 and 1975, and at Langley in winter 1989/90 (perhaps escaped captive birds); and two **king eiders**, seen off Point Roberts in the 1970s.

The mergansers are fish-eating ducks with long saw-edged bills. **Common** and **red-breasted mergansers** are elegant birds with jazzy crests that winter at the coast. Red-breasted mergansers have the record for fastest level flight among birds, clocking 160 kph (100 mph)! Male **hooded mergansers** have spectacular black and white plumage, while the females are much more subdued in colour.

Hooded mergansers prefer quiet lagoons, sloughs and ponds.

Tens of thousands of snow geese winter in the Fraser River estuary marshes.

Geese

Between 30,000 and 80,000 **lesser snow geese** descend every year on the Fraser delta, arriving from late October onwards. Many stay until December, after which most of them fly down to the Skagit River delta in Washington to feed on agricultural fields. Some fly directly to California for the winter. In spring their cries are heard once again, as skeins arrive at the estuarine marshes off Brunswick Point, Westham Island and the Fraser River mouth. Here, they fatten up on sedge and bulrush tubers before heading north to nest.

For more about snow geese see page 37

The lucky observer may spot a lone **Ross's goose** in with the flocks.

The snow geese nest on Wrangel Island, off the northeast coast of Russia, the last remainder of a large Siberian population. They are on the Russian endangered species list. Extreme winter weather in the past gave the geese some disastrous breeding seasons, which kept the population naturally in check. Fortunately, recent years have had good breeding conditions and numbers on the Fraser-Skagit have steadily increased. Fewer geese are wintering in California and climate change is affecting Arctic weather, so it is hard to predict what will happen in future. The best places to see snow geese are Alaksen National Wildlife Area and Reifel Migratory Bird Sanctuary (both on Westham Island) and Sturgeon Bank or Terra Nova, Richmond (*pages 169 - 173*).

The eelgrass beds of Boundary Bay are closely linked with small, dark sea geese known as **brant**, which nest in the Arctic and winter in Mexico. Thousands visit the bay on spring migration in the third week of March and a smaller number stop in fall. Most fly directly across the ocean from Izembek Lagoon, Alaska to Baja California, a distance of 5000 km (3100 mi). In the early 1900s, huge flocks also wintered in the

Brant are marine geese that breed in the Arctic and winter as far south as Baja California.

bay; by the 1920s, market hunting and a shortage of refuges had driven them further south. Today, brant are once again wintering in the bay, and now number around 2000 birds. A further 700 **Western High Arctic brant**, a grey-bellied subspecies, also winter in the delta. The exciting sight of brant flocks feeding, resting and flying in close formation can be enjoyed in season at Beach Grove, Boundary Bay Regional Park and Drayton Harbor, where the regional high count on spring migration is about 4 000 birds. A spring brant festival is held in Blaine to celebrate their presence.

Our local **Canada geese** are more urban than the snow geese and their raucous cries seem to lack the sound of wilderness. However, not so long ago, Canada geese were also migrants, traveling between the Arctic and California, with only a few staying to winter. Sportsmen and other enthusiasts introduced the resident subspecies, a stock of mixed parentage, into Delta and Whatcom County between 1967 - 1977. The large geese soon flourished on the fertile fields of the Fraser Valley.

Names of the various subspecies of Canada goose that once visited these shores, are known to only a handful of birders today. These subspecies are Vancouver, dusky, Taverner's and the tiny cackling goose. It is worth taking a second look at that flock of honking Canada geese, gathered

on the fall stubble fields, to see if a darker or smaller migrant cousin is among them.

In the 1850s the geese were all still wild and plentiful, and thousands of **greater white-fronted geese** used to migrate through Boundary Bay before heading on to winter in the Klamath Basin, Oregon. Today, a few small flocks still stop over in spring and fall, flying down the Fraser Valley and the Serpentine - Nicomekl Rivers to the coast.

People strolling at Crescent Beach in spring 1968 were surprised by a very exotic visitor, a rare **emperor goose**. A few years later, one wintered at Reifel Migratory Bird Sanctuary, and in 1994, one was injured on power lines at Beach Grove, nursed back to health and released to the wild again. June 1998 was the latest sighting of this unusual grey and white goose, which breeds on the Bering Sea coast and winters in the Aleutian Islands.

Further information

Waterfowl on a Pacific Estuary by Barry Leach

Canadian Wildlife Service, Pacific Wildlife Research Centre, 604 940 4700 www.pyr.ec.gc.ca/en/wildlife

Environment Canada ecoinfo www.ecoinfo.ec.gc.ca

Washington Brant Foundation www.washingtonbrant.org

Wintering swans often feed in large open fields, that flood in winter.

Swans

The story of the Fraser delta swans is a happy one. Once dramatically close to extinction, the **trumpeter swan** has made a triumphant comeback, and there are now three established breeding populations on the continent. Wintering flocks visit large fields on Westham Island and beside the Fraser River, arriving in early November. They grub for potatoes and roots, puddling up the mud with their giant feet. At dusk, flocks fly out to roost on the marshes off of Brunswick Point. **Tundra swans** live in the same habitats, but roost on lakes in Whatcom County. Look carefully to see the subtle difference in beak colour and neck shape.

Introduced **mute swans** have taken up residence on the Fraser River, and are sometimes aggressive. Originally from Europe, the **mute swan** has a black knob on an orange beak and is usually seen singly or in pairs. While these beautiful birds do not fit in with the delta ecology, people like them and oppose any restriction on their numbers. Sadly this swan may end up like the Canada goose, a dominant alien becoming a nuisance and a threat to local wildlife.

The Delta Farmland & Wildlife Trust studies waterfowl use of farmland & supports winter cover crop & hedgerow planting programs.
604 940 3392
www.deltafarmland.ca

WATERBIRDS:
LOONS & GREBES

The cry of a loon echoing across the water is an unforgettable sound. **Common loons** nest and spend the summer on interior lakes, later migrating to the coast. Many stay for the winter on Boundary Bay and Roberts Bank. The largest regional concentration of common loons in Washington State is found in Drayton Harbor and huge numbers gather on migration around the mouth of the Fraser River. One or two can sometimes be heard calling at daybreak in early summer before they leave. Loons are fish eaters that prefer deep ocean water. They dive under water to feed.

The **Pacific loon** nests in northern British Columbia and winters on the coast. Peak numbers occur off Kwomais Point and Point Roberts, where the water is deep and the currents are strong. Flocks number in the hundreds during migration, as well as when herring and eulachon spawn in spring. **Red-throated loons** are uncommon, but moulting birds are sometimes seen near White Rock and migrants pass through the bay in spring and fall. The **yellow-billed loon** is a rare winter visitor.

Further Information

Coastal Waterbird Survey
Bird Studies Canada
www.bsc-eoc.org; 1 877 349 2473

Common loon: for many people, the call of the loon is the defining sound of the northern wilderness.

Six species of grebes occur in Boundary Bay, mostly as migrants and winter visitors. **Western grebes** are slim waterbirds, with long graceful necks and brilliant red eyes. They nest on interior lakes and are renowned for their spring courtship ballet; pairs of grebes rise up and patter along the surface of a lake, twisting their heads and necks in beautifully choreographed performances. Boundary Bay is an internationally significant wintering area for these birds, and four percent of the world's population moult here in late summer. Like loons, grebes dive under water to feed.

In recent years, **Clark's grebe**, a close relative of the western grebe, has been distinguished as a separate species. Only a few have been recorded locally, but that may change as birders become familiar with its field marks (the extent of black around the eye is diagnostic).

Red-necked grebes also moult here, with five percent of the North

American population gathering in early fall off Crescent Beach, the largest concentration to be seen in Canada at any one time.

The largest concentration of red-necked grebes in Canada, gathers off Crescent Beach

Horned grebes are common winter visitors, (mid September to April). A large regional concentration of these grebes occurs in Drayton Harbor and they are commonly seen along the Point Roberts coast. The very similar **eared grebe** is a rare visitor, with one or two a year found near White Rock and Blaine piers.

The little **pied-billed grebe** is a year round resident that breeds on freshwater ponds. Look for it in locations like Green Timbers and Brydon Lagoon (*see pages 192, 189*).

Red-necked grebe: look for this elegant waterbird in Boundary Bay and Drayton Harbor.

GREAT BLUE HERON & SANDHILL CRANE

The **great blue heron** is symbolic of the Fraser River estuary. Local birds belong to a non-migratory, dark subspecies, the Pacific great blue heron, occurring on the coast from Puget Sound to southern Alaska.

For many years the largest colony of herons in the Pacific Northwest was on the Point Roberts peninsula, in a grove of red alder trees, overlooking the waters of Roberts Bank. In 2002, an amazing 450 nests were counted there! Just one year later, a breakaway group started a new colony at the Tsawwassen Bluff, on Tsawwassen First Nation land, and by 2005, most of the herons had relocated to the new site. The trees of the old heronry were deserted and left to recover from the onslaught of over thirty years' use.

There are also heronries at Birch Bay, on the Nicomekl River, and at the H-Street wetlands near Blaine. The Birch Bay colony had 350 pairs in 1998, abandoned the site briefly in 1999, and returned the following year. Former heronries existed at Terrell Creek, south Dakota Creek, Crescent Beach, and a short-lived one near Deas Island.

Other herons nest on their own or in small groups elsewhere in the watershed, e.g. Brydon Lagoon. The elegant herons look most

Pacific great blue herons are a Northwest coastal race: pictured is an adult.

incongruous as they balance in their huge stick nests at the tops of trees. Their colonies are noisy, smelly places during the breeding season, their nesting trees splashed with white droppings. Nest building and repairing begins in early March as the water warms up and fish return to the shallows.

Adult herons fly constantly between the colony and the coastal sand flats and river banks where they hunt for fish. They feed their hungry young on fish that have been swallowed and regurgitated, and defend them from attacks by bald eagles. In recent years, these assaults have become a serious problem. When at the nest, most herons are very sensitive to disturbance of any kind.

HERONRY HISTORY

Before 1955, the Point Roberts heronry was located in Douglas-fir forest on the bluffs, just west of 52 Street, Delta. When this forest was clearcut, the herons had to find a new site, but constant disturbance during the 1960s meant that they did not finally settle until they reached the Washington side of the border in 1973.

At its peak, this colony had nearly five hundred nests. A constant stream of herons flew to and from the fishing grounds on Roberts Bank. A golf course development next to the colony in 1993 halved the adjacent 112 ha (280 ac) stand of trees, although a protected buffer zone was left next to the nest trees. The new heronry at Tsawwassen is closer to prime intertidal feeding grounds, so young are not left alone at the mercy of eagles for so long.

At Crescent Beach, a colony of 40 to 50 nests prior to 1967 was abandoned subsequent to human disturbance, a few birds moving to the Nicomekl River. The nascent heronry near Deas Island failed when bald eagles harassed the herons and carried off young.

Adult herons leave the colony after the nesting season and spend the rest of the summer fishing along the shoreline. Juveniles disperse into the delta grasslands and hunt voles, frogs and snakes. In winter, adults also feed in fields and ditches. Adult herons have white, not grey crowns and a black patch on the shoulder; males have a longer beak than females.

People often call herons "cranes" although the two birds belong to quite different families. The **greater sandhill crane** is a tall, leggy grey bird, that is similar in appearance to the heron. It was once a common resident and migrant through the delta, where it inhabited boggy areas between Boundary Bay and the Pitt Valley. Cranes were hunted during the 1850s, being both large and palatable, and were soon almost wiped out. Population recovery has been hampered by the fact that cranes need wide tracts of undisturbed marsh and bog habitat, now rare in the Lower Fraser Valley.

Today, the sight of migrant cranes is a big excitement for local birders. Burns Bog wetlands attract several sandhill cranes every year, and may nest if left undisturbed. Breeding and migrant cranes roost in the heart of the bog and fly out to feed in the surrounding farm fields, especially near Crescent Slough.

The best place to see this elegant species up close is Reifel Migratory Bird Sanctuary, which regularly has resident and migrant cranes.

Sandhill cranes can often be seen at Reifel Migratory Bird Sanctuary.

Further information

The Great Blue Heron by Dr Robert Butler, a local biologist who discovered many interesting aspects of the heron's life history.

The Burns Bog Conservation Society has information on the greater sandhill crane, including a Teacher's Guide: www.burnsbog.org

International Crane Foundation: www.savingcranes.org

GULLS, TERNS & SEABIRDS

Gulls are highly adaptable colonial birds that will eat almost anything, including fish, shellfish, eggs, young birds and human garbage. They pick food out of the water or off the beach, pirate it from other birds and scavenge for scraps, often quite aggressively. They do a fine job of cleaning up the beach and have been a vital part of the Pacific Northwest coastal ecosystem for the area's entire existence.

18 species of gull have been recorded in the Boundary Bay area

Often lumped together as "seagulls", there are in fact approximately 50 species of gull worldwide. Of these, eighteen have been recorded for the Boundary Bay area, ten of them being relatively common.

Gulls are a confusing group of very similar looking birds and present huge identification challenges to even the keenest birder. This problem is compounded by the presence of birds of different age plumages as well as inter-species hybrids. In fact, gulls seriously challenge the biological definition of "species" as a discrete genetic group not producing fertile offspring.

Most gulls take three to four years to grow adult plumage, during which time they change colour from pale brown to pearly grey and white. Small differences like the amount of black or white on wing tips, and the colour of legs, bills and eyes, are the distinguishing marks that birders need for identification. These colours, particularly of eyes and legs, are apparently also crucial to the gulls themselves in distinguishing a potential mate.

Casual observers can enjoy the graceful flight of these accomplished aerialists or watch their bold antics on the beach as they grab at any opportunity that means food.

The most frequently seen is the large, pale **glaucous-winged gull**. The population of these gulls has significantly increased in the last 50 years, thanks to abundant food at the Burns Bog landfill. At dusk and dawn, long straggling flocks of gulls fly in and out of the landfill to feast on the human community's rejects. Glaucous-winged gulls nest

The mew gull is small and neat-featured.

Young glaucous-winged gulls have pale brown plumage in their first year.

on islands in the Strait of Georgia. Juveniles and moulting adults sit around on Boundary Bay beaches through the summer and in winter enormous flocks gather with other gulls in pastures or fields.

Big flocks of **ring-billed gulls** also gather on summer beaches; the Fraser delta is their major congregation point on the coast. Small **Bonaparte's gulls** are quite common in summer, recognized by the adult's chocolate brown head and buoyant, tern-like flight, low over the ocean. Other "seagulls" include: **California gulls**, seen mostly in summer and fall when they disperse after breeding in the Prairies; **mew gulls**, elegant gulls that are common year round; and **Thayer's gulls** that move to beaches during the winter and are very similar to the related

Further Information

Gulls, A Guide to Identification by P.J. Grant

herring gull, with which they hybridise.

Birders watch for **Heermann's gull**, a few of which disperse north from Baja after breeding, **western gull**, a rare visitor from its home on the US west coast, and **Franklin's gull**, a wanderer between the Prairies and southern Chile. **Slaty-backed gull**s from northeast Asia have been rare but regular since the first Boundary Bay sighting in 1989. The best place to spot one is among the mixed flocks in delta fields.

Jaegers are aggressive pirate birds which chase fishing gulls and terns until they drop their catch. All three species are migrants down the Strait of Georgia, and the sudden appearance of these dark streamlined birds swooping in to attack makes for exciting viewing.

Terns are related to gulls but have much slimmer, sharper wings and a more buoyant flight. Increasing numbers of **Caspian terns** now spend the summer on Roberts Bank, loafing at the compensation lagoon next to the ferry terminal. They are easily identified by their blood red bills and raucous cries, heard from June to August. Other terns are less common, and the sight of one is always satisfying to the keen birder.

"Seabirds" are a diverse pelagic group, spending most of their lives at sea. They include guillemots, murres

A pigeon guillemot takes off from the water by paddling over the surface. A few pairs of this seabird nest locally.

and auklets. At nesting season, many seabirds gather in huge colonies on rocky islets and cliffs. An exception is the **marbled murrelet**, which builds a solitary nest on a tree branch, deep in oldgrowth forest. After nesting flocks of seabirds disperse out to sea.

Seabird watching in Boundary Bay can be done from Lighthouse Park at Point Roberts, from Kwomais Point in Ocean Park, from Blaine Harbor pier or Semiahmoo Spit. At all locations it is mostly a matter of luck what the wind and tides bring close to shore.

Pigeon guillemot, a few of which nest locally, are commonly seen in small groups year round, while marbled murrelet and **common murre** are more frequent in winter. **Ancient murrelets** are best found at Lighthouse Park in winter, where **Cassin's auklet**, **tufted puffin** and **rhinoceros auklet** have also been recorded. Drayton Harbor has the only local record for **thick-billed murre**, an outer west coast species.

SONGBIRDS

Pioneer families from Europe were disappointed with the songs of coastal forest birds, finding them harsh and strange. They must have missed the cheerful little red-breasted robin and the melodious thrushes of their homeland.

Here on the mild west coast, robins are present all year.

However, the Boundary Bay area does have some fine songsters, including the unobtrusive **song sparrow**, that has a lovely cascade in springtime, and the **American robin**, a thrush with a wonderful warbling song, heard early on summer mornings and into dusk. It is named after the unrelated European bird. In much of Canada, the robin's arrival presages an end to the bitter cold of winter. However, here on the mild west coast, robins are present all year. A familiar sight on lawns, they find

The spotted towhee may be mistaken for a robin but has a very different song.

Song sparrow

places to nest among the shrubs of residential yards and parks. In winter, they join with others to roam the countryside in loose flocks. The **spotted towhee** is sometimes confused with the similar-plumaged robin, yet has a trilling song, as well as harsh or buzzy calls, quite unlike the robin's melodious fluting. Watch for it scratching on the ground as it forages under shrubs. Streaky, brown song sparrows are also common in gardens and parks. Some birds are resident and others come in fall, setting up territories in blackberry patches for the winter. **Black-headed grosbeaks** and **western tanagers** are other melodious local songsters.

The beautiful trills of the **house finch** brighten up the garden just as the cherry blossom comes into flower. The male's red plumage expands and deepens in intensity with age, and the reddest males have the greatest attraction for the dull-coloured females. **American goldfinches** are brilliant and unmistakable yellow and black birds, and have a cheerful, bubbly summer song. Female finches are tricky to distinguish. They are easily confused with members of the sparrow family, a common group around the bay. Parks with natural, weedy patches and gardens with shrubs, flower beds and feeders are often full of wintering **white-crowned** and **golden-crowned sparrows**, song sparrows and plump **fox sparrows**. These small birds often gather together in loose feeding groups. **Lincoln's sparrows** are regular on migration and **savannah sparrows** nest on the ground in grassy fields.

Coniferous forest birds have calls that carry well among the dense trees. The **varied thrush** delivers its single-pitched, eerie whistles from a hidden perch high in the cedars. These northern thrushes, sometimes called Alaska robins, feed on shady ground where their beautiful mottled plumage makes them almost invisible. The related **Swainson's thrush** has a plaintive, rising call, usually heard at dusk.

Harsh, grating calls from a grove of cedars belong to the little **red-breasted nuthatch**, a small bird with an insatiable appetite for sunflower seeds. Nuthatches like to climb head first down tree trunks, searching for food. **Brown creepers** also climb

White-crowned sparrows are common songbirds around Boundary Bay.

WARBLERS

Warblers are small, beautifully-coloured birds with melodious songs. They often stay well hidden in dense foliage. Most of them arrive in late spring, remain for a few months, then migrate back down to their tropical and sub-tropical homes.

The earliest warbler migrants are the **yellow-rumped warblers**; some even winter locally. They are soon followed by **common yellowthroats, orange-crowned warblers, black-throated grey warblers** and **yellow warblers**. Whatever colour-fixated scientist named them got carried away, forgetting that distinguishing colour is difficult with small, restless birds in poor light! A few features are almost impossible to see, like the crown stripe on the orange-crowned warbler. Other warblers are very bright, like the brilliant yellow **Wilson's warblers** that seem to be everywhere in mid-May.

trees, but only go upwards on the trunk, flying to another tree when they reach the top. They are much quieter birds and rather elusive. The tiny **golden-crowned kinglet**, with its fiery head stripe, flutters among the cedar fronds. Its high calls are beyond the audible pitch of aging birders!

A cold snap will bring lots of varied thrushes, robins and **dark-eyed juncos** down from the mountains to wintering areas on the coast. One partial albino junco, recognizable by the little white patch on its dark hood, visited my garden every winter for three years in a row.

For more about Songbirds see page 61.

Warbler migration keeps pace with the fresh new leaves emerging in woodlots and slough margins. Look for these colourful birds from early to mid-May, when a wide variety of species are passing through or settling into summer territories. Spotting them is a challenge, but bursts of song or insistent call notes alert the observer to their presence.

Warblers spend most of the year in warm climates in the southern states of America, Central America and the Caribbean. Competition for their insect food is intense, as there are hundreds of other migrants there as well as resident birds. By migrating north, warblers gain more daylight and have less competition for bringing up young; however, they need to eat well in winter to have enough energy for the long journey. Birds occupying the richest winter habitats will be the first to arrive and lay claim to nesting territories.

It is difficult to believe that the delicate yellow-rumped warbler has just flown from the mangrove swamps of Central America, or that the common yellowthroat singing beside the dyke may have arrived from a marsh on the Mexican coast. Scientists are only just beginning to understand some of the mysteries surrounding the extraordinary lives of these little birds.

A female common yellowthroat feeding on spiders, in a hardhack thicket at dawn.

In fall, the route is retraced and the passage seems less urgent. Warblers head south in August and September, and strays continue to turn up well into the fall. A few overwintering warblers have been recorded on the Ladner and White Rock Christmas bird counts. As they head to their wintering grounds, warblers form different associations. **Townsend's warblers** that spent the summer in coniferous forests, and Wilson's warbler, which nested on the ground in a montane bog, can be found foraging together in Boundary Bay woodlands. Identifying warblers in fall is a challenging task, because of the now dull-coloured plumages of adults and juveniles.

Rare warblers

These warblers have been recorded very infrequently around Boundary Bay.

Tennessee Warbler
Nashville Warbler
Chestnut-sided Warbler
Palm Warbler
Black and White Warbler
American Redstart
Northern Waterthrush
Prothonotary Warbler

For the latest information, check the Vancouver Bird Alert 604 737 3074

Further Information

Neotropical Migratory Birds
by Richard M. DeGraaf &
John H. Rappole

WOODPECKERS

Woodpeckers are a sign of a dynamic forest ecosystem. Vital members of the recycling process, woodpeckers feed on insects that they find on live trees or in rotting logs. When the birds break up decaying wood, they encourage the growth of fungi and other decomposition agents and redistribute organic matter to the forest floor. The holes of larger woodpeckers provide nest sites for smaller birds and animals, including owls and flying squirrels.

The tiny **downy woodpecker** is a common species that lives in deciduous woodlands, hedgerows

Like all woodpeckers, this downy woodpecker uses its stiff tail feathers to help it perch on the side of a tree.

and gardens. It joins mixed flocks of chickadees and kinglets in winter, sometimes accompanied by its larger relative, the **hairy woodpecker**. Another common species, the **northern flicker**, is a year-round resident, but there are more around in spring and fall as migrants move through. Flickers come in two colour forms, the commonly seen, western, "red-shafted" and the rarer eastern "yellow-shafted". The two races evolved during the Pleistocene Ice Age when they were separated by glaciation. Hybrids are not unusual.

Spectacular **pileated woodpeckers** are large black birds, with a red crest. They have been badly affected by forest clearing on the Boundary Bay uplands. These woodpeckers need mature conifers, ideally with a diameter of more than 43 cm (18 in), for their nests. When trees are felled, the birds move away or die out.

Red-breasted sapsuckers, close relatives of the woodpeckers, tap rows of small holes in tree trunks to reach sticky sap and insects drawn to the sweetness. They visit Boundary Bay when heavy snowfalls bring them down from the mountains. The bird's deep scarlet head and breast are easily seen against the snow.

Further Information

Ecology and Management of Woodpeckers and Wildlife Trees in British Columbia by C. Steeger, M. Machmer and E. Walters

A female rufous hummingbird

HUMMINGBIRDS

The **rufous hummingbird** is one of the first spring migrants to return (*see page 26*). Brightly coloured males arrive first and immediately set up breeding territories. They do this by performing an aerial display, flying vertically in an oval path, and producing a loud buzzing sound with their wings on the downward swoop, accompanied by a wheezing call! They are briefly joined by the greener females, which soon disperse to build nests and raise young, unaided by their mates.

The nests are very tiny, only a few centimetres (1.25 in) in diameter, and rest on an alder or cedar branch, or in a tangle of blackberries or huckleberry. Nests built late in the season are located higher up. Well-camouflaged with lichen, seed tufts and spider webbing, the little nests gradually expand to accommodate the chicks.

The tiny rufous hummingbird is an amazing bird. It is one of only a few hummingbird species that migrate, despite weighing a mere 3.5 g (0.12 oz) and measuring less than 10 cm (4 in) from the tip of its beak to the end of its tail.

Hummingbirds can fly forwards or backwards, their wings blurring as they beat 90 times a second and up to 200 beats a second during a dive, the fastest rate of all birds. (In comparison European starlings average 5 beats/sec and the leisurely great blue heron only 2.5 beats/sec.) As a consequence, hummingbirds must consume half their own weight every day and drink eight times their weight in water. They spend three quarters of their time resting in order to digest, so can often be seen sitting quietly on a tree branch.

Two other species can occur. **Anna's hummingbird** over winter in a few sheltered areas, such as the White Rock ravines, and **calliope hummingbirds** are rare visitors to the region.

Further Information

The Hummingbirds of North America by Paul Johnsgard

Bird facts & figures:
The Bird Almanac by David Bird

For ideas on attracting hummingbirds to your garden *see Wildlife Gardening pages 164 - 166*

SWALLOWS & SWIFTS

On summer days, small insect-eating birds, many with forked tails, swoop over the open fields and along the shore, members of the swallow family. Swallows have had a long association with humans. An archaeological site at Charlie Lake in northern British Columbia has cliff swallow bones dating back at least 10,000 years, alongside human artifacts.

Tree swallows nest in tree snags or nestboxes in wetland areas, and arrive very early in the spring, by the end of February in most years. These glossy dark blue birds leave for the south in the second week of August. Local volunteers have put up nest boxes for them in parks, and monitor them to study breeding success. At the end of the year, the old nests and debris have to be cleaned out and the boxes rehung, ready for the following season. Nestboxes compensate for the shortage of suitable dead or dying trees and snags.

Tree swallow

The **violet-green swallow** is very similar in appearance to the tree swallow but the gloss on its back shines emerald green. It is a widespread and common summer bird in Boundary Bay, especially in residential areas. Arriving at the end of February and leaving in early August, it is the first swallow to depart.

Northern rough-winged swallows are less common around Boundary Bay, usually seen singly or in small groups. They nest under bridges and in culverts. **Cliff swallows** are colonial birds, which can be quite common in wetland areas. Like other swallows, they congregate in flocks before departure in late summer, when they have been observed roosting in cattail marshes.

Barn swallows return every year to nest under the eaves of houses and barns

Barn swallows return each year to build cup-shaped nests of mud, straw and feathers, under the eaves of houses and farm buildings. Some people do not like the mess they make, but swallows eat numerous insect pests and only stay a few short weeks at the nest site, so are worth a little inconvenience.

For more on Bird Migration see pages 41 - 45.

Barn swallow

All five of these swallows are regular summer visitors to the bay, but **purple martins** are only just returning. A common breeding bird until about 1948, these insect eaters declined when marshes were drained and agricultural pesticides became widely used. A few martins now nest each summer in tubular nestboxes in the Nicomekl estuary.

As the summer progresses, flocks of swallows gather on overhead wires and in communal roosts in reed beds. Barn swallows start eating berries and insects to increase their energy levels, and by early September they are ready to depart for the south. Thousands fly low over the fields and up over the Boundary Bay dyke in the first two weeks of September, heading straight out across the water.

A few stay until late into the fall and one or two even winter, but the vast majority head down the continent, through California and Central America, into South America. The exact destination of our local swallows is not known.

Swifts are the ultimate fliers. While rather similar to swallows, they actually belong to a different family. Unlike swallows, swifts' wings are strongly curved in a crescent. Two species can sometimes be seen in the Boundary Bay area.

Black swifts live for months on the wing, only briefly landing to lay eggs and nurse young before heading back into the skies. They do not nest locally but move into Boundary Bay during thundery weather in June and July, during which flocks of several hundred may be seen overhead.

Vaux's swift is a smaller, less common swift. The best time to see one is during migration in September. They used to be more common in summer, but were affected by the loss of freshwater marshes and their attendant clouds of midges. The increased use of agricultural pesticides in the 1950s and 60s, together with habitat loss throughout their range, probably caused the decline of these and other insect-eating birds, such as common nighthawks and western bluebirds.

Volunteer to help with nest boxes?

Some local naturalist groups have nest box building and maintenance programs: contact Federation of B.C. Naturalists at fbcn@telus.net
www.naturalists.bc.ca

This northwestern crow will attempt to open the cockle by dropping it from the air.

CROWS & JAYS

The clever, vocal **common raven** is renowned in the mythology of the Northwest Coast First Nations as a trickster that always outwits other, slower animals. Ravens are recognizable by their black plumage and large size, a wedge-shaped tail and heavy beak. Some are resident in the watershed uplands but most are passage migrants and occasional visitors to the Boundary Bay area. The majority of crows commonly seen are **northwestern crows.** Noisy, conspicuous birds, they forage along shorelines and among suburban garbage bins.

Unique to the Pacific Northwest, these crows are typical of the family. They are scavengers and omnivores, eating anything that looks edible and ganging up to chase away competitors, especially predatory animals like hawks, owls, raccoons and cats. Naturalists know to look up in the trees when a mob of noisily cawing crows starts to fly in from all directions, because often some interesting species will be lurking there.

The ornithologists responsible for species classification are in dispute over the status of the northwestern crow. One group believes that our endemic coastal crow is the same species as the widespread **American crow**. Others point to its slightly smaller size and different call notes as a rationale for separate status. No doubt DNA studies will eventually settle the dispute.

Elsewhere in North America, crows of all kinds have recently died in large numbers as a result of West Nile virus epidemics. As of 2005, the virus had not reached the Fraser estuary and the crow population was thriving. The increase in suburban garbage, particularly the huge pile at the Burns Bog landfill, has translated into more crows over the last twenty years. Versatile and adaptable to urban life, the raucous noise in June of young crows begging their parents for food irritates many people. Don't worry, it is just juvenile behaviour, and in a month or so everything quietens down once more. A good antidote to irritation is to watch them. Crows are intelligent birds, with a varied vocabulary and a mischievous sense of humour. I once saw one give a bogus alarm call, just to watch a dark-eyed junco fly out of the way!

Crows are both resourceful and experimental. They have been seen playing with automatic sensor lights, pulling off garbage bin lids and cracking clam shells by dropping them on the beach. (Invest in a garbage bin with a strong locking lid to stop local crows, gulls and raccoons shredding your trash all down the street.)

Crows are intelligent birds, with a varied vocabulary

Distinguishing between individual crows presents a problem, as both the male and the female are all black and the brownish young ones soon attain the same plumage. Biologists use leg bands to distinguish them in studies and found that crows return to visit relations and help parent the new generation. They live from 6 to 14 years and the pair bond is strong. They begin courtship in early spring, nest around March and raise young through the early summer.

By late summer, groups of young crows are forming loose foraging flocks of several hundred birds. They gather in hedgerows and fields, on river banks and beaches. As fall progresses, both young and adult birds gather locally in staging areas, then fly at dusk to roost in Burnaby, B.C. (*see Roosting Flights page 57*). In spring, the roost breaks up and the crows stay at the nest sites.

The Steller's jay is the provincial bird of British Columbia and a noisy inhabitant of local forests and parks.

Jays are also corvids, members of the crow family, intelligent, canny and vociferous. The common jay resident around Boundary Bay is the **Steller's jay**, the western species and British Columbia's provincial bird. It lives in forested uplands and will come to gardens in search of peanuts. More Steller's jays also migrate through during September, dispersing from mountain and northern forests.

Two other jays sometimes wander into the Boundary Bay region, causing excitement among birders. The **blue jay** is familiar to sports fans and eastern continental residents, and the **western scrub-jay** comes from California and Oregon.

SNAKES & TURTLES

Luckily for those who are phobic, there are only a few species of snake around Boundary Bay. None are poisonous. The most frequently encountered are the garter snakes, a confusing yet colourful family.

Three species, with two subspecies, occur in the watershed. A variety of different names are used, depending on the authority, so the scientific names have been included here. Distinguishing them can be difficult, but behaviour and habitat give useful clues. Avoid handling garter snakes as they all emit a foul-smelling secretion as a defense mechanism, and wandering and common garter snakes will bite.

Slim snakes with lots of red on them, particularly along the dorsal stripe down the centre of the back, are likely to be **northwestern garter snakes** (*Thamnophis ordinoides*). This is an inoffensive, docile species which eats slugs. Unlike other garter

Northwestern garter snakes like upland areas.

snakes, northwesterns very seldom enter water, although they can be found on beaches and dykes, as well as in grass and along woodland edges.

The large **wandering garter snake** (*Thamnophis elegans vagrans*) is the local subspecies of western terrestrial garter snake. This aggressive, aquatic snake is usually found near water and can be recognised by its large size, prominent wavy, yellow dorsal stripe and active behaviour.

Avoid handling garter snakes as they emit a foul-smelling secretion

Widespread, **common garter snakes** (*Thamnophis sirtalis*) are also found in wetlands, where they hunt fish, amphibians and even small birds. Two subspecies occur near Boundary Bay: the **Puget Sound garter snake** (*T.s.pickeringi*), a dark subspecies that inhabits delta wetlands, and the **valley garter snake** (*T.s.fitchi*), barred red on its sides, that is found in Langley.

The only other snake in the area is the inconspicuous, nocturnal **rubber boa**, which squeezes its prey to death like the boa constrictor. Unlike its more famous relative, the rubber boa is only 50 cm (20 in) long. It is no threat to humans.

Only one lizard has been recorded in the Boundary Bay watershed and it is rare. The **northern alligator lizard** is slender and long-tailed, with brown scaly skin. It could be looked for on rocks in sunny areas at woodland edges.

Turtles haul out of ponds in summer to sunbathe on logs. Colourful **western painted turtles** are found in a few places, such as Langley and Drayton Harbor watershed, but they are not common and some local populations may be released pets. Painted turtles are native to large areas of USA and Canada, including parts of the Pacific Northwest.

Many turtles seen in parks are exotic **red-eared slider turtles**. A popular pet, originating from southern USA, the red-eared slider has a splash of red on its head, near the eye, that separates it from the native painted turtle. The slider's shield also has vertical streaking and a serrated rear edge, while that of the painted turtle is smooth, with an olive, yellow or red front border. Red-eared sliders have been released in Diefenbaker Park in Tsawwassen, Crescent Park in South Surrey and other local ponds.

> **Further Information**
>
> The Reptiles of British Columbia by Patrick Gregory and Wayne Campbell
>
> For stewardship ideas for waterfront homes & gardens, see On the Living Edge from www.livingbywater.ca

FROGS & SALAMANDERS

Fishing for frog spawn and newts in freshwater ponds used to be a common summertime pursuit for many children, but both frogs and wetlands are harder to find these days.

The Boundary Bay watershed is fortunate in still having some freshwater wetlands and waterside plants that are perfect habitat for amphibians, including frogs and salamanders. The name "amphibian" means "double-life". Many of these cold-blooded animals live for the first part of their life in freshwater and then emerge onto land as adults. However, one group of salamanders lives entirely on land, hiding under fallen woody debris deep in the forest.

Like most amphibians, **red-legged frogs** lay a mass of jelly eggs, or spawn, in a shallow, shaded pond or stream, early in the spring. The eggs hatch into tadpoles, with fat bodies, long tails and gills for breathing

Red-legged frog

Pacific tree frog

underwater. As the tadpoles grow, they absorb their tails, sprout legs and eventually hop onto land, able to roam some distance from the water. Red-legged frogs are rather quiet callers and their presence is easily overlooked. Look for them in or near freshwater streams.

Pacific tree frogs are tiny but very vocal. The "ribbit ribbit" call of territorial males is a characteristic sound of marshes and ponds on wet spring evenings. Sometimes an enthusiastic frog will call in mid-winter, but the main chorus does not begin until late February or March. Later in the year, tree and red-legged frogs can be found in damp forests, not always close to water, and tree frogs often give a brief rain song when there is a rise in humidity. Pacific tree frogs can change colour from green to grey to brown and are easily hidden in bushes, trees or on the ground.

The deep, booming call of the large **American bullfrog** and the guitar-twang of the **green frog** are heard in the late spring and summer. These two introduced frogs prefer ponds and ditches with grass banks for sunning and deep water with cattail and bullrush beds.

The bullfrog's rapacious tadpoles, up to 10 cm (4 in) long, eat everything in sight. They grow into enormous adults, up to the size of a dinner plate! To discourage the spread of this aggressive frog, it is wise to plant shoreline vegetation around ponds to cool and shade the water.

Bullfrog tadpoles grow into enormous adults, up to the size of a dinner plate

Bullfrogs, released after a failed attempt at farming for frog legs, have probably contributed to the decline of the **Oregon spotted frog.** The latter is no longer found in the watershed.

The **western toad** is in a separate family of frogs. It prefers to walk rather than hop and has a warty-looking skin, containing poison glands. Toads are active only in the night, late evening and early morning from about March to October, and males do not call in this region. According to Rob Rithaler, who made a detailed study of amphibians in Delta, no spawning events have yet been recorded locally, although both toads and tadpoles have been found in a few local areas.

Rough-skinned newt

Although very seldom seen, there are actually five different species of **salamander** living in the Boundary Bay area. These elusive amphibians resemble slimy little lizards and occur as two types. "Aquatics" favour wet meadows, shallow ponds, streams and other freshwater wetland locations, especially those with dense waterside (riparian) vegetation. "Terrestrials" live in the forest soil. They tend to be nocturnal and very secretive.

The aquatic **rough-skinned newt** became notorious in the Pacific Northwest following a fatal incident of human poisoning. Similar to several other species of salamander, this newt has glands on its back that ooze a toxic chemical (tetrodotoxin).

Newts have been found in a number of places in the watershed, but do not normally pose any risk to humans, since the toxin is only released under extreme stress. Nonetheless, as with all wild species, great care should be taken if handling them. The **northwestern salamander** is typically dark, but may occur in a number of forms, including a sexually mature adult that looks like a juvenile. It is found in freshwater wetlands throughout the delta. The different forms that the salamander can assume are believed to be a response to differing environmental conditions and make this species very adaptable. **Long-toed salamanders**, black with a creamy yellow pattern down their backs, are uncommon and may be declining.

Terrestrial salamanders emerge at night, particularly during the heavy rains in November. **Ensatinas** are translucent reddish-brown in colour and occur in damp areas where there is plenty of fallen wood and leaf mould for burrowing. They lay their

Further Information

Amphibians of Oregon, Washington & B.C. by Charlotte Corkran & Chris Thoms

The Amphibians of British Columbia by David Green and Wayne Campbell

FROGWATCH has a cd of frog calls: www.elp.gov.bc.ca/wld/frogwatch

eggs in soil, where the females guard them, brandishing their straight little tails, a feature that gives them their name: "ensatina" means "small sword". Ensatinas live in forests and ravines around the bay, but are seldom seen, preferring to remain below ground most of the time. **Western red-backed salamanders** are also forest-dwelling, terrestrial amphibians, recognized by tan markings on their backs. They have been recorded from Burns Bog, forests and ravines in the watershed.

Amphibians have declined globally since the 1980s. So far, epidemics of chytrid fungus associated with frog extinctions elsewhere have not reached the Pacific Northwest; however habitat destruction, wetland drainage, climate change and air and water pollution by herbicides, pesticides and chemicals such as surfactants, have all been implicated in amphibian declines.

Help to keep frogs and salamanders healthy by encouraging waterside vegetation and restricting the use of chemicals, as far as possible.

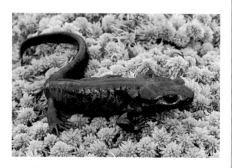

Northwestern salamander

FISH OF ALL KINDS

World famous for its wonderful salmon, the lower Fraser and its estuary support more than fifty other species of fish, including several endangered species. Many more marine fish live out in Boundary Bay and the Strait of Georgia. Delicious, freshly-caught fish are available in local restaurants throughout the region.

The abundance and diversity of fish depend directly on the qualities of the environment, particularly water salinity. Marine fish live in deep, salty, ocean water, and often spawn in shallow eelgrass meadows like those of Boundary Bay, Roberts Bank and Drayton Harbor. They include small shoaling bait fish or forage fish, such as **Pacific sandlance** and **surf smelt**, flatfish, such as **sand sole** and **starry flounder** and long-lived, sedentary groundfish.

Fish that can tolerate some fresh water are found in the lower reaches of the Fraser River, at its mouth and in the small estuaries around the bay. This habitat suits juvenile and adult anadromous fish, such as **eulachon** and the seven species of **Pacific salmon**, that hatch out in fresh water but live their adult lives in the ocean. They adjust in the estuary to the change in salt content and after several years at sea, they return to coastal rivers to spawn and die (*see page 130*).

The Little Campbell River estuary is important fish habitat.

A few fish, such as the **prickly sculpin**, do it the other way around. They are catadromous, living mostly in freshwater and spawning in salt water. Finally, there are a number of native and introduced fish that live all their lives in freshwater, in the streams and tributaries of the Boundary Bay watershed and the lower Fraser River.

Marine Fish

Surf smelt and sandlance occur in shoals and are prey for larger fish, seabirds and marine mammals. Semiahmoo Bay, Semiahmoo Spit and Drayton Harbor are important smelt spawning grounds. Boundary Bay has many members of the sculpin family, well-camouflaged fish ranging in size from the tiny, elusive **spinynose sculpin** to the large, common **Pacific staghorn sculpin**, over 40 cm (16 in) when full grown. Flatfish found in the bay include **lemon sole**, sand sole and **butter sole**. Sole start life looking like ordinary fish, but gradually one eye moves to join the other on one side of the body, and the fish swims on its side, spending more of its life resting on the sea floor. Its upper side becomes speckled to match the sandy floor and the underneath, blind side, turns white and scale-less.

Rockfish, such as the **quillback** and **copper rockfish**, are unusual in giving birth to hundreds of thousands of tiny, live young and for exceedingly long, sedentary lives. The quillback sometimes reaches 95 years old. These colourful red and orange fish prefer marine waters with rocky shorelines, sheltering reefs and crevices. Once abundant in the Strait of Georgia, they proved very vulnerable to overfishing and are now scarce. A few live around Point Roberts and off Roberts Bank, where a rare, giant lingcod can also found.

Freshwater & Estuarine Fish

Freshwater and estuarine fish range in size from tiny minnows to the giant **white sturgeon**, that historically reached lengths of over 6 m (20 ft).

The **white sturgeon** is the largest fish found in North American rivers, able to reach weights of over 500 kg (1100 lb). It is a long-lived, slow growing fish, with a life span well over 120 years. Females take 26 years to reach maturity and produce roe only every four to twelve years, so reproduction rates are low.

Whether the elusive **green sturgeon**, a related fish, spawns in the Fraser is not known, but it has been recorded from Roberts Bank. Sturgeon are bottom feeders, eating the carcasses of spawned-out eulachon in spring and salmon in winter.

The **three-spined stickleback** is found from streams to estuary waters. The male makes a nest in the spring and guards the eggs pugnaciously. It is joined in local rivers by such species as the **peamouth chub, largescale sucker** and the introduced **fathead minnow**, which arrived in the 1950s.

Several freshwater fish were introduced, such as **black crappie, largemouth bass, pumpkinseed** and **brown bullhead.** These had unexpected effects on the aquatic ecosystem. As aggressive predators of smaller fish, they have had a negative impact on native species.

Western brook lampreys are eel-shaped fish with round mouths that latch onto herring or salmon. Lampreys live in open water but come up river to spawn. Mated pairs build stone nests in the river bottom, using their mouths to move the rocks. Larvae live in the mud and eventually metamorphose into small

Ice Age pioneers

Two endangered species, the Nooksack Dace and the Salish sucker, were among the first fish to arrive in the Fraser Valley as the glaciers melted away. They are interesting to biologists as an example of active species diversification. Only a few may now survive in the headwaters of the Boundary Bay watershed.

adults, swimming free to latch onto passing fish. Although considered a delicacy by some cultures, they have not attracted a commercial fishery in North America.

The silvery **eulachon** is an oily little fish, very important to the traditional Coast Salish economy. The "first protein of the year", eulachon arrive in dense spawning shoals during April and May, having spent several years at sea. Their exact spawning location changes from year to year, but seals, sea lions, grebes, mergansers, eagles, crows and gulls always find the shoals. Fry hatch in time to be flushed out with the spring freshet in June and July.

Further Information

The Coastal Fishes of the Pacific Northwest by Andy Lamb and Phil Edgell

The Freshwater Fishes of British Columbia by Carl Clifford, W. A. Clemens and C.C. Lindsay

Marine Resources of Whatcom County has photographs of marine life, distribution maps for Boundary Bay and information on fish life cycles: http://whatcom-mrc.wsu.edu

Department of Fisheries & Oceans Canada www.dfo-mpo.gc.ca

FISH IN TROUBLE

Today's fish are much smaller than their giant ancestors, which had time and space to grow to extraordinary weights. It is difficult to imagine now the excitement of landing a 360 kg (800 lb) white sturgeon or a 136 kg (300 lb) halibut.

In the last century, hundreds of fish species around the world have been brought close to extinction, and it is no different in the Strait of Georgia. **Pacific halibut** were thirty five times as numerous in the Fraser estuary during the 1890s as they are today, and **lingcod** have declined by a factor of thirty in the same period. **Yelloweye rockfish** were once abundant in the Strait, but the fishery closed in 2002. **Cultus Lake sockeye**, that migrate up the Fraser River, are now on the endangered species list. Many coho stocks are struggling. **White sturgeon** were fished out on the Columbia River in the 1800s, after which commercial fishers turned their attention to the Fraser. These long-lived fish were on the brink of extinction by the 1990s, when a recovery program began.

SALMON

The salmon of the Fraser River are so important to the ecosystem that they merit a section to themselves. Their life cycle is well known to residents of the Pacific Northwest.

A spawning pair of chum salmon.

Unlike Atlantic salmon, most Pacific salmon return only once to their natal stream, to spawn and die. Their eggs are laid in gravel beds of shallow, clear water streams, and they hatch in spring. Depending on the species, the fry either linger in the river for a few months or head immediately to the estuary and in due course, the sea. Some stocks then head far out into the northern Pacific Ocean and Bering Sea, while others stay around the coast. Seven species of salmon may be found in the Strait of Georgia, all members of the *Oncorhynchus* genus, meaning "hooked nose". As can be expected of fish that have been hunted and valued for their succulent flesh for millennia, they go by a multitude of names.

Largest of all is the great **chinook**, also known as "spring salmon" in B.C and "king salmon" in the US. They generally spawn at four or five years old. Small chinook, less than 4 kg (9 lb), that come upriver to spawn in their third year are known as "jacks". Most sought by sports fishers are the older, tyee chinook, weighing more than 14 kg (30 lb) and potentially reaching a myth-making 50 kg (110 lb). Recognized by its large size, black spotted tail and dark, speckled back, the chinook also has a distinctive pungent odour. While adults roam far out to sea, young ones, or blackmouths, can be found year round in the Strait of Georgia, often lingering for months at the mouth of the Fraser River. The adults feed at midwater levels on sand lance, herring and squid, rising up to the surface at dawn and dusk and occasionally descending as deep as 80 m (262 ft). Chinook make their way upstream to spawn when the heavy rains begin in November.

The **coho**, or silver, is metallic blue, the black spots on its tail confined to the upper lobe. These salmon spend their first six months to a year in the river then a further two years in the ocean, before returning to spawn. Look for them in small streams from late October through December, at which time they have turned red in colour. Smolts (young salmon) have been found on Roberts Bank, but most juveniles head directly out to sea. At first they eat small shrimp and crustaceans but later switch to bait fish. Coho have suffered high rates of pre-spawn mortality in recent years.

Sockeye or bluebacks are considered by many people to be the best eating of all salmon. Their rich red flesh is a consequence of their diet of euphausiid shrimp and small crustaceans.

As they swim upriver, sockeye undergo extraordinary transformations

Several million sockeye swim up river in the dominant fourth year runs. On the way, the silvery sockeye undergo extraordinary transformations. They stop eating, their scales become bright red, their heads turn deep green, their bodies hump-backed and their jaws hooked and distorted. Because they no longer eat, they cannot be caught with baited hooks. First Nations people used fish weirs, traps and nets to haul them from the water. Today gillnets are the common way of fishing them in the river. Sockeye migrate out as overwintered, year-old smolts, swimming mostly in the fast-flowing centre of the river and not lingering in the estuary at all.

Further Information

Pacific Salmon from Egg to Exit by Gordon Bell

Chum salmon, or dog salmon, are mid-sized 4 to 6 kg (9 - 13 lb) fish, with dark tips to the fins, but no black spots on the tail. In spring, chum fry leave natal streams soon after hatching, heading for the estuary and ocean. Adults return to spawn from mid-September to January.

Pinks, or humpies, are the smallest of the salmon, weighing less than 2.5 kg (5.5 lb) and having a two year life cycle. They spawn only in odd years in the Fraser River and the juveniles also leave the river quickly to rear in the ocean. Their skin is covered in black oval spots, extending over the entire tail.

Sea-run trout that migrate between stream and ocean were identified as members of the Pacific salmon genus in 1988. However, **rainbow** (or steelhead) and **coastal cut-throat trout** differ from the other salmon as they can survive to spawn more than once. Since the 1930s they have been a focus of stocking programs in the tributaries of Boundary Bay. Look for them in Dakota Creek and the Little Campbell River.

Small salmon-bearing rivers and streams around Boundary Bay now have relatively small populations but play an important role in genetic diversity. Clean, clear streams in the watershed are vital for sustaining these special fish, and problems in water flow or quality can mean the end of a local stock.

CRABS, CLAMS & COCKLES

The succulent **Dungeness crab** makes excellent eating and many are trapped commercially. The deeper waters of Boundary Bay and Roberts Bank are prime habitat for this large crab, where it will roam for up to 2 km (1 mi) a day, searching for clams. Crabs mate in subtidal eelgrass meadows and young crabs overwinter in the intertidal. The tiny crabs are said to reach densities of up to 150 per sq m (14 per sq ft) in some areas of the bay.

Crabs moult their pinkish-brown shells each year, which are then washed up on the beaches through the summer. The males will mate with females whose shells are still soft and then guard them afterwards while the shell hardens. One interesting sexual phenomenon was noted by fisherman and author, Terry Glavin: all Boundary Bay and Fraser estuary crabs moult and have sex simultaneously, while those in the Gulf Islands choose their own times! No one knows why this is so.

It is easy to tell male and female Dungeness crabs apart by looking at the underside of the shell; a U-shape is a female and a V-shape is a male. Crabbers are limited to male crabs greater than 165 mm width (in US, greater than 6.25 in) and require a tidal waters sportfishing licence from the relevant jurisdiction.

When the tide is running strongly or the mud is exposed at low tide, the Dungeness crab buries itself under the sand, with just its antennae and eyes protruding.

Most crab shells found on the beach belong to Dungeness crabs, but a search along pebble shores reveals diminutive **shore crabs** hidden among eelgrass leaves, and even smaller **pea crabs** lie concealed inside clam and oyster shells or in the burrows of ghost shrimps.

A stroll on the beach always turns up a variety of shells belonging to the bivalve molluscs: clams, cockles, mussels and oysters.

Butter clams have thick white shells and grow up to 10 cm (4 in) long. They were a favourite of both Coast Salish and immigrants up to historic times. Sadly, harvesting is now closed due to contamination, mostly from agricultural manure.

Clamming

Clam harvesting is not permitted in Boundary Bay, Semiahmoo Bay or elsewhere in the Fraser River estuary.

In many parts of the bay, the strangely warped, clean white shells of the **bent-nose clam** are thickly clustered. When alive, these clams lie on their side, probing and sifting for detritus and bacteria with two separate orange siphons.

Heart cockles have strongly ribbed, equal-sized shells and very short, fused siphons. They bury themselves just below the sand in eelgrass meadows. Like the native **littleneck clam**, which is also a shallow feeder, cockles are slow growing, living to around 7 or 8 years old. Mollusc ages can be told by looking at the number of calcium ridges on their shells; an extra ridge is formed as growth slows, usually in winter each year. Butter clams are very long lived, reaching over 20 years for some specimens.

While many native bivalves are predominantly white, **bay mussels** have an elongated dark blue or black shell and cling in dense clusters to rocks and pilings, securely attached even in strong surf conditions. Tiny deep pink shells, sometimes picked up on the beach, belong to the **Baltic macoma**. Pearly pink, oval shells are likely to be **Carpenter's tellins**. Neither species is very common.

Mudflat snails are just one of many non-native crustaceans on the Boundary Bay mudflats. This Asian snail can be found in huge clusters on higher intertidal areas. They are related to a native snail that lives in similar habitat in southern California. The effect of these invertebrates on the intertidal ecosystem is unknown.

Purple varnish clams have glossy brown shells with purple linings, conspicuous on Boundary Bay beaches since the first record at Semiahmoo in 1991. Native to Japan and Korea, this clam has rapidly spread around the southern Strait of Georgia and into Washington State. They probably arrived in the ballast water of ocean-going ships. The **Japanese mussel** also suddenly arrived in Boundary Bay in 1993, the first record being from Semiahmoo. Since 1994 the Port of Vancouver has required ballast water transfer in mid-ocean to reduce the risk of other alien species introductions.

Rocky beaches are the place to find **acorn** and **thatched barnacles** cemented to the rocks, together with tightly clinging, cone-shaped **limpets**. Another family that stick to rocks, the **chitons,** live deeper in subtidal waters. Their shells are sometimes washed ashore, including the spectacular red **gumboot chiton.**

Further Information

Shells and Shellfish of the Pacific Northwest by Rick Harbo.

Exploring the Seashore by Gloria Snively

The Last Great Sea by Terry Glavin

THE INSECT WORLD

The intricate world of insects is a fascinating one. Over three quarters of species on earth belong to this class, yet even naturalists often overlook them. Insects have an enormous impact on the landscape, as pollinators, defoliators and recyclers, and can be both beneficial and harmful to human activities. They are prey for tens of thousands of species, and they clean up carcasses and waste products that animals leave behind.

In summertime around Boundary Bay, the sharp-eyed observer can expect to find insects belonging to a variety of orders, including butterflies and moths, dragonflies, beetles, bees and wasps, crickets and grasshoppers, bugs, lacewings, flies, aphids and ants. Spiders are also common, but belong to a class of arthropod known as arachnids, quite separate from the insects.

Butterflies and Moths

"*The bright wings of summer*" is how the famous naturalist Roger Tory Peterson described this attractive group. Butterflies live in sunny, sheltered areas. Most fly for a few brief weeks, just time to find nectar, mate and lay eggs.

A few long-lived species, such as the **mourning cloak** and **satyr comma**, survive the winter as adults and are among the first to fly in spring. Most butterflies, however, spend the winter as eggs, caterpillars, or as a pupa, a little tear-drop shaped case. One summer morning, the butterfly breaks free from its pupa and unfurls its damp wings to dry in the sunshine.

Our largest local butterfly is the bright yellow and black **western tiger swallowtail**, which is common and easily seen. It lives near poplars and cedars, and feeds at nectar-bearing plants like honeysuckle and buddleia. A smaller, blacker relation, the **anise swallowtail**, occurs along the Boundary Bay dyke. It lays its eggs and feeds on cow parsnip, wild angelica and fennel.

The ubiquitous **cabbage white** is another common resident of fields and gardens, fluttering around vegetable beds, at home among the broccoli and cauliflower. This non-native butterfly first appeared in Quebec in the early 1900s, but soon made its way west and is often considered a pest. Delicate **pine whites** are similar in appearance but fly in groups around the crowns of Douglas-fir and pine trees.

Woodland skippers are small orange butterflies that hold their front wings at an almost vertical angle to the back pair. They fly from midsummer onwards and contrary to their name, they are found in many habitats, including grasslands.

Stages of the anise swallowtail's life cycle.

The unique habitat of Burns Bog is home to many small butterflies, such as **brown elfin**, **western pine elfin** and **Mariposa copper.** Each species feeds at particular plants in the bog ecosystem, such as salal, lodgepole pine or blueberry.

Butterflies need specific plants for depositing eggs, rearing caterpillars and for sipping nectar as adults. Stinging nettles are a larval food for **Milbert's tortoiseshell, satyr commas** and **red admirals.** Thistles are important for the migratory **painted lady.** This butterfly is much more common every ten years, when peak populations arrive from the south. Some butterflies are strongly territorial around their food plants, like **Lorquin's admiral** that patrols a home patch among spirea, willows or fruit trees.

Butterflies are very good ecological indicators. They are very sensitive to chemicals and many are lost during programs to combat gypsy moth infestations. First flight records can track climate change and can be used to determine if species are at risk.

Dragonflies and damselflies

Dragonfly watching is currently generating a lot of new interest, encouraged by the availability of good field guides and websites. It is not surprising: dragonflies have vivid colours and lively movement, fly for much of the year and offer

Cardinal meadowhawk

some challenging identification puzzles. Dragonfly expert, Rex Kenner of Vancouver, has found about fifty species in the Boundary Bay watershed.

The varieties most likely to attract attention include the large, powerful, blue or green darner dragonflies, the vivid neon-coloured damselflies found around ponds, the cherry red meadowhawks, and the skimmers which have black and white patches or bars on their wings. Identification of species depends on examination of the thorax patterns, the exact shape of the tail and other intricacies for which a really close-up look is necessary.

The earliest flying damselflies, such as the **boreal bluet** and **California bluet,** appear in early April. The other species of damselflies and dragonflies then emerge and fly throughout the summer. Some, such as the **Pacific forktail, spotted spreadwing** and **shadow darner** are still around in late October. They are a beneficial and essential part of the ecosystem, consuming large numbers of mosquitoes and other insects. Both dragonflies and damselflies are associated with freshwater wetlands and lay their eggs in aquatic vegetation or under the soil in ponds and streams. They do not lay in salt water.

The next stage of the life cycle, larvae or nymphs, hatch from the eggs and remain in the water from a few months to over five years, growing into large and aggressive predators. Once they metamorphose and emerge as adults, they live for only a few months, many species staying close to the water, but some flying several kilometres away. The darner dragonflies, for example, can be found in sunny, dry locations far from any ponds. They are masters of the air, constantly patrolling at about 5 kph (3 mph) but able to accelerate to 60 kph (37 mph) in pursuit of a flying insect. In contrast, the damselflies and skimmers tend to spend a lot of time perched on vegetation, soaking up the sunshine.

Look for dragonflies and damselflies in freshwater wetlands throughout the Boundary Bay watershed. Burns Bog has locally uncommon species more often associated with northern habitats, such as the **zigzag darner, subarctic darner** and the **crimson-ringed whiteface.**

Insect information sources, see page 139.

Beetles

There are an astonishing 30,000 species and 111 families of beetle in North America. Some are terrestrial and some are aquatic, some are plant eaters and pollinators, others consume carcasses and efficiently clean up the environment, recycling nutrients into the soil. Boundary Bay's mild climate means that beetles can be found even in the winter months, although late spring and early fall are the best times to look for them. One brightly-coloured group, the ladybirds, are commonly seen on warm sunny days in summer. No one has yet catalogued all the beetles found around Boundary Bay, where both native and introduced species occupy every conceivable habitat.

Ladybirds alone, have about 400 species worldwide. All have complex life histories, behaviours and plant associations, and different numbers of spots. One of the commoner ladybirds found in meadows beside the bay is the **7-spot ladybird**. It is a global generalist, apparently introduced to the region in the 1970s. It can be found on many plants, including vetch, fireweed, consumption plant, and pine trees. Ladybirds often crawl to the top of plants since they are attracted to light and negatively geotactic, which means they walk upwards against gravity. They rely on their bright red warning colour, accompanied by toxic fluids in their bodies, to protect them from predators. This serves well while they are on a plant, feeding on aphids or sipping nectar. When they fly, ladybirds can be caught by swallows and martins, birds that appear to have internal defenses against the toxins.

At the approach of winter, ladybirds seek out sheltered locations to hibernate. **2-spotted ladybirds**, for example, gather in large clusters in buildings. Ladybirds consume vast quantities of aphids, and so are very beneficial to humans. The **convergent ladybird**, a native of the western states of America, is frequently used for pest control.

Beetles are important in forest and hedgerow ecology: look for them in Boundary Bay's forest parks. **Carrion beetles** are boldly marked in red and black. They scurry over the forest floor, burying the carcasses of small animals and other insects. **Ground beetles** and **rove beetles** live under leaf litter, in fallen logs and burrowed into the ground, aerating and fertilizing the soil and

Banded alder borer

Discover the unexpected

The diversity of insect shapes, colour, habitat and behaviour is outstanding. There are plenty of opportunities for both the expert and amateur enthusiast to make new discoveries. A sphagnum bog aphid, *Paraphlepsius varispinus*, was discovered for the first time in British Columbia in Burns Bog during a 1999 ecological study. The study also found a **water beetle**, *Cenocorixa andersoni*, on the British Columbia endangered list, and recorded the scarce *Buenoa confusa*, an **aquatic backswimmer**, for the first time in the Lower Mainland.

Close study of insects allows us to learn more about their very strange lives. The **aphids** that live on our rose bushes have extraordinary sex lives. They initially hatch from eggs as females, then do not mate for up to *thirteen* generations. The females give birth to live young after asexual reproduction. Finally a generation with males occurs once more, and eggs are produced.

Grasshoppers chirp away all summer long, but every once in a while something makes them breed in vast numbers, to the point where swarms can cloud the sky and decimate crop fields.

Take another look at local insects and enjoy them to the full.

transplanting fungal spores. **Wood-boring beetles** and **long-horned beetles** aid decomposition of dead and dying trees. Their larvae are voracious plant-eaters, boring into the sapwood of old or unhealthy trees and felled timber. Epidemic, cyclical infestations of **bark beetles** cause massive economic losses to the timber industry.

Bugs crashing against the porch light on a summer evening might mean a visit from the night-flying **June beetles**, large stripy insects with a thick shell covering their flimsy underwings. Many beetles are most active at night, often being attracted to lights. They are hunted by owls, bats and nighthawks in the air and by raccoons, opossums and shrews on the ground.

Long dry spells send beetles into a summer torpor or "aestivation". Many freshwater ponds have aquatic beetles throughout the summer and, once again, Burns Bog is the ideal location for sighting some unusual species.

Stink bugs are another common family, well known for their characteristic odour.

Bees and wasps

Bees are very beneficial insects for humans: they are responsible for the pollination of our most important plants and honey is a popular food. **Honey bees** have pollinated crops for over 4000 years in Europe and Asia; **orchard mason bees** pollinate plants in North America. Wasps on the other hand are generally viewed as troublesome creatures, disturbers of picnics and always ready to sting the unwary. Both types of insect have fascinating, complex lives.

The honey bee and **bumble bee** are introduced species, active early in the spring when the first fruit trees bloom. They are colourful, social insects, with bands of yellow, black or red on their fluffy bodies. Nearly all the worker honey bees die at the end of the year. Only the queen and infertile female attendants survive to regenerate the hive. Both types of bees sting. In contrast, native mason bees are black, solitary, and do not sting. They nest in holes in wood and can be attracted to a garden by providing them with suitable sites.

Wasps, yellowjackets and hornets die off in cool weather, becoming sleepy and prone to sting in the last days of fall. **Yellowjackets** form colonies in burrows or build hanging nests. The first workers to emerge in spring are sterile females; fertile yellowjackets arrive later in summer in time to pester us on holiday.

In winter, all but the mated queen die. **Paper wasps** are common in fields and gardens. They build nests from chewed and regurgitated wood fibre, creating a comb of paper cells. These wasps will sting if bothered at the nest. The delicate, papery, football-sized globes found in bushes and thickets are not paper wasp nests, but those of the **bald-faced hornet**, a social, non-stinging insect.

Hover flies are small wasp-like insects with a characteristic "stop-and-start", hovering flight. **Black and yellow mud daubers** have large, elongated bodies with thin waists. They collect mud for their nests from ponds and verges.

Further information on Insects

Butterflies of North America by Jim P. Brock and Kenn Kaufman

Introducing the Dragonflies of B.C. by Robert Cannings

Dragonflies of Washington by Dennis Paulson

The Bugs of British Columbia by John Acorn and Ian Sheldon

Beetles by Richard E. White

Bug questions answered at www.whatsthatbug.com

Northwest Odonata Photo Gallery: http://www.ups.edu/biology/museum/WAODphotos.html - dragonfly photos, by Dennis Paulson & Uni. of Puget Sound

SPIDERS

People are often very phobic about **spiders**, and no wonder! This group includes creatures with eight legs that spin deadly traps of silken webbing and inject their prisoners with paralysing toxins. Females of some species even eat the male after mating. No deadly spiders are native to Boundary Bay, but take care when handling spiders as some tropical species might arrive with imported fruit. Despite their unpopularity, spiders' ubiquity and sensitivity to temperature and moisture make them good indicator species for monitoring climate change.

Morning dew highlights the delicate work of an orb weaver spider's web.

There are ten common spider groups. **Cobweb weavers**, a group that includes the **black widow**, make thin, strandy webs inside houses. Colonial **sheetweb weavers** build extensive domes of silk, stretched across low-growing plants and lawns, most noticeable in early morning dew. The **nursery web spiders** build

Boreal cobweb spider, a smaller relative of the black widow. There are more than 3 000 species of spider in North America.

an underwater web, and the **funnel web spiders** build a silk trap within a hole of rocks or logs. The **grass spider** is a funnel web spider and enters houses in the fall. **Orb weavers** make large, circular webs, spun with silk exuded from special organs in their abdomen. They are very clever in positioning their webs, angled to catch flying insects. Among the free-ranging predatory spiders are tiny **dwarf spiders** found in leaf litter, and the large, hairy-legged **lycosas**, or **wolf spiders**. Pink or yellow **crab spiders** are perfectly camouflaged among the flowers in which they live. **Jumping spiders** roam around warm, dry areas stalking and leaping onto their prey. Finally, **gnaphosids** are a group of small, nocturnal spiders.

MICROBES & DISEASES

Microbes are the earth's smallest inhabitants and are both widespread and very abundant everywhere.

Bacteria are extremely simple organisms, neither plant nor animal. They are able to survive in an amazing number of environments. The **cyanobacteria** obtain food by photosynthesis, but other bacteria absorb nutrients directly from the environment. A bacterial cell consists of cytoplasm and a cell wall, and differs from the cells that make up plants and animals in part because the microbial DNA is not enclosed in a nucleus.

Bacteria reproduce by splitting, a process that allows extremely rapid growth of a microbial population. Some of them produce spores which prevent them drying out, so they can remain dormant but alive in soil for many years (e.g. tetanus, anthrax). Bacterial diseases can often be cured by antibiotics.

Viruses can only replicate inside the cells of a host

Viruses are several magnitudes smaller than bacteria and are composed of a nucleic acid in a protein shell. They can only replicate inside the cells of a host animal, plant or bacterium. Many of the world's diseases are caused by viruses, including AIDS, hepatitis, polio, smallpox, rabies, influenza, foot and mouth disease, chicken pox and the common cold.

Viruses cannot be killed by antibiotics, but some viral illnesses can be prevented by vaccination or treated with drugs. The body's own immune system and good hygiene are generally the best defence against them. Viruses are often in the news and here we look at a few headliners.

West Nile Virus

A *Flavivirus* spread by mosquitoes, **West Nile virus** was first detected in North America in 1999, but is common in Africa, parts of Asia and Europe. It is essentially an avian disease but also affects people and other animals, causing flu-like symptoms in about twenty percent of those exposed. A very few people may contract encephalitis, which is potentially fatal.

The virus is transmitted by mosquito bites but not directly between hosts (except through blood transfer). It is therefore most unlikely you would catch West Nile from birds, dogs or other humans. Immunity is gained after a single exposure to the virus, holding out promise of a vaccine in the future. Birds, especially the crow family and small songbirds, have suffered high mortalities in areas badly affected by the virus.

Fortunately, as of December 2005, West Nile had not yet arrived in Washington or British Columbia.

The Greater Vancouver Regional District (GVRD) has taken a precautionary approach to the virus by conducting surveys of mosquito populations. They identified hot spots for breeding Culex tarsalis, Aedes togoi and Culex pipiens. Out of the seventeen or eighteen local species of mosquito, these three are most competent at transmitting the virus. Water bodies with high nutrient levels, for example where manure or sewage have entered the water, are prime breeding grounds for C. tarsalis. Tiger mosquito (Aedes togoi) is an Asian species found near salt water. C. pipiens occurs in wet gutters and tires in urban areas. These mosquitoes do not normally occur in wetlands that are shaded with bankside vegetation and have moving, well-oxygenated water, frogs and fish. The GVRD team treated sites with a bacterial larvicide (BTI) to kill juvenile mosquitoes. This is the preferred method since adulticides are expensive, highly toxic to the environment and not nearly effective enough at reaching the relevant mosquitoes.

Avian Flu

Avian flu, or influenza, is caused by an *Orthomyxovirus*. Like many viruses, influenza has a reservoir in

Wetlands are important for controlling natural pathogens.

wild animals, in this case, waterfowl and other aquatic birds. Wild birds very seldom get sick from influenza. Domestic poultry, however, are extremely susceptible to this virus, which can also infect pigs, people and other mammals. An outbreak in the Fraser Valley in spring 2004 led to the culling of 17 million chickens. There are fears that transmission of Avian flu from chickens to people will cause a global pandemic. To understand the risk one needs to know something about the virus.

This rather rare process is called "antigenic shift"

Influenza A viruses are divided into subtypes based on the presence of two proteins: hemagglutinin and neuraminidase; these are commonly shortened to H and N. These proteins commonly undergo simple mutations, or "antigenic drift". Sometimes, a gene segment will swap with one from a different subtype. This occurs when other flu viruses are already in the host.

If the material incorporated is a coat protein from an animal influenza virus, the new virus subtype will look completely foreign to the human immune system and so will be extremely virulent. This rather rare process is called "antigenic shift" and is the cause of pandemics. Examples of epidemic and pandemic subtypes include H1N1 (Spanish flu), H1N2 and H3N2 (Hong Kong and Asian flu) and the highly pathogenic H5N1 strain.

Transmission of Avian flu, from wild birds to domestic poultry and from poultry to humans, can likely be prevented by good agricultural vaccines and by diligent implementation of security measures. These include the prevention of contact between poultry and wild birds at farms and markets.

Hanta Virus Pulmonary Syndrome

The **hanta virus** belongs to the *Bunyavirus* family. It has caused outbreaks of a rare but potentially fatal respiratory disease, transmitted by deer mice, in countries all around the northern hemisphere. Those likely to be exposed are farmers, biologists and cabin owners who handle mice or inhale dust from their droppings. For more info see Health Canada www.hc-sc.gc.ca. Most outbreaks have occurred in spring and late fall.

Further information

World Health Organization: www.who.int

Centre for Disease Control: www.cdc.gov

All the Virology on the Worldwide Web: www.virology.net

PLANT PROFILES

Unlike so much of the northern half of the continent, the Boundary Bay area offers the plant explorer a rich year-round experience. Plants range from delicate wildflowers to towering conifers, lush mosses and intricate lichens.

WILDFLOWERS

Wildflowers of wet meadows and prairies, such as **Pacific silverweed, fireweed, entire-leaved gumweed, blue-eyed mary, Canada goldenrod** and **Douglas' aster,** create a riot of colour through the summer on the shores of Boundary Bay. The many wildflowers of Burns Bog include the gorgeous pink blossoms of **western**

bog laurel, **cloudberry**, a plant of the northern tundra, and strange carnivorous **sundew**, that catches insects in its sticky trap. **Labrador tea** and blueberries are other more common bog plants.

Native woodland plants include showy **western trilliums,** delicate **bleeding heart,** pale pink **western starflowers, large-leaved avens** and **bunchberry.** A very few woodlands still have **fawn lilies** but they are much scarcer than in former times.

We generally think of wildflowers as the smaller, herbaceous plants, but many native shrubs also produce stunning blooms. The countryside is first brightened by the white bells of **Indian plum** in spring, then the deep crimson petals of **salmonberry,** fragrant, pink **Nootka roses,** creamy cascades of **oceanspray** and the clustered blooms of **Pacific ninebark,** to name just a few. Attractive berries prolong the display: roses have bright red hips that last through the winter, while the small, yellow, tubular flowers of the **black twinberry** are followed by strange, paired fruit, framed by scarlet bracts.

Sundew - a carnivorous plant that grows in Burns Bog.

Salal harvested in the Pacific Northwest is used for flower arrangements locally and throughout the world.

Menzies' larkspur, blue camas and **chocolate lilies** that once bloomed on sunny, upland bluffs have been replaced with exotics from across the world. Only about two-thirds of the local wildflowers are native to the region, the rest have arrived, either accidentally with pioneers, travellers and farmers, or have been introduced by generations of gardeners.

> *Only about two-thirds of the local wildflowers are native*

Introduced plants range from adaptable, weedy species that arrived on cart wheels and oxen with the early European settlers, to some pervasive plants that were introduced deliberately, such as **common dandelions**, Kentucky blue grass, **Scotch broom** and **purple loosestrife**. Dandelions were planted as salad in cottage gardens, but are now common along roadsides. All the Scotch broom in the Lower Mainland spread from just a few seeds, planted by one man in Victoria

in 1850. Purple loosestrife has been labeled "the beautiful killer"for its role in choking wetlands with its prolific growth. **Knapweeds** and **toadflax** rapidly take over grasslands and many woodland trails are fringed with **wall lettuce, meadow buttercups** and clinging **English ivy**. Not all introduced plants are worthless to wildlife. **English hawthorn**, or May, with its dense, fragrant blossoms and abundant berries, is good hedgerow habitat. Even unruly **Himalayan blackberry**, known for its sprawling tendrils and aggressive expansion, gives shelter and food to many songbirds and small mammals.

Alien plants that are generalists can adapt and fit into new surroundings, their aggressive growth habits choking out more specialised plants. Sowing "wildflower" seeds is not a good idea, since packages seldom contain exclusively regional species. Native plants, however, are perfectly suited to wildlife and often have ecological partnerships, or symbiosis, with native insects. They are a crucial part of the ecosystem.

Further information

Plants of Coastal British Columbia by Jim Pojar and Andy Mackinnon

The Native Plant Society of British Columbia 604 255 5719 www.npsbc.org

Watershed forests have a rich understorey of wildflowers and ferns.

NATIVE TREES

Coastal Douglas-fir are spectacular trees with strong, straight trunks. They are highly valued by the timber industry. Regularly growing up to 85 m (280 ft) tall and able to live from 750 to 1500 years, Douglas-fir have tough red-brown bark which thickens and grooves with age, forming a healing growth over cuts and scars. The thick bark protects the trees from all but the hottest fires. The soft cones are easily identified by three-pronged bracts on each segment.

Giant Douglas-fir support bald eagle nests, which may weigh as much as a metric tonne

Douglas-fir prefer sunny, open slopes, where they grow with huckleberries, salal, oregon grape and sword fern. Dozens of plants and animals depend on them. Owls and red-tailed hawks roost among the branches, and the giant mature trees support bald eagle nests, which may weigh as much as a metric tonne (2200 lb). Brown creepers have plumage that exactly matches the mottled brown of the bark, and red crossbills have curiously-shaped beaks that can pull the seeds from the cones.

Douglas-fir seeds are also eaten by deer mice, squirrels, shrews, wrens and chipmunks. The tree, like many

Douglas-fir cone

others, lives in intimate connection with mycorrhizal fungi, existing in symbiosis for their mutual benefit.

Cooling climate around 6000 years ago led to the invasion of **western redcedar** from the south. This spectacular conifer is also called *arbor vitae*, the tree of life. Its medicinal properties, light, decay-resistant wood, fibrous bark and pliable branches were recognised by aboriginal peoples as invaluable resources, thus beginning a unique, four thousand year old, Pacific Northwest cedar culture.

Its drooping frond-like branches shake off winter winds and rain and shade the ground below. Growing to 60 m (200 ft) tall and able to survive for over a thousand years, the western redcedar flourishes alongside western hemlock, bigleaf maple, grand fir and Douglas-fir.

The western redcedar is called the tree of life

Stumps of western redcedar logged from the 1870s onwards can be seen in many of our forest parks, such as Tynehead and Watershed Park. Their enormous size testifies to the immensity of these trees, and even in decay, they act as nurse logs for red huckleberry, ferns, mosses, lichens and others. Large pairs of notches in the sides of the stumps are where the loggers placed springboards for standing on while they used the double handed saw.

Western hemlock is the other dominant tree in our area. Cedar hemlock forests flourish with more than 1250 mm (50 in) of rain a year, a requirement which is met in the more eastern parts of the Boundary Bay watershed. Hemlocks can be recognised by their drooping tops, delicate, lacy boughs of short needles and small cones. Archibald Menzies, the botanist on George Vancouver's expedition, brewed hemlock needles with molasses as a preventative against scurvy, adding a top of rum just before barreling the "spruce" beer. None of Vancouver's

Shore pine and western hemlock in Burns Bog

crew came down with the scurvy in the three year voyage.

Grand fir is the most common native true fir around Boundary Bay. It grows straight and tall in upland forests, such as Watershed Park. Foresters often refer to it as balsam, because of its sweet scent, reminiscent of grapefruit. There used to be many more grand fir around the Fraser delta but many have been felled in recent years.

Short, twisted and gnarled, bent by wind and weather, the **shore pine** grows even on the most exposed parts of the coast and in the acid soil of Burns Bog. A variety of lodgepole pine, it is distinguished from other pines found in the Boundary Bay area by having two twisted needles per bunch, rather than three or five. Lodgepole pine cones need the intense heat of forest fires to release their seeds, and pines are consequently the first trees to regenerate a burn area. Pine wood is an excellent timber with many uses, and its seeds and inner bark feed small animals.

Maples are famous for their display of fall colour throughout eastern North America, but here in the West, native maples are more subdued. The **bigleaf maple**, the largest in Canada, is confined to the mild southwest corner of the province. Its huge leaves, like those of the pretty little **vine maple,** turn a bright ochre yellow in fall but seldom gain the deep orange and red colour characteristic of this family. Maple branches and trunks are often covered with mosses and licorice ferns, a foothold for other plants and animals.

Clustered along the river banks, fragrant stands of **black cottonwood** rustle in the breeze. These fast-growing poplar trees grow more than a metre a year when young and reach 40 m (130 ft) tall. The sweet

Black cottonwood

smell of the woods in spring comes from a gum that covers the orange leaf buds. The gum is collected by bees for sealing their hives and was known and used by First Nations people for its medicinal properties. The catkin flowers emerge before the leaves and later in the year, fluffy, white, hair-covered seeds appear, creating a cottony shower in the air and carpeting the ground.

Cottonwoods are not long-lived trees. They rot from the inside, causing them to shed large branches or suddenly crash to the ground, a dangerous habit that makes them unpopular with parks' managers. Care should be taken when walking under them, especially in windy weather. Many cottonwoods are felled each year, yet they are essential

Further information

The Tree Book, Learning to recognize trees of British Columbia by Roberta Parish, Ministry of Forests, Victoria, B.C. www.gov.bc.ca/for/

wildlife trees, full of songbirds in spring and summer, and flocks of bushtits, chickadees and the little downy woodpecker in winter. The western tiger swallowtail requires poplars as a food plant during its caterpillar stage and the trees shade creeks and sloughs, providing fish habitat. As residents come to understand the value of these trees, they should be given much better protection.

The red alder is a very important component of the landscape

Sometimes referred to as a "weed" tree, the **red alder** is also a very important ecosystem component. It pioneers disturbed sites and acts as a nitrogen recycler. Its roots have nodules that absorb nitrogen from the air and convert it into a useable form within the tree, then return this essential element to the soil through the fallen leaves.

Older stands of red alder, especially along streams and sloughs, attract vireos, warblers and tanagers. These in turn eat the many small flies and larvae found among the leaves. Shading the water, alders keep the stream cool enough for juvenile fish, which feed on insects falling from the branches overhead.

Alder seeds are consumed by pine siskins and American goldfinches and black-capped chickadees feed at the catkins. The leaves are larval habitat for butterflies and moths.

Red alder with horsetails on Deas Island: alders help increase the amount of nitrogen in the soil.

Red alders turn a beautiful warm red in early spring, due to the gradual swelling and blooming of their catkins before their leaves emerge. They produce numerous seeds, an estimated three million during their thirty year lifetime. So many animals and birds feed on the seeds and browse on the seedlings that on average only one will survive to make a mature tree. Nonetheless, red alders are a very common tree around Boundary Bay, particularly in open areas along stream banks and on the floodplains.

For thirty years, the large colony of great blue herons at Point Roberts lived in a grove of these deciduous trees. The huge stick nests balanced on the spindly trunks in a most precarious manner.

The showy flowers of the **Pacific dogwood** delighted plant collectors in the 1790s, when it was introduced to England. It is the provincial floral emblem of British Columbia. It once grew in local Douglas-fir forests, but sadly most of these wild trees succumbed to anthracnose fungus. Garden specimens seem to have more resistance to this blight, and now many dogwood varieties flourish in the suburbs. The berries are eaten by birds, such as thrushes, waxwings and woodpeckers.

Other important tree species around Boundary Bay include **Sitka spruce**, **paper birch**, and **Pacific crabapple** (*see Wildlife Habitats pages 20 - 23*). The interesting variety of local trees contributes to the region's amazing wildlife diversity.

Paper birches provide excellent habitat for many birds, even when they decay.

FERNS & HORSETAILS

Woodlands in early summer are full of fresh, green fern fronds. This ancient order of plants flourishes in the mild and misty coastal climate, particularly along stream banks and narrow ravines.

The large **sword fern** is a very common, evergreen, undergrowth plant in Douglas-fir and cedar hemlock forests, and one of the first plants to appear after a forest fire. Tall fronds of **bracken fern** prefer drier, open areas and die back in winter. Other ferns to look for include the **deer fern**, with its special spore-bearing fronds, as well as the delicate, deciduous **lady fern** and the triangular fronds of the **oak fern** (*see photo page 191*).

Ferns are perennial plants that characteristically have no flowers or seeds. The next generation is produced either from underground stems or from spores, a simple type of cell with only one set of chromosomes.

In mid-summer, ferns develop little brown spots on the underside of the frond leaflets. These are the spore cases. On a dry day when they are ripe, the cases burst open releasing thousands of microscopic spores. Some of these settle in soil and await a shower of rain. This is the signal for the spore, now transformed into a gametophyte, to quickly develop

Sword fern fiddlehead in early spring.

male and female sex organs and for fertilization to take place. After that an egg can develop, complete with two sets of chromosomes, roots are put down into the ground and the stem and leaf gradually push upwards, the frond unfurling in characteristic fiddlehead shape.

Fern groves can be found in most local woodlands and ravines. They generally avoid bogs, where they are replaced with acid tolerant plants like sphagnum moss and swamp cabbage.

Further Information

A Field Guide to Ferns and their related families
by Boughton Cobb.

Horsetails

Horsetails are distantly related to ferns. There is some indication that they did not arrive in the Boundary Bay area until the early 1900s, but they are native across much of North America, flourishing in temperate wetlands and damp woodlands (*see photo page 150*).

Field horsetails are common in early spring along dykes, when they push up clumps of creamy brown stalks, later followed by green frondy branches. Although they do not look similar, both growths surprisingly belong to the same plant. The first is a short-lived fertile stalk, bearing spores, and the other is a photosynthesizing, infertile stalk.

Scouring-rush is a very noticeable horsetail at Deas Island, in the Fraser River. Large thickets of it remain evergreen throughout the winter. Its long, straight stalk is sectioned like a bamboo and topped with a little cone. Bunches are cut for medicinal purposes by Asian families, and many cultures have used the rush as a polishing abrasive, because the cells contain silicon dioxide, the same compound as in sand.

Giant horsetails occur in some damp areas along the foot of the Surrey - Delta uplands. Its young shoots were eaten by Coast Salish people in the spring.

GRASSES, SEDGES & RUSHES

Grasses, sedges and rushes are the dominant plants in the estuary landscape, so learning about them deepens one's appreciation and understanding of the ecosystem.

At first glance, they appear very similar, with green shoots in spring turning to dry, yellow and brown stalks as summer progresses. Closer inspection will reveal a wonderful variety of form, colour and texture, from the chocolate-brown nobble and fluffy spike of the **cattail** or the delicate silver of the **hair grasses**, to soft, red waves of a patch of

Dune grass in Boundary Bay Regional Park

Yorkshire fog or the spiky geometry of the **sawbeak sedge**.

Identification can be a challenge for this group of flowering plants. Several hundred native grass species occur naturally in British Columbia and Washington and many more have been introduced by farmers and gardeners. Wheat, oats and barley have all escaped from the fields and flourish alongside other foreigners such as **Kentucky blue grass**, **orchard grass** and **timothy**.

Closer inspection reveals a wonderful variety of form, colour and texture

Enjoy the colours and textures of grasses like this reed canary grass.

Grasses have fibrous roots, mostly hollow, jointed stems, long narrow leaves and an "inflorescence" or head of many tiny flowers, born on the top of a stalk. The flowers are soon replaced with dozens of little seeds which blow away in the wind, creating next year's field of grass. New plants also grow by budding off thick underground stems called rhizomes. Together these methods of reproduction make the grass family a persistent and widespread ground cover.

Popular species for lawns and forage, such as wheatgrass and bluegrass, are perennials, with creeping rhizomes and the ability to send up new shoots

when repeatedly cut. Common grasses include several species of **bent grass** and **fescues**, and tall clumps of **reed canary grass**, which flourish in ditches, along roads and in other soggy, disturbed areas. The **common reed** is rather uncommon locally despite its name. It grows up to 3 m (10 ft) tall and has large silky plumes, pinkish-purple in flower, fading to yellow-grey as the seeds form.

Sedges belonging to the *Carex* genus, have stems with triangular cross-sections and sharply defined edges. **Rushes**, conversely, typically have

For more about Marshes see pages 7 - 9

smooth, round stems. Both stems are solid, not hollow like grasses and reeds. Sedges are unusual in having different male and female flowers with interesting shapes, colours and textures: look for strange bristly cones, drooping tassels or upright spikes in green, brown or yellow. The habitat gives a clue to species. Dunes at Boundary Bay Regional Park are a good place to see the spiky flower heads of the **big-headed sedge**, rising on short stalks from a rosette of leaves. The female spikes are less conspicuous and grow on separate plants. Their underground rhizomes bind the sand dunes, stabilising the sediment and allowing other plants, such as sheep sorrel and Pacific silverweed to grow.

At the mouth of the Fraser River grow dense stands of **Lyngby's sedge**, a favourite food for snow geese and trumpeter swans. It has four or five drooping spikes, some of which are male and some female, falling from short stalks on each flower stem.

Carex sedges, such as the **slough sedge**, **Kellogg's sedge** and **Merten's sedge** can be found along rivers, streams and ponds, and in boggy wetlands. Striking **sawbeak sedge** forms bright patches of gold in wet meadows, when its spiky flower is in bloom among the silverweed and small-flowered forget-me-not.

Bulrushes are sedges belonging to the *Scirpus* genus. The largest

bulrush is **tule**, in both its soft and hard stemmed forms. The brown flower head springs from the top of a long tubular stalk, so nothing interferes with the smoothness of the stem. It is ideal for weaving into mats and baskets. Coast Salish women gathered bundles in late summer and laid them out to dry, sewing them together with fibre twine. The pithy cores of the stems provided insulation and the mats rolled up easily.

"Sedges have edges and rushes are round, they grow by the water where willows abound" ~ Anon.

Some other *Scirpus* sedges found in marshes and sloughs of the Boundary Bay area are widespread **American bulrush**, **seacoast bulrush** and the attractive **small-flowered bulrush**, with its spray of tiny white flowers. The related **creeping spike-rush** is

Further Information

Field Guide to the Grasses, Sedges and Rushes of the United States by Edward Knobel is still a classic on the subject, with beautiful line drawings.

Richmond Nature Park herbarium www.geog.ubc.ca/richmond/city/plants.htm has information on some of the local species.

distinguished by its solitary blob of a flower at the end of its stalk. Waterfowl eat the seeds of bulrushes, and their dense stands provide cover for mallards, Virginia rails, muskrats and red-winged blackbirds.

Rushes are often confused with bulrushes but belong to a separate family, *Juncus*. There are many species; they typically possess deep green, rounded stalks and leaves. Small brown flowers often grow as a tuft from the side or top of a stalk. The commonest rush around Boundary Bay is the **soft rush**, which grows in tall thick clumps in ditches and marshy areas.

The spectacular and familiar **cattail** belongs to yet another family. This marsh plant has tall, grass-like leaves and a brown, cylindrical, female flower spike topped with a fluffy whitish cone of male flowers.

Cattail marshes are full of wildlife, and the plant has many traditional Coast Salish uses. Generations of babies were raised with diapers of cattail fluff, the leaves were an excellent material for mat-making, whether sewn or twined, charcoal from cattail was used for tattooing and a rolled thread was made from the leaf bases.

MOSSES

Visitors to the upland forests are soon struck by the abundance of emerald mosses, thick on the ground, clustered on tree trunks and draped from branches. The soft, cushiony mosses, with their delicate little fronds and fragile hold on earth, belong to a very ancient group of simple-structured plants, the bryophytes, that reproduce by spores, not seeds.

Mosses possess chlorophyll, the green pigment that enables plants to produce their own food by photosynthesis. Their roots are almost non-existent and they bear no flowers. When they are ready to produce spores, they send up stiff little stalks, often black or red, topped by small, pointed spore cases. The spores scatter, blown on the wind or caught on animals. Rather complex

Cattails

interim stages follow before the new generation produces and sheds spores to carry on the life cycle.

Mosses make a rich habitat. Their spongy surfaces retain fresh water, keeping a damp environment for amphibians and insects. Songbirds and small animals line their nests with soft moss, and deer browse on the greenery. Lacking significant roots, mosses gain their nutrients from water droplets and the air. They absorb nitrogen and carbon dioxide, and recycle them through the forest.

About 40 species of moss have been recorded in the Boundary Bay area. Three of the commonest in upland forests are **oregon beaked moss**, a showy, fern-like species that grows in blankets on shady ground and over fallen trees, **step moss** that is common in seepage areas, and **cat's**

Haircap moss with red spore cases. Many species of moss are present in Boundary Bay forests.

tail moss which can cover a tree, dangling in long, hairy strands from overhead branches. **Red roof moss**, an exposure-tolerant species and perhaps the commonest moss in the world, grows on roofs and roadsides all around Boundary Bay.

Peat mosses

While the greenest mosses belong in the damp and shady west coast forests, a separate yellow-green group, with very prolific growth, is found in our local bogs. These are the **sphagnum**, or **peat mosses**, growing three to four metres (10 - 13 ft) deep in Burns Bog.

Sphagnum requires an extremely wet, acid environment with low nutrient levels, and soon becomes the dominant plant where these conditions are met. Even decay bacteria cannot tolerate such an extreme environment, so sphagnum decomposes at a very slow rate. It keeps accumulating as thick layers of peat, with the lower stems buried

Nurse Logs

Mosses grow so thickly on the woodland floor in damp areas that it is difficult for the seeds of trees and other plants to find a place to germinate.

Nurse logs, fallen trees that lie on top of the mossy carpet, provide a solution. Drier and more accessible than the soil, they act as seed nursery sites, giving more protection from damping-off fungi that kill many seedlings.

deep in the bog. This means that a single sphagnum moss plant can actually be thousands of years old. In Burns Bog, the centre of the bog is wetter than the perimeter, so the sphagnum there grows much faster than it decays. Underlying layers of peat raise the centre of the bog in a dome 5 m (16 ft) above the surrounding delta. The moss acts like a sponge, soaking up rainwater and keeping water levels high.

A single sphagnum moss plant can be thousands of years old

The Coast Salish found many uses for mosses, especially sphagnum, with its superior absorbency and antibiotic qualities. Moss supplied baby diapers, steam pit linings, wound dressings, disposable wipes for removing fish slime, stuffing for pillows and infant bedding. More modern uses include packing for armaments and soil for nurseries and gardens.

Further Information

Some Common Mosses of British Columbia by W.B. Schofield

Plants of Coastal British Columbia, Including Washington Oregon & Alaska by Jim Pojar and Andy MacKinnon

LICHENS

A profusion of lichens is a good indicator of clean air. These subtle coloured organisms grow in crusty masses on trees or ramble across the ground in boggy areas, relying on rain and air for nutrients.

The world of lichens enters the realm of fantasy, with names such as **witch's hair**, **pixie cups** and **dragon cladonia**. There are **frog pelts, lungworts** and **kidney lichens, ragbags, tattered rags** and **forking bones**. The **cladonia** or **bone lichen** family is an abundant one, usually with spiky white branches, topped by a round red fruiting body. There are even lichens that grow on rocks

What is a lichen?

Lichens are not plants, but a bizarre combination of a fungus (ascomycetes or basidiomycetes) and either a green alga or a cyanobacterium. The two types of organism form an association that helps them survive.

The fungus cannot create its own food, for which photosynthesis is necessary, a task only possible for the alga or bacterium. Meanwhile, the simple alga (or bacterium) is protected by the fungus from drying out, especially in summer or on hot rock environments. It is as if the fungus farms the alga for its food.

Pale green reindeer lichen growing amidst bog blueberry in Burns Bog.

at the ocean's edge, such as **sea tar,** a black, stain-like lichen found just above high tide.

Once you start looking closely at lichens, you will get drawn in by the amazing range of shapes and colours. They come in four basic designs: leafy (foliose), spiky (fruiticose), crusts or stains on rocks or trees (crustose) and scaly (squamulose). There are at least 1000 species in the Pacific Northwest and dozens can be found in the Boundary Bay watershed. Some are very noticeable, like the bright orange **xanthoria** or the grey, crinkle-leafed crusts of **hypogymnia** on slow-growing pine trees. Pale antlers of **reindeer lichen** cover the ground in Burns Bog, contrasting with the colourful bog plants and green sphagnum moss. Forest trees are covered with **bitterwort lichen,** the scribbly black designs of **pencil script lichen** and the flat green dusty stains of the **dust lichens,** to name just a few.

Lichens like clean air. According to a recent study in Italy, lung cancer cases correlated with areas in which there were few or no lichens present. This could be just one potential use of these organisms as a biological health indicator.

Further Information

Lichens by William Purvis.

Macrolichens of the Pacific Northwest by Bruce McCune and Linda Geiser

FUNGI

Fungi belong to their own kingdom, neither plant nor animal. There are believed to be several hundred thousand species worldwide. Some of them are microscopically small and others are very large, living mainly underground, and sprouting up colourful fruiting bodies, known as mushrooms or toadstools. An extraordinary diversity can be found in Boundary Bay woodlands, thanks to the mild, damp winters.

While some fungus are renowned for their delicious flavour, others are highly poisonous or hallucinogenic and most are confusingly difficult to distinguish. Beginners beware! Mistakes can be fatal.

Fungi must wait for perfect conditions to emerge, and often

Further Information

Matchmaker: Mushrooms of the Pacific Northwest; Natural Resources Canada website for fungi identification at www.pfc.cfs.nrcan.gc.ca/ biodiversity/matchmaker/

Mushrooms of Western Canada by Helene Schalkwijk-Barendsen

The Vancouver Mycological Society meets regularly at Van Dusen Gardens, Vancouver; www2.icangarden.com/clubs/ VMS

Safety first

All fungus should be handled carefully and treated with caution. Never eat wild mushrooms unless you are thoroughly familiar with them. Every year, Vancouver hospitals treat patients that are suffering toxic effects from poisonous mushrooms.

Animals and birds can consume mushrooms that are poisonous to humans, so do not use this as a guide. Disregard the myth that white-spored mushrooms are edible, as it is certainly not true.

pop up in unexpected places. Tiny fungal spores circulate through the stratosphere on atmospheric currents and blow on the wind, dropping into the soil at random. If the moisture, soil composition and surrounding plants are correct for the particular species, the fungus will start to grow.

The **mycorrhizal fungi**, a network of thin white strands, known as mycelia, spread outwards through the soil, sometimes linking with the roots of trees, shrubs or other suitable plants in a close symbiotic relationship. These networks can cover several square kilometres! In exchange for providing the tree with water, minerals and trace elements from the soil, the fungi obtain some of the sugars made by the tree during photosynthesis. In due season, the mycelia sprout mushrooms containing colourful spores that further propagate the fungus. Northern flying squirrel and Douglas's squirrel consume the mushrooms and spread spores in their droppings (*see page 76*).

Fungi must wait for perfect conditions to emerge and often pop up in unexpected places

Other types of fungus, such as the colourful **sulphur tuft**, decompose and recycle rotten wood, animal and vegetable matter. A third kind is parasitic, growing on trees and sapping them of nutrients, while giving little in return. **Bracket fungi** growing on paper birch and alder are a familiar sight in damp woodlands. Lumpish, grey, **tinder conk fungus** was used by people for many centuries to kindle fires. **Turkey tails** are colourful, striped and banded bracket fungi often seen on fallen logs in the forest.

Sulphur tuft mushrooms

Fairy Rings

Circles of dark green grass on suburban lawns are a sign of the underground network of **fairy ring mushrooms**, slowly growing outwards over the years. A dense crop of small brown mushrooms spring up in the rings, often after rain in September and April.

The **boletes** group of mushrooms have thick, erect stalks, topped by a rounded cap, below which is a spongy structure, often coloured yellow or red. Many other colourful mushrooms, like **agarics** and **honey mushrooms**, have thin or waxy, radiating gills underneath their caps. Placing the cap on a piece of paper overnight will allow spores to drop out, creating a "spore print" with a characteristic colour. This print is essential for fungus identification. The mushroom enthusiast will also look for the presence or absence of a ring on the stalk or slime on the cap, the growth form and location of the clump and of course the colour and shape of the fruiting body.

Not all fungi are shaped like the traditional toadstool. The **orange peel fungus** grows on the ground, looking like its name, and **carbon antlers** grow in little black and white spikes from rotting logs. Skinny little **fairy finger**s sprout straight up from the ground in fall, different species varying from white to deep orange. **Puffballs** grow as perfect spheres, before bursting open to shed their spores into the air. Fungi are very versatile and a few will even live in water, such as the **chitrid fungi** that parasitise freshwater fish and amphibians. They have been implicated in the decline of some amphibians.

SLIME MOULDS

The weird and wonderful slime moulds are neither animals, plants nor fungi, but are provisionally placed by biologists in the *Protista* kingdom. Slime moulds move and eat like animals, but reproduce by means of spores, similar to the simpler plants and fungi.

There are several distinct types: the plasmodial slime moulds are composed of a large single cell, with multiple nuclei, while the cellular slime moulds are single cell organisms that sometimes aggregate into large swarms. One common, golden yellow slime mould, living in damp hemlock forests around Boundary Bay, is the aptly named **scrambled egg slime**. Another slime, found on Douglas-fir logs, is white and almost crystalline, like fallen snow.

Slime moulds are increasingly being used in the study of genetics. This unusual group is certainly worthy of more attention from the amateur naturalist.

WILDLIFE GARDENING

The secret to successful wildlife gardening is having plenty of trees, shrubby, overgrown areas and, best of all, a source of freshwater.

Fallen leaves, log piles and scruffy undergrowth will provide welcome shelter for resident and visiting songbirds, squirrels, shrews, tree frogs and other small animals. Gardens in more densely forested neighbourhoods may have raccoons, flying squirrels, Douglas' squirrels and even black-tailed deer.

Large, mature trees attract owls and hawks, colourful, nectar flowers will bring in hummingbirds and butterflies, and shrubs with seeds or berries, such as crabapple, rowan, red elder and pyracantha, always seem to thrive with life. Birch trees are important for chickadees, woodpeckers and sapsuckers. Poplars, cottonwood, willow and nettle are essential food plants for caterpillars of swallowtail, mourning cloak, red admiral and other beautiful butterflies.

Mourning cloak butterfly

Ponds are wonderful for attracting birds, tree frogs, dragonflies and damselflies, especially if they have running water, a variety of aquatic vegetation and shallow, accessible edges. Even a great blue heron may visit, especially if the pond has fish.

Boundary Bay has a plant zoning classification of 8 and a long growing season.

Pesticides and herbicides are potentially harmful to the health of children and wildlife. Their use is seldom necessary in a garden. Healthy plants, with plenty of compost, humus mulch and air circulation, will naturally repel pest infestations. Furthermore, pulling weeds by hand after spring rain is satisfying exercise. Every garden needs beneficial insects to undertake pollination of all the flowers and to eat smaller, harmful insects, such as aphids. A pesticide-free garden will be full of insect-eating birds like chickadees, warblers, swallows and roaming flocks of tiny bushtits, as well as bright-winged butterflies and dragonflies.

Obtaining native northwestern plants is a little more trouble than buying petunias, but is worth the effort, and they can be intermingled with ornamentals. Plants should not be dug up from the wild. Lots of good books are being written on wildlife gardening, with ideas on planting,

Star-flowered false solomon's seal is a beautiful native ground cover.

pond building and avoiding pests. Long-time naturalist, Bill Merilees' book also includes designs for birdhouses, feeders, orchard mason bee homes and squirrel boxes. Birdhouses are places for birds to build nests and hatch eggs, not year-round homes, although sometimes they are used for winter roosts. Boxes and feeders are easy to make and a fun project for families.

Feeding birds and gardening are great ways to enjoy nature in your own backyard. It is a good idea to only fill bird feeders from late fall to early spring, because there is plenty of natural food around for the rest of the year, and it is healthier for nestling birds to be fed insects, rather than grains. However, having feeders full year-round keeps birds close by. Keep feeders clean to avoid the growth of mould and fungus, and allow them to dry completely before filling with fresh seed.

Attract hummingbirds to your garden by planting red, orange or pink flowers. such as columbine, red-

Chestnut-backed chickadees commonly visit garden bird feeders.

flowering currant, bleeding heart, honeysuckle, twinflower, or Nootka rose. Fuschias, petunias, bee balm and red runner beans also work well. Flowers will supply all the nectar that is needed and maintenance is simple. Hummingbird feeders with a red plastic flower and 1:4 sugar to water solution can be used (some authorities now recommend 1:2). It is essential that they are well maintained, which means very regular, thorough washing with hot water and vinegar. Honey, red food colouring or artificial sweeteners should never be used in feeders.

Bird feeders should be placed clear of windows that the birds might fly into, and out of reach of cats, which kill millions of birds each year across the continent. It is almost impossible to defend against marauding sharp-shinned hawks, that suddenly swoop down and snatch a feeding sparrow. If predators become a problem, it is better to stop using feeders and instead plant shrubs to provide food and shelter.

Further Information

The New Gardening for Wildlife by Bill Merilees

Naturescape British Columbia, Georgia Basin booklets
www.hctf.ca/nature.htm
1 800 387 9853

Washington's Backyard Wildlife Sanctuary Program:
www.wdfw.wa.gov/wlm/backyard/

Douglas College Institute of Urban Ecology for native plant gardening, ethnobotany, demonstration gardens:
604 527 5522   www.douglas.bc.ca

NATURE DESTINATIONS

"There is no other site in Canada that supports the diversity and number of birds found in winter in the Fraser River delta."

~ Rob Butler & Wayne Campbell – The Birds of the Fraser River Delta

This section of the book describes many interesting destinations where nature and scenery can be enjoyed in and around the Boundary Bay watershed. Both British Columbia and Washington State locations have been included: if you intend to cross the international border allow plenty of time, and remember to bring your passport. Destinations are all suitable for day trips from nearby towns and cities, or combined as part of a longer visit.

Season, weather and time of day will determine what wildlife is present. Marine and shoreline destinations are tide sensitive: check local tide tables for best conditions. Nature observation becomes easier with practice, so consider taking a guided walk with one of the local groups mentioned in the text.

Every effort has been made to provide up-to-date information, but changes are bound to occur. Consult tourist guides to this part of the Northwest Coast for travel and accommodation information; a few useful contact details have been provided where possible with each entry. Never leave valuables in your car as unfortunately thefts occasionally occur from parking areas, even in the quietest spots. Map numbers refer to map on page vi - vii.

Enjoy your nature-watching trip!

British Columbia public transportation

Coast Mountain Bus services, TransLink: 604 953 3333
www.translink.bc.ca.

B.C. Ferries 1 888 223 3779
www.bcferries.bc.ca.

The small, brown, western pine elfin can be a difficult butterfly to find.

Sunset on the Strait of Georgia from Lighthouse Park, Point Roberts, WA.

ROBERTS BANK & BRUNSWICK POINT

MIGRATION HOT SPOTS

Roberts Bank is one of the three components of the Fraser River Estuary Important Bird Area, an internationally recognized migration and wintering place on the Pacific Flyway for waterfowl, shorebirds and birds of prey. It is the traditional land of the Tsawwassen First Nation and other Hul'qumi'num-speaking Coast Salish. Brunswick Point at the mouth of the river is low-lying and marshy. The dyke trail leads past the remains of old canneries, blackberry tangles, extensive cattail and sedge marshes and towards the intertidal flats of Roberts Bank, terminating at the railway track to Roberts Bank Port.

ROBERTS BANK

Wildlife highlights

Roberts Bank is known for its birds. Migration time sees the arrival of thousands of shorebirds and waterfowl; many also winter here, together with loons and grebes. Great blue herons nest nearby & feed in the intertidal. Caspian terns gather in summer at the compensation lagoon at the ferry terminal. Black oystercatchers nest, which is unusual for mainland British Columbia. Rare birds recorded include ivory gull and grey-headed rosy finch. Killer whales and sea lions occur seasonally. Eelgrass meadows and subtidal areas are important habitat for Dungeness crab, salmon and waterfowl. The flats are crossed by both the B.C. Ferries' and the Vancouver Port Authority causeways; an increasing number of structures are associated with both operations. Roberts Bank is awaiting formal designation as a provincial Wildlife Management Area.

Common goldeneye displaying.

Access: Cycle lanes along Highway 17 lead to the ferry terminal; a gravel road on the south side of the causeway allows beach access. The compensation lagoon is visible from the cycle trail on the north side; note there is no highway shoulder for pulling over or parking. Access to the port causeway is limited. Be aware of fast-moving, heavily laden trucks at all times. For walking, there is a dyke trail from River Road West, Ladner, to Brunswick Point. Tsawwassen First Nation reserve lies between the two causeways; the salt marsh and shore is private property.

Amenities: Ferry terminal has paid parking, washrooms, cafes & shops, but ocean views are limited due to heavy traffic.

Location: Ferry at SW end of Highway 17, Delta; bus 620 from Vancouver. Roberts Bank port at west end of Deltaport Way, Delta. MAP B4 - B5

BRUNSWICK POINT

Wildlife highlights

In winter, rough-legged hawks, peregrine falcons and short-eared owls join resident northern harriers and barn owls foraging over the point. Snow geese and trumpeter swans gather seasonally at the river mouth to feed on sedge tubers. Other seasonal species include American bittern, marsh wrens, red-winged blackbirds, cottontails and garter snakes. Coyotes hunt for voles in nearby fields. Blackberry tangles have wintering sparrows and finches.

Amenities: Walking & cycling trail along dyke; no washrooms.
Location: Brunswick Point is at the western end of River Road West, Delta. Nearest bus service C86 to River Rd at 46A St. near Ladner Village. MAP B4

Further information
Important Bird Areas
www.ibacanada.ca
VNHS Bird Hotline 604 737 3074

Alaksen National Wildlife Area, on Westham Island, was the first Ramsar Site - a "Wetland of International Importance especially for Waterfowl" - in British Columbia.

The intertidal areas of Boundary Bay, Roberts Bank and Sturgeon Bank far exceed the criteria for Ramsar designation, but have not yet been listed.

WELLINGTON POINT PARK

Wildlife highlights

A small municipal park for boat access to the river mouth, this park has views of Canoe Pass, Westham Island and Fraser River. Look for wintering western grebes, great blue herons, double-crested cormorants, bald eagles and sea lions.

Amenities: Public boat launch, parking.
Location: River Rd West, Delta.
MAP B4

In March and November, the sky above Westham Island is full of snow geese.

ALAKSEN & REIFEL BIRD SANCTUARY

TOP BIRDING ON WESTHAM ISLAND

Famous as the home of the George C. Reifel Migratory Bird Sanctuary and Alaksen National Wildlife Area, Westham Island is a mecca for birders. It is also a fertile farming area, growing crops from strawberries to pumpkins. Farms offer fruit-picking in season, farm-fresh produce and special events. Spectacular flocks of snow geese, over 80,000 in a peak year, fly in from Wrangel Island, Russia, from early October onwards. They can be seen feeding on fields around Alaksen and Reifel, at the mouth of the Fraser River.

ALAKSEN NATIONAL WILDLIFE AREA

Alaksen National Wildlife Area is an internationally recognised bird habitat and Ramsar site, comprising fields and wetlands at the mouth of the Fraser River, on the north shore of Westham Island. Alaksen is also home to the Canadian Wildlife Service's Pacific Research Centre.

Wildlife highlights
Waterfowl here include lesser snow geese, best in October, November, March and April. Also watch for shorebirds, grebes, songbirds, bald eagles, barn owls, Yuma bats, coyotes, beaver and harbour seals.

Amenities: The grounds and walking trails along tree-lined dykes are open to the public on weekdays from 9.00 am to 4.00 pm. Visitors should sign in at the office.
Location: Adjacent to Reifel Bird Sanctuary at Robertson Road, Delta. MAP B3
Information: Canadian Wildlife Service 604 940 4700 or www.pyr.ec.gc.ca

REIFEL MIGRATORY BIRD SANCTUARY

The George C. Reifel Migratory Bird Sanctuary is an attractive destination for keen birders or for a family outing. The shaded, winding trails provide excellent views of birds amidst the beautiful scenery of the Fraser River estuary.

Wildlife highlights
This exciting birding destination is ideally situated to attract early and late migrants and rarities. It has a bird list of 282 species, including shorebirds, waterfowl, owls, hawks, falcons, black-crowned night herons, sandhill cranes, flycatchers and swallows. Bird nesting takes place from March to June, with young ones

> **Reifel Migratory Bird Sanctuary**
> www.reifelbirdsanctuary.com
> 604 946 6980. Bird checklists are available at the gift shop.

active May through June; shorebird migration is at its height in August, and waterfowl flocks start arriving in September and October. The lesser snow geese reach a peak in November. Over 22 species of mammals occur, including mink, beaver, muskrat, river otter, raccoons, Columbian black-tailed deer, Douglas's squirrel, grey squirrel, Pacific jumping mouse, and even killer whales well offshore.

Amenities: Walking trails, wheelchair accessible, viewing blinds, guided tours, Sunday morning walks at 10.00 am, gift shop, warming hut, washrooms, opportunity to feed ducks, small admission charge. November is Snow Goose month. Opening hours are 9.00 am to 4.00 pm daily.
Location: 5191 Robertson Road, Delta, B.C. on Reifel Island off the northwestern end of Westham Island.
MAP B3

Some superlatives about the Fraser River estuary

The Fraser River is the greatest salmon river in the world.

The Fraser River estuary is the largest on the Pacific coast of Canada.

The Fraser River estuary is the top wintering bird site in Canada.

The Fraser River delta is in one of the most seismically active regions in Canada.

The lower Fraser River valley contains some of the most productive agricultural land in Canada.

Reifel viewing tower is framed by the distant backdrop of the North Shore mountains.

THE FRASER RIVER

WORLD FAMOUS SALMON RIVER

The wide main or south arm of the Fraser River brings over three-quarters of the total river flow to the sea. Several fishing bars and parks line the south bank. Juvenile salmon migrate down the river in spring, adults return in summer and fall.

DEAS ISLAND PARK AND SLOUGH

The tall stands of cottonwood and alder along the water, and the fine views of the river, make this Greater Vancouver Regional District park a popular destination. It is an excellent spot in spring to look for early bird migrants, such as hummingbirds, swallows and warblers. Wildlife here is very seasonal and best times are early morning or late afternoon.

Wildlife highlights

Yuma bats have a summer maternal colony in the attic of Burrvilla, one of the pioneer houses in the park. Look for them, and big brown bats, flying at dusk. Up to 1000 females each give birth to a single young in late summer. Also look for nesting bald eagles, great horned owls, migrant warblers, rufous hummingbirds, cormorants, and salmon.

Amenities: Walking and bridle trails, picnic areas, washrooms, group campsite, viewing tower, boat launch, special events and fun nature programs, such as bat watches. Several pioneer era buildings were relocated to the park. Deas Slough is suitable for kayaking, rowing and other boating on a shared space basis. A timetable of advised times is displayed at the Ferry Road boat ramp, Delta, and at the Municipal Hall in Ladner. The south side of Deas Slough can be reached by the Millennium Trail (a public footpath)from Captain's Cove marina on Ferry Road, Ladner. The trail crosses over Green Slough and passes under Highway 99, with the intention of linking in future to Deas Island.
Location: Park entrance River Rd. at 62B St. Delta. Bus 640, limited hours; MAP C3
Information: GVRD Parks 604 224 5739

LADNER VILLAGE

Originally called Ladner's Landing, Ladner was one of the first locations on the Fraser delta to be farmed in the mid-1800s, and had several large

Marsh and black cottonwood along the Fraser River at Ladner.

salmon canneries. Fresh fish can still be purchased off the dock in summer, but sedimentation of the Fraser River and Chilukthan Slough has greatly changed the look of the waterfront since those pioneering days. The Ladner Christmas Bird Count is often Canada's highest.

Wildlife highlights

This area is renowned for its rare bird sightings, (e.g. white-tailed kite, 1995, western scrub-jay, 2004). Wood ducks are regular in local wetlands.

Amenities: Stores and restaurants in Ladner Village and nearby shopping centres; marina and dock at River Road.
Location: west of Highway 17, at 48th Street Delta; Bus 601 from Vancouver.
MAP C4

SOUTH ARM MARSHES

This secluded group of islands, in the middle of the Fraser, is a provincial Wildlife Management Area and only accessible by boat. The low-lying, wetland habitat, covering 810 ha (2002 ac), is ideal for waterfowl of all kinds and hunting takes place on a seasonal basis. Currents on the Fraser River can be strong at certain times of year or tide.

Wildlife highlights

Wetland species: beaver, muskrat, dabbling ducks, marsh wren, great blue heron, red-winged blackbird.

Bird checklists are available for the marshes from B.C. Ministry of Environment: 604 582 5200
10470 152 St., Surrey, B.C. V3R 0Y3

Location: Woodward, Duck, Barber, Kirkwood, Rose Islands in the main arm of the Fraser River, off the Ladner shore, and adjacent Ladner Marsh.
Access: by boat or kayak, but be aware of hunters using the islands during the hunting season (Sept. - March). Community shuttle C88 to Ferry Road, Ladner, or buses 606 and 608 (limited hours). MAP B3, B4, C3, C4

LADNER HARBOUR PARK AND LADNER MARSH

Ladner Marsh lies at the mouth of the Fraser River, a landscape of cattails and tule, riddled with tidal creeks and sloughs and flanked by cottonwoods, alders and Nootka rose. This estuarine habitat really comes to life in the spring. It is a pleasant place to explore by kayak.

Wildlife highlights

Look for nesting Virginia rail, sora, downy woodpecker, mourning dove, western tanager, marsh wren, red-winged blackbird, warblers, vireos, black-headed grosbeak, cormorants, herons and loons on the river, eastern cottontail rabbits, beaver, muskrat, American mink and garter snakes.

Amenities: walking trails, Ladner Harbour Park has picnic tables, washrooms; nearby Ladner Harbour for commercial fishing vessels and an adjacent marina. Kayak and boat tours of Ladner Marsh and the Fraser River are available, see local listings.
Location: Ladner Marsh south entrance, and Ladner Harbour Park: River Road, Ladner; look for binocular logo on blue B.C. Wildlife Watch signs. Ladner Marsh north entrance: Ferry Rd. Delta. Community shuttle bus C88, and bus 606 or 608 (limited hours) to Ferry Rd.
MAP C3 - C4

TAKE A FIELD TRIP WITH NATURALISTS

Federation of BC Naturalists
604 737 3057   www.naturalists.bc.ca

Young Naturalists Club of BC
604 737 3057   www.ync.ca

Vancouver Natural History Society
www.naturalhistory.bc.ca/VNHS

Green Club (Mandarin & English)
604 327 8693   www.greenclub.bc.ca

TERRA NOVA, RICHMOND

Wildlife highlights
Terra Nova, beside Sturgeon Bank, is a characteristic delta ecosystem with old fields, wetlands and woodlot. Look for northern harrier, Virginia rail, short-eared and long-eared owls, snow geese, dabbling ducks, sparrows, vireos and swallows.

Location: West end of Westminster Hwy, Richmond. Buses 401, 491. MAP B2

IONA BEACH REGIONAL PARK, RICHMOND

Located at the tip of Lulu Island, just outside the Boundary Bay watershed, and with about 300 listed species, Iona is such a hot spot for birders that it deserves inclusion here. Habitats at this 114 ha (282 ac) park range from marsh to deep water.

Wildlife highlights
Shorebirds, gulls, loons, waterfowl, longspurs and snow buntings can be seen here, best in fall and winter. Many rare birds have been observed, especially after southerly gales.

Amenities: Washrooms, walking path. The 4 km (2.5 mi) South Jetty reaches into the mud flats of Sturgeon Bank. Sewage ponds (limited access).

Location: on Ferguson Road, Sea Island, Richmond, northwest of the Vancouver International Airport. The nearest public transport is C90 from Airport Square to McDonald Beach park. Cycling is possible on flat roads and cycle paths through out Richmond. Do not leave valuables in car. MAP B2

STEVESTON & RICHMOND DYKES

Steveston is a historic fishing village at the mouth of the Fraser River. Nearby Sturgeon Bank is a vast area of marshes and mud flats lying between the Main and North arms of the river. The marshes are bordered by a dyke trail between Garry Point Park and Terra Nova, linked to other trails throughout Richmond.

Wildlife highlights
Snow geese, ducks, bald eagles in winter, herons, nesting marsh wrens, red-winged blackbirds, coyotes and harbour seals are local highlights.

Amenities: Steveston Village has Georgia Cannery National Historic Site, restaurants, shops, fishing harbour (fish sales in season).
Location: Garry Point and dyke entrance at west end of Chatham Rd. Steveston; other entrances from side roads on west side of Richmond, consult local maps. Bus numbers 401, 490, 491 and others. MAP B3

Further information

UBC Geography department website www.geog.ubc.ca/richmond has lots of information on Richmond nature.

The Birder's Guide to Vancouver & Lower Mainland, edited by Catherine Aitchison

BOUNDARY BAY

GLOBALLY IMPORTANT BIRD AREA

A vast sweep of sand and ocean beneath open skies characterizes Boundary Bay, an unspoiled wetland only thirty minutes from Vancouver. The intertidal flats and salt marsh are protected as a provincial Wildlife Management Area. This is a premier bird watching location on the Pacific Flyway with a wide variety of habitats. Boundary Bay is one of the three component areas in the Fraser River Estuary Important Bird Area, a top site in Canada.

Northern harrier

BOUNDARY BAY REGIONAL PARK & CENTENNIAL BEACH

Boundary Bay is reputed to have the warmest water north of California; the soft sand and shallow water of Centennial Beach is a nice place for family picnics and swimming.

The beach is part of 160 ha (395 ac) Boundary Bay Regional Park on the west shore of the bay, much of which is reserved exclusively for wildlife habitat. This in an excellent location for birds and flowers at all times of year.

Wildlife highlights
Winter and migration times are best for birding and 225 bird species have been recorded within the park, including brant, sanderling, avocet, Wilson's snipe, mountain bluebird, western meadowlark, savannah and Lincoln's sparrows, short-eared owl, nesting northern harrier. Coyotes, Townsend's voles, eastern cottontails, Pacific tree frogs, two or three bat species and a locally distributed butterfly, the anise swallowtail also live here. Notable plants include: big-headed sedge, one-sided sedge, small-flowered blue-eyed mary, redstem spring beauty, consumption plant and salt marsh dodder.

Amenities: Facilities at Centennial Beach in the south end of the park include: washrooms, sandy beach and picnic area, playground, concession; Cammidge House, a restored, historic farmhouse, is available for function rentals.
Location: Tsawwassen, South Delta. Entrances and parking off Boundary Bay Rd. and at the east end of 12 Ave. Buses 601, 604 (limited hours). MAP C5
Information: GVRD Parks, 604 224 5739; bird checklists available.

BOUNDARY BAY SHORE AND DYKE TRAIL

Good views of the bay can be obtained by hiking the 16 km (10 mi) Dyke Trail from Beach Grove to Mud Bay Park. The flat, exposed terrain can be very bracing in winter, when a northeast wind howls down from the mountains, but the walk will be enlivened by the spectacle of dunlin flocks wheeling in clouds over the salt marsh, chased perhaps by a peregrine falcon or bald eagle.

Wildlife highlights

Boundary Bay is one of the top destinations on the continent for birds of prey, shorebirds and winter waterfowl. The dyke foreshore and farmland at 64 St. and 72 St. in Delta, have the greatest diversity of raptors in Canada in winter. Ones to watch for are short-eared owl, northern harrier, snowy owl, northern shrike, rough-legged hawk, peregrine falcon, merlin and rare gyrfalcon.

Waterfowl are best viewed at high tide in winter when dabbling ducks occur in the tens of thousands. High tides in August and September are good for shorebirds, especially near the 96 St. and 112 St. dyke entrances (*see note below about access*).

Migrant shorebirds can include black-bellied plovers, western, least, semipalmated, Baird's and pectoral sandpipers, ruddy turnstone and the occasional red knot, bar-tailed godwit or American golden plover.

An old field in June in Boundary Bay Regional Park.

Other wildlife include butterflies, (anise swallowtail, skippers), garter snakes, coyotes and the occasional ermine or mink. Gumweed, fireweed, Douglas aster and silverweed bloom along the banks.

Amenities: Trail for walking, horseriding, cycling, ; washrooms at Heritage Air Park, 104 St and Beach Grove. Some waterfowl hunting September to mid-March, (March 1-10 offshore for brant). Be aware of some quicksand and soft sections on the beach.
Location: The dyke runs along the north shore of Boundary Bay. MAP C4 - E4
Access: Entrances at south end of 64 Street and 72 Street off Highway 10, and 104th Street off Hornby Drive, Delta; also at Mud Bay Park, Surrey & at 17A Ave, Beach Grove: park at Beach Grove Park and walk through alley at corner with Beach Grove Rd. Bus 601 stops at South Delta Recreation Centre; a walkway behind the centre leads to 17A Ave. Community shuttle C76 runs along Highway 10 between Ladner Loop and North Delta. Note: the public cannot drive along the dyke and there is limited parking at road ends, with absolutely none at 112 St., 96 St. or 88 St. To reach prime birding areas in this area, you have to walk or cycle.

BEACH GROVE PARK

A cottonwood grove that is often semi-flooded by winter rains, this is a treasure of a habitat for birds. The park is also a favourite of dog walkers, so birders will want to visit at quiet times of the day or week.

Wildlife highlights
Look for nesting great horned owls, bald eagles, downy woodpecker, northern flicker and wide variety of songbirds, including Hutton's vireo, Lincoln's sparrow, willow flycatcher, western wood pewee, Bewick's wren. Indian plum growing here is one of the first native shrubs to bloom in spring. Coyotes are often seen and heard in the adjacent forest and fields.

Amenities: A small municipal park with washrooms; adjacent woodland is private property.
Location: 6051 17A Ave, Beach Grove, Tsawwassen. Bus 601 to nearby South Delta Recreation Centre. MAP C4

Female gadwall with ducklings.

TSAWWASSEN

Once covered with forests and potato farms, this community, just north of the International Border on the Point Roberts peninsula, has been developed over the last forty years.

Wildlife highlights
Look for bald eagles, turkey vultures, band-tailed pigeons, bushtits and resident raccoons. There is a large great blue heron colony in trees below English Bluff on Tsawwassen First Nation land.

Amenities: Town centre at 56 St. and 12 Ave. B.C. Ferry Terminal for ferries to Vancouver Island and Southern Gulf Islands reached from Highway 17. Point Roberts, WA, land access is only through the International Border on 56 Street, Tsawwassen.
Location: Tsawwassen is off Highway 17, south on 56 St. or 52 St., Delta. Buses 601 & peak time, 602, 603, 604. MAP C5

DIEFENBAKER PARK

Wildlife highlights
The park was once a gravel pit owned by the Kirkland family in the 1920s. It has a small pond and a stand of Douglas-fir on the gravel cliffs. Wildlife includes frogs, dusk-flying bats and introduced red-eared slider turtles.

Amenities: picnic tables, washrooms
Location: 1 Ave., at 56 St. Tsawwassen
MAP C5

Delta Naturalists
www.naturalists.bc.ca/clubs
Boundary Bay Conservation Committee
Box 1251, Delta, B.C. V4M 3T3

FRED GINGELL PARK AND TSAWWASSEN BEACH

This small cliff top park is named for a popular Member of the Legislative Assembly. Watch the evening sun sink behind distant islands or take the steep path down to Tsawwassen Beach.

Wildlife highlights
Watch for bald eagles, osprey, winter wren, loons, surf scoters, harlequin ducks and horned grebes. Great blue herons fly down from nests on the bluff to the tidal flats of Roberts Bank.

Amenities: Viewpoint and pedestrian access by stairs down English Bluff to Tsawwassen Beach. This is the only public access to this beach, other than via Tsatsu Shores Road off Highway 17. All side roads leading down English Bluff are private.
Location: 200 block, English Bluff, Delta. MAP C5

O.W.L (ORPHANED WILDLIFE REHABILITATION)

This is a treatment centre for injured hawks, eagles and owls. Trained volunteers look after up to 300 raptors a year, many of which are then released into the wild. This is a good place to get a close look at these remarkable birds.

Amenities: School programs, special "release" events, gift shop. Wheelchair accessible. Public opening times: Sat-Sun 10.00 am - 3.00 pm; every day July, August.
Location: 3800 72 Street, Delta. MAP D4
Information: O.W.L: 604 946 3171 or visit www.owlcanada.ca

WHITE ROCK & OCEAN PARK

BEACHES & RAVINES

The seaside community of White Rock, with its extensive sandy beaches and sunny south-facing views, is a popular destination for sunbathers and swimmers. Winter is the best time for birding trips, when high tides bring grebes, loons and diving ducks close to shore. Conspicuous on the shoreline is the large white rock after which the town is named; a glacial erratic, it is now regularly painted white. Panoramic views of Mount Baker and the southern Gulf and San Juan Islands are visible from the hillsides and beach.

Take care when crossing the Burlington Northern Railway that follows the coast. Amtrak express trains, particularly, are surprisingly quiet. Do not walk along the line.

Canada geese pair for life and live up to 25 years in the wild. These geese used to all migrate south in winter, but introduced stock now live here year round.

WHITE ROCK BEACH & PIER

Wildlife highlights
Look for rare eared grebe, diving ducks, loons in winter, gull species anytime. Eelgrass meadows shelter marine life and are nursery habitat for salmon & other fish. Resident Anna's hummingbirds can be seen in ravines, sheltered gardens.

Amenities: sandy beaches, pier, restaurants, shops; the main townsite is around North Bluff Road at the top of the cliffs. White Rock Museum and Archives is in the old station building on the waterfront.
Location: Beach access 8 Ave & Marine Drive; Community shuttles C51 and C52 from White Rock Centre. MAP E5 - F5

Further information

Friends of Semiahmoo Bay Society and the *Birds on the Bay* celebration & events: 604 536 3552 or visit www.birdsonthebay.ca

White Rock & Surrey Naturalists www.naturalists.bc.ca/clubs

White Rock Visitor Info Centre: www.whiterockchamber.com 604 536 6844

1001 STEPS, KWOMAIS POINT & OCEAN PARK

Beautiful views of blue sea, distant islands and snow-capped Olympic mountains can be had from the top of the extravagantly named 1001 Steps. This steep trail, with actually only 265 steps, leads down Ocean Park bluffs and under the Burlington Northern Railway line to a rocky beach on the shores of Boundary Bay. Kwomais Point, a spiritual site for the Coast Salish, is the southwestern point of the bluff. Be careful to respect no trespassing signs on the railway track, which is in constant use, and be aware of the tide when hiking the shoreline.

Wildlife highlights

Bald eagles, grey whales, grebes & sea ducks are seen seasonally off the rocky beach at the foot of the bluff. Singing fish (plainfin midshipman) spawn in April. Rock pools have purple ochre stars, bay mussels, acorn and thatched barnacles not generally found around Boundary Bay's predominantly sand beaches.

Amenities: A long flight of steps to the beach. No washrooms in this area.
Location: West end of 15A avenue, Ocean Park, South Surrey. More steps and a bridge over the railway from Christopherson Rd., at the west end of 24 Ave., South Surrey, making possible a beach hike and loop back through suburban streets. Nearest bus 351, Crescent Beach to White Rock, then on to Vancouver. MAP E5 - E4

Kwomais Point, Ocean Park, has been a spiritual site for the Coast Salish people for thousands of years.

CRESCENT BEACH & MUD BAY

PACIFIC FLYWAY BIRD DESTINATION

An attractive seaside village in South Surrey, Crescent Beach enjoys sunshine, ocean and wide sandy beaches. Its long Coast Salish history is recalled by the Semiahmoo petroglyph (rock carving) on display in Heron Park at the entrance to the village.

Blackie Spit is a gravel beach jutting into the Nicomekl estuary, bounded by the aptly-named Mud Bay and a marshy lagoon. This whole area is a very important resting and foraging habitat for waterfowl and shorebirds and consequently a protected Wildlife Management Area and part of the Fraser River Estuary Important Bird Area. It is a stopping point on the Pacific Flyway and many unusual and rare species have been seen here, particularly in the fall. Birders and naturalists are advised to go at quiet times of the week and day, as this area is very popular with dog walkers and other beach users.

Sunlight breaks through January storm clouds in the salt marsh of Mud Bay.

BLACKIE SPIT NATURE PARK

About 200 bird species are recorded at Blackie Spit every year. The spit itself is a gravel bar that extends north from Crescent Beach across the mouth of the Nicomekl River. It is managed by Surrey Parks. The eastern side of the spit has salt marsh, lagoons and sloughs, lined with hedgerows and walking trails.

Wildlife highlights

The spit is renowned for rare bird sightings, especially shorebirds, such as long-billed curlew, marbled godwit and willet, and even a brown pelican has paid a visit. Summer songbirds include common yellowthroat, Lincoln's sparrow, warbling vireo, yellow warbler and cedar waxwing.

Harbour seals are particularly common in the waters of Mud Bay, muskrats swim in the sloughs and raccoons and several bat species can be observed after dark.

The Nicomekl estuary is the only location around the bay where purple martins breed; look for them in summer at nest boxes over water near the marina. Hundreds of moulting red-necked grebes gather in the estuary in fall.

Greater and lesser yellowlegs and dowitchers are among shorebird species regularly seen in the tidal lagoons, together with large numbers of waterfowl. Dabbling ducks gather to moult and feed in the sloughs in good numbers.

Blackie Spit is a shingle bar stretching into Mud Bay.

Amenities: Blackie Spit: boat, kayak launch, car parks, washrooms; walking trails.
Dogs should not be allowed to disturb wildlife in this important migratory site. Please respect dog on leash signs.
Crescent Beach village has several cafes and restaurants; public washrooms.
Location: Blackie Spit 3124 McBride Ave. Crescent Beach; Crescent Beach village is at the west end of Crescent Road, South Surrey. Bus 351 runs between Crescent Beach, White Rock, South Surrey Park and Ride, and Vancouver. MAP E4

Further information

For more about Migration *see pages 41 - 45*, Pacific Flyway *see page 42* Spits and sand dunes *see page 5*

Fraser River Estuary Important Bird Area: visit www.ibacanada.ca

Purple martins also nest at Maplewood Flats in North Vancouver, a Wild Bird Trust of B.C. reserve. www.wildbirdtrust.ca

MUD BAY PARK AND DYKE

Mud Bay Park has views of fields, shorelines and two river estuaries, all excellent wildlife habitat. The Boundary Bay Dyke Trail, bordered by farmland, runs along the bay. It connects Mud Bay Park and Beach Grove, Delta. There is no public access to farmland, dyke or railway bridges between the Serpentine and Nicomekl rivers.

One of the best placess for shorebirds is the salt marsh at the south end of 112 Street, Delta, near the site of an old oyster cannery. A few wooden pilings are all that remain of this once thriving industry.

Wildlife highlights
Mud Bay is visited by thousands of wintering and migrating waterfowl and shorebirds every year. Birding is best an hour or two before high tide, when birds are forced inshore by the rising water. Depending on the season, look for big flocks of dunlin, black-bellied plover, western and least sandpipers and smaller groups of Baird's and pectoral sandpipers. Rarities are regularly spotted, especially in the salt marshes during August and September.

At high tide, shorebirds move to fields behind the dyke, where rare buff-breasted sandpipers and American golden plovers can occur. In February, flocks of trumpeter swans can be seen feeding near here.

A drake (male) mallard flies in to land. Mallards are common residents. Tens of thousands also migrate through or spend the winter.

Other interesting species include Pacific great blue herons, northern harrier, short-eared owls, green-winged teal, northern pintail, coyotes, ermine and garter snakes.

Amenities: Gravel walking and cycling trails; the Dyke Trail from Mud Bay Park to Beach Grove (17A Avenue) is 16 km (10 mi) long. Parking, washrooms at Mud Bay Park and at Delta Heritage Air Park at 104 Street and dyke (part of the Boundary Bay Regional Park).

Location: Mud Bay Park entrance is reached from Colebrook Rd., Surrey, then south on 127A St. and east onto the park access road (Railway Rd.). Parking lot is at the end of the road, just after the bridge under highway 99. View the 112 St. saltmarsh by hiking or cycling the Dyke Trail.

Access: There is absolutely no parking along 112 Sreet. Back roads are used constantly by farm vehicles; do not impede traffic when parking or pulling off to observe wildlife. All agricultural land north of Boundary Bay is private property and wildlife on it can only be viewed from the roadside.

The closest public transport to this area is the White Rock to Vancouver bus 351, that stops at Matthews Exchange at the intersection of Highway 99 and Highway 10.

MAP E4

LITTLE CAMPBELL RIVER VALLEY

WOODLAND PATHS & SALMON STREAMS

The Little Campbell River, barely more than a stream for much of its length, winds through rolling pastoral country. The diminutive "little" distinguishes it from its larger cousin on Vancouver Island, but is not part of the officially gazetted name.

LITTLE CAMPBELL HEADWATERS

Rising in South Langley, only 61m (200 ft) above sea level, the upper streams are lost in marshy fields and woods, where they merge with the waters of Bertrand Creek, a tributary of the Nooksack River.

Wildlife highlights

Look for rare mountain beaver, American beaver, black-tailed deer, garter snakes and salamanders. Birds include green and great blue heron, red-winged blackbird and dabbling ducks.

Amenities: A rural area with quiet back roads for cycling.
Location: South Langley around 16 Avenue & 240 Street. MAP H5

LANGLEY NATURE PARK & IRENE PEARCE TRAIL

Wildlife highlights

Look for fungi, especially in fall, butterflies, dragonflies, garter snakes, woodland flowers, Columbian black-tailed deer, songbirds. Black bears are sometimes seen in this area.

Amenities: An undeveloped, 37 ha (91 ac), nature park with a winding 1.5 km (1 mi) footpath, the Irene Pearce Trail, named after an active local volunteer. It links with the South Langley Regional Trail that runs for 11 km (6.8 mi) from Campbell Valley Park to Zero Avenue at 256 St., in the Nooksack watershed. It is accessible to pedestrians, cyclists and equestrians. Dogs on leash.
Location: 232 St. at 4 Ave. Langley Township MAP H5

SEMIAHMOO FISH & GAME CLUB HATCHERY

The volunteer-run Little Campbell River hatchery raises and releases salmon. The riparian woodland setting is a nice place for a stroll at any season: check at the hatchery for access permission.

Wildlife highlights

Coho, chinook, steelhead and cutthroat trout can be seen from October to January (adults) and in spring (juveniles); also freshwater crayfish, American mink, blacktail deer are common.

Amenities: Fish hatchery, path along river.
Location: 1284 184 Street Surrey. MAP G5
Information: Semiahmoo Fish & Game Club http://sfgc.ca

CAMPBELL VALLEY PARK

One of the most popular of the Greater Vancouver Regional District (GVRD) parks and a designated B.C. Wildlife Watch site, Campbell Valley can be crowded on summer weekends. Wildlife watchers will do best to visit early or late in the day. Vine Maple and Ravine Trails are generally quietest and best for wildlife. The scenic trails wind through woodlands, open fields and wetlands.

Wildlife highlights

A wide variety of species can be found here. Look for Columbian black-tailed deer, Douglas's and grey squirrels, shrews, Hutton's vireo, bushtits, black-capped and chestnut-backed chickadees, spotted towhees, fox and song sparrows, migrant and nesting warblers, Cooper's hawk, red-tailed hawk, barred and great horned owls, salamanders, banana slugs, dragonflies and butterflies. Rare sightings of bobcat have occurred in nearby areas.

Amenities: Walking and horse-riding trails; boardwalk over marsh; the Annand/Rowlatt farmstead dating from 1886, Lochiel Schoolhouse (1924), Demonstration Wildlife Garden (White Rock and Surrey Naturalists), Visitor Centre, Camp Coyote group camp. The Little River loop trail is wheelchair accessible.

Location: The park lies between 200 St. and 216 St., accessed from 8 Ave. and 16 Ave, Langley. Community shuttle bus C63, from Langley City, goes to 20 Ave. in Fernridge, at the northwest corner of the park.

MAP G5

Vine maples in Campbell Valley Park.

Campbell Valley Park

Camp site reservations:
GVRD East Area 604 530 4983
www.gvrd.bc.ca/parks.

B.C. Wildlife Watch bird checklists:
www3.telus.net/driftwood/checklst.

LITTLE CAMPBELL RIVER ESTUARY

The estuary was substantially altered in the early 1900s by the addition of the Burlington and Eastern railway crossing, and later by filling of salt marsh all along the northern bank. The stretch of 8 Ave. between Stayte Road and Maple in White Rock was once tidal water. A beautiful woodland on the south shore of the river remains as valuable wildlife habitat and is private property, part of the Semiahmoo First Nation Reserve. Birds and animals that shelter there can be observed feeding in the estuary from the public park across the river.

Wildlife highlights

Waterfowl, shorebirds, swallows, herons, belted kingfishers are seen near the water; Columbian black-tailed deer, songbirds, woodpeckers, hawks are also local.

Amenities: Public park with manicured lawns, river view, beach access, washrooms.
Location: 8 Ave and Stayte Rd, White Rock, at border with Surrey. Community shuttle buses C51 and C52 from White Rock Centre. MAP F5
Information on the Little Campbell Valley: Little Campbell Watershed Soc. 604 514 4552
A Rocha: www.en.arocha.org/canada

SERPENTINE & NICOMEKL RIVERS
EXPLORING THE WATERSHED

Both the Serpentine and Nicomekl Rivers arise almost 30 km (19 mi) east of Boundary Bay, in a network of narrow tributaries flowing through Surrey and Langley. Several streamside parks provide an opportunity to admire spring flowers, trees and songbirds. The rivers then descend to the floodplain, which is mostly agricultural land.

In its lower reaches, the Serpentine is dyked and straightened. The Nicomekl winds through tree-lined banks for at least some of its length, and the lowest reaches can be paddled by kayak. Spring and fall are particularly pleasant seasons for exploring these river valleys.

ALONG THE SERPENTINE RIVER

TYNEHEAD REGIONAL PARK

Close to the headwaters of the Serpentine River, this spacious 260 ha (642 ac) Surrey park includes second growth woodland, meadows, several creeks, the winding Serpentine River and a salmon hatchery. The park was once a family farm; it is now a B.C. Wildlife Watch site and an excellent place for a family outing.

Amenities: Walking trails (some wheelchair accessible), washrooms, dog off leash area, picnic sites, camping (reservations: 604 432 6352) and salmon hatchery (see below).
Location: Just south of the Trans-Canada highway, between 161 and 176 Sts., Surrey. Only the area west of 168 St. is open to the public. Entrances on 96 Ave, 168 St. and 161 St. Surrey. Buses 501, 509, C74 at East Guildford Park and Ride, and 355, but none go right to the park entrance.
MAP F2

Great horned owl

Wildlife highlights
The forest has Douglas's squirrels, eastern grey squirrels, raccoons, woodpeckers, songbirds, fungi, ferns and woodland flowers. Fish include coho, chum & chinook.

Further information
GVRD Parks 604 520 6442
www.gvrd.bc.ca/parks
Surrey info: www.tourismsurrey.com
Serpentine Enhancement Society
604 589 9127 www.serpentineriver.org

Steelhead fry

TYNEHEAD SALMON HATCHERY

The hatchery in Tynehead Park was built in 1987, and operates as a volunteer enterprise by the Serpentine Enhancement Society.

Wildlife highlights

Coho, chum and chinook are all raised here. Best times for viewing spawning activity are late October and November following fall rains; juvenile coho in March - May, chum fry, April to May, juvenile steelhead year round. The society also offers advice on protecting the watershed, preventing storm drain and ground water pollution, and restoring the health of salmon streams.

Location: 16585 96 Ave. Surrey. MAP F2
Info: www.serpentineriver.org/tynehead

SURREY LAKE

This is a new lake that was created for flood control.

Wildlife highlights

Look for cutthroat, chum, coho, steelhead, Douglas's squirrel, Pacific tree frog, waterfowl, great blue heron, belted kingfisher, dragonflies.

Location: 152 St. between 72 and 76 Ave. Surrey. Approach park by driving north on 152 St. MAP F3

SERPENTINE FEN

A rich habitat of lagoons, meadows, fresh and salt water marshes lying near the mouth of the Serpentine River, this is an excellent area for birding year round. Over 175 bird species have been seen on the 71.3 ha (176 ac) property, including rarities. Officially known as the Serpentine Wildlife Area, this B.C. Wildlife Watch site is managed by Ducks Unlimited but owned by the provincial government.

Wildlife highlights

Look for nesting and migratory waterfowl and songbirds, herons, hawks, eagles and harriers, harbour seal, muskrat. American avocet and yellow-headed blackbird are rare visitors.

Amenities: Walking trails, viewing towers. Location: South of the Serpentine River at 44 Ave., South Surrey; enter from King George Highway, turn west on 44 Ave. and proceed to parking lot down the road, on the left. Entrance to walking trails is on opposite (north) side of 44 Ave. Bus 321, from White Rock to Surrey Central, stops at King George Highway and 44 Ave.
MAP E4 - F4

Further information

BC Field Ornithologists www.bcfo.ca

B.C. Wildlife Watch bird checklists: www3.telus.net/driftwood/checklst

White Rock & Surrey Naturalists www.naturalists.bc.ca/clubs

BC Ministry of Environment 604 582 5200

Ducks Unlimited www.ducks.ca

NICOMEKL RIVER WATERSHED

A series of peaceful parks line the Nicomekl River in an area once known as Langley Prairie. This stretch of the river is rich in both history and wildlife. The Nicomekl is a traditional First Nations route through to the Salmon and Fraser Rivers, and the portage was used by the first Hudson Bay Company explorers.

Further downstream, Elgin Heritage Park borders the south bank shortly before the estuary and Crescent Beach.

NICOMEKL HATCHERY

The Nicomekl Enhancement Society has taken care of the river since 1989, rearing and releasing over two million salmon and providing eggs for classroom incubation. It has re-established chinook and chum salmon runs that were fished out before world war one.

Volunteers participate in regular river clean-ups, restoration work and streambank stabilization. They have mapped the entire Nicomekl system with the assistance of the Langley Environmetal Partners Society, and started a Pacific Salmon Foundation scholarship fund.

Location: 5263 232 St. Langley, B.C.
MAP H4
Access: Open Sundays 09.00 - 13.00.

PORTAGE PARK

James McMillan, his Hudson Bay Company men and Coast Salish guides, stopped here in 1824 to lift their canoes from the Nicomekl River and carry them on a 6.5 km (4 mi) portage to the Salmon River. Later, pioneer settlers Joseph and Georgiana Michaud and their seven children homesteaded on the river bank; their house is now the oldest remaining in Langley.

Wildlife highlights
Find here beaver, raccoons, eastern cottontails, hooded merganser, common goldeneye and songbirds. Fish include coho, chinook, chum, pink, cutthroat, red-sided shiners, sticklebacks, western brook lamprey & brown bullheads.

Amenities: Walking & wheelchair accessible trails, washrooms. Historic Michaud house at Portage Park, 204 St. Interpretive wildlife signage by the Nicomekl Enhancement Society and Langley Field Naturalists is located at the 203 St. entrance.
Location: Along the Nicomekl River through Langley City, from 200 St. to 208 St., adjacent to Brydon Lagoon in the west. Entrances from nearby roads. Langley City is served by buses 320, 501, 502, 590 and by community shuttles C60 - C64. MAP G4

Want to get involved?

Langley Field Naturalists
www.naturalists.bc.ca/clubs
Langley Environmental Partners
www.leps.bc.ca 604 514 4552
Nicomekl Enhancement Society
www.geocities.com/nicomeklh

American coot

REES-CALLARD PARK

This little park has an open meadow and a natural woodland. It was donated by Richard and Laura Rees to Langley Township in 2004, under a new Natural Park area designation. Elementary students participate in enhancement projects.

Amenities: A small 2 ha (5 ac) park with walking trail. Demonstration drought, nectar and shade gardens are planned.
Location: 202 St. and 32 Ave. adjacent to St. Catherine's School, Langley.
MAP G4

BRYDON PARK NATURE LAGOON

The Langley Field Naturalists voluntarily maintain this quiet, 2.5 ha (6.2 ac) wildlife sanctuary and a series of ponds near the Nicomekl River. One activity has been purple loosestrife control; this non-native, invasive flower threatened to choke out the ponds. The wetlands are good for waterfowl and many birds nest here, including great blue herons. Increasing numbers of shorebirds, e.g. dowitchers, are being seen.

Wildlife highlights
Look for American beaver, muskrat, river otters, coyotes, wintering waterfowl, including ruddy duck and hooded merganser, green heron, belted kingfisher, nesting pied-billed grebe, wood duck, great blue heron and bald eagle, as well as painted turtles, American bullfrogs and Pacific tree frogs. Salmon swim up nearby McLellan Creek.

Amenities: Wildlife viewing and walking trails that connect with the river floodplain, Portage Park and Hi-Knoll Park.
Location: 53 Ave. at 198A St. Langley City. Baldi Creek flows into the first pond. A footpath leads from here to Brydon Lagoon and across the Nicomekl floodplain.
MAP G4

HI-KNOLL PARK

This park has a small forest and seasonal wetland at the west end of the Nicomekl River parkland.

Wildlife highlights
Renowned for spring flowers, such as western trillium, white and pink fawn lilies, yellow wood violets. Look also for woodpeckers, owls, Wilson's snipe, songbirds, American beaver and muskrat.

Amenities: This is a natural park with a 1.5 km (1.2 mi) walking trail. The northern part of the park is often closed by flooding in winter.
Location: Colebrook Rd., just west of 196 Street on Surrey, Langley border. MAP G4

Further information
Langley Parks: 604 532 PLAY
Langley Township: www.tol.bc.ca

Vanilla leaf covers some parts of the forest floor of Sunnyside Acres in April.

ELGIN HERITAGE PARK

The massive oldgrowth Douglas-fir around Elgin were the first forests to be logged in Surrey. Trails and settlement soon followed. An attractive period farm house still stands on the bank of the Nicomekl, flanked by tall second growth trees and tidal flats. Walking trails wind through woods and along the river.

Wildlife highlights

Look for forest birds, shorebirds, waterfowl, great blue heron, bald eagles, occasional osprey. Chum, coho and chinook salmon swim up river in late fall.

Amenities: 16 ha (40 ac) park, walking trails, kayak and boat launch at Ward's Marina; washrooms, picnic areas, Stewart Farm House, 1894, pole barn, bunkhouse (open mid-Feb. to mid-Dec. hours vary), Hooser Weaver Centre (limited hours). Info 604 502 6456.
Location: 13723 Crescent Road, South Surrey. Bus 352 from Vancouver.
MAP E4

SEMIAHMOO TRAIL

A winding path across South Surrey - White Rock, this trail leads through leafy residential areas. It traces the route said to have been used by the Semiahmoo and early settlers. A large glacial erratic rock is evidence of the last Ice Age.

Amenities: Walking trail; Elgin Community Hall (1878), schoolhouse (1921).
Location: Trail heads at Crescent Road, 144 St. and 22 Ave., 150 St., South Surrey.
MAP E4 - F4

SURREY WOODLANDS

FORESTS & FLOWERS

Surrey is one of the most extensive cities in Canada; its jurisdiction ranges across much of the watershed of the Serpentine, Nicomekl and Little Campbell rivers. Despite intensive logging, draining and building over the last 150 years, some remnant habitats have survived in parks or on private property, providing shelter for all kinds of wildlife.

CRESCENT PARK

Crescent Park has many of the characteristic trees, ferns, mosses, fungi and flowering plants of the original forested uplands. It is a good place to look for spring migrant songbirds, especially early in the morning.

Wildlife highlights
This is a good location for migrating warblers, vireos and other songbirds in May. Several woodpecker species, band-tailed pigeon, great horned owl, Douglas's squirrel, eastern grey squirrel and flying squirrel (nocturnal) live in the park. Look for black-tailed deer and bats on summer evenings. A naturalised pond has frogs, introduced red-slider turtles, dragonflies and damselflies.

Amenities: Walking trails; picnic sites; public washrooms; children's playground; sports facilities.
Location: Entrances on Crescent Road, 128 Street and 132 Street, South Surrey; bus 352 from Vancouver.
MAP E4
Information: Surrey Parks, Recreation and Culture hotline 604 501 5000

SUNNYSIDE ACRES

Sunnyside Acres Urban Forest has groves of cedar, hemlock and maple, with a rich understorey of ferns, shrubs and wildflowers.

Wildlife highlights
Look for black-tailed deer, Douglas's squirrel, woodpeckers, songbirds, and spring flowers: western trillium, bleeding heart, rattlesnake-plantain.

Amenities: Over 3 km (2 mi) of walking trails; Wally Ross trail is wheelchair accessible. Link with Semiahmoo Trail at 28 Ave. Sports complex, washrooms at 24 Ave. Restricted access to Wildlife Nature Reserve, west of the sports facility.
Location: 148 Street and 24 Avenue in South Surrey; bus 352. MAP F4
Information: Surrey Parks, Recreation and Culture 604 501 5000 www.surrey.ca

Oak fern

GREEN TIMBERS

The last vestige of the great lowland forests that once covered the Fraser valley, the oldgrowth of Green Timbers was all felled in the 1920s. Constant public outcry eventually ensured that trees were replanted in the 1930s, making the park British Columbia's first reforestation project. The dense, second growth forest was designated as a protected park in 1996.

Green Timbers lies in the Serpentine River watershed, on the King Creek tributary. Look for the springboard notches from pioneer loggers on the stumps of giant conifers.

Wildlife highlights

At least 234 species of plants, from 52 plant families, are found here. Specialities include western trillium, Indian pipe, coral root orchid, vanilla leaf and rattlesnake plantain. Fungi colour the ground in fall. Columbian black-tailed deer, Douglas's squirrel, northern flying squirrel (nocturnal), eastern cottontail, raccoon, striped skunk and shrew-moles have been recorded. Herp highlights are four species of salamander and three species of frogs. A constructed lake hosts waterfowl, including nesting pied-billed grebe.

Amenities: Walking trails, lake fishing for rainbow trout (provincial fishing regulations apply), self-guiding nature trail.
Location: Parking at 100 Ave. between 144 & 148 Sts., Surrey. Several buses come fairly close: 345, 502, 325, 326. MAP E2, F2

Towering Douglas-fir at Green Timbers.

BEAR CREEK PARK

A chance to see nature in the heart of the city, this small urban park is noted for its fall salmon run in November, on both Bear Creek and King Creek.

Amenities: Walking trails, picnic sites, washrooms, Surrey Arts Centre, recreational facilities (swimming pool, sports fields, summer water playground).
Location: 88 Avenue east of King George Highway, Surrey. Buses 321 and 394. MAP E2 - E3

Further information

Green Timbers Heritage Society
www.greentimbers.ca

Surrey Parks, Recreation & Culture hotline 604 501 5000

REDWOOD PARK

Peter and David Brown were the twin sons of a pioneering family, who later in life became eccentric recluses in this woodland they planted from seed. The towering trees are testimony to their love of the forest.

Wildlife highlights

The park has the largest stand of Sierra redwood north of the border, two dawn redwoods, clumps of Spanish chestnuts, Chilean monkey puzzle trees, Siberian elm, European beech and many native Canadian trees.

Amenities: Walking trails, washrooms.
Location: 17900 20 Avenue, South Surrey. There is no public transport. MAP G4

The **Sierra redwood**, also known as giant redwood, giant sequoia, or wellingtonia, is native to the inland mountains of California. It can reach a massive size, up to 77 m (253 ft) tall and 6 m (20 ft) diameter!

Dawn redwoods were once native to North America: fossil remains dating back 30 to 60 million years have been found in both British Columbia and Washington. These trees were known only from the fossil record until living trees were discovered in China in 1945. They are deciduous conifers and shed their needles in the fall.

Western trillium and false lily of the valley cover the forest floor at Green Timbers in late April.

Reindeer lichen hummocks on a foggy winter morning in Burns Bog. This lichen gets its name because further north it is a major food source for caribou (called reindeer in Europe).

BURNS BOG

UNIQUE FRASER DELTA WETLAND

A premier wildlife habitat in the heart of the Fraser River delta, Burns Bog is about 4000 ha (10,000 ac) of domed sphagnum bog, birch and pine forest, home to numerous resident and migratory birds and animals. After numerous development attempts over 2000 ha (5000 ac) was purchased as parkland in 2004. The challenge will now be to protect the bog's ecological treasures. Fires, for example, are difficult to extinguish here, and the bog must be maintained as a wetland if it is to survive.

BURNS BOG ECOLOGICAL CONSERVANCY AREA

Wildlife highlights

Find here greater sandhill cranes, wintering and nesting waterfowl and raptors, black bear, Columbian black-tailed deer, coyote, ermine, bog-loving dragonflies, damselflies and butterflies, yellow pond-lily, sphagnum moss, Labrador tea, bog laurel, cloudberry, round-leaved and long-leafed sundews and many other unusual bog plant and invertebrates, more typical of northern latitudes.

Amenities: No developed trails in most of the bog. Sphagnum moss soaks up water and is dangerous to walk on; sinking up to the thighs is not uncommon. Some industrial remnants of the peat mining operations, dating from the 1940s, can be seen.
Location: Delta, north of Highway 99.
MAP D3.

> **Guided walks, school tours:**
> Burns Bog Conservation Society
> www.burnsbog.org; 604 572 0373 or toll-free 1 888 850 6264.
> GVRD Parks 604 224 5739

DELTA NATURE RESERVE AND GREENWAYS TRAIL

This is a well-established park on the eastern fringe of Burns Bog. Visitors can enjoy a stroll along boardwalk trails built by volunteers from the Burns Bog Conservation Society, or cycle the Greenways Trail from the Fraser River to Mud Bay.

Wildlife highlights

Look for Labrador tea, bog laurel, and skunk cabbage. The forest has Columbian black-tailed deer, barred owl, warblers, vireos, flycatchers and other songbirds; rough-skinned newt, salamanders and Pacific tree frogs occur in damp vegetation in stream corridors. Coyotes and occasional black bear also pass through.

Amenities: Boardwalk and walking trails; Greenways cycle trail running north-south, between the Fraser River and Mud Bay.
Location: Northeast side of bog, east of Highway 91 and just south of River Road. Take the Nordel Court turning off Nordel Way and park at the SE corner of the Great

Pacific Forum parking lot. The footpath to the Nature Park and entrance to the Greenway is under the Nordel Way overpass. Bus Routes: 301 and 640. MAP D3

RICHMOND NATURE PARK

Lying in the heart of Richmond, this park is another remnant of the vast bogs that once covered much of the Fraser Delta.

Wildlife highlights
Bog plants like blueberry, cranberry, Labrador tea and sphagnum moss are highlights here. Look for butterflies, dragonflies, waterfowl, turtles, frogs, fungi and the "quaking bog".

These tiny bog cranberry flowers were photographed in June.

Amenities: A boardwalk and trails wind through 80 ha (200 ac) of forest, pond and bog. The Nature House has activities, displays, several live animals, a herbarium and other nature information. School tours and interpretive programs are available. Open dawn to dusk, daily.
Location: 11851 Westminster Hwy, Richmond.
MAP C2

Further information

Richmond Nature Park
604 718 6188
City of Richmond 604 276 4000
www.richmond.ca

Rain drops on bog blueberry.

DELTA - SURREY ESCARPMENT

VIEWS FROM THE UPLAND EDGE

JOE BROWN PARK

A small park on the western side of the escarpment adjacent to the Surrey City landfill, Joe Brown is a surprisingly peaceful place for a late afternoon stroll.

Wildlife highlights
Look for eastern cottontail rabbits, coyotes, woodpeckers, songbirds, woodland flowers. Sand hills are relics of Pleistocene era beaches.

Location: 125A St and 54 Ave, Surrey, south of Highway 10. Nearest bus number 322. MAP E3

PANORAMA RIDGE

This is a recently acquired park and as yet undeveloped. It consists mostly of low-lying floodplain below the Surrey escarpment. The fields are overlooked by forested, south-facing bluffs.

Wildlife highlights
Ferns, mosses, woodland flowers and insects, Pacific tree frogs, warblers, winter wren, flycatchers, swallows, woodpeckers, hawks.

Location: North of Colebrook Rd, Surrey. At present habitats can only be viewed from surrounding roads. MAP E3

> *For more about Bluffs and Escarpments, see page 23 - 24.*

Colourful vine maple flowers in April.

WATERSHED PARK

This densely timbered part of the North Delta escarpment is noted for its artesian freshwater springs and mountain biking trails. The upland forest has dense, second growth western redcedar, hemlock, Douglas-fir and bigleaf maple. Lower, wetter areas have skunk cabbage, salmonberry & thimbleberry.

Wildlife highlights
Look for ferns and fungi, warblers, vireos, chickadees, kinglets, winter wren, Swainson's thrush, spotted towhee, northern flying squirrel (nocturnal), raccoon, black-tailed deer and three-spined sticklebacks.

Amenities: Walking and mountain biking trails, artesian springs (tap on 72 St. not in use), picnic areas, public washrooms, Greenway path connects to Burns Bog Nature Reserve.
Location: Entrances on Kitson Parkway and 72 St., Delta; Greenway cycle and pedestrian trail from River Rd., North Delta. Bus 340 along Kitson Parkway, numbers 311 and 318 travel Hwy 10. MAP E3

BLAINE, SEMIAHMOO & BIRCH BAY

WASHINGTON IMPORTANT BIRD AREA

Beautiful views out over the water and a pleasant walking trail await the visitor to this stretch of the Whatcom County shoreline, close to the international border. A key resting and foraging area for shorebirds and waterfowl, it is a premier birding destination, one of only 53 designated Important Bird Areas in Washington State and an anchor site for the northern loop of the Great Washington State Bird Trail. Tidal conditions and season determine the number, diversity and location of birds and other marine wildlife.

BLAINE MARINE PARK

This attractive little park, jutting into Semiahmoo Bay, was built on land reclaimed from an old municipal landfill and the remains of nineteenth century mills and canneries. A waterside trail connects to Marine Drive, Blaine and a public pier in deep water at the entrance to Drayton Harbor. The pier is a favourite crabbing spot for locals. There are views to Semiahmoo Spit and across Boundary Bay to Point Roberts.

Wildlife highlights

Watch for harbour seals, wintering loons, grebes, scoters, northern pintail, American wigeon and other waterfowl, bald eagles, gulls, migrating brant in spring and fall. Migrating shorebirds can be seen Aug-Sept, especially at Cain Creek, from two hours before high tide. Double-crested cormorants nest on breakwaters in Drayton Harbor.

Enjoy birding?

Follow the *Great Washington State Birding Trail*; see Audubon Washington www.wa.audubon.org

Amenities: Interpretive signage; picnic shelters; bike trail; visitor centre, visitor boat moorage and public washrooms at Blaine Marina; public pier on Marine Drive, several restaurants and cafes in Blaine town centre. Historic ferry, the H.V. Plover, takes foot passengers, cyclists to Semiahmoo Spit weekends, Memorial Day to Labor Day.

Location: Marine Drive, Blaine; Take I-5 exit 276. MAP F5

Further information

Whatcom Parks 360 733 2900
www.co.whatcom.wa.us/parks

North Cascades Audubon Society
www.northcascadesaudubon.org

Washington Brant Festival
www.washingtonbrant.org

Blaine Chamber of Commerce
www.blainechamber.com
360 332 4544 or toll-free
1 800 624 3555

SEMIAHMOO SPIT, DRAYTON HARBOR

Semiahmoo County Park lies on a 2.4 km long (1.5 mi) sandy spit forming the western side of Drayton Harbor. It provides panoramic views of Mount Baker, the North Cascade Range and Boundary Bay from Birch Point to the distant cliffs at Point Roberts. Good views of eelgrass meadows and open water can be obtained from both sides of the spit.

Wildlife highlights

Highlights include intertidal life, bald eagles, wintering diving ducks, grebes, loons, marbled murrelet, migrating brant, whimbrel, double-crested & pelagic cormorants, ospreys, harbor seals. Harbor porpoises are sometimes seen off Birch Point. The shoreline is an important smelt and Pacific sand lance spawning location.

Amenities: beaches on both sides of the spit, walking, cycling trails, washrooms. Semiahmoo Museum, run by the Drayton Harbor Maritime Association features a restored Bristol Bay sailboat and other artifacts of the Alaska Packers Association (APA) salmon cannery era. Museum open from Memorial Day to Labor Day.
The site of the APA cannery is now a resort, with accommodation, restaurants and moorage. The historic ferry, H.V. Plover, departs from here on summer weekends to Blaine Harbor. Nearby Birch Point and adjacent woodlands are private property, but the quiet roads are pleasant for walking or cycling.
Location: Semiahmoo County Park, 9261 Semiahmoo Parkway, Blaine, WA. The park is 11 km (7 mi) north of I-5, exit 270.
MAP F5

Old cannery pilings at Semiahmoo.

BIRCH BAY STATE PARK

Somewhat south of the Boundary Bay region, this 78 ha (192 ac) park, situated 13 km (8 mi) south of Blaine features mixed woodland, 1800 m (6000 ft) of shoreline and marshy Terrell Creek estuary, used by Native Americans over many millennia.

Wildlife highlights

Look for intertidal life, bald eagles, shorebirds, ducks, black brant, nesting great blue herons, songbirds, harbor seals, beaver, muskrat.

Amenities: Hiking trails, camping, boat launch, public washrooms.
Location: Birch Bay Drive, Birch Bay, WA; exit 270 from I-5. The park is just south of the area shown on the Boundary Bay map.
Information: Washington State Parks
1 800 233 0321 www.parks.wa.gov

HOVANDER PARK & TENNANT LAKE

This nature park and historic site offers a variety of facilities, 16 km (10 mi) south of Blaine. A boardwalk leads out to the lake and wetlands, where there are waterfowl and songbirds.

Amenities: Wetland wildlife, interpretive centre, washrooms and a Fragrance Garden, with 200 varieties of flowers and herbs, braille signage and raised beds for easy wheelchair access. The adjacent Hovander Homestead Park has a historic farmhouse listed by National Register of Historic Places, hiking and cycling trails along river bank, fishing, picnic areas.

Location: 5236 & 5299 Nielsen Road, Ferndale, WA 98248; I-5, exit 262. This park lies just south of the area shown on the Boundary Bay map.

Washington State public transportation

Whatcom Transit Authority
www.ridewta.com
360 676 7433

Greyhound bus service
www.greyhound.com
360 733 5251

There are opportunities for boat charters out of Bellingham.

DRAYTON HARBOR WATERSHED
RURAL HINTERLAND TO BOUNDARY BAY

The twin river valleys of Dakota and California Creek flow in a northwesterly direction into Drayton Harbor. Their watershed, comprising the narrow creeks and numerous tributaries, is still very rural in nature. The rolling countryside is covered with woodlands, pastures and working farmland, interspersed with smallholdings and acreages.

DRAYTON HARBOR WATERSHED

The highlands around the north and south forks of Dakota Creek have second-growth forests of alder, birch, Douglas-fir and cedar. The streams cut deep channels through the hillsides. California Creek and its network of tributaries flow across a wider floodplain, scattered with farms and small communities. The countryside here is predominantly pasture or other agricultural fields and small patches of forest. Quiet back roads are suitable for cycling.

Wildlife highlights
Forested parts of the watershed have Columbian black-tailed deer, striped skunk, red-tailed hawk, owls and songbirds. Coho, chum, sea-run cutthroat & salamanders are found in creeks; Dakota Creek also has chinook and steelhead. Conservation

"sensitive plants" found here include few-flowered sedge and water-hemlock.

Amenities: Most of the watershed is privately-owned, rural land and farm acreages, but beautiful views of Mount Baker can be obtained from roads on higher ground. Some farms sell produce in season.
Location: Lying east and south of Blaine, WA, the watershed is 160 sq km (62 sq mi), encompassed by H Street in the north, Markworth Road in the east and the intersection of Grandview Rd. & Vista Drive in the south. The main highway, I-5, runs between Dakota & California Creek valleys. MAP G5, G6, H5, H6

CALIFORNIA CREEK - DAKOTA CREEK ESTUARY

The two creeks broaden out in their lower reaches and become tidal, entering the eastern side of Drayton Harbor within 1 km (0.5 mi) of each other. Their tree-lined banks and shallow, brackish waters are attractive wildlife habitat.

Limited views of California Creek for birding are possible from Loomis Trail Rd. The bridge is a favourite spot for sports fishers in fall.

Wildlife highlights
Shorebirds, waterfowl, great blue heron, belted kingfisher, salmon and trout species are highlights here.

Amenities: Bridges across the creeks, shallow banks for fishing, kayak launch. Other amenities at nearby Blaine.
Location: Drayton Harbor Road, south of Blaine. MAP F5 - F6

See pages 13 - 14 for more about California and Dakota Creeks

Large-leaved lupines

LINCOLN PARK

This small park on the outskirts of Blaine has towering Douglas-fir on the south-facing slope and bigleaf maples on the north. A trail leads uphill and smaller footpaths wind through the woodland on either side. Visit nearby Peace Arch Park for formal gardens on the international border.

Wildlife highlights
Look for woodland flowers, fungi, and songbirds such as chickadees, kinglets and red-breasted nuthatch.

Amenities: Footpaths, parking.
Location: East Blaine, access at D-Street and H-Street. MAP G5

POINT ROBERTS

WHALES & WATERBIRDS

A major nature destination at all seasons, Point Roberts is known for its rich marine life, exciting birding, and relatively rural landscape, compared with the Canadian end of the peninsula. This is perhaps the best place around Boundary Bay to view deep water wildlife. The Point is an isolated corner of Whatcom County, flanked by Boundary Bay and the Strait of Georgia and reached either by boat or by road through British Columbia.

Wildlife highlights

Head to the southern and western shores of Point Roberts to see marine life typical of the rocky shoreline. Diving ducks, grebes, loons, gulls, auklets and murres occur in the kelp beds and deep offshore waters. Watch for jaegers and terns on migration. Wooded areas around the back roads are home to Columbian black-tailed deer, raccoons, bald eagles, turkey vultures, hawks, owls and numerous songbirds, including Hutton's vireo. The largest colony of Pacific great blue herons in the Pacific Northwest was located on the Point until 2004, when it moved to Tsawwassen. Herons are still seen regularly and some still nest on the Point.

Orcas, or killer whales, are regularly seen in summer from Lighthouse Marine Park.

Amenities: Boat, kayak launches, marina, restaurants. Quiet back roads for cycling.
Location: Point Roberts is about 13 sq km (5 sq mi) of land south of the International Border, accessed at 56 Street, Delta, (Tyee Drive and Roosevelt, Point Roberts). Note that you will need a passport for crossing the border. Public transport from Vancouver: bus 601 to 2 Avenue, Tsawwassen, then walk or bike to the border (several blocks).
MAP C5

Further information

Lifeforce (education about orcas)
www.lifeforcefoundation.org

Georgia Strait Alliance
www.georgiastrait.org

Chamber of Commerce: 360 945 2313
www.PointRobertsChamber.com

LIGHTHOUSE MARINE PARK

Lighthouse Marine Park is ideally located for wildlife viewing on the extreme southwest tip of Point Roberts, overlooking the deep waters of the Strait of Georgia.

Wildlife highlights
Depending on the season, this is an excellent place to spot killer whales, harbour seals, California and Steller sea lions or harbour porpoises.

Winter bird watching here is very exciting, when harlequin and long-tailed ducks, horned grebes, alcids, surf scoters, loons and cormorants can be seen offshore. Three species of jaeger, elegant terns and other rarities have been recorded. The park is a good location for occasional Heermann's gull in summer. Shore pines and shrubs behind the beach are worth checking for songbirds on migration.

Amenities: Public washrooms, barbecues, sheltered picnic sites, a boat launch and a campsite across the road. Curiously, despite its name, the park lacks a traditional lighthouse. There is a small parking fee for non-county visitors. Lifeforce Foundation provides interpretive information about killer whales in summer.
Location: 811 Marine Drive, Point Roberts, WA 98281. No bus service. Access by foot, kayak, bike, boat or car. MAP C5

Further information
Whatcom Parks   360 733 2900
www.co.whatcom.wa.us

Vancouver Natural History Soc. Rare Bird Alert 604 737 3074

Large driftwood washed ashore at Lighthouse Park, Point Roberts.

LILY POINT

The pale-coloured cliffs of Lily Point are composed of attractively-layered, Pleistocene era sands and gravels, exposed in a large land slip on the eastern face. The point is the original site of Straits Salish reef net fisheries and the ancient village of Chelhtenem, dating back thousands of years; there are many important spiritual and cultural values associated with the cliffs and headland. Also known as Cannery Point, the shoreline has remains of old cannery pilings and orchards, witness to the varied inhabitants through the ages (see photo page 62).

Location: Southeast tip of Point Roberts. Lily Point is private land: view cliffs by kayak or boat. MAP C5

OFFSHORE WATERS

WILDLIFE WATCHING AFLOAT

Caspian tern

Scheduled services on B.C. Ferries between Tsawwassen, Vancouver Island and the southern Gulf Islands give an excellent opportunity to enjoy coastal scenery and watch for wildlife. All trips give good views of the Strait of Georgia and a chance to see killer whales, seabirds and seals. Active Pass between Mayne and Galiano Islands is particularly scenic. Steep forested cliffs descend to turbulent waters, and bald eagles perch in the overhanging trees. This is the route taken by ferries bound for Swartz Bay, near Victoria.

Wildlife highlights

Look for harbour porpoises off Galiano Island, killer whales near Roberts Bank, Dall's porpoise, harbour seals and sea lions. Birds seen here include double-crested, pelagic and Brandt's cormorant, pigeon guillemot, rhinoceros auklet, ancient murrelet, surf scoters, Caspian tern, Bonaparte's gull, Heermann's gull, parasitic jaegers and rarities, such as fork-tailed storm-petrel and shearwaters.

Amenities: Car ferries are fully serviced on Vancouver Island routes, with restaurants, gift shop, washrooms, etc. Gulf Island routes use smaller ferries and can have limited food services; reservations required for vehicles. Foot passengers can wheel on kayaks or bicycles, for an extra charge.
Location: Tsawwassen Ferry Terminal, south end of Highway 17, Delta. Bus 620. MAP A5, A6, B5, B6

Further information
B.C. Ferries 1 800 223 3779
www.bcferries.com

Steller sea lions

CONSERVATION

"Ours to Preserve by Hand and Heart" ~ Delta Municipality Motto

The more we learn about nature, the more we can appreciate its incredible beauty, complexity and uniqueness. We live on a very special planet and often we take it too much for granted. Nature can be strong and resilient, yet it is also under constant pressure from human expansion and development. Every day, all around the world, animals and plants become extinct. They are erased from the web of life with no thought for their role or the future.

Conservation means protecting what is valuable. Today more and more people are realising the true value of nature. Without the living, global, inter-connected network of plants and animals, human life would be impossible. To protect plants and animals, it is vital to protect their habitat. Boundary Bay and the Fraser River estuary have habitat that is internationally-recognized: it is a priority for protection. While some excellent work has been done in achieving designations, this has not always translated into on the ground retention of wetlands, fields, forests and streams. Large shifts in temperature and humidity patterns are already causing changes in habitat and wildlife declines all

Boundary Bay: International, National & Regional Habitat Designations

• Western Hemispheric Shorebird Reserve Network Site (WHSRN)

• Wetland of International Importance especially for Waterfowl (Ramsar Site) - UN designation Alaksen; Boundary Bay, Roberts Bank, Sturgeon Bank meet criteria.

• Important Bird Area - BirdLife International Program: Fraser River estuary, including Boundary Bay is the top site in Canada.

• Important Bird Area - BirdLife International Program: Blaine, Semiahmoo and Birch Bay

• Alaksen National Wildlife Area: Canadian federal protected area

• Boundary Bay Wildlife Management Area (WMA) South Arm Marshes WMA Sturgeon Bank WMA Roberts Bank WMA nominated: B.C. Provincial protected areas

around the world. Climate change is thus an enormous threat to our planet. As well as protecting habitat, we must address the sources of direct and indirect mortality.

Sadly, there are many threats to wildlife. Killer whales are on both the US and Canadian endangered species lists, due in part to toxic chemicals in the water and to fish declines. Sandpipers and great blue herons perish on overhead wires, and songbirds collide with windows or are caught by domestic cats. Barn owls have a limited distribution in Canada, and many in the Fraser delta are killed by traffic. Overfishing and wasteful bycatches have meant the loss of dozens of fish species in the Strait of Georgia, in the same way that commercial whaling once wiped out the humpback whales. Fish stocks are in peril, and illegal harvesting threatens clams, crabs, and consequently all intertidal life. Some losses are not easy to explain.

Once common animals, such as the western spotted skunk and red fox, have disappeared in the last twenty years from Boundary Bay. Shorebird populations are plummeting across North America: sandpiper numbers have declined by 80% on Roberts Bank since 1994.

Among these setbacks, there have also been success stories. Trumpeter swans, once hunted nearly to extinction, have made a remarkable comeback, thanks to regulations adopted both in Canada and USA. Wood duck have also rebounded due to conservation measures, and bald eagle numbers have recovered since fatal pesticides were banned. Farmers made the switch to integrated pest management, and their efforts have

This great blue heron with its fish represents one connection between the land and water. Successful conservation protects all the connections of an ecosystem.

meant a far healthier environment for both humans and wildlife. The public have regularly voted for an increase in habitat protection, as demonstrated by the cooperative purchase of Burns Bog.

A key factor in the protection of wildlife is local knowledge; we value what we know and love. A deeper understanding of the natural world leads to a strong desire to protect its numerous life forms.

My hope is that this book will both open the door to an appreciation of Boundary Bay's natural beauty and encourage its wise conservation.

Without our bogs we would have no Labrador tea.

LEARN MORE

We hope you have enjoyed this introduction to Boundary Bay's natural wealth. There is so much to see and enjoy, whatever the time of year.

For additional information on the topics in A Nature Guide to Boundary Bay, check out:

www.natureguidesbc.com

The site has endnotes and sources for the text, a full bibliography, annotated checklists of birds, animals and plants, with common and scientific names, and links to nature and conservation organizations mentioned in the text.

All photographs in this book were created by Dr. David Blevins. To find out more about where and how the images were created, to see more images that did not fit in this book, or to purchase prints of your favourite images, visit David's website:

www.blevinsphoto.com/boundarybay.htm

INDEX

Illustrations are shown in **bold**.

Species lists for Boundary Bay are available at **www.natureguidesbc.com**
Names follow Wilson and Ruff 1999, ABA 2005, Cannings & Harcombe 1990.